RECONSTRUCTING THE BALKANS

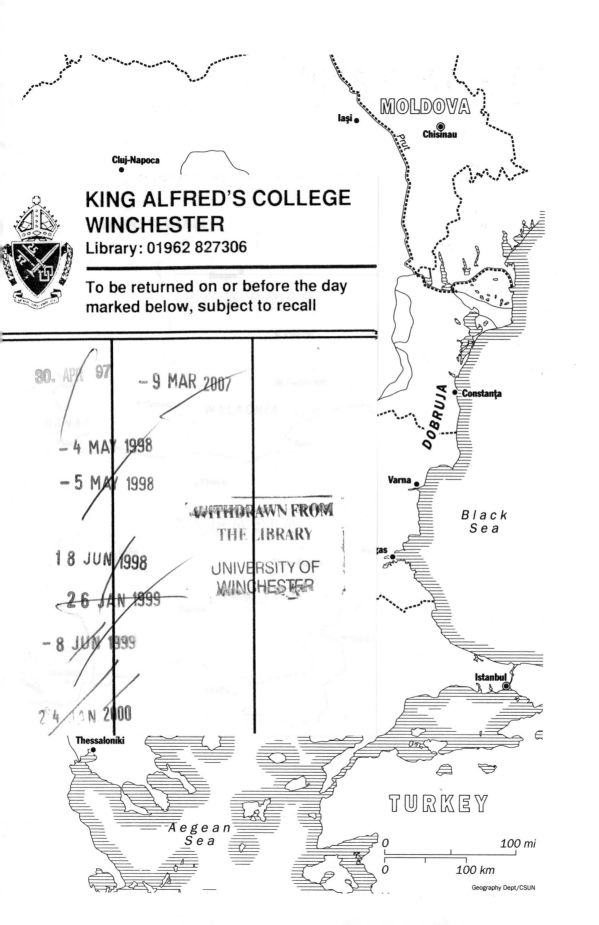

MOLDOVA

Iaşi

Chisinau

Cluj-Napoca

Prut

DOBRUJA

Constanţa

Varna

Black
Sea

...as

Istanbul

Thessaloniki

TURKEY

Aegean
Sea

0   100 mi

0   100 km

Geography Dept/CSUN

RECONSTRUCTING THE BALKANS

A Geography of the New Southeast Europe

Edited by

Derek Hall
Scottish Agricultural College, Ayr, Scotland

and

Darrick Danta
California State University, Northridge, California, USA

JOHN WILEY & SONS
Chichester · New York · Brisbane · Toronto · Singapore

Other Wiley Editorial Offices

John Wiley & Sons, Inc., 605 Third Avenue,
New York, NY 10158-0012, USA

Jacaranda Wiley Ltd, 33 Park Road, Milton,
Queensland 4064, Australia

John Wiley & Sons (Canada) Ltd, 22 Worcester Road,
Rexdale, Ontario M9W 1L1, Canada

John Wiley & Sons (Asia) Pte Ltd, 2 Clementi Loop #02-01,
Jin Xing Distripark, Singapore 129809

Library of Congress Cataloging-in-Publication Data
Reconstructing the Balkans : a geography of the new Southeast Europe
/ edited by Derek Hall and Darrick Danta.
       p. cm.
    Includes bibliographical references and index.
    ISBN 0-471-95758-5 (cloth)
    1. Balkan Peninsula—Geography. 2. Geopolitics—Balkan Peninsula.
I. Hall, Derek R. II. Danta, Darrick
DR11.R43 1996   96-12816
914.96—dc20   CIP

British Library Cataloguing in Publication Data

A catalogue record for this book is available from the British Library

ISBN 0 471 95758 5

Typeset in 10/12pt Times by Dobbie Typesetting Ltd, Tavistock, Devon
Printed and bound in Great Britain by Bookcraft (Bath) Ltd
This book is printed on acid-free paper responsibly manufactured from sustainable forestation,
for which at least two trees are planted for each one used for paper production.

Contents

Contents

List of tables

List of figures

List of plates

Glossary

A	Austria
AAG	Association of American Geographers
ACY	Adriatic Club Yachting (formerly Adriatic Club Yugoslavia)
AL	Albania
AML	Archives of Megiste Lavra
ARCE	Romanian Energy Conservation Agency
a.s.l.	above sea-level
ATA	Albanian Telegraphic Agency
BG	Bulgaria
BH	Bosnia and Hercegovina (Bosnia–Hercegovina)
BIS	Bank for International Settlements
BSZEC	Black Sea Zone for Economic Cooperation
CAP	Cooperative Agricole de Producţie (cooperative farms, Romania)
CEDEFOP	European Centre for Development of Professional Training
CMEA (COMECON)	Council for Mutual Economic Assistance (or Aid)
CRO	Croatia
CSCE	Conference on Security and Cooperation in Europe
CZM	Comisia Zonei Montane (Commission for Mountainous Regions, Romania)
D	Germany
DA	Dalmatian Action
DDR	(former) German Democratic Republic
DM	Deutschmark
DON	digital overlay network
EBRD	European Bank for Reconstruction and Development
EC	European Community/Commission
ECRE	European Council on Refugees and Exiles
ECU	European currency unit
EFTA	European Free Trade Area
EIB	European Investment Bank
EIU	Economist Intelligence Unit (London)
EU	European Union
FBIS	Foreign Broadcast Information Service (Washington, DC)
FSU	Former Soviet Union
FYR	Former Yugoslav Republic
FYROM	Former Yugoslav Republic of Macedonia
G-7/G-24	Group of 7/24 'Western' (including Japan) most industrialised countries
GATT	General Agreement on Tariffs and Trade
GDP	gross domestic product

Glossary

GNP	gross national product
GR	Greece
H	Hungary
ha	hectare
HAM	Historical Archives of Macedonia
HDZ	Hrvatska Demokratska Zajednica (Croatian Democratic Community)
HND	Croatian Independent Democrats
HR	Croatia (Hrvatska)
I	Italy
IBG	Institute of British Geographers
IBRD	International Bank for Reconstruction and Development (World Bank)
ICEMENERG	Energy Research and Modernising Institute (Romania)
IDS	Istrian Democratic Convention
IUCN	World Conservation Union (International Union for the Conservation of Nature)
IMF	International Monetary Fund
IREX	(US) International Research and Exchanges Board
JV	joint venture
km	kilometres
LOUFL	Law on Ownership and Use of Farm Land (Bulgaria)
LTD	limited liability firm (Bulgaria)
m	metres
MLC	municipal land commission (Bulgaria)
mm	millimetres
MTS	machine and tractor station
NATO	North Atlantic Treaty Organisation
n.d.	no data, or not dated
NDH	Nezavisna Država Hrvatska (Independent State of Croatia, 1941–45)
OECD	Organisation for Economic Cooperation and Development
OSCE	Organisation for Security and Cooperation in Europe
PHARE	Poland/Hungary Assistance for Restructuring Economies
R	Romania
RFE/RL	Radio Free Europe/Radio Liberty
RGS	Royal Geographical Society
RGS(IBG)	Royal Geographical Society (with the Institute of British Geographers)
ro-ro	roll-on, roll-off (ferry transport facility)
SAA	Serb autonomous area
SBHS	Slavonia–Baranja Croatian Party
SHE	state hunting enterprise (Bulgaria)
SLO	Slovenia
SME	small and/or medium-size enterprise
SOE	state-owned enterprise
SOPEMI	Système d'Observation Permanente sur les Migrations (OECD (q.v.), Paris)
SQ	Slovakia
SU	(former) Soviet Union
t	tonnes
TEL	Trans-European (telecoms) Line

TEM	Trans-European Motorway
TEMPUS	Trans-European Mobility Programme for University Studies
TER	Trans-European Railway
TKZ	Bulgarian collective farm
TR	Turkey
UCPTE	Union for Coordination of Production and Transmission of Electricity in Western Europe
UDF	Union of Democratic Forces (Bulgaria)
UN(O)	United Nations (Organisation)
UNDP	United Nations Development Programme
UNESCO	United Nations Educational, Scientific and Cultural Organisation
UNHCR	United Nations High Commission for Refugees
UNIPEDE	Union of European Producers and Distributors of Electricity
UNPROFOR	United Nations Protection Force
US(A)	United States (of America)
USSR	(former) Union of Soviet Socialist Republics
UYR	Union of Yugoslav Republics ('rump' Yugoslavia: Serbia and Montenegro)
WBTF	World Bank Task Force
WEU	West European Union
WHO	World Health Organization
WTO	World Tourism Organization
WWF	Worldwide Fund for Nature
YU	(former) Yugoslavia

Notes on the contributors

Dr Michael Chapman is Lecturer in the School of Planning, Heriot-Watt University, Edinburgh, Scotland.

Dr Darrick Danta is Professor in the Department of Geography, California State University, Northridge, California, USA.

Dr Alan Dingsdale heads the Centre for European Awareness and Cooperation, Nottingham Trent University, England.

Dr Anton Gosar is Associate Professor in the Department of Geography, University of Ljubljana, College of Arts and Sciences, Slovenia.

Dr Derek Hall leads the Department of Leisure and Tourism Management, Scottish Agricultural College, Auchincruive, Ayr.

Stella Kostopoulou is in the Department of Economics, Faculty of Law and Economics, Aristotle University of Thessaloníki, Greece.

Dr Boian Koulov is in the School of International Service, The American University, College of Arts and Sciences, Washington, DC, USA.

Dr Mieke Meurs is in the Department of Economics, The American University, College of Arts and Sciences, Washington, DC, USA.

Sarah Monk is Lecturer in the Division of Geography at Anglia Polytechnic University, Cambridge, England.

Jerome Oberreit is in the Department of Geography, California State University, Northridge, California, USA.

Dr Alex G. Papadopoulos is in the Department of Geography, DePaul University, Chicago, USA.

Dr Scott M. Pusich is in the Department of Geography, University of Kansas, USA.

Dean S. Rugg is Professor Emeritus in the Department of Geography, University of Nebraska at Lincoln, USA.

Dr Theano S. Terkenli is in the Department of Human Geography, University of the Aegean, Mitilíni, Lesvos, Greece.

Dr David Turnock is Reader in Geography at the University of Leicester, England.

Dr George W. White is at the Frostburg State University, Oregon, USA.

Dr Allan M. Williams is Professor of Human Geography and European Studies at the University of Exeter, England.

Preface

This example of transatlantic collaboration represents a timely, and we hope, important contribution to the debate and understanding of contemporary Balkan affairs. The participants in this venture are varied not only in their continental background, but represent a balance of young researchers, academics from the region in question, first- and second-generation *émigrés*, and long-established Western analysts. What the authors of this volume have in common is the experience of practical empirical activity in, and an intimate knowledge of, the areas and subject-matter dealt with in their respective chapters.

The material in this book was brought together during 1994 and 1995 by authors and editors armed with the most recent sources and field-work experience. The anchoring introductory and concluding sections of the book were written by the editors during 1995. The other chapters are derived from three major original sources, during the collaboration for which, the nature and purpose of this volume took shape. These represent the transatlantic collaborative efforts of the editors, who, working within the framework of their respective national geographical professional societies, convened gatherings aimed to attract the latest research on Balkan destruction/deconstruction/reconstruction/restructuring.

The core of this book is therefore made up of revised and edited versions of original research papers presented at:

1. The January 1994 Institute of British Geographers (IBG: since merged with the Royal Geographical Society (RGS)) Annual Conference session 'Reconstructing the Balkans', held at the University of Nottingham, which was convened by Hall and included contributions from Danta.
2. The March–April 1994 San Francisco American Association of Geographers (AAG) Annual Conference session 'The Balkans: destruction or reconstruction?', convened by Danta and including contributions from Hall.
3. The San Francisco gathering's 'Yugoslav update' panel discussion, also convened by Danta and including Hall.

While we have structured this volume in such a way that the four sections are meant to present coherent sets of chapters, in no way do we claim comprehensiveness or balance. For one thing, not all of the research areas, nor indeed researchers, were sufficiently accessible for us to represent all aspects and interpretations of contemporary Balkan issues (even if we had wanted to); and for another, it is implicit that each author within this collection, including ourselves, has their own biases and prejudices, witting or otherwise. We thus neither claim neutrality for the interpretations in this book, nor the necessity to even attempt to remove what some may regard as controversial interpretations. A volume on the Balkans, however crafted, will never please all readers, particularly in the current climate imposing itself on many of the region's peoples. What we have attempted, however, is the bringing together of a set of assessments and interpretations which can act to stimulate constructive debate on the present and future nature of the Balkans. While the book is written mostly by geographers, and its intent is to present a geographical—and essentially political geographical—perspective, we have also been pleased to draw upon the skills and insights of anthropologists, sociologists, economists and historians.

Both editors gratefully acknowledge the support of colleagues, family and friends, the cooperation of the contributors to this volume, and the indefatigable encouragement of Iain Stevenson and the production team at John Wiley.

Derek Hall, Newcastle upon Tyne, UK
Darrick Danta, Northridge, California, USA

Section A
The Balkan context

1

The Balkans: perceptions and realities

Derek Hall and Darrick Danta

1.1 Introduction: Balkans!

This first chapter attempts to explain and identify the essential defining characteristics of 'the Balkans', both in terms of spatial extent and ethnic complexity. This is followed, in Chapter 2, by a historical evolution and encapsulation of the 'Balkan problem' as a point of departure for the book's essential role of providing a series of (largely geographical) perspectives on contemporary Balkan issues as a basis for discussion of regional reconstruction. The latter term is employed in a self-consciously ambivalent manner: physical, economic, political and psychological reconstruction and a post-deconstruction reconceptualisation of the Balkans represent a broad agenda which, wittingly or otherwise, keep Balkan affairs to the forefront of Western thinking and concern well into the twenty-first century.

A geographical conundrum we firstly need to confront is the ambiguity surrounding the spatial semantics of the region. What is (are?) the Balkans? Lewthwaite's Law,[1] which states that the shorter the definition, the longer the explana-

---

1. Gordon Lewthwaite is Professor Emeritus in the Department of Geography, California State University, Northridge, USA, where he began teaching in 1959.

tion, applies all too well here. A short(-ish) definition may follow thus. The Balkans is a mountain range in Bulgaria whose name over the years has come to refer to a larger region coincident with the Balkan peninsula, which in turn makes up the majority of Southeast Europe. In terms of physical demarcation the region may be defined as the territory lying south of the Danube–Sava river boundary (Figure 1.1), which corresponds roughly to the 45th parallel (degrees north of latitude). In political terms the Balkans may also be defined as the territory constituting the states of Albania, Bulgaria and the former Yugoslavia; Romania, Greece and European Turkey may also be included (see Table 1.1).

The long answer, however, is more complicated. First, the term 'Balkans' is of relatively recent origin. From classical times to the early nineteenth century, the mountains now called the Balkan range were known as the 'Haemus' (Schevill, 1922, p. 14; Todorova, 1994, p. 462). Likewise, the region now referred to as the Balkans was for centuries known by the names of its Roman provinces, Illyricum in the west and Thrace in the east. Later,

Medieval European travelers knew several Balkan regions as Romanie, while the Ottoman Turks called the eastern and central portions Rumelia. . . . In the eighteenth century, European travelers called most of the area Turkey-in-Europe, in obvious reference to its

---

Reconstructing the Balkans: A Geography of the New Southeast Europe. Edited by Derek Hall and Darrick Danta.
©1996 John Wiley & Sons Ltd

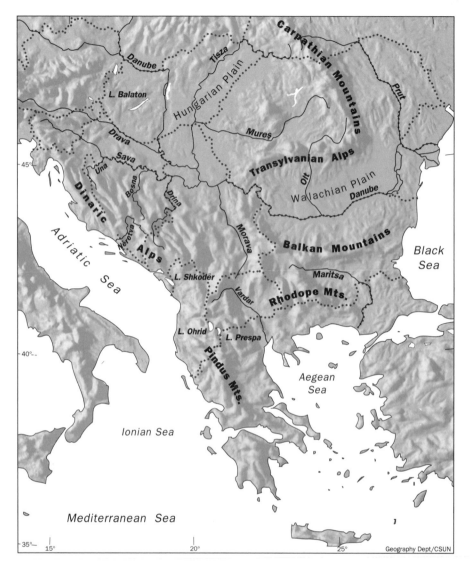

Figure 1.1 *The physical geography of Southeast Europe*

inclusion within the Ottoman Empire . . . (Stoianovich, 1994, p. 1).

Not only was the word 'Balkans' not used until relatively recently but no single geographical term was applied to the whole territory we now call the Balkan peninsula.

'Balkan', which is derived from the Turkish *balak* (Magocsi, 1993, p. 2), although of Persian origin meaning 'high house', 'mountain' or 'wooded mountain', was first used in 1809 by the German geographer A. Zeune (Hoffman, 1963, p. 11). Todorova (1994, pp. 462–463) notes that the terms 'Haemus' and 'Balkan' were used interchangeably from the early nineteenth century, with the latter becoming preferred after 1820. Only in 1827, however, was 'Balkan' used to refer to the whole peninsula. The term was in

Table 1.1 *Political components of selected definitions of 'Balkans'/'Balkan peninsula'*

Source	Political components										
	AL	BH	BG	CR	GR	MA	MO	RO	SR	SL	TR
Anon (1891)	×	×	×	×	—	×	×	—	×	×	—
Forbes *et al.* (1915)	×	×	×	—	×	×	—	×	×	—	×
Wallis (1924)	×	×	×	—	×	×	×	○	×	—	×
Shackleton (1954)	×	×	×	×	×	×	×	—	×	×	×
Hoffman (1963)	×	×	×	×	—	×	×	—	×	×	—
Hösch (1972)	×	×	×	×	—	×	×	—	×	×	—
Blanc (1977)	×	×	×	×	×	×	×	—	×	×	×
Jelavich (1983)	×	×	×	×	×	×	×	×	×	×	×
Webster's (1984)	×	×	×	×	×	×	×	×	×	×	×
Cviic (1991)	×	×	×	×	—	×	×	×	×	×	—
Sjöberg and Wyzan (1991)	×	×	×	×	—	×	×	×	×	×	—
Poulton (1994)	×	×	×	×	×	×	×	—	×	×	—
Carter *et al.* (1995)	×	×	×	×	×	×	×	×	×	×	×

Notes
AL: Albania; BH: Bosnia–Hercegovina; BG: Bulgaria; CR: Croatia; GR: Greece; MA: Macedonia; MO: Montenegro; RO: Romania; SR: Serbia; SL: Slovenia; TR: Turkey (in Europe).
×: full inclusion; ○: part inclusion; —: exclusion.

common use by the early part of this century. Shortly after the Balkan Wars, Schevill (1922, p. 13) introduced the term 'Balkania', but this did not find favour, although it was used, in passing, by Wallis (1924, p. 688).

In a survey of classic geographical texts of the late nineteenth and early twentieth centuries, 'Balkan peninsula' is regularly used almost to the exclusion of all other terms for the region. But disagreement over the spatial extent of such a construction is evident. Anon (1891) included the Ottoman Empire in Europe, Romania, Serbia, Montenegro, Bulgaria, Bosnia–Hercegovina, and Greece. Wallis (1924, p. 636), however, viewed the 'Balkan peninsula' as embracing Greece, Bulgaria and Albania, 'the major portions of Yugoslavia' but only the Dobruja (Dobrogea) portion of Romania, and Turkey in Europe. Slovenia was regarded as the 'boundary line' with Central Europe in both physical and cultural terms:

. . . while the Serbs are peasant proprietors with a patriarchal (*zadruga*) culture in old Serbia, the Croats are peasants with central European methods, the Slovenes are peasants who have evolved an additional stimulus, many of them are business organisers and traders; the Slovene, thus, is outside Balkan limitations (Wallis, 1924, pp. 688–9) (see also Mijatovich (1915), Cvijić (1918), Stamp (1930), Vujević (1930) and Byrnes (1976)).

There is perhaps an implication here that the interplay of cultural difference and 'modernisation' could contribute to a dynamic 'Balkan' boundary. In other words, in a strongly ethnocentric sense, as 'progress' and 'modernisation' overtake (diffusing spatially?) the peoples of the Balkans, might we expect the constituency of 'Balkan', as both a spatial indicator and pejorative label, to contract and eventually disappear, as the peoples of Southeast Europe are accepted/absorbed into 'civilised' Europe?

Certainly, the interplay of environmental factors, human migration and ethnic complexity are essential components which have weighed heavily upon those attempting to characterise, not always unambiguously, the 'Balkan peninsula'. According to Shackleton (1954, p. 390):

Owing to its position and shape the Balkan peninsula is the least Mediterranean of the three southern peninsulas of Europe, though paradoxically it includes

Greece, parts of which provide text-book examples of a Mediterranean country.

As Wallis (1924, p. 635) put it,

Unlike Italy and the Iberian Peninsula, the Balkan Peninsula is not shut off from the continent of Europe by a lofty mountain barrier.

While Ellen Semple (1913, p. 404) considered that

The Balkan Peninsula . . . owing to the great predominance of its continental section and the confused relief of the country, has not protected its distinctively peninsular or Greek section from the southward migrations of Slavs, Albanians, Wallachians, and other continental peoples. It has been like a big funnel with a small mouth; the pressure from above has been very great. Hellas and even the Peloponnesus have had their peninsularity impaired and their race mixed, owing to the predominant continental section to the north.

By the early 1920s, those with a strong academic interest in the region, such as the famous karst expert Jovan Cvijić, already realised that although 'Balkan peninsula' was neither a correct regional term nor had anything to do with the most important mountain of the region, it was too late to influence a change in terminological use (Hoffman, 1963, p. 11). Indeed, fellow Yugoslav Josip Roglić (1950) vainly sought adoption of the term 'Southern European peninsula'.

Subsequently, the terms 'Balkans', 'Balkan peninsula' and 'Southeast Europe' have been used seemingly interchangeably (Hoffman, 1989, pp. 15, 498; McDonald, 1992, p. 351), with variations in use and occasional additional terms perpetuating inconsistency. Hubbard (1952), for example, restricted the use of the term 'Balkans' to the mountain range (Stoianovich, 1994, p. 1), while referring to the region of the peninsula as 'lower Danube states'. By contrast, Unstead (1957, pp. 148, 188) simply talked about peoples of 'the Balkan region'. Emphasising both a spatial and psychological marginalisation, as part of his regionalisation of the European continent, Jordan (1988, pp. 401–2) refers to the area as the 'Balkan periphery',

although he appears to be alone in this attribution.

Taking a politically framed perspective, *Webster's* (1984, p. 110), for example, defines the Balkans in terms of the states occupying the Balkan peninsula: Albania, Bulgaria, Greece, Romania, (former) Yugoslavia and Turkey west of the Bosphorus. A more restrictive political definition of the Balkans embraces the territory of those states which formerly pursued centrally planned economies. In this categorisation, Greece and Turkey are implicitly excluded, typically to be instead regarded as part of southern Europe and Southwest Asia respectively. That Greece is an EU member, and both Greece and Turkey belong to NATO, has hitherto set them apart from the other countries of the region in the post-war period (see Chapter 18).

An alternative approach to defining the Balkans is to look not at the edges but at the centre or core of the region, in pursuit of which one might expect to be confronted with less controversy or ambiguity. The geographical centre of the Balkans is in the vicinity of 42°N latitude, 22°E longitude, within the territory of present-day Macedonia (FYROM) just east of Skopje. Indeed, many of the important events relating to the Balkans, such as the Battle of Kosovo Polje and the Balkan Wars, have occurred in or close to the surrounding core area. Indeed, Hösch (1972, p. 11) addresses a 'central Balkans' comprised of Yugoslavia, Bulgaria and Albania. However, the problem of where to draw the outer boundaries still exists.

If we consider the way in which inhabitants of the area, not least geographers, define the region, we tend to find Romanians insisting that the Balkans start south of the Danube, and Slovenians casting the region to the east of themselves. That Croats, Greeks and Turks have also been known to disassociate themselves from a Balkan identity may suggest restricting any notion of the 'Balkans' to contemporary Serbia, Montenegro, Albania, Macedonia and Bulgaria. The argument of Stoianovich (1994, pp. 1–2) that the region can be defined in terms of a Balkan culture, does not, however, correspond with this demarcation of contemporary states in that, he argues, such a culture does not extend to the sea nor onto the plains of Central Europe.

In truth, the terms 'Balkans' and 'Balkan peninsula' are often employed (particularly by outsiders, not least 'Westerners') as points of reference without resort to definitional clarification. For example, Mellor and Smith (1979) and Bateman and Egan (1993)—who do not cite 'Balkans' or 'Balkan peninsula' in their index—use these terms variously and undefined in their texts, as do all of the contributors to Held (1992). The terms appear to have become sufficiently familiar for these authors not to feel the need to elaborate their areal extent, even though there is far from being a consensus over the region's delineation.

This volume pragmatically fudges any notion of a single Balkan definition by recognising an areal hierarchy of Balkanness—a veritable Balkan nest of geographical 'Russian' dolls consisting of at least three layers. The first, most territorially circumspect of these, 'the Balkans', encompasses Croatia, Bosnia–Hercegovina, Albania, Serbia, Macedonia, Montenegro and Bulgaria. Second, a somewhat larger extent of territory is implied by the term 'Balkan peninsula', which adds Slovenia and Greece to the above list. Finally, the largest areal unit is 'Southeast Europe', which can also be taken to include Romania and European Turkey. Further, of course, there are also those neighbouring countries which have been involved with, or have felt the direct impacts of, Balkan affairs, such as Hungary (Chapter 17) and Italy (see Chapter 10).

1.2 Europe's back door

The Balkans begin in Istria, the peninsula jutting into the Adriatic Sea in the border of Italy. There the northern Italian landscape of cypress trees, pink and tawny stucco farmhouses and green fields passes shockingly into a savage caricature of itself. It becomes a contorted landscape of barren limestone hills and desolate upland pastures under a light so hard and a sky so piercingly blue that in summer the eye is blinded.

All that is easygoing and prettily charming ends in Italy . . . where the Balkan zone begins we enter a

world of the tragic . . . an area cut off from the West not so much by distance as by time (Stillman *et al.*, 1964, p. 9).

Few regional terms pack the emotional punch of 'the Balkans'. Indeed, it is an appellation with which few appear to want to be associated, and about which conferences often degenerate into name calling and curses uttered in any one of a dozen tongues. Todorova (1994, pp. 460–1) asks:

How could a geographical appellation be transformed into one of the most powerful pejorative designations in history, international relations, political science and, nowadays, general intellectual discourse?

She offers three reasons:

1. 'Inaccuracies' in geographical description led to a misperception of the region.
2. This purely geographical term acquired political, social, cultural and ideological overtones so that the name 'Balkan' came to possess pejorative connotations.
3. Dissociation of the designation from its object occurred, which furthered its negative connotation. In other words, the term for the region was taken out of its context, a separate intrinsic meaning evolved, and now as the term is reapplied to the region it carries added baggage to confuse the semantics.

Adding to the problem of perception and definition was the expectation of early travellers to the region. It was in the Balkans where the first European civilisation arose; where Pericles walked and Olympian gods played out their intrigues; where science, the arts and democracy flourished. Élitist European visitors who came here in the eighteenth and nineteenth centuries expecting to find a continuation of classical heritage were sorely disappointed. Their less than enthusiastic reports reflected intellectual frustration and personal distaste with what they found, thereby establishing a precedent for viewing the region negatively, a position which has tended to persist to the present, becoming seemingly ever more entrenched.

Cartographers have played their part in shaping images of the region. In classical times, maps were crafted portraying a large mountain range—the 'Haemus'—stretching the length of the peninsula from the Black Sea to the Adriatic. This range, which in reality did not exist, acted as a conceptual barrier against the barbarians living to the north: a natural, if mythical, construction to compare with the Great Wall of China or Hadrian's Wall. Later cartographers replicated this range, only by now the implication of the construction was that the barbarians lived to the south.

Yet the perceived 'primitiveness' and 'savage' nature of the region took on for some travellers a new chic. The 'wild and lawless countries between the Adriatic and the Black seas' of de Windt (1907, p. 2) were also 'wild' to Olivia Manning (1985). It was here that Edith Durham (1923) sought out head-hunters and often required personal detachments of bodyguards (Durham, 1904, 1909, 1928), while Edward Lear marvelled at such rare European sights as teeming pelican colonies (Lear, 1851; Noakes, 1985; Hyman, 1988). Not the least of the ingredients in this characterisation is the strong element of 'orientalism' (e.g. Said, 1978):

The Balkans are the gateway of the East, through which one catches one's first glimpse of the languorous land . . . three quarters psychic, one quarter mystic, wholly sensuous (Anon, 1912, quoted in Allcock and Young, 1991, pp. xv–xvi).

By the early part of this century (Bowman, 1921, p. 30), the term 'Balkan' had been transformed into a verb, 'balkanisation' referring to the 'parcelization of large and viable political units' and at the same time used as 'a synonym for a revision to the tribal, the backward, the primitive' (Todorova, 1994, p. 433). The twentieth-century picture of the Balkans that emerges is therefore one of a region where violence and hatred are endemic, where civilisation is all too easily overshadowed by impulses for revenge, and hence where peaceful solutions to tensions and conflicts appear unrealistic. This is the region upon which 'sick man of Europe' and 'tinderbox of Europe' have been among the milder epithets to have been bestowed (Newman, 1945, p. 1).

These internal variations play a significant role in the external portrayal of the conflicts and tensions enveloping the region. At least one attempt to convene a 'Balkan peace conference' has been aborted because sufficient of the potential participants did not want to admit to being 'Balkan' by virtue of their attendance. Indeed, for many outsiders, Balkan problems may seem intractable and hence not worth the bother of seeking solutions. However, even a cursory examination of history reveals instances of problems that have seemed equally intractable, conflict no less brutal and mystifying, involving individuals whose minds were equally closed. Unfortunately, the Balkans region does not hold a monopoly of such characteristics.

Allcock and Young (1991) point to the 'sense of otherness' generated by impressions of the Balkans being separated from 'the West' by an apparent unbridgeable gulf of misunderstanding (but see also Meštrović, 1994). They argue that in both geographical and cultural terms, what most characterises the Balkans, its images and the often disparate interpretations of its extent and nature, is the region's 'multiple marginality':

The Balkan countries stand at the overlapping edges of several different aspects or points of view from which the identity of the region might be constructed. The definitions of marginality may have shifted over time; but nevertheless, significant cultural, economic or political frontiers have met here at least since Roman times (Allcock and Young, 1991, p. xvi).

While this theme is elaborated, in historical perspective, in the next chapter, one dimension of the characteristic may be highlighted here with reference to Hösch (1972, p. 21), who, building on the work of Cvijić and others, notes that at least four 'culture areas' can be identified within the Balkans:

1. A Balkan–Byzantine culture with a strong oriental element which is present in the continental and eastern parts of the region.
2. In the upper regions of the western Balkans, is

an area typified by a patriarchal way of life, with people of pronounced physical and social features who believe in the heroic male as an ideal. Here the most favourable conditions have prevailed for keeping alive archaic national characteristics (Hösch, 1972, p. 21).

3. Along the Adriatic coast, a zone of Italo-Slav culture persists.
4. In the north, a Central European cultural zone or Pannonia (northeast Slovenia, north Croatia, Slavonia, Srem, Vojvodina) connects the Balkan peninsula with the European continent.

1.3 Ethnic complexity and territoriality

Indeed, in terms of ethnic, linguistic and religious composition, the Balkan peninsula is one of the world's most complex areas (Table 1.2). Three of the region's peoples claim descent from classical times: Greeks, Vlachs (descended from the original Thracians) and Albanians (claiming descent from the ancient Illyrians). Others, notably Slav groups, have been attracted to the region more recently.

The observation that a nation is a group of people united by a common error about their ancestry and a common dislike of their neighbours (Kedourie, 1960; King, 1973) would appear particularly pertinent in the Balkans. Although language, literature, religion, customs and historical antagonisms assist the definition of ethnic groups' national ideals, territorial exclusiveness and integrity are vital to assert a separate identity. In the Balkans, however, complicated patterns of migrations have intermixed groups geographically over a long period, rendering territorial exclusiveness often elusive (Jelavich and Jelavich, 1965).

Albania and Slovenia are the most ethnically homogeneous countries in the region, a tendency which appears to have been increasing over the past 70 years. Greeks still comprise a significant population in the 'northern Epirus' area of southern Albania, although their numbers have been diluted by recent emigration. Situated along a religious fault line, Roman Catholicism took hold in the north of Albania, inhabited by Gegs,

while Orthodoxy was characteristic of the southern Tosks. With Turkish domination from the fifteenth century, Islam was widely adopted over Albanian lands subsequently (see Chapter 10) (Norris, 1993; Hall, 1994).

As the other major Islamic area in the Balkans outside of Turkey, Bosnia–Hercegovina, in contrast to Albania, has been characterised by a pluralistic society (Irwin, 1984; Malcolm, 1994). Indeed, until 1991 proportions of the three main groups—Muslims, Serbs and Croats—had remained reasonably stable, although the effects of a higher Muslim birth-rate were not insignificant (Table 1.2) (Donia and Fine, 1994).

Although relatively homogeneous, Croatia's concentration of ethnic Serbs along the border with Bosnia in the 'Krajina' region has been the source of recent notable conflict (Magaš, 1993; Križan, 1994; Carter *et al.*, 1995; Cohen, 1995). The relatively heterogeneous Former Yugoslav Republic of Macedonia (FYROM) has experienced limited ethnic problems (Perry, 1992, 1993; Poulton, 1993, 1994). Although many (not least Greeks) would question their legitimacy as a separate ethnic group (see Chapters 6 and 7), Macedonians comprise the largest proportion of the country's population, but with significant Turkish and Albanian minorities (Wilkinson, 1951). The latter are concentrated in the western part of the country and comprise perhaps one-third of the total population: many of the official census figures depicted in Table 1.2 are contestable. The separate ethnic identity of Montenegrins can also be called into question, since although their political histories have differed in recent centuries, cultural affinities with Serbs are close. Dominant in Serbia, Serbs make up just over half the population in the constituent region of Vojvodina in the north, where up to 40% of the population is Hungarian, Romanian or Roma (Gypsy), but in Kosovo to the south, ethnic Albanians predominate (Pipa, 1989; Harris, 1993).

Under the Communists, the Bulgarian government used various implicit and at times explicit means to 'Bulgarise' its ethnic Turkish minority, and in the early post-war years several thousand

Table 1.2 *Ethnicity in selected Southeast European countries*

Albania

	1923	1980	1989
Albanians	90.4	97.0	98.0
Greeks	n.d.	n.d.	1.8
Others	—	—	0.2
Total population	814 385	2 670 500	3 182 416

Bosnia–Hercegovina

	1921	1981	1991
Muslims	30.9	39.5	43.6
Serbs	43.5	32.4	31.4
Croats	21.5	18.4	17.3
Others	4.1	9.7	7.7
Total population	1 890 440	4 124 008	4 364 574

Bulgaria ('Bulgarians' includes Macedonians)

	1920	1980	1992
Bulgarians	81.7	88.0	85.0
Turks	15.0	8.4	9.7
Roma	1.7	2.6	3.4
Others	1.6	1.0	1.9
Total population	5 096 530	8 876 600	8 472 724

Croatia

	1921	1981	1991
Croats	68.1	75.1	78.1
Serbs	17.4	11.8	12.2
Others	14.5	13.1	9.7
Total population	3 447 594	4 601 469	4 784 265

Macedonia

	1921	1981	1991
Macedonians	62.4	67.0	64.6
Albanians	13.9	19.8	21.0
Turks	12.7	4.5	4.8
Roma	—	2.3	2.7
Serbs	2.3	2.5	2.1
Others	8.7	3.9	4.8
Total population	798 291	1 912 257	2 033 964

Montenegro

	1921	1981	1991
Montenegrins	75.8	71.9	61.8
Muslims	12.3	13.4	14.6
Serbs	(included with Montenegrins)		9.3
Albanians	5.5	6.5	6.3
Croats	5.8	1.2	1.0
Others	0.6	7.0	6.7
Total population	311 341	584 310	615 267

(continued)

Table 1.2 *(continued)*

Romania

	1920	1977	1992
Romanians	78.4	89.1	89.4
Hungarians	10.7	7.6	7.1
Roma	0.8	0.4	1.8
Germans	5.3	1.5	0.5
Others	4.8	1.4	1.2
Total population	13 270 105	21 559 910	22 760 499

Serbia (including Vojvodina and Kosovo; 'Serbs' includes Montenegrins)

	1921	1981	1991
Serbs	64.5	67.8	67.7
Albanians	6.4	14.0	16.7
Hungarians	7.8	4.2	3.3
Muslims	2.1	2.3	3.2
Roma	—	1.0	1.3
Croats	2.6	1.6	1.1
Others	16.6	9.1	6.7
Total population	4 808 077	9 313 677	10 345 464

Source: Various national censuses. See also Hadzivuković (1989), Harris (1993) and Poulton (1994).

Turks were expelled. Romania's Hungarian (both Magyar and Székely) minority is found in significant numbers in Transylvania. Numbers of Saxons (ethnic Germans), however, have declined dramatically, having provided a lucrative trade in Deutschmarks for the Ceauşescu regime through transfer agreements with Bonn, and, from 1990, having been able to emigrate to Germany in a relatively free manner.

The reasons for the region's ethnic complexity, though greatly reduced this century as a result of population exchanges and expulsions, may be summarised as:

1. The ease of land- and seaward accessibility of the Balkans from neighbouring regions.
2. The abundance of mountain fastnesses and remote upland plateaux which have assisted local isolation of groups within the region.
3. The deliberate policy pursued by previous imperial powers of moving loyal groups to border areas and of administratively dividing potentially hostile subject peoples.
4. Population pressures exerted by neighbouring peoples.
5. The later demarcation of political boundaries, particularly by the great powers, with little

regard for, or knowledge of, the detail of ethnic group distributions.

As a consequence of these factors, ethnic minorities in the Balkans are geographically disposed in one or both of the following ways:

1. Those which have been separated from their main ethnic group by an international boundary, but which otherwise live in a contiguous area, such as Hungarians and Romanians in Vojvodina, Albanians in Kosovo, Macedonia (FYROM) and Montenegro, Greeks in southern Albania, Turks in southeastern Bulgaria, Italians in Istria (Slovenia and Croatia), Slovenians in Austria and Italy, Croats in Bosnia and Serbia, and Serbs in Croatia, Bosnia, Montenegro and FYROM.
2. Those which live in non-contiguous areas, such as the Germans in Vojvodina, Hungarians and Germans in Transylvania, Serbs in pockets of varying size in Croatia, Bosnia and Albania, and scattered Vlachs and Gypsies.

In either case, no one ethnic group may be in the majority in any given area: groups may be intermixed at a regional level, within individual settlements and even within individual housing blocks. On the other hand, even neighbouring villages may possess distinctly separate ethnic identities, as characterised by, for example, one village being clustered around a Roman Catholic church, the next around a mosque and a third hard by an Orthodox church, each of the three dominating buildings acting as both symbols of cultural separation and of the continuing role of religion as one defining ethnic characteristic. Most significantly, such complexities were characteristic of many parts of the former Yugoslavia (Hondius, 1968; Banac, 1984; Lydall, 1989).

Yet such patterns have always been dynamic, and one of the implicit flaws in any Balkan peace settlement based on an imposed 'ethnic map', is that such a construction, by sustaining the myth of monopoly claim to territory, ignores both the complicated and ever-changing patterns of interethnic spatial and social relations. Recent events have telescoped the temporal dynamism of such processes and have, infamously, reduced spatially expressed ethnic complexity in several parts of the former Yugoslavia. The historical background to, and evolution of these events are discussed in the next chapter.

1.4 References

Allcock, J. B., Young, A. eds, 1991, *Black lambs and grey falcons: women travellers in the Balkans*, University of Bradford, Bradford.

Anon, 1891, *The 'Regina' geographical reader. Book five: Europe*, George Gill, London.

Anon, 1912, Why the Balkans attracts women, *The Graphic*, 26 October.

Banac, I., 1984, *The national question in Yugoslavia: origins, history, politics*, Cornell University Press, Ithaca and London.

Bateman, G., Egan, V., 1993, *Encyclopedia of world geography*, Barnes and Noble, New York.

Blanc, A., 1977, *L'économie des Balkans*, Presses Universitaires de France, Paris, 2nd edn.

Bowman, I., 1921, *The new world: problems in political geography*, World Book Company, New York and Chicago, 4th edn.

Byrnes, R. F. ed., 1976, *The zadruga*, University of Notre Dame Press, Notre Dame and London.

Carter, F. W., Hall, D. R., Turnock, D., Williams, A. M., 1995, *Interpreting the Balkans*, Royal Geographical Society, Geographical Intelligence Paper No. 2, London.

Cohen, L. J., 1995, *Broken bonds: the disintegration of Yugoslavia*, Westview, Boulder, Colo.

Cviic, C., 1991, *Remaking the Balkans*, RIIA/Pinter, London.

Cvijić, J., 1918, *La Péninsule Balkanique, géographie humaine*, Paris.

De Windt, H., 1907, *Through savage Europe; being the narrative of a journey through the Balkan states and European Russia*, Fisher Unwin, London.

Donia, R. J., Fine, J. V. A., 1994, *Bosnia and Hercegovina: a tradition betrayed*, Hurst, London.

Durham, M. E., 1904, *The burden of the Balkans*, Nelson, London.

Durham, M. E., 1909, *High Albania*, Edward Arnold, London. Reprinted by Virago, London, 1985.

Durham, M. E., 1923, Head-hunting in the Balkans, *Man*, **11**, 19–21.

Durham, M. E., 1928, *Some tribal origins, laws and customs of the Balkans*, Allen and Unwin, London.

Forbes, N., Toynbee, A. J., Mitrany, D., Hogarth, D. G., 1915, *The Balkans: a history of Bulgaria, Serbia, Greece, Rumania, Turkey*, Clarendon Press, Oxford.

Hadzivuković, S., 1989, La population de la Yougoslavie: structure, développement et perspective, *Population*, **44**(6), 1189–212.

Hall, D. R., 1994, *Albania and the Albanians*, Frances Pinter, London.

Harris, C. D., 1993, New European countries and their minorities, *Geographical Review*, **83**(3), 301–19.

Held, J., ed., 1992, *The Columbia history of Eastern Europe in the twentieth century*, Columbia University Press, New York.

Hoffman, G. W., 1963, *The Balkans in transition*, Van Nostrand, Princeton NJ.

Hoffman, G. W., ed., 1989, *Europe in the 1990s: a geographical analysis*, John Wiley, New York and Chichester.

Hondius, F., 1968, *The Yugoslav community of nations*, Mouton, The Hague.

Hösch, E., 1972, *The Balkans: a short history from Greek times to the present day*, Faber and Faber, London.

Hubbard, G. D., 1952, *The geography of Europe*, Appleton-Century-Crofts, New York, 2nd edn.

Hyman, S., ed., 1988, *Edward Lear in the Levant*, John Murray, London.

Irwin, Z. T., 1984, The fate of Islam in the Balkans, in Ramet, P., ed., *Religion and nationalism in Soviet and East European politics*, Duke University Press, Durham, NC.

Jelavich, B., 1983, *History of the Balkans: twentieth century*, Cambridge University Press, Cambridge.

Jelavich, C., Jelavich, B., 1965, *The Balkans*, Prentice-Hall, Englewood Cliffs, NJ.

Jordan, T. G., 1988, *The European culture area*, Harper and Row, New York.

Kedourie, E., 1960, *Nationalism*, Hutchinson, London.

King, R. R., 1973, *Minorities under communism*, Harvard University Press, Cambridge.

Križan, M., 1994, New Serbian nationalism and the Third Balkan War, *Studies in East European Thought*, **46**(1–2), 47–68.

Lear, E., 1851, *Journals of a landscape painter in Greece & Albania*, Hutchinson, London.

Lydall, H., 1989, *Yugoslavia in crisis*, Clarendon Press, Oxford.

McDonald, J. R., 1992, *The European scene: a geographical perspective*, Prentice-Hall, Englewood Cliffs, NJ.

Magaš, B., 1993, *The destruction of Yugoslavia: tracking the break-up 1980–92*, Verso, London and New York.

Magocsi, P. R., 1993, *Historical atlas of East Central Europe*, University of Washington Press, Seattle and London.

Malcolm, N., 1994, *Bosnia: a short history*, Macmillan, London

Manning, O., 1985, *The Balkan trilogy*, Penguin, London.

Mellor, R. E. H., Smith, A., 1979, *Europe: a geographical survey of the continent*, Macmillan, London; Columbia University Press, New York.

Meštrović, S. G., 1994, *The Balkanization of the West: the confluence of postmodernism and postcommunism*, Routledge, London and New York.

Mijatovich, C., 1915, *Servia of the Servians*, Pitman, London.

Newman, B., 1945, *Balkan background*, Macmillan, London and New York.

Noakes, V., 1985, *Edward Lear 1812–1888*, Weidenfeld and Nicolson, London.

Norris, H. T., 1993, *Islam in the Balkans*, Hurst, London.

Perry, D. M., 1992, The Republic of Macedonia and the odds for survival, *RFE/RL Research Report*, **1**(46), 12–19.

Perry, D. M., 1993, Politics in the Republic of Macedonia: issues and parties, *RFE/RL Research Report*, **2**(23), 31–7.

Pipa, A., 1989, The political situation of the Albanians in Yugoslavia, with particular attention to the Kosovo problem: a critical approach, *East European Quarterly*, **23**(2), 159–81.

Poulton, H., 1993, The Republic of Macedonia after UN recognition, *RFE/RL Research Report*, **2**(23), 22–30.

Poulton, H., 1994, *The Balkans: minorities and states in conflict*, Minority Rights Publications, London, 2nd edn.

Roglić, J., 1950, O geografskom položaju i ekonomskom razvoju Jugoslavije, *Geografski Glasnik*, 11–12, 11–26.

Said, E. W., 1978, *Orientalism*, Routledge & Kegan Paul, London.

Schevill, F., 1922, *The history of the Balkan Peninsula*, Harcourt, Brace and Company, New York. Reprinted as *A history of the Balkans*, 1991, Dorset Press, New York (page references are to the reprinted edition).

Semple, E. C., 1913, *Influences of geographic environment*, Constable, London; Henry Holt, New York.

Shackleton, M. R., 1954, *Europe: a regional geography*, Longmans Green, London, New York, Toronto, 5th edn.

Sjöberg, Ö., Wyzan, M. L. eds, 1991, *Economic change in the Balkan states*, Frances Pinter, London.

Stamp, L. D., 1930, *Slovene studies*, Faber and Faber, London.

Stillman, E. *et al.*, eds, 1964, *The Balkans*, Time Incorporated, New York.

Stoianovich, T., 1994, *Balkan worlds: the first and last Europe*, M. E. Sharpe, Armonk, NY and London.

Todorova, M., 1994, The Balkans: from discovery to invention, *Slavic Review*, **53**, 453–82.

Unstead, J. F., 1957, *A world survey: from the human aspect*, University of London Press, London, 5th edn.

Vujević, P. ed., 1930, *Royaume de Yougoslavie, aperçu géographique et ethnographique*, Belgrade.

Wallis, B. C., 1924, *Europe*, Vol. 1 *The Peninsula*, Edward Stanford, London.

Webster's New Geographical Dictionary, 1984, Merriam-Webster, Springfield, Mass.

Wilkinson, H., 1951, *Maps and politics*, Liverpool University Press, Liverpool.

2

Contemporary Balkan questions: the geographic and historic context

Darrick Danta and Derek Hall

2.1 Introduction

This chapter aims to present a picture of the complex geography—both physical and human—of Southeast Europe, as a backdrop to the discussions which follow. This is not intended to supersede the much longer discourses found in more extensive treatments such as those of Shackleton (1959, pp. 350–417) or Hoffman (1989, pp. 537–50).

2.2 Physical background

The stage upon which the Balkan drama has been played is a paradox: at once complex and diverse. The land is often poor, offering scant reward to those who toil in its fields to eke out a living. Most observers would agree, however, that the Balkan physical environment has been a significant factor in the evolution of the region's ethno-territorial patterns.

The relief of Southeast Europe is dominated by a series of rugged mountain chains dividing river basins and plains, and often separating coastal lands from the interior (Figure 1.1). Running the length of the Adriatic coast of the Balkans are the northwest–southeast-trending Dinaric Alps, which extend into Greece as the Pindus Mountains. Bulgaria contains two ranges, the Rhodope and Balkan Mountains, which run generally east–west to the Black Sea. Much of Romania is dominated by the horseshoe form of the southern extension of the Carpathians and Transylvanian Alps; these in turn cradle the Bihor Mountains. Maximum elevations of these mountains are in the range 2600–2800 m, though heights around 2000 m are more typical.

This relief is influenced greatly on the one hand by the complex tectonic environment of Southeast Europe, especially its numerous fault, fold and joint systems; and on the other hand by the predominance of limestone lithology, especially across the western half of the peninsula. The porous and, in the cool, humid environments found over much of the region, easily eroded rock, has had a great impact on landform development. Steep, rugged slopes are the norm rather than the exception, especially along watercourses. Furthermore, subsurface solution weathering creates the karst topography for which part of this region is famous (Cvijić, 1918). Characteristic of this landscape are underground caves, travertine terraces (e.g. at Plitvice),

Reconstructing the Balkans: A Geography of the New Southeast Europe. Edited by Derek Hall and Darrick Danta.
©1996 John Wiley & Sons Ltd

saucer-shaped depressions (sinkholes), larger closed hollows (dolines), and poljes. These latter features form when several dolines in an area coalesce to produce a generally flat area that can stretch for several kilometres; poljes, which appear frequently in place names, are often the only viable agricultural land in otherwise mountainous areas.

Topography and lithology also greatly influence Balkan hydrology. The major river of the Balkans is the Danube, which flows south from Hungary to Belgrade, thence eastward to the Black Sea forming the borders between Serbia, Romania and Bulgaria along the way (Figure 1.1). Major tributaries of the Danube system include the Sava, which in turn has the Drina, Bosna and Una as tributaries: the Drava, Tisza, Morava and Olt. Other important rivers include the Neretva, Vardar and Maritsa. However, the predominance of limestone in the peninsula has resulted in greater subsurface flow, and hence lesser surface river development, than might otherwise have been the case. In particular, apart from the Danube, only the Vardar is capable of supporting any type of water-borne transport, the others being too shallow, rapid or rocky to allow the passage of even small boats. Few large lakes are found in the region, the three on Albania's borders being exceptional (Figure 1.1).

Climate is another important component of the physical make-up of the Balkans. The three main types of climate are humid continental, extending from Hungary, across Romania, to northern Bulgaria; humid subtropical, covering the lowlands from Slovenia to southern Serbia; and Mediterranean, occupying coastal areas from Dalmatia to the Black Sea and all of Greece. Since Southeast Europe is too far from the Atlantic to experience directly maritime influences, these climates mainly reflect the dominance of cold, continental air masses in winter, subtropical high pressure developed over the Mediterranean and Black Seas in summer and higher than expected humidity from the Adriatic. Of course, climates are significantly colder at higher elevations, especially in the Dinaric Alps where winter snowfall is the norm.

Natural vegetation corresponds to these climate types, with grasslands and mixed forests predominating in plains, coniferous forests in higher elevations, and scrub and/or sclerophyl forests covering coastal and the more southerly portions of the peninsula. Throughout much of the Dinaric Alps vegetation is sparser than might be expected given the humid climate, because of the porous, limestone lithology and associated karst features. Likewise, soils are generally deep and fertile in the plains and river valleys, but are thin on the numerous hillslopes and are additionally acidic over limestone. Consequently, agriculture is limited in much of the region.

2.3 Evolution of the ethno-territorial landscape

The contemporary configuration of the human geography of the Balkans is the result of more than 3500 years of complex change involving the interplay of migrating tribes, expanding kingdoms, conquering empires and developing nations, as cartographically expressed in Magocsi (1993). Standard works portraying this evolution include Jelavich (1983), Carter (1977), Jelavich and Jelavich (1965) and Schevill (1922); more specific focus on the various ethnic groups of the region can be found in Kocsis (1992) and Bugajski (1994) (see also section 1.3 above).

Any review of Balkan ethno-territorial history is complicated by several factors. First, accurate archaeological evidence for much of this region is lacking. This means that a clear picture of many of the important groups that have had such an impact on the peninsula in prehistoric times, especially regarding their distributions, is not available. Ordinarily, this lack of accurate information would not pose much of a problem; however, individuals and even governments in Southeast Europe have long pointed to history, no matter how distant, as a means of laying claim to territory and identity. Second, unravelling notions of 'ethnicity' is often quite problematic. Indeed, the region has experienced thousands of years of migration and an inter-mixing of the indigenous and incoming peoples. Of greater import, though, is the fact that in several cases claims to 'ethnicity' are based not on physical, but rather on cultural traits such as religion, language and alphabet. Given the fluidity of these traits, identification becomes an arbitrary pursuit at best. Finally, trying to disentangle the political–territorial history of the Balkans is fraught with difficulties. A modern mindset seeks to draw boundaries on maps with utmost precision based on uncontroversial authority. However, the science of boundary demarcation generally grows more imprecise and indistinct the further back in history one travels. Further, boundaries which existed within empires—the form of political–territorial organisation which has dominated most of the Balkans' recorded history—were much more fluid than those of present-day nation states. Complicating this problem is the existence of vassal states and other types of shadowy territorial arrangements. Often, deciding whether a region belongs within one empire at a particular point in time becomes an arbitrary exercise, especially given the sometimes rapid change of boundaries and their deliberate manipulation. Also, many institutions, such as the Orthodox Church, maintained a high degree of autonomy and authority even during periods when their control officially vanished, as during Ottoman times. Overlapping institutions greatly complicate the picture and render virtually meaningless the task of deciding who controlled a particular tract of land and its people at any specific time.

Mindful of these caveats, the following review will attempt to present a picture of the patterns of ethnic groups in Southeast Europe and their evolution into political entities. The review will follow an essentially historical approach, tracing developments during the classical and Byzantine periods, the growth of medieval kingdoms, expansion of the Ottoman Empire, contraction and the emergence of nation-states. Finally, building on the discussion of ethnicity and territoriality in Chapter 1, some of the key political geographical elements in the disintegration of Yugoslavia are examined.

2.3.1 *From earliest times to the Greeks*

The first discernible human spatial organisation of Southeast Europe dates from the Neolithic period, for which time Stoianovich (1994, pp. 21–2) identifies five distinct culture areas:

1. A central culture in what is today Serbia and Macedonia;
2. A northern Danubian culture in southern Hungary and Transylvania;
3. An eastern steppe culture in Moldavia and western Ukraine;
4. A southern Aegean culture;
5. A northwestern culture in Bosnia.

Later, several sites throughout the Balkans became significant for metal extraction and production. However, the real story of the Balkans begins with the rise of the great classical civilisations.

The various peoples and civilisations commonly referred to as Greek sprang from the islands of the Aegean and Mediterranean seas; they were the dominant force on the Balkan peninsula from around 1500 to 200 BC. Largely seafaring, these peoples had their greatest impact on coastal areas, mainly around the Peloponnesos and Attica, although they eventually extended along the edges of the Aegean, Ionian and Black seas. The territorial organisation practised by the early Greeks, based on near-autonomous city-states with their associated agricultural hinterlands, was accompanied by well-known achievements in architecture, politics and the arts. However, Greek influence did not extend far inland, with the result that much of the Balkans remained outside its civilising effects.

The furthest penetration of the Balkan interior by Greek civilisation occurred during the reigns of Philip and especially his son, Alexander, of Macedonia, during the third century BC. From his capital at Pella, just north of present-day Thessaloníki, Alexander marched all the way to the Indus River, founding cities and introducing other elements of Greek influence along the way. However, the great leader was never able to 'Hellenise' the Thracians or Illyrians, tribes

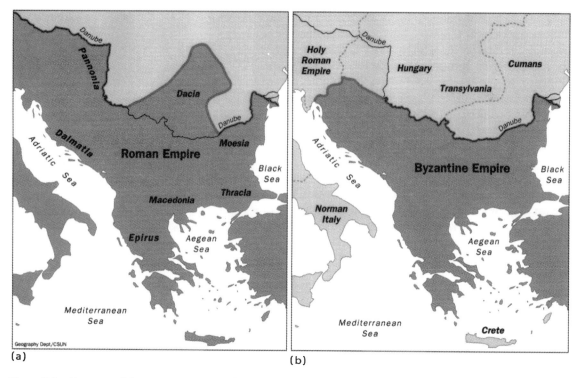

Figure 2.1 *Roman and Byzantine empires at their greatest areal extent: (a) Roman Empire: second century AD; (b) Byzantine Empire: twelfth century*

inhabiting the more mountainous areas to the north and east of Macedonia.

2.3.2 The rise of empires

Much of Balkan history is dominated by the flow and ebb of empires, beginning with the Romans. One important fact to keep in mind during the history of the Balkans is that conquering empires were not universally opposed by 'indigenous' groups. For example, the Thracians and Illyrians supported the campaigns of the Romans against the Macedonians, their longtime enemies; while much later Russians, Britons, Germans and French played Bulgarians, Serbs, Greeks and Turks against one another for their own purposes. This habit of indigenous peoples using stronger allies from afar, and of foreign powers exploiting existing animosities, helps to explain the lack of allied resistance and hence the

relative ease with which various empires have expanded into and within the Balkans.

Whereas influence of the Greeks was felt mainly in coastal locations, the Romans, who dominated the region from 200 BC to around AD 500, took a much more active role in conquering and organising the whole extent of the Balkan peninsula. After defeating the Macedonians in 197 BC, the Romans quickly spread over the region. By the second century AD, they controlled all of the territory south of the Danube, and under Trajan had even taken most of present Transylvania, which was then known as Dacia after the tribe inhabiting the area (Figure 2.1 (a)). As elsewhere, the Romans set about constructing towns, garrison outposts, aqueducts and roads, the most famous being the Via Egnatia, which connected Dyrrhachium (Durrës) on the Adriatic coast to Thessaloníki and on to Byzantium (Constantinople).

Despite the many cities and other architectural and archaeological features attributed to it, the cultural impact of the Roman Empire on the Balkan peninsula proved to be short-lived. Only two groups—the Dacians, who would later become the Romanians, and the Vlachs—adopted Roman speech and culture. For the most part, Greek language and culture was retained in coastal regions, and the Illyrians and other tribes found throughout the interior carried on much as they had done before, albeit in more restricted mountainous areas. Conversely, the Thracians appear to have disappeared during Roman occupation: whether killed off in continual conflict or assimilated to extinction, the cause is not certain.

Fractures in the Roman armour became more pronounced during the third, fourth and fifth centuries as Germanic (Goth) and Asiatic (Hun) tribes pounded the Empire from beyond the Danube. Coincidentally, the Empire was undergoing internal change, largely through the adoption of Christianity, which became the official religion in 392. These and other events led, in 326, to the relocation of the Roman capital to Byzantium, which was quickly renamed 'New Rome' then Constantinople after the reigning Emperor. The subsequent split in the Empire between west and east soon led to two essentially separate realms; the dividing line, which passes north to south through present-day Bosnia, has from its inception remained a major European cultural, political and religious chasm.

As control slipped from the grasp of Italian rulers to those hailing from the city on the Bosphorus, the story of Balkan history shifts from the Roman to Byzantine empires. Rather than marking a reinvigoration of classical heritage, though, the Byzantine is remembered mainly as a stagnant and ultimately corrupt period of Balkan history. The Eastern Empire succeeded in maintaining Roman law, administrative practice, tradition and the army and navy; however, it had a decidedly more ecclesiastical bent and was far less interested in territorial organisation and administration than were the Romans.

Problems for the Byzantines began almost at once. Pressure from the Persians from the east

and Avars from the west reached a climax in 626 with the first siege of Constantinople. Renewed pressure from Islamic Arabs led to another siege in 717; simultaneously, advancing Slavs from the north restricted the zone of Byzantine influence to coastal areas, in particular to the safety of walled cities. The practice of Christianity by this time had degenerated to little more than fetish worship. Furthermore, the birth of the Holy Roman Empire in the west in 800 called into question the legitimacy of Byzantine authority. Two and a half centuries later, Seljuk conquests in Asia Minor robbed the Empire of its richest granaries. On the other hand, during the eleventh and twelfth centuries the Byzantine Empire expanded into the Balkan interior, reaching its greatest extent under Basil II (Figure 2.1(b)). Furthermore, Constantinople, capital of the Empire and centre of oriental trade with Europe, was able to remain the leading city of the world for five centuries.

The Byzantines were essentially Greek: therefore, Greek language, culture, government and church provided the cement holding the Empire together. By the early Middle Ages most Balkan groups acknowledged the rule of the Phanariotes, which explains the use of the Cyrillic alphabet in Serbia, Montenegro, Macedonia and Bulgaria (Romania also used Cyrillic until the late 1800s). However, the capture and sacking of Constantinople in 1204, ostensibly as part of the Fourth Crusade although orchestrated by the power-hungry Venetians, dealt the Empire a near fatal blow. Technically, though, the Byzantine Empire lasted until 1453, when the capture of Constantinople by the Ottoman Turks put an end to what remained. Greek authority over the Orthodox church continued throughout the Ottoman period, however, and lives to this day in the person of the Prelate of Istanbul.

2.3.3 Medieval kingdoms

Overlapping with the rise and fall of empires is the appearance of other peoples on the Balkan scene. Slavic peoples moved into Southeast Europe mainly during the seventh century from their homeland on the Russian plain, thereby

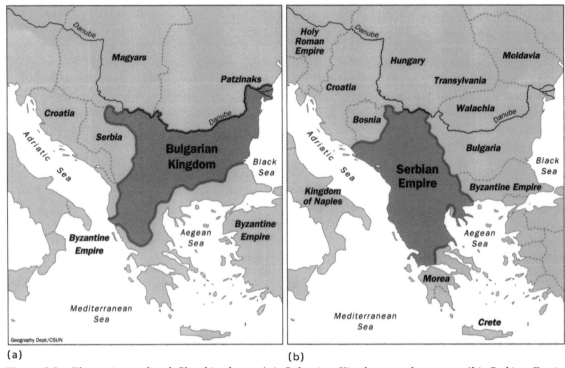

Figure 2.2 *The major medieval Slav kingdoms: (a) Bulgarian Kingdom: tenth century (b) Serbian Empire: fourteenth century*

considerably changing the ethnic make-up of the Balkans. Slavs were not at all welcome by the Byzantine authorities; indeed, as early as the mid-sixth century Justinian tried to use the Avars in a scheme to halt their progress. As they entered the peninsula, the Slavs displaced, annihilated and/or intermixed with existing groups. The same process occurred later in history when various waves of Asiatic tribes arrived in the region. Initially, south Slavs formed what can be regarded as a single group.

Over the centuries, however, more specific 'ethnicities' sprang from this common ancestry. The mutual distinctiveness of Slovenes, Croats, Serbs and Bulgarians as recognised today is the result of historic processes operating differentially across the region.

Slavs gradually came to occupy the northern Balkans from the Adriatic to the Black Sea. However, they remained only loosely organised into clan territories called *zupa*, which were headed by a chief or *zupan*. The first branch to

split from the main Slavic trunk belongs to the Bulgars, whose homeland is generally considered to be the area bounded on the north by the Danube, the east by the Black Sea, the west by an indeterminate line around the Morava River, and the south by the region of the Maritsa River, although settlement at various times extended to the Aegean Sea. The term 'Bulgar' actually refers to an Asiatic (Mongolian) tribe that overran the eastern Balkans during the seventh century. However, the conquerors were themselves assimilated by the more advanced Slavs; therefore, the Bulgars, although possessing Asiatic racial features, maintain Slavic language and culture. Soon, Bulgar leaders, beginning with Boris in the 860s, embraced Christianity and Greek trade and culture, and initiated a process of territorial expansion. This reached its greatest extent during the reign of Tsar Simeon (893–927), when most of the Balkans were united under one banner (Figure 2.2(a)). Bulgar power waned subsequently, and the early kingdom slowly faded first into the Byzantine Empire, when it became a Greek province from 1018 to 1186, then disappeared under the Ottomans after a brief revival, not to re-emerge as a separate nation until the late 1870s.

The next group to consider are the Serbs, who have long been the central players of the Balkan drama. The Serbs are generally associated with the region south of the Danube, west of the Morava, and extending at times to the Adriatic.

Serbia reached its greatest territorial extent during the reign of Stephan Dušan (1331–55) (Figure 2.2(b)). At this time, Serbs controlled nearly all of the Balkans west of Bulgaria, north of the Greeks and east of Bosnia (see Chapter 3). This zenith of empire, usually referred to as 'Greater Serbia', was quickly eroded by the advancing Ottomans—especially following Serb defeat at the Battle of Kosovo Polje in 1389— also to be completely blotted from the map for a time and resurrected in the 1800s. A closely related group, the Montenegrins, are essentially Serbs who held out against the Ottomans in their mountain strongholds near the Adriatic coast in a region referred to as Zeta.

The south Slav group known as Croats have historically occupied the region between the Drava River and Adriatic Sea. Originally indistinguishable from Serbs, the Croats differ today only by virtue of a different history: they fell within the western zone of Christendom following the Great Schism of 1054, and so have adhered to Roman Catholicism as opposed to Orthodoxy; their history has been closely associated with the Central European powers, especially Austria-Hungary; and they use the Latin alphabet.

A special group lying between the Serbs and Croats have come to be known as the Bosnian Muslims. Ethnically Slav, these are people who converted to the Islamic faith during Ottoman occupation. Most, but certainly not all, of those who converted were previously Bogomils: heretics who rejected strict Orthodoxy, but who were severely persecuted prior to the Ottomans. Conversion to Islam generally led to enhanced possibilities for social/economic mobility within

the Empire: a basis for animosity from other groups that has lasted to the present.

The most westerly south Slav group of the Balkans is the Slovenes, who occupy the region at the head of the Adriatic Sea. Similar to the Croats, they also are Roman Catholic and have long been associated with Western and Central European powers. Under the Habsburgs they were linked to Vienna when the Croats were associated with Budapest.

Non-Slav Balkan peoples of the region tend to have strong identities. Greeks maintained their language and identity during Roman occupation, especially on the islands, and again came to the fore during Byzantine times, when Greek culture, language and religion became dominant across the Balkans. The Albanians, who are descendants of the Illyrians, experienced territorial contraction, such that by medieval times they were restricted to their present location along the Adriatic coast, although they did not begin to aspire to nationhood until the second half of the nineteenth century, and only achieved statehood earlier this century (see Chapter 10).

The Vlachs were Romanised natives (Thracians and/or Illyrians) who took to the mountainous reaches of the Balkans at the approach of the Slavs during the sixth century. Sephardic Jews arrived in the Balkans after being expelled from Spain in 1492. Settling mainly in coastal cities of the Aegean, they had a major impact on the development of trade and other economic activities from the late medieval period. Finally, although strictly not part of the Balkans, various Asiatic tribes—Avars, Cumans, Huns, Magyars and others—have made incursions into the Balkans and settled along its flanks, as have Gypsies or Roma.

2.3.4 The Ottoman Empire

The Ottomans, a Turkic (Asiatic) people whose name derives from Osmanli ('Sons of Osman', the dynasty founder), have had a tremendous impact on the development—or, as many would argue, the under-development—of Southeast Europe. Their story is clearly an integral part

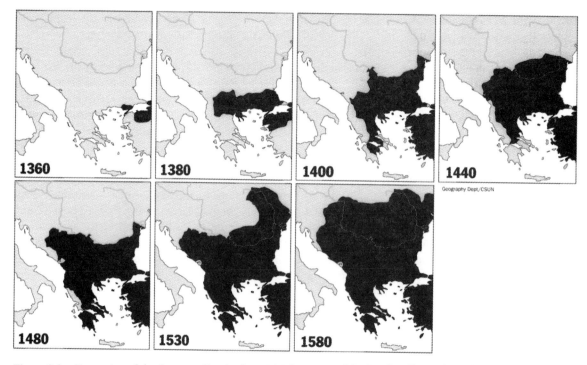

Figure 2.3 *Expansion of the Ottoman Empire from initial capture of the Dardanelles in the mid-fourteenth century to the failed siege of Vienna in the mid-sixteenth century*

of the Balkans; however, popular notions often contradict reality (Kinross, 1977).

The date 1453 is typically seen as marking the end of the Byzantine and the beginning of the Ottoman period of Balkan history. In fact, Ottoman expansion across the Dardanelles began in 1354 and *at the invitation* of the Constantinople leaders, who wanted to use the Turks in their internal struggle with unruly subjects, in particular the Serbs (Figure 2.3). Once unleashed in the region, the military superiority of the Ottomans soon overcame the decaying Byzantine Empire and the disorganised Slav groups, who were unable to mount any concerted efforts at defence. The Turks' expansion across Southeast Europe, although checked in places by the heroic efforts of such individuals as the Albanian Skënderbeg and Vlad IV in Wallachia, was relentless. They had advanced into Thrace by 1361; defeated the Serbs at Kosovo Polje in 1389; stamped out the Bulgars

by 1393; taken Thessaloníki in 1430 and controlled almost all of Hellas by 1460. By 1462 they had pushed into Bosnia and in the same year Wallachia succumbed. Moldavia was taken by 1512; under Suliman the Magnificent (1520–66), the Turks defeated the Hungarians at Mohács in 1526, and were at the gates of Vienna by 1529. Degrees of control, however, varied widely. Bulgaria under the Ottomans ceased to exist; Wallachia, Moldavia and Transylvania were tributary states which retained their own princes and enjoyed a large measure of independence; the mountainous parts of present-day Albania remained largely outside the grasp of Ottoman authority; while Zeta, the precursor of Montenegro, held out against the Turks, though in a much reduced state. Furthermore, ecclesiastical institutions, either the Greek Church in Constantinople or the other Orthodox churches, retained almost complete autonomy and thus were able to exercise a degree of authority over their followers. On the other hand, the many converts to Islam in Bosnia, who soon rose to positions of power, became the most fanatical and staunchest defenders of Ottoman rule.

Much of the lasting impact of the Ottomans on the Balkan peninsula derives from their various forms of administration. Technically, the Ottoman Empire was run by the Sultan, but sacred Islamic law, as interpreted by the *Ulema*, was the ultimate authority. Furthermore, the army, which in the mid-1500s numbered around 60 000–70 000 and which grew to 200 000 in times of war, was the real power behind the throne. The military was administered by *beglebegs*, whose territorial units were *sandjaks*. Large estates were called *ziamets*, smaller ones *timars*. Every four years, villages were visited and boys aged 14–18 were selected to be converted to Islam, educated and trained and then pressed into the service of the Empire. Service could be in the military as janissaries ('new troops'), or in other aspects of public administration or public works. After a time, many, if not most, of the high-ranking officials of the Ottoman Empire were ethnic Slavs or Greeks; during the nineteenth century, Greeks actually kept the Ottoman Empire afloat, particularly in some areas such as Romania, where they, and not the Turks, were the immediate enemies. At the bottom of the social and economic ladder were *rayahs* (a pejorative term meaning 'herd' or 'flock'), Christian or Jewish subjects who were forbidden from carrying arms and who were taxed more heavily than Muslims.

Under the Ottomans, the peninsula was stable, received generally good administration and security, benefited from many improvements to the infrastructure, notably the construction of bridges and public buildings, and was probably better off economically than under the Byzantines. The sultans understood the importance of trade; after capturing Constantinople, the city was quickly repopulated with merchants, while commerce was relatively unhindered in other cities, such as Thessaloníki and Ragusa (Dubrovnik) (Carter, 1972). However, the relatively independent nature of administration, especially with regard to religion, allowed for the historical divisions present in the peninsula to persist and widen.

The inevitable decline of the Ottomans set in during the 1600s as the economy faltered and the military swelled and became increasingly independent. A second failed siege of Vienna in 1683 was followed by Austria, Poland and Venice joining forces to push the Turks out of Europe. The once fearsome army of the Sultan crumbled under the offensive, so that by 1690 most of Hungary, Transylvania, Belgrade, and the Morea including Athens was taken. During the 1700s, the Austrians continued the push, securing the Banat by 1718; Russia joined in, and was able to gain for itself access to the Black Sea and protectorate status for Moldavia and Wallachia.

At this point in the story, Balkan history becomes increasingly tied to the larger European picture, particularly in terms of the ambitions of the powerful nations. Until her revolution, France was the only Ottoman ally. Afterwards, British policy towards the Balkans increasingly sought to support 'the sick man of Europe' as a means of checking Russian expansion and in particular to prevent St Petersburg from gaining control of the Bosphorus. Austria was left to fill the vacuum of the crumbling Ottoman Empire in Central Europe; the result was an expansion of Habsburg control over Hungary, Transylvania and Croatia. As Venetian power rose generally in the eastern Mediterranean, they took control of larger numbers of islands and territory of the south Balkan mainland.

2.3.5 The formation of states

While the great powers of Europe were busy either buoying up the Ottoman Empire or feeding from its carcass, visions of nationhood were beginning to stir among the various groups in the Balkans. By 1800, four centres of Serb culture existed:

1. Raška, now confined to the *pashalik* of Belgrade in the area between the Morava, Danube and Sava rivers;

2. Bosnia, where Muslim converts ruled over Orthodox Serbs;
3. Southern Hungary, where some 30 000 Serbs settled at the end of the seventeenth century at the approach of the Turks; and
4. In Zeta, where, from the 1360s, Serbs held out in mountain strongholds.

Somewhat later, a fifth area of Serb settlement arose along the border between Croatia and Bosnia in the area known as the Krajina (see Chapter 4). In addition, many individuals maintained an ongoing guerrilla war against the Turks; these Serb *hayduks* had their counterparts in other areas, such as Greek *klefts*. Beginning in the early 1800s, the Serbs revolted first under Karageorge (1804) then under Milos (1815); autonomy was finally granted in 1834 with the help of Russia. This Serb state, centred on Belgrade and bounded by the Danube, Drina, Tirnok and Morava rivers, though, was still far from unified and remained a pawn in Austrian and Russian schemes.

The Greeks also agitated for independence during the early 1800s. Several societies of different types were formed and their struggle became something of a *cause célèbre* in European liberal circles. After a revolt (1821) and another Russo-Turkish War (1828–29), Greece gained independence in 1830; however, the territory of this state did not include Epirus, Macedonia, Thessaly nor most of the islands.

In the 1850s, France joined Britain in an attempt again to block Russian designs on Constantinople. Russia's defeat in the Crimean War (1854–56) resulted in her having to give up the role as protector of Balkan Orthodoxy and of Wallachia and Moldavia, which opened the way for Romanian statehood in 1862. The Peace of Paris (1856) also opened trade along the Danube and on the Black Sea, while elevating Christians to the status of Muslims.

The Bulgarians, though, represent a different story. They were the most suppressed peoples under the Ottoman yoke, ceasing to exist as a separate political entity from 1393 for some 400 years. During this time, Greek became a common

language and many Bulgars lost their national consciousness (Schevill, 1922, pp. 384–5). The first Bulgarian school was not founded until 1835, and the Bulgarian Church was not made independent until 1870. However, statehood was still beyond reach.

Bosnia–Hercegovina stayed a part of the Ottoman Empire during this period, on the one hand because of its isolation from European involvement, and on the other because of tight control by ethnic Slav Muslims. Albanians, who did not even have a unified alphabet until the end of the nineteenth century, had yet to make much of a move towards the creation of a nation, while Croatia and Slovenia became more firmly enmeshed within the Austro-Hungarian Empire.

The most significant event of the nineteenth century for the Balkans was the Congress of Berlin (1878) following the Turko-Russian War of 1877 (Figure 2.4). In all, the treaty awarded full sovereignty to Romania, Serbia and Montenegro, gave Bosnia–Hercegovina to Austria to 'occupy and administer', although the Sultan technically still held control, and allowed Austria to station troops in the *sanjak* of Novi Pazar between Serbia and Montenegro. The treaty also created the Principality of Bulgaria, albeit within a limited frame since the Dobrudja region of the Black Sea coast was awarded to Romania, and East Rumelia and Macedonia, which Bulgaria had acquired in the Treaty of San Stefano (1877), were given back to the Turks. Greece received Thessaly and part of Epirus. In the final analysis, the Congress of Berlin, which on the surface appears to be mainly concerned with nationalist aspirations in the Balkans, proved to be more a vehicle for the imperialist expansion of European powers eager to secure new markets for their growing industries.

By the late 1880s, Bulgaria united with East Rumelia and then vied with Serbia for control of Macedonia. This area, long a corridor for migrating peoples along the Vardar River, was (and remains) the most ethnically complex Balkan region: *macédoine*, the French salad composed of a medley of fruits or vegetables, is aptly named. The region contained Greeks in the

Figure 2.4 *The Balkans at the time of the Congress of Berlin, 1878*

south, though Sephardic Jews were the overwhelming majority in Thessaloníki, and Slavs in the north with pockets of Vlachs in some mountain areas. The race to 'win over' the inhabitants of Macedonia was largely won by Bulgarian propaganda in the latter part of the nineteenth and early twentieth centuries. However, friction erupted in the First Balkan War (1912), which pitted Turkey against Bulgaria, Greece, Serbia and Montenegro. The quick victory led to

the creation of an Albanian state and the splitting of Macedonia between Serbia and Bulgaria. However, no sooner had fighting subsided when Bulgaria attacked Serbia (the Second Balkan War, 1913), but was soundly defeated, thereby losing any hope of gaining the long-sought prize.

Serb nationalism, in particular with regard to dreams of establishing a 'Greater Serbia', led to increasing friction with Austria over the Habsburg hold on Bosnia–Hercegovina. The assassination of Archduke Ferdinand in Sarajevo in 1914 by a Serb was the match that lit the flame of the First World War. However, to say that the war began in the Balkans underestimates the degree to which the competing great powers of Europe were already preparing for conflict, and in some cases at least, were merely looking for an excuse to go to war. The Balkans yet again bore the brunt of European folly.

The Treaties of Versailles (1919) and Trianon (1919–1920) mark the beginning of the contemporary period of Balkan history since the boundaries set forth in these documents remained in place, apart from a few minor and in most cases only temporary changes, until 1990. In the wake of the break-up of the Austro-Hungarian Empire, the post-war settlement sought to allow for the self-determination of recognised national groups within acceptable boundaries. Essentially, the treaties rewarded Serbia, Greece and Romania at the expense of Bulgaria, Turkey, Austria and especially Hungary, which lost some 67% of its former territory. In particular, Transylvania was awarded to Romania; Slovenia, Croatia, Bosnia–Hercegovina, Serbia and Macedonia were formed into the kingdom of Serbs, Croats and Slovenes (later Yugoslavia), and the borders of Turkey were pushed back to their current position.

Since 1989, events have encouraged a balkanisation of the region into smaller states than hitherto, a process arising notably from the dismantling of Yugoslavia, the land of the South Slavs, of whom Serbs have constituted the largest group. For some time in the inter-war period and most notably after the Second World War, the country was territorially divided into six republics, each based on a Slav 'nation'. The capital of Yugoslavia, Belgrade, was located within, and also acted as the capital city of, Serbia. The country's post-war president, Josip Broz Tito, a Croat, attempted to mitigate this dominance and to deflect traditional Serb–Croat enmities through various economic and administrative policies (Bebler, 1993).

Yugoslavia's two non-Slav 'nationalities' (Albanians, predominant in Kosovo, and Hungar-

ians in Vojvodina), almost by definition, could not be given republican status, with the result that their inhabited areas were latterly considered as 'autonomous regions' within the republic of Serbia. The boundaries which acted as the internal divisions of the Socialist Federative Republic of Yugoslavia (SFRY) now serve as the international boundaries of the new ex-Yugoslav states. This has been a major cause of concern, particularly for Serbs who were distributed, often in large numbers, outside of the boundaries of Serbia (Mitrovič, 1983).

2.4 Serb nationalism and territoriality

The relatively static nature of the state system established in the Balkans in the earlier part of the century, and the post-war federal structure of Yugoslavia were seen by Serb nationalists to have frustrated the 'natural' expression of Serb nationalism in a number of ways (Glenny, 1992; Magaš, 1993):

1. Although constituted in 1918 as the Kingdom of Serbs, Croats and Slovenes, from its inception, Yugoslavia (a name formally adopted in 1929) acted as a framework for constraining Serb aspirations, most notably when the Vojvodina and Kosovo regions were granted substantial autonomy by the 1969–74 constitutional changes.

2. In Kosovo, a sustained high Albanian birth-rate had been complemented by a steady emigration of Serbs (Mladenović, 1978). The 1981 Albanian demand for upgrading Kosovo to republic status was seen by Serbs as a potential first step towards incorporation into a Greater Albania (Moore, 1992).

3. The continued economic disparities between the advanced northwestern republics (Slovenia and Croatia) and the rest of the country represented a challenge to Serb pride: particularly apparent following the crumbling of communism elsewhere in Eastern Europe. This raised substantial fears in the ruling

apparatuses of the then Yugoslav state—the Communist Party, the People's Army (JNA) and the secret police, all organisations characterised by an over-representation of Serbs. Any diminution of Yugoslavia threatened the Serbs' benefiting from subsidies generated by the country's more advanced republics.

4. Attempts to shore up the integrity of Yugoslavia, either through Communist or Serbian hegemony, begun by Slobodan Milošević in 1987, were an abject failure.

While Slovenes and Croats brushed aside both Communist and Serb interference in their pursuit of independence, non-Serb Bosnians and Macedonians chose separation only after it became obvious that to remain in a truncated Yugoslavia would result in second-class citizenship. Henceforth, nationalist Serbs cultivated a self-perceived 'heroic' image of Serbs fighting alone against the rest of the world. Two key documents heralded this position:

1. The January 1986 petition 'Against the persecutions of Serbs in Kosovo', signed by 212 Serb intellectuals and addressed to the parliaments of Serbia and Yugoslavia, demanding radical changes in Kosovo;
2. The September 1986 'Memorandum' of the Serbian Academy of Sciences and Arts, reinforcing Serb nationalist claims through an extensive critique of the structure and functioning of Yugoslavia, denouncing earlier constitutional reforms, and defining 'enemies' of the Serbs. This was 'rejected by Yugoslavia's non-Serbs as a tendentious, propagandistic compilation' (Cviic, 1991, p. 66).

Taken together, these documents appeared to justify armed conflict as a means of securing Serb national (territorial) interests. They provided a simplistic ideological pretext for conflict 'solutions' to socio-spatial complexities. In 1987, the then Communist Milošević seized political power in Serbia and both adopted and substantially invigorated pan-Serb nationalism (Bennett, 1995). The appeal of such an ideology was extended particularly to the more than 2 million Serbs who lived within the federation in republics other than Serbia, most notably in Croatia and Bosnia–Hercegovina.

With the simultaneous crumbling of communism in much of the rest of Eastern Europe, in the autumn of 1989, the most Westernised republic, Slovenia, drafted a new constitution which explicitly declared its right to secede from the Yugoslav federation. Both Slovene and Croat leaders vainly attempted to negotiate with the other republics for a peaceful transformation of Yugoslavia to a looser confederal structure. But Serbs sought not only the maintenance of a Yugoslavia dominated politically by themselves, but one in which internal boundaries could be redrawn to incorporate into Serbia the Serb-inhabited regions of Croatia and Bosnia–Hercegovina, with corridors to link non-contiguous Serb areas.

Long resentful of their requirement to subsidise the other republics, Slovenia and Croatia became fearful of Serb intentions. European Community (EC) recognition of the independence which the two western republics sought required clearly established democratic political systems and respect for human rights. Domestic expression of support for independence, a third requirement, saw positive declarations through referenda of 89% in Slovenia and 92% in Croatia. In Slovenia, attempts to reassert Yugoslav sovereignty in July 1991 were curtailed after 10 days of conflict, when an EC-negotiated cease-fire saw the Yugoslav Army (JNA) withdraw from the country. This intrinsically Serbian humiliation encouraged Croatia's subsequent declaration of independence.

2.5 Croatia and the 'Krajina'

Serbs were in the majority in large areas of Croatia, and in particular lands abutting Bosnia known as the 'Krajina' (borderland). Croatia's horseshoe shape arches around a long north Bosnian border, eventually abutting Serbia in the northeast (eastern Slavonia) and narrowing into a strategically vulnerable strip between the

Adriatic and Bosnia–Hercegovina southwards down the Dalmatian coast, an area long coveted by land-locked Serbs for access to the sea, past Dubrovnik to Montenegro. Croatian Serbs felt both that their territories needed to be protected and that they were in a position to help forestall the establishment, or disrupt the functioning, of an independent Croatian state, and to contribute to a potential 'Greater Serbia', being able to call upon support from neighbouring Bosnian Serbs. Serbs in Croatia also faced a loss of authority: although comprising only 12% of the population of Croatia, they constituted 40% of the republic's Communist Party membership and two-thirds of its police force.

Following Croatian nationalist success in the April 1990 elections, Communist Party functionaries began to be dismissed, and local Serb leaders were not alone in viewing this as a process of purging all non-Croats from key positions. Following Croatia's declarations of autonomy from the Yugoslav federation in the summer of 1991, orders were given to disarm Serb police and militia units, such as the commune-based local defence associations in the Krajina. In response, the Serbs proclaimed the autonomy of their areas in Croatia from republican authority. Krajina Serbs felt threatened by newly ascendant Croatian nationalism, while Croats felt threatened by Serb irredentism and the potential disruption and possible disintegration which Serb control of one-third of Croatian territory might bring.

What began as a Serb–Croat conflict within one republic overspilled into an 'international' war between Croatia and Serbia over both the Krajina and parts of Slavonia. Early in 1992, United Nations (UN) and EC intervention attempted to negotiate a peace. Overriding the advisory opinions of its own Badinter Commission, which questioned the readiness of Yugoslav republics for independence, on 15 January 1992 the EC recognised the independent status of Slovenia and Croatia.

As UN negotiator, the former US Secretary of State, Cyrus Vance, was now to give his name to a plan covering the withdrawal of the JNA from Croatia and the establishment of a United Nations Protection Force (UNPROFOR) presence to protect a buffer zone between Croats and Serbs. Such a plan, which, from April 1992, brought 14 000 UN troops to Croatia, recognised the Krajina Serbs as equal signatory partners with Croatia and (rump) Yugoslavia. Outbreaks of conflict continued until a ceasefire agreement was reached in March 1994 which re-emphasised the UNPROFOR presence to protect a 2 km buffer zone and to oversee 19 crossing points. The most important road and rail links between Serbia and Croatia, however, remained in abeyance for the normal transit of goods and people. These included the principal rail route to Dalmatia which passed through the Krajina town of Knin, and the main international road and rail links through the spine of former Yugoslavia from Western Europe to the Black Sea and the Middle East via Zagreb and Belgrade. By the time of the agreement, some 400 000 people were living in the Krajina.

Subsequently the Croatian leadership indicated that it did not wish to renew the agreement when it expired at the end of March 1995, and that it wished the UNPROFOR peacekeeping forces to leave. An inability to assist the return of refugees was put forward as one reason for viewing the UN presence as a 'failure'. But to the Croatian leadership, the UN presence had merely sustained Serb territorial gains of 1991, and Zagreb was intent on winding up the unfinished business of having 30% of Croatian territory remaining in 'foreign' (Serb) hands.

Despite a continued UN presence, Croatian forces subsequently took the Krajina and western Slavonia by force in the summer of 1995. This was accompanied by the destruction of Serb property and settlements and the evacuation of large numbers of Serb refugees to Serbia, with a knock-on effect for some Croats in Serbia and an attempt to resettle a number of displaced Serbs in Kosovo. The question of Serb-occupied eastern Slavonia, the last part of the EC-recognised Croatian state not to be 'liberated', abutting Serbia, remained.

2.6 Bosnia divided

With a complicated mix of ethno-religious communities (Table 1.2, Figure 2.5(a)), Bosnia–Hercegovina was the Yugoslav republic most likely to succumb to the irredentist pressures of ascendant neighbouring nationalisms. Fearing that either or both Serbia and Croatia would seek to redraw the local map, a special meeting of the Bosnian assembly met in March 1990 to denounce any notion of changing Bosnia's borders, emphasising the need to preserve Bosnia's unique character as a multinational, multi-religious republic.

In demanding the secession of large parts of northern and western Bosnia which could then join up with the Krajina, Bosnian Serbs clearly had the full support of the Belgrade leadership. With appalling conflict taking place on several fronts, the September 1991 UN arms embargo imposed on the whole of Yugoslavia had little effect on the well-stocked Serb-dominated JNA, but seriously impeded the Serbs' opponents, most notably the Bosnian government forces. International recognition of Croatia and Slovenia meant that it was now necessary for Bosnia to seek independence also, otherwise it would be left to the mercy of Serbia in a rump Yugoslavia. In response to an EC invitation, a referendum on the question took place in February 1992, in which Bosnian Muslims and Croats voted overwhelmingly for independence; Bosnian Serbs abstained.

One dimension of the worst conflict in Europe since the Second World War, saw Serbs and Croats competing with each other to devise territorial 'solutions' to the Bosnian question. The EC and Lord Carrington even chaired negotiating sessions on the question. All they achieved was to emphasise that such plans would disadvantage hundreds of thousands of Bosnians, the majority of whom had 'voted for a democratic and independent Bosnia of equal citizens' (Malcolm, 1994, p. 233).

The EC recognised Bosnia–Hercegovina as an independent state on 6 April 1992. Three weeks

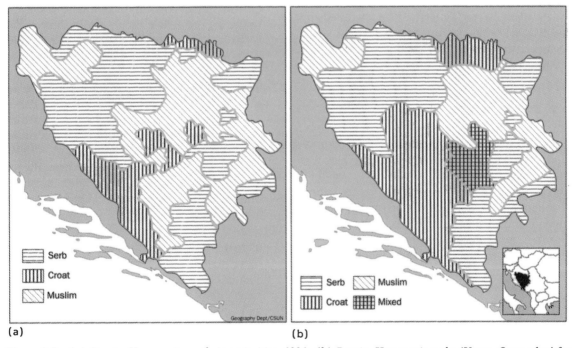

(a)

(b)

Figure 2.5 *(a) Bosnia–Hercegovina: ethnic majorities, 1991; (b) Bosnia–Hercegovina: the 'Vance–Owen plan' for partition, 1992–93. Source: Jordan (1993, p. 181)*

29

later the declaration of a new federal state of Yugoslavia, comprising Serbia and Montenegro alone, meant that the JNA's presence in Bosnia could no longer be justified as that of a peace-keeping force, and the role of paramilitaries in achieving Serbian aims in Bosnia now became more critical.

International condemnation of the way in which paramilitaries set about modifying Bosnia–Hercegovina's cultural geography appeared to have little effect, even when comparisons were drawn between the methods euphemistically referred to by some as 'ethnic cleansing' and the Nazi 'final solution' for the Jews (Gutman, 1993). The West appeared not to fully appreciate that grotesque 'ethnic cleansing' genocidal activities were not a by-product of the conflict but that the dismantling of pre-existing administrative–territorial structures, and the obliteration of settlements, culture and human life were axial to the major Yugoslav wars of succession now being acted out. This was no conventional 'civil' war, but a series of conflicts embodying very definite territorial ambitions within and against an independent sovereign state as recognised by the EC, set within a framework of even wider (competing) territorially expressed newly unleashed nationalist aspirations.

2.7 The Vance–Owen plan

October 1992 saw the first cartographical expression of a proposed political settlement. This was put forward on behalf of the EC and UN negotiators, now Lord Owen and Cyrus Vance. It sought to represent midway points between the individual demands of the Serbs, Croats and the Bosnian government. As a consequence, the Bosnian government was led to believe that Serbs and Croats were being rewarded for their aggression, while to the aggressors it appeared that by continuing their hostile acts they would place themselves in a stronger position to claim more territory (Malcolm, 1994, p. 247).

The plan sought to create a system of cantons which could pursue most governmental func-

tions. When the plan was reissued at Geneva in January 1993 (Figure 2.5(b)), it also insisted that the cantons established in Serb-occupied areas would not be geographically linked with Serbia in a way which could permit a single contiguous territory, and that refugees be allowed to return to their homes unimpeded throughout Bosnia. But giving full legislative, judicial and executive powers (including policing) to the cantons would make it virtually impossible for Muslim refugees to return safely to Serb-ruled cantons. Further, the Serb-held areas were already joined by links which were crucial for the Serb military leadership (Malcolm, 1994, p. 248). In geographical terms, the plan was unsuccessful:

1. By partitioning the country along ethnic lines, which was the key purpose, a high percentage of all groups would have been left in the 'wrong' ethnic area, as suggested by a comparison of Figures 2.5(a) and (b).

2. Being based on commune-level data, the plan completely masked patterns at village level. For example, most of the villages and hence territory of a particular commune could be settled by one ethnic group, yet in the plan be assigned to another because that group would be more numerous by virtue of its dominance in a nearby city.

3. The proposed areas did not conform to geographically functional or coherent areas. They ignored mountains, rivers and other natural boundaries, while not conforming to agricultural areas. Further, Jordan's (1993) map of functional economic regions (Figure 2.6(a)) shows the overall economic landscape of the country has been focused on cities acting as regional centres. Overlying this map with that of the Vance–Owen plan (Figure 2.5(b)) produces a composite with virtually no correspondence (Figure 2.6(b)): the proposed Vance–Owen regions were not based on cities, they truncated pre-existing commuting sheds, and would otherwise destroy the spatial landscape of the country.

In short, the Vance–Owen plan was both a cartographical embodiment of the statement that

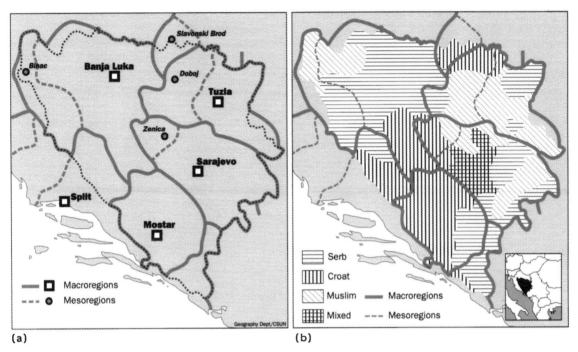

Figure 2.6 *(a) Bosnia-Hercegovina: functional economic regions; (b) Bosnia–Hercegovina: composite map of functional economic regions and the Vance–Owen plan. Source: Jordan (1993, p.183)*

the functional relationships which had characterised an effectively multicultural Bosnia–Hercegovina could not be reinstated, and an appeasing acquiescence to the territorial consolidation sought by nationalist aggressors.

Further, on the January 1993 version of the plan the cantons were given 'ethnic' labels on the map, but at the same time the impression was given that precise boundaries were not yet fixed, a context which had the (predictable) effect of inciting renewed competition for territory. Most damagingly, it provoked conflict between Croat and Muslim forces over parts of central Bosnia where hitherto a mixed Muslim–Croat population had lived in relative harmony. In May 1993 the UN human rights representative, Tadeusz Mazowiecki, warned that the published plan was actually encouraging 'ethnic cleansing'.

In those areas where ethnic identity and territory are disputed, as in Bosnia–Hercegovina, the imposition of static maps which naïvely apportion territory according to group strength, provides no lasting answer to an almost intractable problem. Owen–Stoltenburg, Contact Group and Holbrooke plans followed the Vance–Owen solution, all of which continued to be seen as little more than Western appeasement and covert surrender to aggressors' ambitions.

When any notion of attempting to enforce the Vance–Owen plan was abandoned, the deployment of 75 000 UN peacekeeping troops became focused on half a dozen so-called 'safe areas' where it was decided that the remnants of Bosnia's 2 million Muslims would be allowed to congregate. However, the Muslims' safety was far from guaranteed in such designated areas: the UN mandate entitled the Muslims' 'protectors' to return fire not if the Muslims were shot at but only under circumstances where the UN soldiers themselves came under attack. Sarajevo was notoriously subject to indiscriminate shelling and sniper fire. This apparent symbol of UN impotence was further emphasised with the subsequent taking of a number of 'safe areas' by Bosnian Serbs. UNPROFOR's ground withdrawal from other designated areas highlighted the West's sense of humiliation and focused the Bosnian government's sense of outrage. The subsequent resort to NATO air strikes only helped to re-emphasise the longer-term and diverging positions taken by Russian and Western interests.

The question remains as to whether old Balkan enmities can be overcome on the region's long path of modernisation when so many ethnic complications and Western misperceptions persist. And if they cannot, what is the future for Southeast Europe, and indeed, what are the implications for the rest of Europe and for post-cold war Western alliances? The following chapters may go some way in addressing and putting such questions in context.

2.8 References

Bebler, A., 1993, Yugoslavia's variety of communist federalism and her demise, *Communist and Post-communist Studies*, **26**(1), 72–86.

Bennett, C., 1995, *Yugoslavia's bloody collapse*, Hurst, London.

Bugajski, J., 1994, *Ethnic politics in Eastern Europe: a guide to nationality policies, organizations and parties*, M. E. Sharp, Armonk and London.

Carter, F. W., 1972, *Dubrovnik (Ragusa): a classic city state*, Seminar Press, London and New York.

Carter, F. W., 1977, *An historical geography of the Balkans*, Academic Press, London.

Cviic, C., 1991, *Remaking the Balkans*, RIIA/Pinter, London.

Cvijić, J., 1918, *La Péninsule Balkanique: géographie humaine*, Paris.

Glenny, M., 1992, *The fall of Yugoslavia: the third Balkan war*, Penguin, London.

Gutman, R., 1993, *A witness to genocide*, Element, Shaftesbury.

Hoffman, G. W., ed., 1989, *Europe in the 1990s: a geographic analysis*, John Wiley, New York, 6th edn.

Jelavich, B., 1983, *History of the Balkans*, 2 vols, Cambridge University Press, Cambridge.

Jelavich, C., Jelavich, B., 1965, *The Balkans*, Prentice-Hall, Englewood Cliffs, NJ.

Jordan, P., 1993, Is there a coincidence of ethnic and functional regions in Croatia and Bosnia–Hercegovina? *Geographica Slovenica*, **24**, 179–89.

Kinross, Lord, 1977, *The Ottoman centuries: the rise and fall of the Turkish empire*, Morrow Quill, New York.

Kocsis, K., 1992, Changing ethnic, religious and political patterns in the Carpatho-Balkan area, in Kertész, Á., Kovács, Z., eds, *New perspectives in Hungarian geography*, Akadémiai Kiadó, Budapest, pp. 115–42.

Magaš, B., 1993, *The destruction of Yugoslavia: tracking the break-up 1980–92*, Verso, London and New York.

Magocsi, P. R., 1993, *Historical atlas of East Central Europe*, University of Washington Press, Seattle and London.

Malcolm, N., 1994, *Bosnia: a short history*, Macmillan, London.

Mitrovic, A., ed., 1983, *Istorija Srpskog naroda*, Srpska Knjizevni Zadruga, Belgrade.

Mladenović, M., 1978, The policy and system of stimulating faster development in economically underdeveloped republics and the autonomous province of Kosovo in the period 1976–1980, *Yugoslav Survey*, **19**(1), 55–68.

Moore, P., 1992, The 'Albanian question' in the former Yugoslavia, *RFE/RL Research Report*, **1**(14), 7–15.

Schevill, F., 1922, *The history of the Balkan Peninsula*, Harcourt, Brace and Company, New York. Reprinted as *A history of the Balkans*, 1991, Dorset Press, New York (page references are to the reprinted edition).

Shackleton, M. R., 1959, *Europe: a regional geography*, Longmans Green, New York, 6th edn.

Stoianovich, T., 1994, *Balkan worlds: the first and last Europe*, M. E. Sharp, Armonk and London.

Section B
Emerging from the Yugoslav vortex

Introduction

Darrick Danta

B.1 Yugoslavia unravelling

Yugoslavia—land of the South Slavs—rose from the ashes of the First World War to fulfil the long-held dream of uniting the kindred peoples of Southeast Europe under a single banner. Born of conflict and raised on strife, the country became the embodiment of Wilsonian self-determination. Yugoslavia also achieved economic success: during the 1970s, people throughout Eastern Europe looked with envy at the relative prosperity enjoyed by large numbers of the country's inhabitants.

That the Yugoslav experiment ultimately failed gives stark testimony to the difficulty in creating national identity among peoples that have experienced disparate development paths. Indeed, Yugoslavia was sometimes described as six republics, five nations, four languages, three religions, two alphabets and one party (Lewis, 1987, p. 504). A sense of mistrust bordering on paranoia also seems to have been present; schoolchildren supposedly remembered the names of neighbouring countries (Bulgaria, Romania, Italy, Greece, Albania, Hungary [Magyarország] and Austria) by the word *brigama*, which means 'troubles' or 'worries' in Serbo-Croat.

The fabric of Yugoslavia began to unravel following the death of Tito, wartime partisan leader and the country's post-war fountainhead, in 1981. The decentralised economy overheated and then declined, and slumped as resentment grew over the continued need of richer republics, especially Slovenia and Croatia, to subsidise the poorer ones. Economic scandal and political catharsis appeared to take hold at federal level, just as from the mid-1980s, Serbian nationalism was in the ascendant. Finally, as the wave of revolution swept across Eastern Europe in the waning months of 1989, individuals in some of the republics made known their desire for independence. Of course, the break-up of the former Yugoslavia, briefly examined in Chapter 2, has generated a substantial literature: English-language books on the subject published since 1992 include Almond (1994), Biberaj (1993), Cohen (1993), Crnobrnja (1994), Denitch (1994), Dragnich (1992), Drakulić (1993a,b), Glenny (1992), Hall (1994), Magaš (1993), Mojzes (1994), Rieff (1995), Thompson (1992), Seroka and Vukasin (1992) and West (1994). Other works that address aspects of refugees, policy or the war experience have included Amnesty International (1992), Gutman (1993), Dizdarenic (1993), Frelick (1992), Larrabee (1994) and Zlata (1994).

B.2 Evaluating the components

Although each of the chapters which follows in this section of the book addresses a different aspect of the ex-Yugoslav problem in a different manner from a different perspective and with a different emphasis, in sum the studies go a long way towards elucidating and clarifying significant aspects of the territory under consideration.

Reconstructing the Balkans: A Geography of the New Southeast Europe. Edited by Derek Hall and Darrick Danta.
©1996 John Wiley & Sons Ltd

In doing so, the various authors also demonstrate the contribution that geographers can make to an understanding of such complex regional settings.

George White, in the first chapter in this section, demonstrates the role of place in defining Serbian national identity. He argues that place and territory are more than mere commodities: they become, through shared experience and deep emotional–psychological bonds, the ground from which collective consciousness springs; they are not only 'in' a place, but 'of' it. When place becomes part of the fundamental definition of a people, removing them from the place in large measure destroys that identity. Such is the case with the Serbs: little wonder, then, for the apparently irrational attachment held by most Serbs for places that are of historical significance to them. As White demonstrates so well, an appreciation of the significance of these places is essential for understanding Serbian national character; such a perspective is also needed for any viable solutions to problems that grip the region.

Scott Pusich examines the political–territorial structure of Croatia in Chapter 4. After reviewing the development of the state and its current structure, he proposes a new, regionally based arrangement. This structure, which is composed of five regions, takes into account historical development along with political, economic, demographic and ethnic criteria. The proposed units also conform to landform and agricultural regions. Given the current situation in the area, though, chances for implementing this structure are slim.

In the next chapter, Jerome Oberreit examines the battle over Dubrovnik in terms of its causes and consequences. In particular, he documents levels of destruction to villages surrounding the city and goes on to analyse reconstruction efforts with an eye to uncovering priorities on the part of the Croatian government. He concludes that damage suffered in the region was not random, and that villages with the highest tourism potential seem to be receiving most resources for repair and reconstruction.

Alex Papadopoulos in Chapter 6 analyses the role of the Orthodox (Byzantine) Church in the development of Macedonian political–territorial identity. He is able to demonstrate how the Church not only maintained itself during Ottoman times, but was an active institution shaping practice and identity in the region. More important, though, is the elucidation of the manner in which affiliations among the people of Macedonia arose, and how these affiliations support what appear to the West European mind as absurd, overlapping territorial claims.

The theme of indeterminant identity in Macedonia is also addressed by Theano Terkenli. In this study, she argues that political legitimacy of Macedonia based on nationalist affiliation is misguided. Rather, the region should be viewed as a functioning geographical entity; a collective 'home' for its people. Terkenli concludes that the political context of Macedonia needs to be seen as a collage of overlapping and ever-transforming subcultural or personal affiliation and relations, which acquire differential intensity in space, time and society.

In Chapter 8, Anton Gosar gives an 'insider's' view of recent changes that have taken place in Slovenia with an eye to predicting future development paths. After placing the new country in the European context, Gosar evaluates the role of Slovenia as a transport corridor, then outlines some development scenarios. Finally, he discusses problems associated with border regions before pointing to increased economic ties with other Central European countries as the most important future development path.

The final chapter of this section is by Mike Chapman and also concerns Slovenia. Chapman brings the discussion back to a consideration of the 'ethnic' problem, specifically with regard to the importance of cultural identity in the context of changing economic and social conditions. After reviewing some background on the historic evolution and economic structure of Slovenia, he goes on to examine some key elements of change, such as housing privatisation and the growth of the tourism industry. He concludes that independence, while a positive step, has brought economic and cultural costs.

Taken together, the messages that emerge from these chapters are that the former Yugoslavia is a complex region and that simple solutions to problems are doomed to failure. However, rather than presenting a hopeless situation, the authors have identified several key issues—place, territoriality, ethnic and cultural identity, strategic location and development potential—as essential geographic components of the conflicts. Frances Schwartz of the *Toronto Star* has pointed out that 'War is the devil's method of teaching geography'; perhaps the following pages will demonstrate the importance of considering geographic factors in regional conflict and the need to get past the obvious to uncover more significant underlying factors.

B.3 References

Almond, M., 1994, *Europe's backyard war: the war in the Balkans*, Heinemann, London.

Amnesty International, 1992, *Yugoslavia: further reports of torture and deliberate and arbitrary killings in war zones*, Amnesty International Publications, New York.

Biberaj, E., 1993, *Kosova: the Balkan powder keg*, RISCI, London.

Cohen, L. J., 1993, *Broken bonds: the disintegration of Yugoslavia*, Westview, Boulder, Colo.

Crnobrnja, M., 1994, *The Yugoslav drama*, McGill–Queen's University Press, Montreal.

Denitch, B. D., 1994, *Ethnic nationalism: the tragic death of Yugoslavia*, University of Minnesota Press, Minneapolis, Minn.

Dizdarevic, Z., 1993, *Sarajevo: a war journal*, Fromm International, New York.

Dragnich, A. N., 1992, *Serbs and Croats: the struggle in Yugoslavia*, Harcourt Brace Jovanovich, New York.

Drakulić, S., 1993a, *Balkan express: fragments from the other side of war*, W. W. Norton, New York.

Drakulić, S., 1993b, Falling down: an elegy for the bridge at Mostar, *The New Republic*, 13 December.

Frelick, B., 1992, *Yugoslavia torn asunder: lessons for protecting refugees from civil war*, US Committee for Refugees, Washington, DC.

Glenny, M., 1992, *The fall of Yugoslavia*, Penguin Books, London and New York.

Gutman, R., 1993, *A witness to genocide*, Macmillan, New York.

Hall, B., 1994, *The impossible country: a journey through the last days of Yugoslavia*, D. R. Godine, Boston, Secker & Warburg, London.

Larrabee, F. S., 1994, *Western strategy toward the former Yugoslavia*, Rand Corporation, Santa Monica, Calif.

Lewis, F., 1987, *Europe: a tapestry of nations*, Simon and Schuster, New York and London.

Magaš, B., 1993, *The destruction of Yugoslavia: tracking the break-up 1980–92*, Verso, London and New York.

Mojzes, P., 1994, *Yugoslavian inferno: ethnoreligious warfare in the Balkans*, Continuum, New York.

Rieff, D., 1995, *Slaughterhouse: Bosnia and the failure of the west*, Simon & Schuster, New York and London.

Seroka, J., Vukasin, P., eds, 1992, *The tragedy of Yugoslavia: the failure of democratic transformation*, M. E. Sharpe, Armonk, NY.

Thompson, M., 1992, *A paper house: the ending of Yugoslavia*, Pantheon Books, New York.

West, R., 1994, *Tito and the rise and fall of Yugoslavia*, Sinclair-Stevenson, London.

Zlata, F., 1994, *Zlata's diary: a child's life in Sarajevo*, Penguin Books, London and New York.

3

Place and its role in Serbian identity

George W. White

3.1 Introduction

In an attempt to stop the warfare in Bosnia–Hercegovina, diplomats, politicians and other experts are attempting to develop peace plans that divide people into a number of small territorial units based on ethnicity. The attempt to divide people territorially is based on the assumption that people of different ethnic backgrounds are incapable of living together and, therefore, must be divided. Such an assumption overlooks the fact that the various ethnic groups of the Balkans, particularly those in Bosnia–Hercegovina, have lived together in peace longer than they have lived in war. Indeed, many individuals from the various ethnic groups have intermarried. More importantly, despite the war, many Serbs and Croats are still living together with Muslims in Sarajevo and other towns, and are serving together in the Bosnian government and army. Yet the peacemakers, and indeed many researchers, have not tried to explain why people with varying cultural beliefs and practices are able to live together in a place.

In addition to the assumption that people with differing ethnic backgrounds cannot live together peacefully, the peacemakers have had to over-simplify the current Balkan conflict in other ways before they were able to begin their task of drawing new lines on the political map. In particular, the peacemakers have found the need to treat both ethnicity and nationalism as unproblematic and static concepts. They have begun from the premise that ethnic groups and nations simply exist and always have existed. They have ignored the fact that ethnic and national identities are very dynamic and evolve over time. Ethnic and national identities are shaped by a number of phenomena, including new events, changes in technology and governmental policies. Such stimuli force groups to think about themselves in new ways and even redefine their identities. For example, almost every census in Yugoslavia has contained a different listing of ethnic and national identities. The category 'Muslim in the ethnic sense' did not appear until 1961 and the category 'Muslim in the national sense' was introduced first in 1971 (Burg and Berbaum, 1989, p. 538). Certainly, individuals and groups have had to think about themselves in new ways as they have been forced to recategorise themselves. The proposals of the peacemakers likewise have challenged the people of the Balkans to re-evaluate their senses of ethnic and national identities. Not surprisingly, many people in the Balkans, feeling that these proposals threaten their sense of identity, have reacted violently. They simply do not want their

Reconstructing the Balkans: A Geography of the New Southeast Europe. Edited by Derek Hall and Darrick Danta.
©1996 John Wiley & Sons Ltd

communities and territories to be redefined and reconstructed for them by diplomats with foreign beliefs and values. Instead, they would rather define their own communities and territories based on their own sense of who they are.

By treating ethnic groups and nations as unproblematic and static, the peacemakers, along with many researchers, have given themselves the opportunity to define groups primarily in terms of easily identifiable cultural characteristics such as religion and/or language. Rightful territories of a group then are assumed to be synonymous with the spatial distributions of religions and/or languages. As a further assumption, groups then only have the right and desire to claim places and territories inhabited by their members as defined by these criteria. By treating place and territory as phenomena that play no part in the development of ethnic and national identities, place and territory come to be viewed as mere commodities, objects to be traded or sold. As a consequence, no one has explained why various ethnic groups have lived together peacefully in the Balkans, particularly in Bosnia–Hercegovina. Moreover, no one has explained why many Serb leaders are claiming, and indeed tenaciously are trying to hold on to or to obtain, territories that are not inhabited by Serbs. In an attempt to provide an explanation not based on the religion/language distribution idea, it may be tempting simply to adopt geostrategic or economic arguments. However, such arguments do not suffice either. Contested territories such as Bosnia–Hercegovina, Kosovo and Macedonia are geostrategically and economically some of the least valuable territories in the Balkans. Geostrategic and economic arguments fail in this case because they also treat places and territories as commodities.

The important issue is indeed place and territory. However, place and territory are not mere commodities. Place, as Yi-Fu Tuan (1977, p. 179) points out, is 'an organized world of meaning'. Over time, as people shape and alter the places they inhabit, they develop strong emotional–psychological bonds to such places and even come to think of themselves in terms of the places they inhabit. The shared experience of place is instrumental to the development of larger group, e.g. ethnic and national identities. In fact, the shared experience of living together in a place can transcend religious and linguistic differences and become the basis for a common group identity. The elements of a place (e.g. monuments and historical artefacts) reinforce a group's identity by reminding its members of who they are; place and territory 'comes to be viewed as the repository of shared collective consciousness, the place wherein memory is rooted' (Williams and Smith, 1983, p. 503). Place testifies to a group's abilities by heralding past achievements; by doing so, place also points to a future direction by illustrating a group's potential for success and by reminding a group of its responsibilities.

In this chapter, the place component of group identity is illustrated through an examination of Serbian ethno-national identity. The examination is carried out by looking at those places that have been used to define Serbian ethno-national identity, places with which the Serbian nation has developed strong emotional–psychological bonds. The list of places is extensive; discussing each individually would be too cumbersome. However, many of these places function in regional groupings and, therefore, will be presented together. Moreover, since one of the aims of this chapter is to shed some light on the nature of ethnic and national conflict in the Balkans, Serbia proper and Montenegro are not discussed because these regions are not in dispute. Instead, attention is given to regions that many Serbs value greatly yet are inhabited by substantial numbers of other ethnic groups. These regions include the Vojvodina and Srem, Old Serbia (Raška and Kosovo), Macedonia, northern Albania, Bosnia–Hercegovina, Dalmatia, the Banat and areas of western and southern Bulgaria, northern Greece, Croatia–Slavonia and the Pannonian Plain.

Before analysing the places that are important to the Serbian nation, it is important to remember that Serbian ethno-national identity began to develop from the end of the eighteenth century and the early part of the nineteenth century, during the Romantic period. Romantic nationalism places great emphasis on language and religion as national characteristics, but just as importantly, Romantic nationalism emphasises history as well. Unfortunately for many Serbs, no one had kept an authenticated record of Serbian history. Indeed, since nations did not exist before the rise of modern nationalism at the end of the eighteenth century, national histories simply did not exist, but had to be written. National histories were written by recasting the events of the past into a modern national context. Serbian Romantic nationalists, like many other Romantic nationalists of Eastern Europe, wrote a Serbian national history by using folklore and folk-songs. This practice of reinterpreting the folk practices of the past was actually encouraged by the famous Romantic Johann Gottfried Herder (Kohn, 1955, p. 31; Wilson, 1973, p. 825). Since the past is such a crucial element to Serbian ethno-national identity, the places discussed in this chapter were identified through an examination of Serbian history and folklore. These places are plotted on two maps (Figure 3.1 and 3.2).

3.2 The Vojvodina and Srem

One of the most important regions to Serbian ethno-national identity is the Vojvodina and Srem. While Serbia proper and Montenegro are the political centres of Serbia, the Vojvodina and Srem were the early intellectual–cultural centres of modern Serbia (Petrovich, 1976, vol. 1, pp. 344–5). It was the South Slavs of the Vojvodina and Srem who, from the end of the eighteenth century, wrote the history of the Serbian nation and codified the Serbian language. Even after a fledgling national state was founded in Serbia proper in 1817, the Serbs of the Vojvodina and Srem played key roles in the growth and development of their nation's institutions. The Serbian identity that developed among the South Slavs of the Vojvodina and Srem was distinctly different from that of either

Serbia proper or Montenegro. Therefore, in order to understand why the Serbs of the Vojvodina and Srem wrote the history of the Serbian people as they did, it is important to understand how their regional form of Serbian identity developed.

The Serbs of the Vojvodina and Srem were descendants of South Slavs who, unwilling to live under Ottoman rule, migrated north of the Sava–Danube line into the Kingdom of Hungary. However, they did not escape Turkish domination for long. The Ottoman advance continued steadily until much of the Hungarian lands was occupied by the middle of the sixteenth century. By that time, most South Slavs did not flee further northwest but, instead, remained clustered in colonies. Szentendre was the colony furthest to the north, but most migrants settled in the Vojvodina (including the areas of Baranja, Bačka and Banat), with the highest concentrations of migrants settling between the Sava and Danube rivers in an area known as Srem. Within Srem, the Fruška Gora, a low mountain range of parallel ridges with heights under 1250 m extending 30 km in an east–west direction located just south of the Sava River, became an important refuge. Srem was actually the eastern extension of Slavonia, but, with the immigration of more and more people from the southern Balkans, it forged a closer association with the regions to the southeast. Eventually, Srem became part of the Vojvodina.

After the Ottoman Empire reached its zenith of territorial expansion in Europe, the Vojvodina and Srem emerged as an important region for Serbian culture. In the beginning, the Vojvodina and Srem were simply a cultural preserve, but, with the waning of the Ottoman Empire, the area became the first of the Serbian-inhabited areas to become liberated. More and more Serbs migrated into the region from the south, including the mass migration to Sremski Karlovci led by the Patriarch of Peć in 1691 (Holton and Mihailovich, 1988, pp. 37–8). With the centre of the Serbian Church in the region, towns such as Kosovska Mitrovica (now Sremska Mitrovica), Novi Sad, Pančevo, Sremski Karlovci, Sombor,

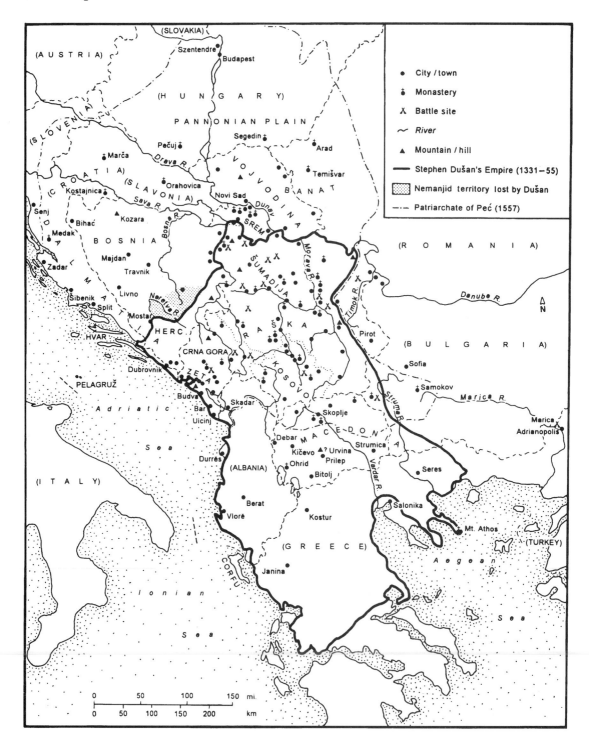

Figure 3.1 *Places significant to Serbian national identity: Balkan peninsula*

Figure 3.2 *Places significant to Serbian national identity: central Balkans*

43

Vrdnik and Zemun as well as monasteries such as Novo Hopovo, Krušedol (in Novi Sad), Nova Ravanica (or Sremska Ravanica in Vrdnik) and Šišatovac began to flourish. Even places as far to the east as Kikinda, Vršac and Temišvar (at the time Temesvár, Hungary, now Timişoara, Romania) achieved some significance. In time, many Serbian intellectuals and leaders were born and grew up in the numerous small towns of the territory and then were buried in such places as Krušedol and Nova Ravanica. In fact, Nova Ravanica, meaning 'New Ravanica', came to represent the original Ravanica, supposedly built by Prince Lazar outside of Kruševac in Old Serbia. Even the Prince's body, his shroud, and an older relic, Jefimija's golden prayer, were located here from 1683 until the Second World War. The Vojvodina and Srem were also the first of the Serb-inhabited regions to have schools, publishing houses, theatres and literary societies on a large scale.

The involvement of Serbs from the Vojvodina and Srem in the universal education system that emerged in the nineteenth century not only enhanced their influence but allowed them to dominate. Thus, when Serbia proper began to exert its independence from the Ottoman Empire, Serbs from the Vojvodina and Srem were recruited as administrators and teachers. By the end of 1835, of the 28 schoolteachers in Serbia proper, 20 were from the Vojvodina, Srem and other Austrian-controlled lands, 2 were from other places outside Serbia proper, and only 6 were from Serbia proper (Petrovich, 1976, vol. 1, p. 222). The overwhelming influence of Serbs from the Vojvodina and Srem in the literary fields and the arts, coupled with their anti-Turkish sentiments, resulted in a Serbian national myth that was anti-Turkish. In their works, the Serbs of the Vojvodina and Srem totally glossed over the fact that many Serbs, whether in Bosnia–Hercegovina, Serbia proper or Macedonia, lived peacefully and prosperously under the Ottomans and were decidedly anti-Austrian and even anti-West European. Prince Marko was made into a national hero despite the fact that he was a vassal of the Turks. Clan leaders, from medieval to modern times, were depicted as Serbs with a clear Serbian national consciousness despite the fact that many of them were primarily concerned with their own familial clans and often betrayed other so-called Serbian leaders to the Turks.

If Serbian history had been written by Serbs of Serbia proper, Serbian national identity would have been much different. The Serbs of Serbia proper generally found life under Ottoman rule to be much more tolerable than life under Austrian rule. When the Austrian armies first crossed over the Sava–Danube rivers and pushed the Ottoman armies further to the southeast, the Serbs of Serbia proper welcomed the Austrians with enthusiasm. However, after living under Austrian rule only for a short time, they found life to be unbearable. The Austrians were less tolerant than the Turks and pursued vigorous policies of conversion to Roman Catholicism. The Islamicisation policies of the Ottomans were, by comparison, much milder and less dogmatic. While the Austrian armies had reached as far as Skoplje (now Skopje, Macedonia), the continuing loss of support of the Serbs south of the Sava–Danube meant that the Austrian armies were eventually pushed back over these rivers. The Serbs of Serbia proper decided to push for independence without Austrian aid. None the less, the anti-Austrian and even anti-West European feelings of many Serbs are not clearly noticeable in Serbian ethnic and national identity. Only in times of crises with the West have they expressed themselves.

3.3 Old Serbia (Raška and Kosovo)

In light of the fact that modern Serbian national identity is a product of the Romantic period, history and historical regions cannot be over-emphasised. When the Serbs of the Vojvodina and Srem wrote the history of Serbia and the Serbian people, they brought to life a multitude of historical sites. Old Serbia not only contains one of the densest concentrations of places significant to modern Serbian national identity, it contains some of the most significant places (Dragnich and Todorovich, 1984, p. 29). In addition, Old Serbia is the oldest territory that any Serb can possibly claim as a place that is distinctly Serbian.

Old Serbia was the early centre of the Nemanjid dynasty as it arose in the twelfth century (Clissold, 1966, p. 91). The territory of the Nemanjids initially extended to Zeta and the cities of Skadar (now Shkodër, Albania) and Kotor. The Lim River is in the centre of the region; however, the region extended as far to the southwest as the Tara and Drin (Drina in Albanian) rivers, and to the northeast as far as the Ibar and western Morava rivers (Tempereley, 1919, p. 19). The major towns of the territory were Raška, Novi Pazar and Peć (Ipek). While the town of Raška has not survived into modern times, the significance of this early capital city led to the establishment of a town with the same name in the nineteenth century (Tomašević and Rakić, 1983, p. 388). Novi Pazar has remained important throughout the centuries and is a large city today. To the northwest of Novi Pazar is Goleš Mountain, which is often cited in epic poems and considered to be the 'very heart and royal fortress of Old Serbia' (Holton and Mihailovich, 1988, p. 74).

Many of the earliest places of great religious significance are also in Old Serbia. In the thirteenth century, the autocephalous Serbian Church was centred on Ziča (in Kraljevo). Later, under continual threat of Tartar raids, the religious centre was moved to Peć (Clissold, 1966, p. 93); Peć eventually became the Patriarchate of the Serbian Orthodox Church in 1346. Peć, however, was not the only significant religious centre. Dečani, Mileševa, Sopoćani and Studenica were important as well. When Stephen Nemanja abdicated his throne in 1196, he retired to Studenica and was later buried there (Fine, 1987, p. 39; Koljević, 1980, p. 98).

In its early days, Old Serbia was an isolated mountain kingdom. Its contact with the outside world came primarily via transport routes that followed the Beli Drin and Zeta rivers down to the town of Skadar on the Adriatic coast (Tempereley, 1919, p. 20). Skadar had great economic and strategic value and also is emphasised in epic poetry. The earliest epic poem of the Serbs, one that stands alone in its prominence in this time period, is called *The Building of Skadar* (Butler, 1980, pp. 429–41; Holton and Mihailovich, 1988, pp. 86–94). The city is referred to in the phrase 'white Skadar on the Bojana [River]'. Skadar was built by three great Serbian figures: King Vukašin, Duke Ugljesa and Gojko; the latter is actually a fictional character. It is important to note that King Vukašin is a figure that appears often in Serbian mythology. His son, Prince Marko or Kraljević Marko and a greater mythological figure, was supposedly born in Skadar. In another poem, *The Marriage* [or Wedding] *of King Vukašin* (Low, 1968, pp. 1–9), Skadar is once again highlighted. The poem centres around an incident between King Vukašin and Duke Momcilo. The Duke originally had a stronghold in the Rodopa and was killed in a battle against the Turks in 1361 in the town of Peritheorion. Chroniclers began to refer to him as the Duke of Peritheorion. Over time, the name was reduced to Pirlitor and moved from the coast to the vicinity of Durmitor Mountain, now in Montenegro but formerly in Hercegovina (Pennington and Levi, 1984, p. 85). The poem therefore refers to Duke Momcilo of 'the white stronghold of Pirlitor'. Also figuring prominently in the poem are Durmitor Mountain and the Tara River.

The importance of Skadar is reinforced by the name of a street and district in Belgrade, Ulica Skadarska and Skadarlija. In the nineteenth century, Skadarlija, a quarter of the city where painters, poets and writers lived, became a centre of Serbian culture (Holton and Mihailovich, 1988, pp. 156–7). Although Skadarlija has lost much of its influence in this century, the district remains a distinct area of Belgrade that is frequented by tourists. More importantly, names in the landscape, such as Ulica Skadarska and Skadarlija, remind modern-day Serbs of the importance of Skadar in Serbian history and reinforce any beliefs that Skadar is rightfully a Serbian city.

Of all the places in Old Serbia, not to mention all of Serbia, Kosovo Polje is the most significant. It was on Kosovo Polje, 'the field of blackbirds', in 1389 that the combined Christian forces of the Balkans were defeated by the Turks. The battle was one of many military campaigns of the Ottomans during their occupation of Southeast Europe. In fact, it was only one of several battles that determined the fate of Serbia. The earlier Battle of Maritsa in 1371, three more battles (1402, 1448, 1689) on Kosovo Polje, the Battle of Smederevo in 1459, the conquering of Bosnia in 1463, the fall of Hercegovina in 1482 and the defeat of Montenegrin forces in 1499 were crucial as well, not to mention several other battles in the Balkan peninsula fought by other Christian armies that could have halted the Ottoman advance. Some historians argue that the Battle of Maritsa in 1371 was the most significant (Fine, 1987, pp. 379–88). If the Turks had lost the battle, they may have never entered Europe. Moreover, half of the forces from Dušan's Empire were annihilated; the Empire was defenceless afterwards. Over time, however, the significance of the Battle of Kosovo Polje in 1389 mushroomed in importance. Serbian ethnic and national identity has focused on, and become preoccupied with, this event and place more than any other event or place in Serbian history (Matthias and Vučković, 1987). More epics have been written about Kosovo than any other event. Serbian identity also has been moulded by this event more than any other event in Serbian history (Emmert, 1990, vol. 1; Kotur, 1977, pp. 131–9). Kosovo Polje is an event and a place that serves as a major milestone in history. Many modern Serbs feel that they had one of the greatest empires in all of Europe before the Battle of Kosovo Polje. The disastrous and debilitating defeat on Kosovo Polje explains the difficulties that the Serbian nation has had to face in modern history. Kosovo Polje also has provided many modern Serbs with a sense of purpose and direction as they have tried to define their nation's role in the modern world order.

Besides Kosovo Polje itself, other places are mentioned with reverence in the Kosovo epics.

Most of these places fall within the state of Prince Lazar, who was one of the Serbian leaders who began to act independently after Stephen Dušan's death. Lazar organised Serbian resistance to the Ottomans and led the Christian armies at the Battle of Kosovo Polje, where he died in battle. Lazar's state was in the northern part of Dušan's realm with its capital in Kruševac. Besides Kruševac, towns such as Banjska, Majdan, Niš, Prizren, Priština, Prokuplje, Vučitrn and Zvečan are often mentioned in the Kosovo epics (Emmert, 1990; Koljević, 1980, pp. 97–176; Matthias and Vučković, 1987; Pennington and Levi, 1984, pp. 1–29; Subotić, 1976, pp. 51–93).

Ravanica is the monastery most honoured in the epics; sometimes it is referred to as the 'Church of Kosovo'. The epic poem *The Building of Ravanica* is written about Prince Lazar's decision and plans to build the great monastery (Koljević, 1980, pp. 143–6; Pennington and Levi, 1984, pp. 104–12). After his death, Lazar's body, his shroud and Jefimija's golden prayer (all three of which are the holiest of Serbian relics) were placed in Ravanica until 1683, when they were moved to Nova Ravanica in Srem and then finally to Belgrade during the Second World War (Holton and Mihailovich, 1988, p. 23). The monastery of Samodreža is the site where Lazar's army took communion before the battle (Holton and Mihailovich, 1988, p. 23). The Sitnica River is mentioned often in the epic poems of Kosovo Polje: the Turkish leader first pitched his tent along the banks of the river; by the end of the battle, many bodies were thrown into the river, including King Vukašin's (Noyes and Bacon, 1913, p. 128) in spite of the fact that he actually died 18 years earlier in the Maritsa River at the Battle of Maritsa. Yet the Battle of Kosovo Polje became so important that epic poets also began placing the death of one of their great leaders at the Sitnica River in the Battle of Kosovo Polje as well.

After most of the Serbian lands were conquered by the Ottomans, the fortress of Stalać and the prosperous mining town of Novo Brdo continued to resist the Ottoman advance. The resistance of Stalać is heralded in the epic poem *The Death of Duke Prijezda*. As in many Serbian poems, rivers are spoken of with great reverence. Towards the end of the poem, when Stalać is eventually overrun and burned, the poem focuses on Prince Prijezda and his wife Jelitsa and reads:

Each of them took the other by the hand,
they went out high onto the high wall of Stalach,
and the lady Jelitsa spoke:
'Prince Prijezda, my dear, my Lord,
Morava water bred us up,
let Morava water bury us'.
And they leapt into Morava water
(Pennington and Levi, 1984, pp. 28–9).

3.4 Macedonia

Round the Struma and the Vardar
a lovely flower blooms,
it is the flower of the Serbian tsar:
the holy blossom of Tsar Dušan.
   Round the Struma and the Vardar
   bloom the flowers of the Serbian tsar.
   —Stevan Kaćanski, 1885
   (Banac, 1984, p. 307)

When the Romantic nationalists of the Vojvodina and Srem constructed a history for the Serbian people, Macedonia figured prominently. Macedonia and the many sites within it served as the power centre of Dušan's Empire, the Empire heralded as the greatest political–territorial achievement in Serbian history according to Serbian Romantic nationalists. As a result, many of the specific places within Macedonia that were important in the medieval empire became important to modern Serbs. For example, under King Uroš II (1282–1321), Skoplje (now Skopje, the modern capital of Macedonia) became the capital of the Nemanjid dynasty. Dušan had himself crowned Emperor here on Easter 1346. In addition to Skoplje, Seres, the location of Dušan's second residence, became a centre of power in the Empire (Dedijer *et al.*, 1974, p. 87). Also during Dušan's reign, monasteries such as Andreja, Gračanica, Ohrid and Sušica flourished.

After Dušan's death, his Empire began to disintegrate. His son Uroš V could not hold the Empire together as the various leaders of the regional substates began to act independently. The activities of these leaders or the exact nature of their states is unclear. What emerged over time among the Balkan Slavs, after living under Turkish occupation for centuries, was an interest in the demise of the medieval Serbian Empire of Dušan. Much was written, even fictitiously, of those southern states which were the first to be threatened by the advance of the Ottoman Turks. King Vukašin's state, with the capital in Prilep and later ruled by his son Prince Marko (Kraljević Marko), became one of the most popular subjects of Serbian epic poetry (Petrovich, 1976, vol. 1, p. 15).

Vukašin was part of a coalition of Balkan forces which first engaged the Ottomans outside Adrianople (now Edirne, Turkey) in 1371 in what has become known as the Battle of Maritsa (or Cernomen). The Balkan forces were defeated and many leaders were killed, including Vukašin. Subsequently, many references have been made to the Maritsa River in light of the battle that was fought along its banks (Holton and Mihailovich, 1988, p. 74). However, while it can be argued from a political–strategic point of view that the Battle of Maritsa signalled the end of Serbian independence and prestige in the Balkan peninsula and the beginning of centuries of Ottoman Turk domination, the battle actually never became that significant in Serbian national consciousness.

After King Vukašin died, his son Prince Marko inherited his lands. Of all the medieval historical figures, Prince Marko probably has been written about the most in folk epics (Low, 1968; Pennington and Levi, 1984; Popović, 1988). Other than the Šar Mountains in the northwest (the current boundary between Macedonia and the autonomous region of Kosovo in Serbia), the exact limits of Marko's state are unknown in any detail. The epic poem *Prince Marko and Mina of Kostur* indicates that Marko's state extended as far south as Kostur (now Kastoria, Greece) (Popović, 1988, pp. 108–9). Another, albeit less precise, reference has been made to the Vardar River gorge, which was supposedly cut by Marko's sword (Popović, 1988, p. 41).

3.5 Bosnia–Hercegovina and Dalmatia

Bosnia–Hercegovina and Dalmatia, like Macedonia, are territories that have been closely associated with the core territories of Serbia, at times even sharing in the same predicaments. Close associations were likely given that substantial numbers of Balkan Slavs migrated to and from these territories. From the Serbian perspective, Bosnia–Hercegovina is indeed a Serbian land. Areas of eastern Bosnia, paralleling the Drin River, and most of Hercegovina were within the medieval state of Dušan or the states of his predecessors. In fact, the great leader Dušan lost a portion of Bosnia when he tried to incorporate all of Bosnia into his state (Figure 3.1). Despite the failure to gain complete control of the territory, it was and still is considered to be a Serbian land by many Serbs. Indeed, the famous King Tvrtko of Bosnia is simply considered to be one of the many Serbian rulers of one of the numerous Serbian lands (Jelavich, 1990, p. 189).

Serbian leaders and their Slavic predecessors have expressed great interest in Dalmatia for centuries. Dalmatia provides an outlet to the sea for many of the Serbian lands, which otherwise would be land-locked. Of course, Montenegro has had periodic access to the sea, but such access always has been problematic. Even during favourable times, the coastal cities of Montenegro never reached the level of prominence of those in Dalmatia. Again, early interest by South Slavic leaders existed as far back as medieval times when the Nemanjids ruled the southern areas of Dalmatia. During that time, Dubrovnik (Ragusa) served as the major trading centre for Nemanjid goods, particularly for the silver and other precious metals mined in their territory. The Nemanjids depended heavily on Dubrovnik and its navy for building their wealth and power

(Koljević, 1980, p. 33). Great leaders such as Emperor Dušan, Prince Lazar and Prince Marko visited Dubrovnik. However, Dubrovnik was able to maintain a high degree of autonomy during medieval times despite the attempts of many outside rulers to subjugate the city. Dubrovnik even expressed its strength and independence by its control of the major mining town of Novo Brdo.

Dalmatia and Bosnia–Hercegovina, like Montenegro, became symbols of Turkish resistance. The rugged terrain prevented the Ottomans from achieving complete control of these regions. In addition, the entire coast of Dalmatia remained a zone of conflict between the Ottoman, Austrian and Venetian empires for centuries. The continual waxing and waning of imperial boundaries gave many South Slavs the opportunity to find refuge, usually from the Turks, in such Dalmatian cities as Dubrovnik, Split, Zadar and Senj. These cities even became the bases from which South Slav refugees could launch raids, particularly on the Turks.

The anti-Turkish, Romantic nationalists in the Vojvodina and Srem glorified the raiders, bandits and outlaws of the Dalmatian coast and Bosnia–Hercegovina; they were generally known as *hajduks* and *uskoks*. The difficulties that these people created for the Turks became heralded as examples of a greater Serbian struggle against the Ottoman Empire. Dalmatia and Bosnia–Hercegovina, with their rugged terrain, were seen as protectors of the Serbs. The people and these regions worked together to overcome the Turks; subsequently, Dalmatia and Bosnia–Hercegovina were viewed as important Serbian lands. The stories of these raiders were then used to write the history of the Serbs in these lands. Those places within Dalmatia and Bosnia–Hercegovina that were important to these raiders became important to the Serbian nation. For example, during the periods of favourable weather, particularly summer, the *hajduks* and *uskoks* would camp in the mountains (Koljević, 1980, pp. 219–20). One of these most cited in epic poetry is the Romanija, a range of mountains on the eastern side of Sarajevo.

In many epic poems, the enemy is referred to as the Bosnians, not the Turks. Indeed, many of the native Slavs of Bosnia, whether converts to Islam or continuing Catholic or Orthodox Christians, did not oppose Ottoman occupation as much as the Slavs in Serbia proper. In fact, many Bosnians not only adjusted to Ottoman rule but adapted to it and accepted it. Consequently, while Bosnia as a whole, and even many specific places within it, came to be viewed as a refuge for Serbs, these same areas were viewed as something foreign and hostile. Towns, such as Bihać, Livno, Travnik, Sarajevo and Zvornik (the location of the largest Turkish fortress in what was to become Yugoslavia), were of major concern to the *hajduks* and *uskoks*. Many captured *hajduks* and *uskoks* were brought to fortresses in these towns and tortured (Koljević, 1980, pp. 243–4). Many of these places are referred to often in epic poetry and song, but in negative terms.

3.6 Peripheral territories

In addition to the regions already mentioned, a number of noteworthy places exist in a broader peripheral zone that consists of western and southern Bulgaria, northern Greece, central and southern Albania, Croatia–Slavonia and the Pannonian Plan. While Serbian identity is only marginally derived from this zone, the periphery, with its considerable size, delineates a broad geographical range that is important to many Serbs. Although each of the individual places within the periphery is relatively unimportant, taken as a whole the periphery illustrates the greatness of the Serbian nation, for to prove one's nation great is a fundamental concern of Romantic nationalists. In addition, the periphery reinforces claims to territories that play more of a 'core' role in Serbian identity. Dušan's Empire and the Patriarchate of Peć are two territorial configurations that contribute to a large periphery and thereby show the greatness of the Serbian nation. Dušan's Empire extended far to the southeast and included such important

medieval cities as Durazzo (now Durrës, Albania), Berat, Valona (now Vlorë, Albania), Janina (now Ioánnina, Greece) and Seres (now Sérrai, Greece). It also included the religious centre of Mount Athos with Hilander Monastery, founded by Stephen Nemanja. While Dušan's Empire stretched far to the southeast, the Patriarchate of Peć extended far to the northwest. Orthodox churches were founded in Kostajnica, Marca, Orahovica, Pečuj (Peć, Hungary), Segedin (Szeged), Budapest and Szentendre. In addition, one of the earliest teacher training colleges for Serbs was founded in Szentendre in 1812, and the first Serbian literary society, Srpska Matica, was founded in Budapest in 1826 (Hanák, 1988, p. 111). The Patriarchate of Peć also extended to the east, to Samokov and the area around it. In addition to the territories of Dušan's Empire and the Patriarchate of Peć, the Maritsa River and the battle against Ottoman forces that took place along it attained some significance as well; many passing references to both the river and the battle site exist in Serbian epic history. None the less, while the periphery is significant because it illustrates the greatness of the Serbian nation, few Serbs have developed strong emotional bonds with the periphery. Consequently, little effort has been made to obtain it.

The periphery, however, is also important to Serbian sense of territory in another context. It helps to create a close link between a Serbian identity and a broader pan-South Slav, or Yugoslav, identity. However, all of the significant places to Serbian identity in the periphery are within territories that are significant to other national groups, many of which are not even South Slav; the most noteworthy of these are the Croatians, Bosnians, Macedonians, Bulgarians, Hungarians, Romanians, Albanians and Greeks. The intermingling of Serbs with the other South Slav peoples and the intermingling of significant places led to the rise of a few different pan-South Slav identities.

The Greater Serbian idea is one that has great appeal among Serbs. Many Romantic Serbian nationalists, conscious of the broad geographical distribution of significant Serbian places, particularly Dušan's Empire, developed the belief that all South Slavs were essentially Serbs. In the nineteenth century a number of prominent Serb nationalists, such as Ilija Garašanin, noting how the Piedmont united the Italian territories into a single state, developed the idea that Serbia was likewise the natural unifier of the Balkans. In other words, Serbia was seen as the 'Piedmont of a South Slavic union' (Petrovich, 1976, vol. 1, pp. 231–2). In fact, Garašanin believed that Serbia's destiny was to unite the South Slavs into a Greater Serbian state (MacKenzie, 1985, p. 44; Stavrianos, 1941–42, p. 52). Later in the nineteenth century, a second pan-South Slav idea emerged, the Yugoslav idea. Those advocating a Yugoslav idea believed that a common identity should emerge out of all the South Slav groups, with no particular group's characteristics dominating. It is important to note that many Serbs did not see a difference between Greater Serbian ideas and Yugoslav ideas. Many Serbs interpreted the willingness of other South Slavs to develop a common pan-Slav identity as a desire of other South Slavs to become Serbs and to be incorporated into a Serbian state.

The emergence of both a Greater Serbian identity and a Yugoslav identity reflected a broader level of Serbian sense of territory. While most Serbs are not willing to fight tenaciously for control of the periphery, the political status of the periphery is, nevertheless, important to many Serbs; a positive political orientation of the periphery towards Serbia is important.

The dissolution of Yugoslavia in the 1990s has been a challenge if not a threat to Serbian ethno-national identity from the perspective of sense of territory. The desire of non-Serbs to be independent of Serbs and a Serbian state runs contrary to the Serbian belief that Serbia is the natural 'Piedmont' of the Balkans. Much in the same way that many Serbs reacted violently to the rise of a Bulgarian state in the late nineteenth century, many Serbs have reacted violently to the independence movements of Slavs within the Yugoslav state. In both cases, the questioning of

Serbian sense of territory is likewise the questioning of Serbian ethno-national identity. While many Serbs will eventually relinquish control of the periphery, many will not be willing to do the same with the territory more intimately tied to Serbian identity.

3.7 Conclusion

By identifying and spatially delineating the places that are important to Serbian ethno-national identity, the significance of territory is cast in a different light. While religion and language distribution maps suggest that the Vojvodina, Old Serbia (Raška and Kosovo), Macedonia, Bosnia–Hercegovina and Dalmatia should be less important to the Serbian nation because relatively few Serbs live in these territories, a 'place' distribution map shows otherwise. Indeed, these territories have played crucial roles in Serbian history and, nationally speaking, Serbs subsequently have developed strong emotional–psychological bonds with these territories. The Vojvodina (and Srem) served as the cultural–intellectual centre of modern Serbia. Many of the modern national institutions of the Serbs had their origins here.

Old Serbia, particularly Kosovo, provides a physical link to the earliest beginnings of the Serbian people. The places within Kosovo testify to a medieval grandeur and illustrate the abilities of the Serbian people by showing that they once built an empire which rivalled any nation in European history. In particular, Kosovo Polje (the location of the Battle of Kosovo in 1389) illustrates the sacrifices that the Serbs have made for all of Europe and also explains how and why the Serbian nation went into a period of decline. Kosovo Polje contributes greatly to a sense of Serbian ethno-national identity as modern Serbs struggle to define their national identity and their role in the modern world. The fact that Kosovo Polje has become a national meeting-place where thousands of Serbs assemble annually testifies to the importance of this place.

Macedonia plays a similar role to that of Kosovo because it too was one of the centres of the medieval Serbian Empire. Moreover, one of Serbia's greatest historical figures, Prince Marko, came from and ruled much of Macedonia. To say that Macedonia is not rightfully part of Serbia is to say that Prince Marko was not really Serbian; the Serbs would be deprived of one of their greatest national heroes and many of their notable historical accomplishments. The Serbs would have to redefine their sense of national identity. By the same token, Macedonia is also a territory of great importance to the Bulgarian and Greek nations. Not only do specific places hold particular significance but important historical figures for each of these peoples come from Macedonia as well. For example, the Bulgarians consider Prince Marko to be a great Bulgarian figure, while the Greeks consider Alexander the Great to be a great Greek figure. Therefore, as in the Serbian case, to say that Macedonia is not rightfully part of Bulgaria or part of Greece is to say that Prince Marko was not really Bulgarian or that Alexander the Great was not Greek. The Bulgarians and Greeks also would have to redefine their respective national identities before they could believe that Macedonia was neither Bulgarian nor Greek. Considering that Macedonia is so fundamentally tied to Serbian, Bulgarian and Greek identities, it is no surprise that all three peoples have come into sharp conflict over this territory. Likewise, considering that Macedonia has its own unique set of historically significant figures and places, it is no surprise that a separate Macedonian national identity may be emerging.

Bosnia–Hercegovina and Dalmatia play a different role in Serbian national identity. Both of these territories, like Montenegro, have served as the physical refuge of the Serbian people throughout time. They are also territories where Serbs maintained their freedom and even successfully resisted the occupations of vastly superior military forces. Quite simply, the Serbs would not have survived throughout history without territories such as Bosnia–Hercegovina, Dalmatia and Montenegro. Subsequently, the Serbian nation has developed strong emotional–psychological bonds to these territories and, indeed, all three of these territories represent important elements of Serbian ethno-national identity.

The Serbian nation would not be what it is today without the Vojvodina (and Srem), Old Serbia (Raška and Kosovo), Macedonia, Bosnia–Hercegovina and Dalmatia, despite the fact that Serbs may be ethnic minorities in most of these places today. One of the reasons that the peacemakers are having difficulty solving the conflict in the Balkans stems from the fact that they treat place and territory as mere commodities. They fail to recognise the long-held relationships that ethnic groups and nations have with places and territories, and that ethnic groups and nations define much of their identities in terms of the places and territories that they inhabit.

3.8 References

Banac, I., 1984, *The national question in Yugoslavia: origins, history, politics*, Cornell University Press, Ithaca, NY.

Burg, S. L., Bergbaum, M. L., 1989, Community, integration, and stability in multinational Yugoslavia, *American Political Science Review*, 83, 535–54.

Butler, T., 1980, *Monumenta Serbocroatia: a bilingual anthology of Serbian and Croatian texts from the 12th to the 19th century*, Michigan Slavic Publications, Ann Arbor.

Clissold, S., ed., 1966, *A short history of Yugoslavia: from early times to 1966*, Cambridge University Press, Cambridge.

Dedijer, V., Božić, I., Ćirković, S., Ekmečić, M., 1974, *History of Yugoslavia*, McGraw-Hill, New York.

Dragnich, A. N., Todorovich, S., 1984, *The saga of Kosovo: focus on Serbian–Albanian relations*, Westview Press, Boulder, Colo.

Emmert, T. A., 1990, *Serbian Golgotha Kosovo, 1389*, East European Monographs, Boulder, Colo.

Fine, J. V. A., 1987, *The late medieval Balkans: a critical survey from the late twelfth century to the Ottoman Conquest*, University of Michigan Press, Ann Arbor.

Hanák, P., ed., 1988, *One thousand years: a concise history of Hungary*, Corvina Press, Budapest.

Holton, M., Mihailovich, V. D., 1988, *Serbian poetry from the beginnings to the present*, Yale Center for International and Area Studies, New Haven, Conn.

Jelavich, C., 1990, *South Slav nationalisms—textbooks and the Yugoslav Union before 1914*, Ohio State University Press, Columbus.

Kohn, H., 1955, *Nationalism: its meaning and history*, Van Nostrand, New York.

Koljević, S., 1980, *The epic in the making*, Clarendon Press, Oxford.

Kotur, K., 1977, *The Serbian folk epic: its theology and anthropology*, Philosophical Library, New York.

Low, D. H., trans., 1968, *The ballads of Marko Kraljević*, Greenwood Press, New York.

MacKenzie, D., 1985, *Ilija Garašanin: Balkan Bismarck*, Westview Press, Boulder, Colo.

Matthias, J., Vučković, V., trans., 1987, *The Battle of Kosovo*, Swallow Press/Ohio University Press, Athens.

Noyes, G. R., Bacon, L., trans., 1913, *Heroic ballads of Servia*, Sherman, French and Company, Boston, Mass.

Pennington, A., Levi, P., trans., 1984, *Marko the prince: Serbo-Croat heroic songs*, Duckworth, London.

Petrovich, M. B., 1976, *A history of modern Serbia, 1804–1918*, Harcourt Brace Jovanovich, New York, 2 vols.

Popović, T., 1988, *Prince Marko: the hero of South Slavic epics*, Syracuse University Press, Syracuse, NY.

Stavrianos, L. S., 1941–42, Balkan federation: a history of the movement toward Balkan unity in modern times, *Smith College Studies in History*, **27**, 1–338.

Subotić, D., 1976, *Yugoslav popular ballads: their origin and development*, Folcroft Library Editions: reprint of 1932 Cambridge University Press, Cambridge, edition.

Tempereley, H. W. V., 1919, *History of Serbia*, G. Bell, London.

Tomašević, N., Rakić, K., eds, 1983, *Treasures of Yugoslavia*, Yugoslaviapublic, Belgrade.

Tuan, Y.-F., 1977, *Space and place: the perspective of experience*, University of Minnesota Press, Minneapolis.

Williams, C. H., Smith, A. D., 1983, The national construction of social space, *Progress in Human Geography*, **7**, 502–18.

Wilson, W. A., 1973, Herder, folklore, and romantic nationalism, *Journal of Popular Culture*, **6**, 819–35.

4

The case for regionalism in Croatia

Scott M. Pusich

4.1 Introduction

For most of its history, Croatia has been a nation without a state. It is one of the smaller nations on the European stage, and its role has usually been determined by more powerful neighbours. Croatia's previous experience with statehood has been both sporadic and unsuccessful. The current Croatian state, which is the primary focus of this study, nevertheless seems to have attained a measure of stability and international legitimacy, although both are compromised somewhat by the loss of territory and economic devastation associated with the recent war of secession.

The purpose of this study is to explain why the current Croatian state would function better with a regional state structure than with the unitary structure it has presently. The chapter begins by reviewing the three examples of Croatian statehood and how the latter two examples emerged from the context of a Yugoslav state. There then follows a description of the current unitary structure, the ideology behind it and the problems confronting it. The study then explains what factors make a regional structure appropriate for Croatia, and offers a possible model for restructuring Croatia as a regional state. Finally, the possibilities for implementation are considered, given the internal and external political environment.

4.2 Croatian statehood

The first example of Croatian statehood was the medieval kingdom, which lasted from 924 to 1102 (Figure 4.1). The various Croatian duchies and principalities were united by Duke Tomislav, who then became the first king of Croatia (*Webster's*, 1988, p. 300). At this time Croatia expanded inland to Slavonia from its core area along the central Dalmatian coast (Rogić, 1991, p. 171). In fact, the cities of Nin and Biograd-na-moru on the Zadar coastal plain were the most important centres of the medieval Croatian kingdom. Zagreb did not develop into the centre of the Croatian nation until much later.

Faced with enemies on all sides—Venice, Hungary and Byzantium—Croatia gradually weakened until the late eleventh century, at which time the Croatian nobles faced the choice of either electing one of their own as king, or accepting the dynastic successor, the Hungarian Crown Prince Kálmán. In 1102 the nobles accepted Kálmán as their king, uniting Hungary and Croatia in a personal union through the monarchy (Singleton, 1985, p. 29).

Reconstructing the Balkans: A Geography of the New Southeast Europe. Edited by Derek Hall and Darrick Danta.
©1996 John Wiley & Sons Ltd

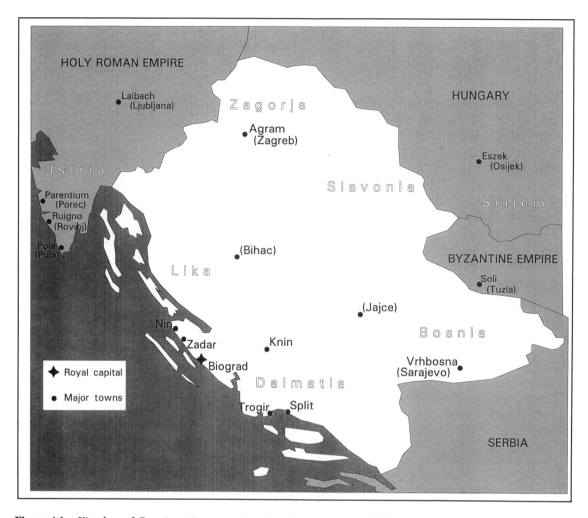

Figure 4.1 *Kingdom of Croatia at its greatest territorial extent, c. AD 1070*

While Croatia had a great deal of autonomy under Hungarian rule, keeping its diet and governor, 1102 effectively marked the end of the first Croatian state, and the start of centuries of foreign rule.

The concepts of 'state' and 'nation' in the medieval period referred to the monarchy and nobility; nobles in the medieval European kingdoms had more in common with their peers in other kingdoms (such as a level of literacy and the use of Latin) than with their own serfs and peasants, who were usually considered as property and not as co-nationals.

After the dissolution of the Austro-Hungarian Empire in 1918, the Croatian intelligentsia pressed for either complete independence or federation with other South Slav nations. To the dissatisfaction of both groups, the Kingdom of Serbs, Croats and Slovenes was proclaimed instead, with the Serbian monarchy as the governmental authority.

Croat intellectuals who considered themselves Yugoslavs accepted the new state, but they were a definite minority and quickly became disillusioned. The Yugoslav kingdom did not make any concession to Croatia until 1939, when it granted limited autonomy, but by then the opportunity for establishing a viable state had already passed. The Croatian extreme right had surpassed the moderate centre in political influence due to the connections with Fascist Italy and Germany, and it implemented a truly Fascist state in 1941 by riding in on the coat tails of the Axis invasion (Singleton, 1985, p. 175).

The second example of Croatian statehood was the Independent State of Croatia (Nezavisna Država Hrvatska, or NDH), which lasted only four years from 1941 to 1945 (Figure 4.2). The NDH was seen by the Croatian Fascists as the rebirth of Tomislav's kingdom, even to the point of proclaiming the Italian Duke of Spoleto as Tomislav II (Singleton, 1985, p. 177). But in reality the NDH was a quisling state which owed its existence to the Axis invasion, and indeed the NDH was split into German and Italian occupation zones.

The actions the Croatian extremists (known as Ustaše) carried out in the name of Croatia poisoned that name for generations to follow. The state itself was illegitimate; had it been

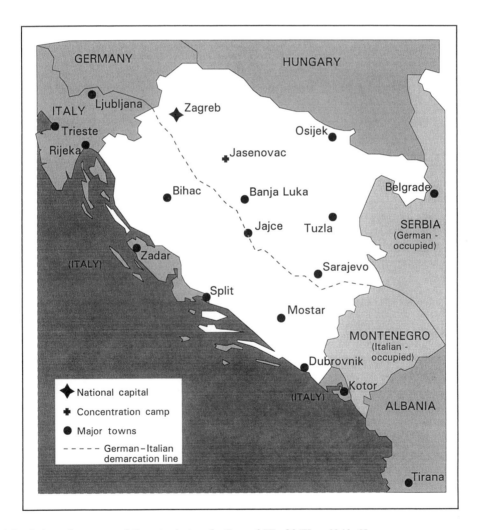

Figure 4.2 *Independent state of Croatia during the Second World War, 1941–45*

created legitimately, it would not have collapsed so quickly once the Axis withdrew. In fact, a large part of the Croatian government attempted to flee near the end of the war. Some succeeded, but most were executed or jailed by the Communist partisans, who became the legitimate government of post-war Yugoslavia. Croatia, like Slovakia, achieved its longed-for independence at the wrong time and in the wrong way; not only was the NDH dependent upon the Axis for its existence, but its genocidal anti-Serb actions ensured future suspicion of an independent Croatia (however legitimate) and a desire for revenge among many Serbs.

The third (and current) example of Croatian statehood is the Republic of Croatia, which proclaimed its sovereignty in May 1990 shortly after the Croatian Democratic Community (Hrvatska Demokratska Zajednica, or HDZ) came to power in the first post-war multi-party elections. The new Croatian government, in cooperation with the new government in Slovenia, proposed a loose confederation to replace the Yugoslav structure, but negotiations stalled (Cohen, 1993, p. 178).

When it became clear that Serbia would not negotiate, Slovenia and Croatia both declared their independence in June 1991. The war that ensued in Slovenia ended after two weeks, but the war in Croatia raged for six months after which an uneasy UN truce took effect in January 1992, freezing the gains of the rebel Serbs in Krajina, who had been assisted by the Yugoslav army. At the time of writing, the truce lines were still guarded by UNPROFOR and although a peace agreement was signed in March 1994, it was not being enforced. Once it became clear that the Yugoslav federation was beyond the point of rescue, the EC and USA recognised Croatia; it became a UN member in May 1992.

4.3 Current structure

The Republic of Croatia has a unitary state structure with moderate centralisation. This structure closely parallels that of revolutionary France, in which the traditional provinces were replaced by departments (Taylor, 1989, p. 149). In France, the new structure was meant to eliminate loyalties to provincial authority and replace them with loyalty to the centre, i.e. Paris and the revolution. Combined with the military expansionism of the Napoleonic Wars, the new structure succeeded in creating a popular French nationalism. This is no doubt an example of which Croatian President Franjo Tudjman (a military historian and former Yugoslav Army general) was aware when he came to power, as the new government attempted to consolidate its control over the police forces and the media, both of which employed many Croatian Serbs during the Communist era.

In 1992, the unitary approach was formalised with the creation of a new county (*županija*) structure (Figure 4.3). This structure replaces the old commune (*općina*) system of the unitary but non-independent Socialist Republic of Croatia, which was part of the Yugoslav federation. The county governments have their power restricted by the central government; they must rely on the powerful central ministries in Zagreb for funding and direction. As intended, this new system ignores regional identity in favour of a local identity, which is much less threatening. In many cases, the county boundaries disregard boundaries of the historical regions, and also disregard the ethnic minority areas.

The Croatian government may see this structure as necessary in a wartime situation (much as the French revolutionaries fought enemies both internal and external), but perhaps the unitary structure and the attempt to centralise control have actually served to harden Croatian Serb opposition to Croatia's independence. Indeed, many Croatian nationalists do not want to share power with Serbs or allow them autonomy. Their level of influence in the current government means that negotiations with the rebel Serbs usually end in failure, since neither side is willing to compromise.

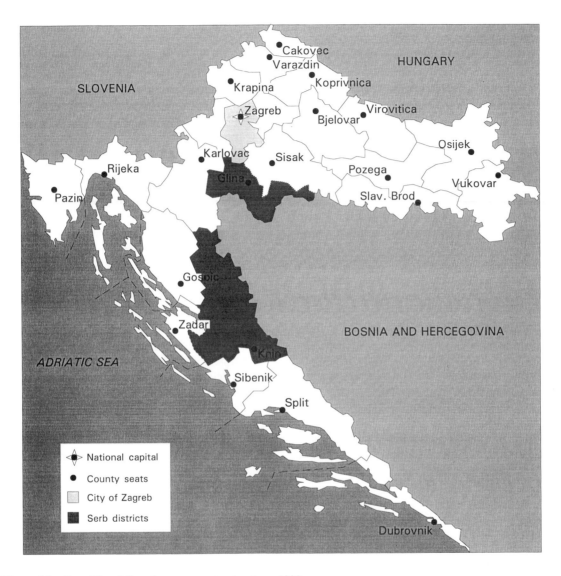

Figure 4.3 *Republic of Croatia: new county structure, 1992*

4.4 Unitary vs regional

While Croatia has a right to determine its own state structure, one can argue that the unitary structure it now has is inappropriate. A unitary state is ideally realised under certain conditions: a compact shape with no fragmentation or proruption; a high and even population density, with no large gaps; and one central core area with no rivals (Glassner, 1993, p. 100). Other important criteria are ethnic homogeneity and a shared national culture.

When a unitary state fails to meet most of these criteria, it may tend to become overcentralised and authoritarian to compensate for a lack of genuine unity. States of this sort often tend to be relatively new in the political sense and ethnically fragmented or heterogeneous (Pusich, 1991, p. 7).

Croatia does not meet many of the conditions for a unitary state. It is prorupted in shape, like a

'C' or a reverse '7'. The Dinaric Mountains, which run through the centre of Croatia separating the coast from the inland basin, are sparsely populated and are experiencing depopulation. Zagreb is clearly a central core, but not overwhelmingly so. And while there is a common Croatian identity, it overlays very significant regional differences in culture. Croatia is ethnically relatively homogeneous (75% Croats), but the Serbs are a large minority (12%) (Bertić, 1988, p. 123) and the Croat majority is spatially fragmented.

The need for a regional administrative structure in Croatia is evident. Croatia fulfils many of the conditions associated with regional states. A regional state combines elements of both unitary and federal structures, and is defined essentially as a unitary state which grants a degree of autonomy to at least one region within its territory (Ferrando Badia, 1978) based on ethnic distinctiveness or remoteness from the central core area. For Croatia, Serb Krajina matches the first criterion and Dalmatia matches the second. A regional state also tends to have regional subcores complementing the central core; for Croatia, the cities of Split, Rijeka and Osijek fulfil this condition.

The location of the Serb minority is probably the most immediate reason why a regional state structure should be adopted. The Serbs have been present in Croatia for centuries, and they are an integral part of the Croatian state: not just in the area known as Krajina ('frontier'), but throughout most of the republic (Figure 4.4). The Krajina area itself is a legacy of the Austrian military frontier established against the Ottoman Empire. Serbs fleeing Ottoman rule were encouraged to settle along the frontier in the 1600s and 1700s (Rogić, 1991, p. 175).

The Kordun–Banija area is especially noteworthy; Serbs in this area are less than 80 km from Zagreb. Kordun–Banija was a crucial part of the defence of civil Croatia, especially Zagreb, from Turkish invasion. The Serbs have constituted a majority in almost every commune in this area between the Kupa and Una rivers.

Krajina Serbs from Kordun–Banija (and, to a lesser extent, from the Knin area) had grown accustomed, first under Habsburg rule and then in Yugoslavia, to a privileged status within Croatia, or at least to a degree of local autonomy. They were likely to refuse direct control, especially by a central government in Zagreb. The NDH faced its stiffest resistance during the Second World War in Krajina, and this was the same area which saw the first rebellion against the Republic of Croatia in 1990 (Glenny, 1992, p. 91). The course of events in Kordun–Banija best illustrates the unsuitability of a unitary approach for Croatia, and the status of the area is an important part of the regional structure proposed below.

4.5 Proposed regional structure

The Communists in former Yugoslavia gave some recognition to the logic of a regional structure for Croatia (and other republics), but this regionalism was only 'socio-economic', not administrative or political (*Enciklopedija Jugoslavije*, 1988, p. 214). The historical regional names were avoided, and the regional subcores were neglected as seats of regional government; the central government in Zagreb was the next level after the communes.

The proposed regional model in this study is based on both political and economic regional autonomy, combined with ethnic autonomy *where appropriate* (Figure 4.5). The five regions (*banovine*) are delineated according to historical, political, economic, demographic and ethnic criteria.

The two Serb autonomous areas (SAAs)—North SAA with a capital at Glina, and South SAA with a capital at Knin—represent the communes which in 1991 had an absolute majority Serb population (with the exception of Petrinja). They should be allowed local control of services such as police and education; that is, they may require that education and prominent signage be in Serbian/Cyrillic, with Croatian/Latin secondary. The police force should be primarily Serb; this pre-empts the regional

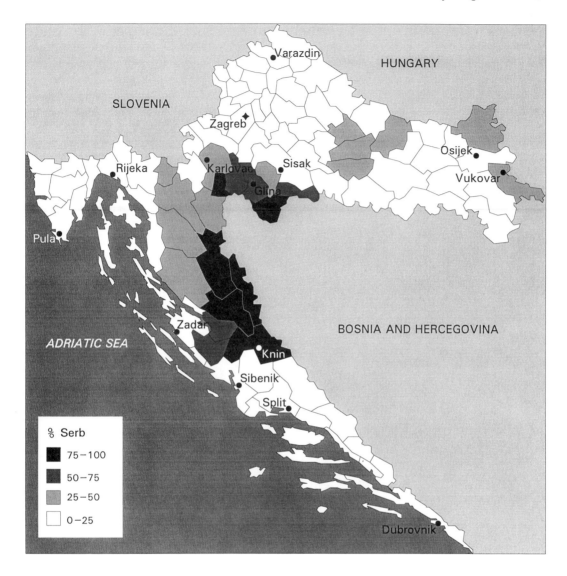

Figure 4.4 *Republic of Croatia: ethnic Serb minority, 1991*

government where appropriate. However, in return the SAA governments must accept Croatian sovereignty in order to be reintegrated with the economic and political activity of the regions, which is the only way they can return to a decent standard of living.

In terms of administration, the regions themselves should each have their own legislature with one representative per municipality/city to conduct regional affairs, especially concerning economic activity (regional taxes, investment programmes, transport networks, communications, energy, etc.). Also, each region should have a governor (*ban*) elected by the population of each region and responsible to that region. Appropriately, appointed positions (lieutenant-governor, vice-president, etc.) may be allocated specifically to Serbs in order to guarantee them a voice in regional government decisions affecting the SAAs.

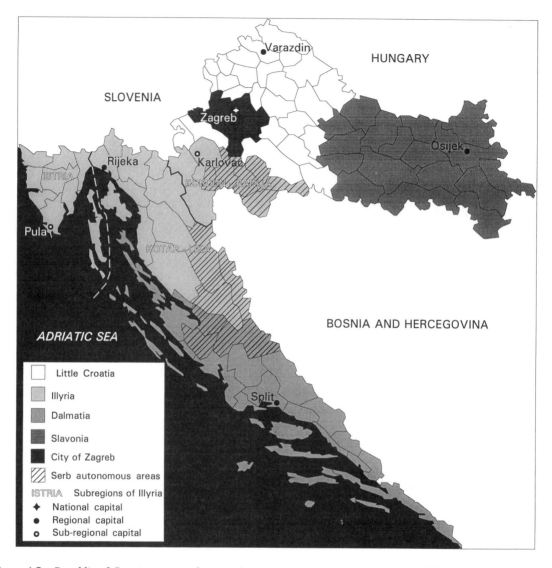

Figure 4.5 *Republic of Croatia: proposed regional structure*

The central government in Zagreb, i.e. the president and bicameral Parliament (Sabor), would retain many centralised functions, such as national defence, foreign policy, national banks, customs regulations, social services and the like. Unlike a federation, the central government would decide which powers to allocate to the regions, not vice versa. Certain state functions, particularly taxation and fund allocation, would be more efficient if devolved to regional governments. The SAAs should be granted special exemptions from central government requirements, such as defence (no Croatian Army troops stationed there) and taxation (incentives for investment in the SAAs).

Various European examples can be used by Croatia should it opt for regionalism: Spain, Italy, Belgium and even France have made efforts within the past few decades to decentralise

60

their states in a logical fashion, not into federations, but into regional states (Glassner, 1993, p. 107). As delineated in the model, each of the five regions has close to 20% of the total population of Croatia (Table 4.1), placing them on an equal footing demographically, if not in other respects.

4.6 Geographic features

The logic of a regional approach is also reflected in seven geographic features of Croatia and how they correspond with the proposed model: urban, rural, economic, political, ethnic, historical and physical.

The urban geography of Croatia comes very close to the regional system ideal. It definitely has a

major core, Zagreb (population about 700 000); but it also has the three regional subcores of Split, Rijeka and Osijek (population between 100 000 and 200 000) (Table 4.2). In addition, there are two important regional subcores in the proposed Illyria region: Pula and Karlovac (about 60 000 each). The name 'Illyria' for this region is derived from the Illyrian provinces established by Napoleon, of which this region was a part, and also the Illyrian movement among Croats and Croatian Serbs in the mid-1800s which gave rise to the multinational Yugoslav idea.

Finally, the city of Zagreb itself is separate from the surrounding rural region, which has always had an ambivalent relationship with the city. The oldest parts of Zagreb, Gradec and Kaptol, were declared a free royal city and an archbishopric, respectively, in 1242 (Bertić,

Table 4.1 *Croatian regional population data*

Region	1981	Share (%)	1991	Share (%)	Share change
Slavonia	990 146	21.5	1 006 249	21.1	−0.4
'L' Croatia	976 613	21.2	962 698	20.2	−1.0
Dalmatia	898 003	19.5	961 024	20.2	+0.7
Zagreb	873 353	19.0	950 232	20.0	+1.0
Illyria	863 354	18.8	880 141	18.5	−0.3
Istria	227 967	5.0	244 402	5.1	+0.1
Kotar–Lika	386 901	8.4	393 108	8.3	−0.1
Kordun–Banija	248 486	5.4	242 631	5.1	−0.3
Total	4 601 469		4 760 344		

'L' = 'Little' Croatia.
Source: Križovan and Štefanac (1991).

Table 4.2 *Area and urban population data for Croatia*

Region	Area (km²)	Share (%)	Capital	Population	
				1981	1991
Illyria	18 092	32.0	Rijeka	159 433	167 757
Kotar–Lika	9 962	17.6	Rijeka	48 249	45 409
Kordun–Banija	4 487	8.0	Karlovac	55 031	59 658
Istria	3 643	6.4	Pula	56 153	62 690
Slavonia	13 344	23.6	Osijek	104 775	104 553
Dalmatia	12 158	21.5	Split	169 322	189 444
'L' Croatia	11 016	19.5	Varaždin	39 545	41 728
Zagreb	1 928	3.4	Zagreb	649 586	703 799
Total	56 538			1 122 661	1 207 281

'L' = 'Little' Croatia.
Sources: Bertić (1988); Križovan (1993).

1992). In addition to remaining the seat of the central government in the proposed model, Zagreb would have a separate regional/metropolitan government.

The rural region surrounding Zagreb comes closest to fulfilling the nationalist ideal of the Croatian peasant working his own farm in an ethnically homogeneous land, and it was the main portion of Croatia left unoccupied by the Turks; it is given the name 'Little' Croatia to prevent confusion. Its regional capital, Varaždin (population about 40 000), was the capital of Habsburg Croatia from 1756 to 1776, at which time it was severely damaged by fire (Marković, 1990, p. 281). It still retains a baroque identity.

The rural geography of Croatia also shows considerable regional variation and identity (*Enciklopedija Jugoslavije*, 1988, p. 251). In fact, the main agricultural regions match the proposed regions almost perfectly (Figure 4.6). 'Little'

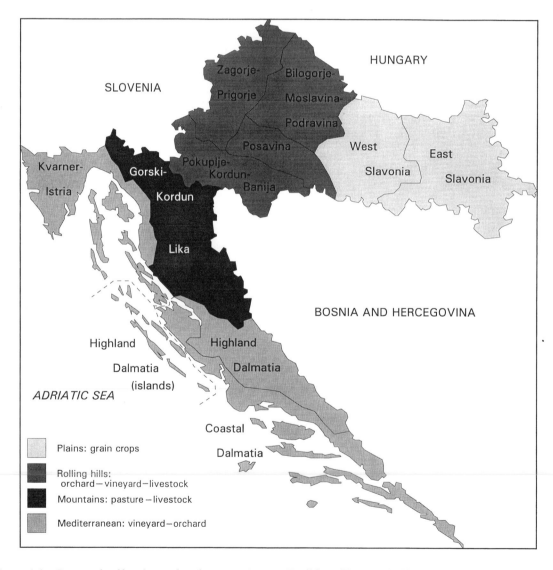

Figure 4.6   *Croatia: landform/agricultural regions. Source:* Enciklopedija Jugoslavije *(1988, p. 251)*

Croatia is characterised by farming adapted to the landscape of rolling hills and hollows; Slavonia is dominated by mechanised plains agriculture, much of which was collectivised in Yugoslavia; Dalmatia is represented by variants of Mediterranean agriculture; and Illyria is extremely diverse, with Mediterranean agriculture in Istria, hilly agriculture in Kordun–Banija and its own mountain-plateau farming in Kotar–Lika.

The economic geography also varies by region (Bertić, 1988, pp. 102–3, 108–9, 119). Each region has its own strengths: Dalmatia was a major tourist destination before the war, and grows specialised Mediterranean crops and has a major fishing industry. Slavonia is strongly orientated towards grain crops, food processing and oil extraction. Illyria even now has a booming tourist industry in Istria, and a major shipping and manufacturing centre in Rijeka. 'Little' Croatia has some petrochemical and textile industries, along with its traditional strength in private, small-plot agriculture. Zagreb is the economic hub and a centre of finance, trade, education and advanced manufacturing. The regions differ considerably in national income per capita as well (Bertić, 1988, p. 123) (Table 4.3).

The political (in particular, electoral) geography of Croatia reveals some interesting regional patterns. In the 1990 multi-party elections, the HDZ had solid support in 'Little' Croatia as well as rural Slavonia and Dalmatia, but in Illyria the leftist and non-nationalist parties were quite

successful (Mrdjen, 1993, p. 120). Regional differences were evident even in the 1920 elections for the first Yugoslav Parliament. 'Little' Croatia at that time supported the Croat Peasant Party more than did other regions (Banac, 1984, p. 228). The Serb-inhabited areas of Illyria, however, supported the Serb Democratic Party (Banac, 1984, p. 176). Presently, the major national parties in Croatia vary regionally in their levels of support, and there are also specific regional parties (mentioned later), which are rather weak in the current unitary structure.

The proposed regions differ in their degree of ethnic homogeneity (Table 4.4). 'Little' Croatia is the most homogeneous (90% Croat) and Illyria is the least (61% Croat). Their common border is drawn so that the Serb minority in Kordun–Banija (41% Serb) is not overwhelmed by nationalist Croats in 'Little' Croatia, and so that a multi-ethnic environment of cooperation can be fostered in Illyria (22% Serb), with an avowedly anti-nationalist capital in Rijeka. While less of a dividing factor, the differences in spoken dialects are also visible (Banac, 1984, p. 48) and further help to identify the region of 'Little' Croatia, as it closely matches the area of the Croatian *kajkavian* dialect.

The historical geography of Croatia is important in identifying the region of Dalmatia, since its boundaries as a region date back through centuries of Venetian rule. Istria also has a long and distinct history as a separate region, also under Venetian rule (*Webster's*, 1988, pp. 312, 556). The other parts of Illyria have specific local histories more than they share a common regional history. Slavonia has a distinct identity due to its long period under direct Hungarian rule (Jelavich, 1983, p. 25).

The physical geography of Croatia is the most pertinent feature in giving Illyria its regional identity: it is a mountainous region with scattered and isolated farming villages coinciding with the scarce arable land. Here is a karst terrain where much of the precipitation from the harsh winters is inaccessible, as it quickly seeps into underground caverns; and the area is subject to

Table 4.3 *Index of national income per capita, 1981 (Yugoslavia = 100)*

Zagreb	186.3	Croatia SR	128.3
Illyria	134.0	Slovenia SR	178.2
Kotar–Lika	154.2	Bosnia SR	69.2
Istria	148.0	Macedonia SR	65.5
Kordun–Banija	89.5	Serbia SR*	95.7
'L' Croatia	110.1	Vojvodina SAP	127.6
Slavonia	108.8	Kosovo SAP	32.7
Dalmatia	106.1	Montenegro SR	77.4

'L' = 'Little' Croatia; SR = Socialist Republic; SAP = Socialist Autonomous Province; *Excluding SAPs.
Source: Bertić (1988).

Table 4.4 *Croatian ethnicity*

Proposed regions	Croat (%)	Serb (%)	Yugoslav (%)	Other (%)
1981				
'L' Croatia	88.2	3.7	3.7	
Zagreb	82.2	4.9	7.0	
Dalmatia	78.4	11.3	6.8	
Slavonia	64.2	16.6	11.8	1.0 Hungarian
Illyria	62.0	20.5	10.9	1.2 Italian
Istria	72.4	3.6	11.7	3.1 Italian
Kotar–Lika	64.3	18.6	11.6	
Kordun–Banija	48.8	39.0	9.0	
Total	75.1	11.6	8.2	0.6 Hungarian
1991				
'L' Croatia	89.8	4.6	1.4	
Zagreb	85.7	5.4	1.7	1.6 Muslim
Dalmatia	82.2	11.6	1.5	
Slavonia	70.0	17.8	2.6	0.9 Hungarian
Illyria	60.5	21.5	2.2	4.2 region, 1.6 Italian
Istria	58.3	4.5	2.4	15.0 region, 5.9 Italian
Kotar–Lika	67.7	20.0	2.2	
Kordun–Banija	51.1	41.2	2.1	
Total	77.9	12.2	2.2	1.0 Muslim

'L' = 'Little' Croatia.
Sources: Bertić (1988); Križovan and Štefanac (1991).

periodic cycles of flood and drought (Singleton, 1985, p. 6) which make even subsistence agriculture a struggle. This explains both Illyria's experience of depopulation and its increasing urbanisation (Table 4.2). The other regions have distinct climates: Mediterranean for Dalmatia; continental for Slavonia and 'Little' Croatia, with landforms (rocky bare mountains, rolling hills, flat plains) which lend them a recognisable appearance.

4.7 Possibilities for implementation

The regional model proposed here makes sense, but in order to be implemented it requires considerable compromise. Implementation is unlikely given the current political stance of the Croatian government, and will not even have a chance of success unless the parties moderate their positions or are replaced by more moderate political leaderships. The current government in Zagreb remains in the control of the nationalist wing of the HDZ, with Croats from Hercegovina (Bosnia) in some important ministerial positions.

This has led to regional dissatisfaction with the central government and particularly with the HDZ. The visibility of regional parties, such as the Slavonia–Baranja Croatian Party (SBHS), the Istrian Democratic Assembly (IDS) and Dalmatian Action (DA), is growing (*EEN*, 2 November 1993, p. 3). The moderate wing of the HDZ split from the main party and formed a new party, Croatian Independent Democrats (HND), which is now part of the opposition in the Sabor (RFE/RL, 2 May 1994). The HND was critical of Croatia's involvement in the Bosnian war and its increasing authoritarianism (*EEN*, 13 April 1994, p. 2), and if it could have formed a centre–left coalition with other opposition parties, the HDZ might have been defeated in the 1996 parliamentary elections.

To resolve its ambivalent position in Europe, the Croatian government needs to be willing to compromise. It would be possible to achieve a regional state and enter into economic confederation with Bosnia, but this requires both that the Bosnian Serbs reach an agreement with the Bosnian federation and that rump Yugoslavia abandons its Greater Serbian policy in deed as well as word.

Any agreement will require trust and also the encouragement and sponsorship of major powers: a possible arrangement would be the USA and Russia on behalf of the UN, with Austria and Greece on behalf of the EU. The SAAs will need both constitutional guarantees of territorial autonomy and a minimal international presence; but reintegration into Croatian economic and political life is necessary as well if both Croatia and the SAAs are to recover from the war.

Mutual dependency is a fact; ignorance of this fact is detrimental to both Zagreb and Knin. Cooperation is needed if Croatia ever hopes to achieve economic recovery and political stability. The events of recent years and the present situation in Croatia show that the question to be asked is not whether Croatia should have a regional structure, but why such a structure has not yet been implemented; and will it ever be attempted?

4.8 References

Banac, I., 1984, *The national question in Yugoslavia: origins, history, politics*, Cornell University Press, Ithaca, NY.

Bertić, I., 1988, *Geografski atlas Jugoslavije*, Sveučilišna naklada Liber, Zagreb.

Bertić, I., 1992, *Zemljopisna karta Republike Hrvatske*, Školska Knjiga, Zagreb.

Cohen, L. J., 1993, *Broken bonds: the disintegration of Yugoslavia*, Westview, Boulder, Colo.

EEN (Eastern Europe Newsletter), London.

Enciklopedija Jugoslavije, 1988, Jugoslavenski leksikografski zavod 'Miroslav Krleza', Zagreb, 2nd edn, vol. 5.

Ferrando Badia, J., 1978, *El Estado unitario, el federal y el Estado regional*, Editorial Tecnos, Madrid.

Glassner, M. I., 1993, *Political geography*, Wiley, New York.

Glenny, M., 1992, *The fall of Yugoslavia: the third Balkan war*, Penguin, London.

Jelavich, B., 1983, *History of the Balkans*, vol. 1: *18th and 19th centuries*, Cambridge University Press, Cambridge.

Križovan, Z., 1993, *Republika Hrvatska: županije, gradovi, općine*, Naklada C., Zagreb.

Križovan, Z., Štefanac, S., 1991, *Republika Hrvatska: zemljopisna karta*, Cankarjeva Založba, Ljubljana/Zagreb.

Marković, J. Dj., 1990, *Enciklopedijski geografski leksikon Jugoslavije*, Svjetlost, Sarajevo, 2nd edn.

Mrdjen, S., 1993, Pluralist mobilization as a catalyst for the dismemberment of Yugoslavia, in O'Loughlin, J., van der Wusten, H., eds, *The new political geography of Eastern Europe*, Wiley, New York, pp. 115–31.

Pusich, S., 1991, Political boundaries and ethnic nationalism in Yugoslavia, 1918–1990, unpublished Master's thesis, Florida State University.

Rogić, V., 1991, Croatian military border: fundamental historical–geographical problems, *Geographical Papers*, **8**, University of Zagreb, pp. 167–87.

RFE/RL (Radio Free Europe/Radio Liberty) *Daily reports*, Munich.

Singleton, F., 1985, *A short history of the Yugoslav peoples*, Cambridge University Press, Cambridge.

Taylor, P., 1989, *Political geography*, Wiley, New York, 2nd edn.

Webster's new geographical dictionary, 1988, Merriam-Webster, Springfield, Mass.

5

Destruction and reconstruction: the case of Dubrovnik

Jerome Oberreit

The 1991 war waged by Serbia against Croatia has been rightly described as the first classical war in Europe since 1945. It has involved the destruction of cities, villages and economic infrastructure by heavy artillery, mortar, rocket, tank and aircraft fire; the seizure of territory and expulsion of population; the blockading and bombardment of ports and their immediate hinterland; the call-up of thousands of reservists; a death toll running in the thousands (Magaš, 1993, p. 336).

5.1 Introduction

Since the disintegration of the former Yugoslavia and the onset of conflict, whether in Slovenia, Croatia or Bosnia–Hercegovina, the landscapes of areas that suffered or are suffering the brunt of war are undergoing major changes (e.g. Pierson, 1992; Magaš, 1993). Displaced populations, destruction due to armed conflicts and reconstruction have played a role in changing these landscapes. This chapter intends to look at the possible reasons why a certain area would be the target for conflict, the causes that have led to certain patterns of destruction and influences that lead to patterns of reconstruction.

While much was documented about the plight of the city of Dubrovnik in the winter of 1991/92, little has been said about the town and its surroundings in the aftermath of the conflict which has been termed by some the 'Dubrovnik War' (Poljanic, 1992; Obradovic, 1993). Dubrovnik is now a free province belonging to the Republic of Croatia although it is still dealing with the toll of the 1991/92 war. Reasons why this area came under attack, and patterns of destruction and reconstruction can now be analysed, as well as looking at what the future holds for places that have suffered a similar predicament.

Dubrovnik is an area of particular interest due to its economic, cultural and historical importance to the former Yugoslavia and today's Croatia. What also makes the province an attractive case study on the causes and patterns of conflict, and the future prospects of such a war-torn city on a micro scale, is the

Reconstructing the Balkans: A Geography of the New Southeast Europe. Edited by Derek Hall and Darrick Danta.
©1996 John Wiley & Sons Ltd

available data on the situation within the province. Data have been collected by local authorities in an attempt to monitor the exact levels of structural destruction and population displacement. The data on levels of destruction were made available by the Institute for the Reconstruction and Renewal of Dubrovnik and information on patterns of reconstruction come from personal observations on visits made to the region in the summer of 1993 and winter of 1993/94, and other reported observations since federal troops have moved out of the province.

5.2 Location

The province of Dubrovnik is located in southern Dalmatia, which is an integral part of Croatia. The region is divided into three parts, the north, central and southern areas. The area of Dalmatia covers 11 758 km² and, according to the 1981 census, had 889 126 inhabitants. Before the recent conflict 78.3% of the inhabitants of Dalmatia were Croats and 11.7% Serb. Most of the southern part of the 'Krajina' region, a former self-declared Serb republic, is within Dalmatia. Today's Dalmatia consists of 22 provinces, of which 5 are islands, 11 are coastal, and 6 are inland. The provinces of Dubrovnik, along with Korčula and Lastovo, make up southern Dalmatia.

Dubrovnik is the most southern province of Croatia. This narrow strip of land, located at the foot of the Dinaric mountain range with the town of Dubrovnik as its administrative centre, reaches from near the tip of Peljesa peninsula down to the northern part of the Gulf of Kotor. Since independence from Yugoslavia, the administrative borders within Croatia have been revised: new county boundaries have been created. The new administrative borders now extend further north than the former province and contain the area now designated as Zupanija Dubrovacko-Neretvanska county, but this still retains Dubrovnik as its administrative centre. The data collected and examined in this chapter relate to the geographical extent of the former province and not the new county limits.

5.3 Why Dubrovnik?

The first question that comes to mind when looking at the evolution of the events in the former Yugoslavia is why certain areas should have come under attack while others were spared. The media targeted ethnic issues as the main underlying reason for conflict within the whole of the former Yugoslavia. While the fighting has occurred between distinct ethnic groups, in the case of Dubrovnik, where conflict involved Croats fighting against a federal army consisting mainly of Serbs and Montenegrins, the reasons for engaging in conflict cannot be seen as purely ethnic. Unlike the Krajina region, which has a Serbian majority, the population of the province of Dubrovnik, as most of the rest of the Dalmatian coast, is a highly homogeneous Roman Catholic one. Insubstantial numbers of Serbs—only 6.7% of the total population—lived within the area, yet the area was targeted as a major front in the early days of the conflict.

Then why Dubrovnik? Although there is no single reason for the onslaught on the province, the overriding causes were certainly the importance of its geographical location and its historical and cultural heritage. These are what transformed the province into an important economic entity within the former Yugoslavia and the Balkans as a whole and which promise the region great economic potential for the future. These attributes provide Dubrovnik with its ability to attract tourism as few other places in the world can. Prior to the conflict Dubrovnik was the prime destination for tourists within the former Yugoslavia. Today it arguably remains perhaps the most fascinating and certainly one of the most beautiful towns of the world. Its location and past bring together culture, a beautiful setting and the riches of art and history.

In the long term, just as with the secession of Slovenia, Serbia had much to lose with the declaration of independence of Croatia. Not only did these two republics share a disproportionate concentration of Yugoslavia's industry (Ash, 1992a), but they were also important economic growth poles attracting substantial foreign investment. The economic potential of the region of Dubrovnik as a point of ingress and egress, especially for land-locked Serbia, as well as its economic value through its ability to attract hard currency tourism, was certainly a strong motive for the federal government to retain the region within the federation, regardless of its ethnic composition. By the mid-1980s the number of foreign tourists entering Yugoslavia had risen to 7 200 000 from 270 000 in 1939, generating an estimated income of $US1054 million. Croatia accounted for 50% of national tourists and 75% of foreign tourist markets for the former Yugoslavia as a whole. In 1984 some 9 124 000 tourists came to Croatia, 57% being foreign (Bobot, 1985; Ash 1992b). The simple geographical proximity to Serbia and Montenegro, which are the only two republics remaining with Yugoslavia, also made the Dubrovnik province an easy target for the federal offensive.

Branka Magaš (1993, pp. 341–2) distinguishes three phases in the development of the Serbia/Croatia War, each reformulating but not abandoning earlier aims. The first phase was to create an armed base within the Krajina region of Croatia leading to a *de facto* control over the area, thus challenging the authority of Croatia's government. Clearly this lulled areas such as the Dubrovnik province into a false sense of security at the outset of the conflict due to its overwhelming Croatian population. The second phase was fought in the name of Yugoslav unity, the extent of the entity 'Yugoslavia' diminishing to what can loosely be defined as 'Greater Serbia' the more the conflict dragged on. The province of Dubrovnik did come under threat during this phase (beginning with the unsuccessful war on Slovenia), due partly to its proximity to Serbia and Montenegro and its economic importance within the former Yugoslavia. The third phase is the federal army's frontal attack on Croatia. Croatia was seen as the pivotal republic; with its defeat a reconquest of the whole Yugoslav federation was viable, or at least attainment of part of the aspirations of a Greater Serbia under the banner of Yugoslavia would be possible.

Clearly, in this phase Dubrovnik and its surroundings were a major target.

One of the early aims of the federal army in the conflict was to create a blockade of the seven major Croatian harbours Pula, Rijeka, Sibenik, Split, Zadar, Ploče and Dubrovnik. Submitting Croatia to an early economic blockade and military siege was the strategy employed to show that survival independent of Serbia was impossible. Zadar and Dubrovnik were to suffer the most from federal shelling, while Split became the main humanitarian centre for the coastal region. Many of the tourist resorts in the area were made into refugee centres (Plate 5.1). Split has been sheltering refugees and displaced persons (both Croatian and Muslim) from a wide geographical area, many coming from Bosnia–Hercegovina, while Dubrovnik has had to deal with a more local population who were driven from villages within the province.

5.4 Destruction

During the period of conflict, three main fronts developed within the province of Dubrovnik. One was from the south as the federal army advanced from Montenegro, and two fronts moved in from Bosnia–Hercegovina, one directly above the Old Town through the region known as Zupa Dubrovacka, and the other northwest of the Old Town, above Slano (Figure 5.1). The early days of the war began with tension between Croats and federal army forces located at the Prevlaka barracks, near the entrance of the Gulf of Kotor to the southeast, and units stationed at Trebinje, to the northeast of Dubrovnik close to the Bosnian–Hercegovinian border. The southern road to Dubrovnik was rapidly cut off by federal forces, who then forced past Croatian troops to gain access to the Adriatic at the height of Slano, blocking the northern access to the city.

These events led to heavy fighting in the Slano/Lozica region, causing high levels of destruction in the region to the northwest of Slano. Over 50% structural destruction was recorded for all villages located between Slano and Ston for

Plate 5.1 *Muslim refugees from Bosnia in a former tourist camp near Split (Jerome Oberreit, August 1993)*

which data were available (Figure 5.1). Access by sea was also blocked by the federal navy (*Le Monde*, 3, 4 October 1991).

The aim of the federal forces apparently was to strangle Dubrovnik into submission by implementing a total siege over the city and its direct surroundings. In order for this siege to be effective, control over the main points of ingress and egress within the region had to be complete; this made the capture of Cavtat, Slano and Cipili crucial as, aside from Dubrovnik's port of Gruz, these are the area's largest two ports and airport.

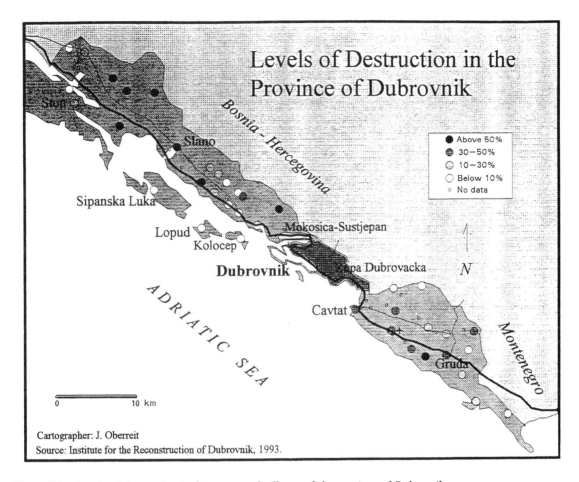

Figure 5.1 *Levels of destruction in the towns and villages of the province of Dubrovnik*

The southern area of the province suffered less than the northern areas (Figure 5.2), as few believed in the threats of aggression coming from the federal government at the beginning of the disintegration of Yugoslavia. The homogeneity of the local population led many to believe that federal forces would not move into the area. The initial approach of federal forces into the province from Montenegro took much of the local population by surprise and time was needed for local Croatian forces to organise a resistance against the federal army. Because of this lack of organised military capability, many of the southern enclaves put up very little resistance. A month after tensions began to grow between federal and Croatian forces 75% of the province of Dubrovnik was under Serbian control (*Le Monde*, 22 November 1991).

5.4.1 Classification

Individual households have been classified by the Institute for the Reconstruction and Renewal of Dubrovnik into six categories relative to their levels of destruction as follows: category 1: below 5% structural destruction; category 2: 5–25%; category 3: 25–45%; category 4: 45–65%; category 5: 65–85%; category 6: 85–100%. Of

71

the 20 925 households surveyed, 58% suffered structural damage from the Federal onslaught on the province, leading to a total structural destruction of 21% (19% in category 1, 15% in category 2, 10% in category 3, 4% in category 4, 7% in category 5, and 3% in category 6). The data were then converted into percentages for entire villages and classified into four categories as seen in Figure 5.2.

Certain villages suffered far higher levels of destruction than the rest of the province. Osojnik, located directly north of the Mokosica–Sustjepan region close to the Bosnian border, suffered 75% total structural damage (Plate 5.2): not a single house remained untouched (of 107 households, 71 fell into category 5). Slano, the largest coastal village after Ston and Cavtat with a total of 545 households, suffered 63% structural destruction with as many as 208 households falling into category 6. The high levels of destruction within these two villages is attributable to the strong nature of resistance mounted by Croatian forces here.

The fact that the Gruda–Cilipi–Cavtat area suffered high levels of destruction comes as no real surprise due to two main factors. First, as mentioned, Cilipi is the location of the airport, the largest airfield in Croatia south of Split. The airport was of obvious strategic importance for both Serbs and Croats, as the control of an operational airfield in a war zone enables easier troop movement, faster evacuation and crucial relief access. This led federal forces to attempt either to capture the airfield or at least to render it non-operational. Second, the area is also located along the only main road coming in from Montenegro, which was the main thoroughfare for the bulk of the federal army, again making the area highly vulnerable to high levels of fighting and destruction. Cavtat's role as the largest harbour south of the Old Town increased the strategic importance of gaining or retaining control of the area. This led to the airport and its surroundings experiencing between 45 and 65% structural destruction.

Patterns of destruction can also be seen within individual settlements as specific structures were targeted by federal troops. From the onset of the conflict, the federal army was successful in targeting key objectives within towns and villages, such as fire stations, port depots/storage, and factories (*Le Monde*, 22 November 1991), and in crippling the infrastructure. Since religion is the main cultural difference between Serbs and Croats, churches and other Roman Catholic edifices were systematically vandalised within

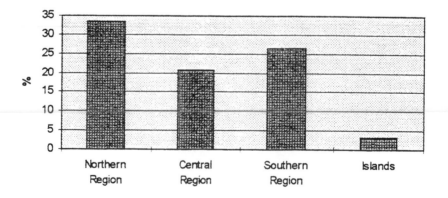

% of Structural Destruction by Region

Figure 5.2 *Dubrovnik province: levels of destruction by region*

Plate 5.2 *Interior of a house in Osojnik destroyed by shelling (Jerome Oberreit, August 1993)*

the district (Plate 5.3). A notable exception to this onslaught on the Roman Catholic faith was the church of Cilipi. Although, as mentioned, the town itself suffered high levels of destruction, the church was spared due to its symbolic significance to the Orthodox faith. Being dedicated to St Nicholas, patron of the Orthodox faith, prevented it from being destroyed and vandalised to the extent other churches were. (This did not, however, prevent soldiers from decapitating other saints' images located on the outside of the church.) A sign was placed on the wall of the church stating 'God protects the Serbs'. This shows the importance of religion as a fuel for driving one ethnic group against another for purposes and ends that more often than not have very little to do with religion.

Plate 5.3 *Destruction of a Roman Catholic church in Osojnik (Jerome Oberreit, August 1993)*

Federal forces left the province between May and October of 1992. The region has not been able to return to normality, however, as all infrastructure, whether industrial or other, was either completely or partially destroyed. As the area primarily relied on tourism, the economic situation is catastrophic. Estimates in 1992 for the reconstruction of the district have been put at $US2 billion (Poljanic, 1992).

5.5 Reconstruction

Dubrovnik must be seen as an atypical case in terms of reconstruction. Two main factors distinguish it from much of the rest of the former Yugoslavia. The first stems from the substantial media attention the town received when under siege by the federal army. Other areas were suffering the same fate, yet far less attention and outrage from the international community were directed towards these other locations. Much the same can be said for the reconstruction effort. International donations have been geared specifically towards Dubrovnik Old Town, as charities, governments and individuals were shocked into action by the onslaught on an area recognised by the international community as unique, having been placed on the UNESCO Register of World Cultural Heritage sites in 1979. The second factor is that the unique source of wealth and development potential that the Dubrovnik region can generate has been recognised by the Croatian Ministry of Economic Development (Ministry of Economic Development, 1992), making Dubrovnik a priority for reconstruction. A final and important aspect has been the enthusiastic rebuilding effort undertaken by the local population: the pride they possess of their own cultural heritage can be witnessed through the very substantial restoration efforts in the Old Town.

Since the end of the fighting in and around Dubrovnik, clear patterns of reconstruction have emerged. Between the summer of 1993 and winter of 1993/94, certain areas were left on the wayside, while others were built anew. Priority for the reconstruction effort has been given to Croatian cultural symbols, infrastructure and a regeneration of the economy.

Areas that were primary targets for the federal offensive have also been those that have undergone rapid reconstruction. These mainly include the infrastructure of the province, namely public facilities and services, roads, filling stations, hospitals, fire stations, port facilities and the like. As mentioned above, points of ingress and egress suffered very high levels of destruction. These have also been some of the first areas to undergo reconstruction, including the harbour of Dubrovnik, the airport and the main north–south road. While these are necessities for the day-to-day survival of the province, they are also vital for the regeneration of the economy.

At the time of writing, Dubrovnik's economy remains in a shambles. Two main reasons have prevented the local economy from returning to normality: the state of the infrastructure, and the ongoing conflicts and tensions in both Croatia and neighbouring Bosnia–Hercegovina. With tourism being the main source of income for the province as a whole, there is little prospect for a return to the pre-1991 situation until peace has returned to the region. However, there has been a strong effort to rebuild areas linked to tourism in an attempt to attract foreign visitors once again. The infrastructure of the province is of obvious importance for tourism and, as mentioned above, has been one of the early targets of reconstruction. Other areas of specific tourist interest that have been or are undergoing reconstruction include the marina and the numerous hotels. The marina, located just to the north of the Old Town, is a former Adriatic Club Yugoslavia (ACY) marina now renamed Adriatic Club Yachting (also ACY). It was heavily damaged, and up to the summer of 1993 remained unattended. Between the summer and winter of 1994, the marina was renovated and although it remains for the most part empty, it is once again prepared to receive visitors.

The Old Town has also been a main area of reconstruction, not only due to its importance in once again attracting tourism but also due to the funding that has been directed specifically towards it by various private and public organisations around the world. Here again the reconstruction of Dubrovnik's cultural heritage has been combined with economic need.

The renovation of Dubrovnik's cultural heritage has been vital for the morale of the local population, whose pride in ethnic identity has grown with the pain inflicted by what the

Plate 5.4 *Reconstruction of St Blaise, the Roman Catholic landmark in Old Town Dubrovnik (Jerome Oberreit, August 1993)*

population sees as an evil force. Religion being the main way for the population of Croatia to express its ethnic identity, churches have again been a focal point and are often the first structures to undergo reconstruction within villages, again partly as a symbolic gesture promoting the Croat victory in gaining its independence, and also due to the importance a place of worship has on the morale of a community undergoing civil unrest (Plate 5.4). The Roman Catholic Church symbolises victory over both Communism and the Orthodox faith. The people of Dubrovnik have an extreme sense of pride in their cultural heritage passed down over the generations. Never before had Dubrovnik suffered such destruction, and the local population has made an enormous effort in attempting to return to the Old Town a sense of normality. Remote villages, on the other hand, have had far less, if any, specific help directed towards them by the international community. Two years after the worst of the fighting, many villages remained much as they did in the winter of 1991/92.

Most rural dwellers are at the mercy of international donations as the individual effort for reconstruction that many try to undertake amounts to little due to the lack of funds, construction material and tools. Most of the displaced population have no income, and for those who do with an average wage of DM100 (US$60) a month there is barely enough for personal survival, let alone the reconstruction of a home. Although the army is actively helping in the reconstruction of certain more remote areas, with the ongoing conflict in neighbouring Bosnia–Hercegovina, and the remaining tensions within Croatia itself (close to a third of the country at the beginning of 1995 was still under Serbian control and monitored by the UN), the government has few resources to allocate.

5.6 Prospects

While it is clear that the coastal villages of the province and the town of Dubrovnik will once again flourish due to the beauty of its cultural heritage, climate and natural environment, one can only wonder what the future holds for the more remote villages of the interior. If reconstruction does not occur rapidly, the very existence of many of these villages could come under threat. Many of the displaced people from the hinterland express little hope of ever

residing again in their former villages, let alone their homes. With the new-found vitality that tourism offered in the coastal areas in the second half of the century, many of the more remote villages experienced an out-migration of the younger population leaving a predominant old-age structure. The longer reconstruction takes, the fewer, if any, of the population will remain to return to their villages.

Economic indicators point much the same way as demographic ones. The hinterland has little to offer when compared with the coastal region. While decline was already in progress prior to the war and was merely accelerated by the conflict, imposing such a sudden death on these remaining hubs of untouched Dalmatian culture will leave a void in our cultural geography and a painful feeling in the hearts of Dalmatians. While most towns and cities of the former Yugoslavia will once again return to normality, it seems that if attention is not directed towards the less known villages of the hinterland they will remain unknown and buried, never to have existed but for the few who once lived there.

5.7 References

Ash, N., 1992a, Fighting on two fronts, *Euromoney*, May.
Ash, N., 1992b, Staying afloat, *Euromoney*, May.
Bobot, R., 1985, *Données sur la Yougoslavie*, Beogradski izdavacko-graficki zavod, Belgrade.
Le Monde, daily, Paris.
Magaš, B., 1993, *The destruction of Yugoslavia*, Verso, London.
Ministry of Economic Development (Croatia), 1992, Sponsorship statement, *Euromoney*, May.
Obradovic, D., 1993, *Suffering of Dubrovnik*, University Press, Split.
Pierson, J.L., 1992, *La Yougoslavie disintegrée*, GRIP, Brussels.
Poljanic, P., 1992, *Dubrovnik war, Croatia 1991*, Nasa Djeca Offset, Zagreb.

6

Single human geography, multiple Macedonian histories

Alex G. Papadopoulos

6.1 Introduction

Research on the historic issue of ethnic territoriality of Macedonia can and should be extended back to the classical, Byzantine and Ottoman periods because the philological and historical records of the Hellenic world provide us with notions of territoriality that are completely alien to the sensibilities of Western-style ethnonationalism and are perhaps more appropriate in this context. This retrospective exploration seeks to discover useful concepts, terms and socio-spatial linkages that explain the proliferation of subjective histories of Macedonia in the face of a single, objective historical geography.

Of the relevant complex of philological evidence, I would like to focus on instances of ritual practice that may underline one of the fundamental characteristics of the historic ethno-territorial dispute over Macedonia between Greeks, Bulgarians, Serbians, Albanians, Vlachs, Turks, and now also Macedonians. These cultural elements involve the quality and substance of the land–society relationship of the resident citizen population of a *polis* and are encapsulated in the term 'autochthony'. Greeks were not simply 'indigenous' or 'native' but, as the etymology of the term suggests, they were of

the earth as plants and rocks were. This intimate association of 'being' and 'place' makes all others 'heterochthonous', and if also not Greeks, then also 'barbaroi'.

6.2 Autochthony and landscape signification

Ritual behaviour involved in the signification or symbolic and material appropriation of a territory as belonging to one *polis* or another, or to one deity or another, was practised by the Greeks as early as the sixth century BC, and by the Byzantines as late as the fifteenth century AD. The strong sense of 'placeness', which permeated Hellenic society and gave rise to a distinctive political territoriality, had as its basis the great significance which Greeks placed on the *oikos* (house or home). The meaning of *oikos* extended well beyond the understanding of shelter to include metaphysical and metaphorical qualities of kinship, lineage and citizenship, and, consequently, the continuing connection with a locale. It is therefore reasonable to assume that the wilful destruction of an *oikos* had, at least partially, as symbolic or actual objective, the

Reconstructing the Balkans: A Geography of the New Southeast Europe. Edited by Derek Hall and Darrick Danta.
©1996 John Wiley & Sons Ltd

termination of a lineage and its alienation from the locale.

Connor (1985, pp. 80–3), in his survey of the practice of *kataskaphé* (the razing of a house) in archaic and classical Greece, underscores its connection with punishment for major offences. The need to expunge the physical vestiges of a condemned person's *oikos* is likely connected to the ancient Greeks' attitudes towards guilt and *miasma* (pollution). Moulinier (1952; Parker, 1983, p. 122) notes that pollution, although invisible, permeates physical objects that come into contact with the guilty person, including dwellings, the soil upon which that person treads, and the place in which the person is buried. It is then most important for the *polis* to eliminate the possibility of generalised *miasma* by purification of the site. Moreover, as Connor (1985, p. 94) states:

the razing of the house of someone who has violated the most important norms of the society and who was thought polluted, could be a powerful symbolic act, affirming the ability of the community to impose its own values, and legitimized by the pollution beliefs of the community.

The physical removal of the house demonstrates the ultimate authority of the *polis*. The island of Rhenia, or Greater Delos, on the Aegean Sea was reserved as the birthplace for pregnant, and as the necropolis for dying, Delians expelled from their island by the Athenians. In 426 BC, the Athenians ordered the purification of Delos, which mandated the removal of all the coffins of the dead from the island. The removal of the substance of Delian autochthony from the island was meant to remove the substance of the Delians' political and territorial claim to it.

Kataskaphé appears also to be a wartime practice and extended to the destruction of fortifications, sanctuaries and entire cities. As in Philip of Macedon's destruction of the cities of Phocis and Olynthus, and Alexander's destruction of Thebes, the city of the vanquished may be liquidated to the point that a visitor may not recognise that a city once stood there. The Macedonians were quick to seize on religious

infractions as a justification for conquest and destruction (Connor, 1985, p. 98).

An alternative method of resignification of territory by a conqueror—entailing both *realpolitik* and pecuniary dimensions—involved *exandrapodismos*, or the liquidation of the male population, and the selling of the female population and children to slavery. Often, *exandrapodismos* and *kataskaphé* were used together.

Both in the Delian and the Olynthian cases, as in the practice of *kataskaphé*, the dissolution of the land–society relationship is of paramount importance to conquest and resignification. The signifier—in the former case Athens, and in the latter Macedon—invests the territory with his own land–society paraphernalia: necropoleis, temples to deities specific to the signifier's cultural identity, modes of production and a new vernacular landscape.

This autochthony-based notion of ethnoterritoriality opens a methodological window for understanding the Macedonian issue, albeit a narrow and treacherous one. Since the hypothesis elaborated above suggests that different peoples in the Hellenic world and its environs—including Thrace and Macedonia—vest a fundamental value on the signification of territory through the manipulation of symbols of autochthony, it is sensible to assume that the interpretation of landscape features of such a nature would reveal the true cultural identity of the region. In other words, the stratigraphy of autochthony-revealing landscape features would suggest whether modern-day Strumica, Kilkis, Petrich and Prilep are truly part of one or another of the antagonists' homelands: Bulgarian, Greek, Serbian, Albanian or, indeed, Macedonian.

6.3 Multiple identities

The emphasis the antagonists place on the cast of sites they identify as their own would recommend such an approach to the study of Macedonian ethno-territoriality. As noted in a previous chapter, it is the duplicate, or sometimes multiple, designation of these sites that confuses the issue of territorial signification, making landscape interpretation a scientifically questionable enterprise.

On the one hand, as Angelopoulos (1980, pp. 53–61) notes, the relics of the Fifteen (Orthodox) Martyrs of Tiberioupole—modern Strumica, situated in the southeast of the Republic of Macedonia—are identified by both Greeks and Bulgarians as fundamental to their historic territorial claim to Stromnista/Strumica and were the object of contest and theft in the nineteenth century. The relic arm of the Martyr Peter—one of the 15—is currently part of the reliquary of a Church of the Fifteen Martyrs built in 1913 in the city of Kilkis in Greece, a symbol of expatriate Greek Stromnitsan culture and the focus of a transplanted folk tradition that perpetuates the original territorial claim.

On the other hand, the process of resignification of territory required the liquidation of the symbolic landscapes of the 'Other'. For example, the selective destruction of the Greek inscriptions of the Church of Saint Leontios, 3 km west of Strumica, during the height of the covert struggle for Macedonia, suggests that elements which assigned the site to the Greek Byzantine tradition needed to be removed to reinforce a running Bulgarian cultural and demographic claim that probably could have been documented had a legitimate census been held in the territory.

Censuses, however, had not been held at the time of the Congress of Berlin of 1878, when the Great Powers were shaping the southern Balkans. Each national group gathered data which served its political aspirations in Macedonia, or interpreted the statistics collected by the Ottomans in accordance with those aspirations. In 1890, the entire *kaza* (broadly defined as 'subprefecture' in the Ottoman administrative hierarchy) of Stromnitsa contained a population of 31 491. Of these, 12 505 were Muslim, 13 486 Roumeliot (broadly defined as Greek and/or adhering to the dicta of the Patriarchate of Constantinople), 3082 Bulgarian (broadly defined as Bulgarian speakers and/or adhering to

the dicta of the newly established Bulgarian Exarchate), 569 Jewish and 1849 Gypsy. In 1910, the same authorities distinguished the following groups among a population of approximately 26 000: 10 000 Muslims, 15 000 Christians and 1000 Jews (Vakalopoulos, 1988).

Statistics with changing classification schemes appear in the archives of the Greek Ministry of Foreign Affairs and the Greek Consulate of Ottoman Salonika as handwritten notes supported by an official copy of the tabulated data from the records of the Ottoman *vilayet* (district) of Salonika. In spite of their authenticity as official Turkish data, they are highly unreliable, as they lump together Greeks and Bulgarians who subscribe to the authority of the Patriarchate of Constantinople as Greek or Roumeliot, and, moreover, describe as Bulgarian Greeks who inhabited the bishoprics of the Exarchate. Indeed, these are only a few of the many possible permutations of religious–linguistic–administrative complexes that described individuals in Macedonia at that time.

Wilkinson (1951, pp. 314–26) has illustrated this methodological nightmare. He examined maps of Macedonia dating from 1730 to 1945 produced by interested, and often politically motivated, foreigners, such as the British, the French, the Germans and the Russians, as well as maps produced by the main antagonists and their spokespersons. He concluded that the striking diversity of opinion on ethnographic distributions in Macedonia—and consequently, the production of multiple histories—was due to four factors:

1. Misrepresentation of facts or even wilful falsification of data;
2. Ignorance of the ethnographic situation—especially due to the lack of reliable, centrally managed time-series census data;
3. The passage of time that clearly changed the ethnographic profile of the Macedonian territories after 1912–13 under the suzerainty of Bulgaria, Serbia and Greece;
4. The vast array of inconsistent classification criteria used by ethnographers and ethnographic cartographers.

Ultimately, the maps are less a guide to the true cultural geography of Macedonia than a vade mecum to the geopolitical imperatives of Bulgaria, Greece, Serbia and Turkey. Perhaps a more accurate intimation of distributions can be gleaned when one controls for the classification criterion upon which each group places most emphasis: religion, language or administrative/commercial sway.

6.4 The Church as signifier

If we were to isolate, however, the single force that shaped *autochthony* (not necessarily political *identity* in every instance in Macedonia), it would have to be the Christian Orthodox religion, its folk traditions, as these related to the Byzantine and Ottoman cultural and geopolitical experiences, and the symbolic spatial linkages it crafted among Orthodox Christian peoples. It is, therefore, important to grasp the events that lie at the foundation of a symbolic geography of the southern Balkans, in which Macedonia plays an important, albeit not necessarily pivotal, role.

The profound connection that Orthodox peoples have had with the southern Balkans is unquestioned. In this, the attachment to Macedonia is subsumed under the attachment that Greeks, Serbians, Bulgarians, Vlachs and even distant Russians felt towards the *axis mundi* of Eastern Orthodox Christendom, the city of Constantinople. This attachment is anchored both in the city's time of expansion and prosperity and in its defeat on 29 May 1453 at the hands of the Ottoman Sultan Muhammed II. While Constantinople was not in Macedonia, Macedonia represented an important portion of its hinterland. Thessaloníki (Salonika), the most important city in Macedonia, was Constantinople's forward bastion, as it was situated on the Aegean Sea and at the junction of north–south and east–west routes. Macedonia's expansive, fertile cultivated plains, its olive groves, flocks and cities were connected to Constantinople by the Via Egnatia. Its sustenance in times of expansion was partly dependent on Macedonia

and partly foodstuffs ferried from as far as Trapezous and Wallachia on the Black Sea. The fates were thus connected: the loss of Macedonia made the loss of Constantinople all the more probable.

The loss of Constantinople was a tremendous blow to Orthodox Christians. The events that led to its fall to the Ottoman Turks, the actual chronicle of the siege, and the fall and subsequent occupation became the source of epic writings which influenced the crafting of national identity and foreign policy in the southern Balkans in later centuries. One should not discount the symbolic significance that the capturing of Constantinople had for the Russians as late as 1917. Until the Bolshevik victory, a gigantic cast cross awaited in the port of Odessa for Russian forces to place on the main dome of a 'liberated' Hagia Sophia. Even when one allows for the cold calculation of Russian imperial strategists, one becomes astonished by the endurance of the imagery of Byzantium and Christian Orthodoxy as a common reference among Orthodox peoples; a reference kept alive and embellished in Russia as martial epic poetry in the *Legend of Czargrad* of 1553, reputedly by one Nestor Iskander (Afigenov, 1994, p. 223).

Slav attachment to the southern Balkans has three bases:

1. Dynastic allegiance and obligations;
2. Geopolitical exigencies;
3. Religious affiliations.

The Hegemon of Serbia at the time of complete Ottoman absorption of the Balkans was George Brankovič (1427–56). He was a descendant of Stephan Dušan on the distaff side, and the grandson of Prince Lazarus, a revered figure of the 1389 Battle of Kosovo Polje, the Serbians' unsuccessful attempt to stop the progress of the Ottomans into the Balkans. Following the long-standing Byzantine tradition of marrying members of the imperial family with Slav royalty for the purpose of consolidating alliances, Brankovič married Irene Cantacuzene, a descendant of Emperor Ioannes V Cantacuzenos. He later arranged the marriage of his son to Eleni Palaiologa, niece of Byzantine Emperor Ioannes VIII Palaiologos. These links assured a dynastic connection between the houses of Serbia and Byzantium, and a possible basis for future territorial claims. It is quite significant that in Serbian epic poetry, as in Konstantin Mihailovič's late-fifteenth-century chronicle of the fall of Constantinople, the Byzantine Emperor Constantine XI, although a Greek, is given the Serbian eponym 'Dragatses', in remembrance of the dynastic linkages between the two peoples (Ostrogorsky, 1969, p. 567).

Similar bonds are forged by Muskovy in 1472 with the marriage between Tsar Ivan III (1462–1506) and the Princess Zoe Palaiologa, daughter of the last Despot of Moreas. The marriage, 19 years after the fall of Constantinople, no longer has the objective of an alliance with Byzantium, but presents the incalculably valuable opportunity to appropriate the Roman imperial imagery subsumed by Byzantium, the autocratic and solemn tone of the Byzantine regime as protector of the true faith, and the physical paraphernalia of a grand old empire, which could help Asiatic Muskovy recast itself as an important European kingdom. It is at this time that the double-headed eagle of the Palaiologi becomes the coat of arms of Muskovy.

By contrast, intermarriage between Christian royalty and Ottoman sultans did not yield similar attachments. Murad II, for example, had taken as one of his official wives the Serbian Princess Maria, daughter of Hegemon Brankovič and niece of the Emperor Trapezous Ioannes. Although this specific arrangement contributed to an uneasy peace between the two parties, ultimately it never amounted to cultural or political association or *rapprochement* of any permanence. The role of the Ottoman sultan as Muslim religious leader made any deeper association impractical and unlikely.

The second basis of attachment with Byzantium, especially for Serbia, was the precarious geopolitical position of Christian Orthodox populations who were trapped be-

tween the ambitious Vladislav III of Hungary and Poland and the *voivode* of Transylvania under Corvinus Hunyadi in the north, and the Ottoman Turks, expanding with *élan* into the heart of the Balkans and into the power vacuum created by a withering Byzantium, in the south. In the middle of the fifteenth century, Brankovič's Serbia was essentially an interface territory for major powers, its land used frequently as a battlefield. The Hungarians' indecision to dedicate the necessary resources to oust—if possible—the Ottoman Turks from the Balkans, obliged the Serbs to reach an accommodation with Murad II in 1444 (Ostrogorsky, 1969, p. 565; Kalic, 1994, pp. 196–7). From that point on, Serbia's survival appeared to depend on the balance of power between Hungary and the Ottomans, rather than on its own resources. The negotiated peace with Murad II afforded the Serbs merely a 15-year respite before their complete defeat and absorption into the Ottoman Empire.

Dynastic bonds with Byzantium ultimately amounted to little more than symbolic gestures of amity and solidarity, as exemplified in Brankovič's financing of repairs in 1448 of one tower and a small portion of the ramparts of Constantinople (Kalic, 1994, p. 201). The Serbs were fully aware of the strategic significance of the loss of Constantinople for Serbia's survival. Indeed, within six years of its fall, Ottoman troops were occupying the Serbian capital of Smederevo, putting an end to their independence for nearly four centuries.

The importance of Constantinople to Western European defensive strategy was significant, although obvious only to those who were more directly involved in trade and military operations in the eastern Mediterranean, essentially the Venetians and Rhodian Hospitaller Knights. Constantinople as a maritime stronghold straddling Europe and Asia at the Bosphorus was the only possible and sufficient point of entry that could serve, from a tactical standpoint, a Western crusade against the Ottomans. Its loss meant that any Western military challenge to the

Ottomans would either need to be made overland and with the cooperation of Hungary, or staged from the sea without the benefit of a massive fortress beachhead. In contrast to conventional wisdom, Pope Nicholas V made a great—although unsuccessful—effort to rally the Western kingdoms and feudal nobility against Ottoman expansionism in Europe (Brandmüller, 1994, pp. 170–8; Ostrogorsky, 1969, p. 568).

The Slavs' religious affiliation with Byzantium, the third basis for attachment, stems from their common Orthodox roots. Bulgarian 'historical–apocalyptic' literature of the fifteenth to seventeenth century points, again, to the fall of Constantinople as a fundamental gauge of the attachment of Bulgarians to the Byzantine experience and its iconography. Tapkova-Zaimova and Miltenova (1994, p. 213) describe the frequently vague references to the 'fall of the Kingdom' as intimately linked to the fall of Constantinople. As in the case of Serbia and Russia, Bulgaria has its own dynastic bridges to Byzantine imperial houses. Furthermore, however, already at the turn of the fourteenth century another important literary image makes its appearance: if Constantinople falls, the end of time will arrive. In other words, the essence of the Christian Balkans is contained in, and mediated by, Constantinople as the centre of the Orthodox ecumene. Similar fantastical apocalyptic imagery allegedly prophesying the fall emerged as early as the tenth century in both Bulgarian and Greek folk-songs and legends. The allegorical announcement of the impending fall to the King and Queen made by birds (usually a hawk, dove or crow) evokes New Testament imagery; while folk traditions about the martyrdom of 'the last King' as a Christ-figure dying for the sins of his subjects, again, underscores the significant spiritual common ground among the beleaguered Orthodox (Tapkova-Zaimova and Miltenova, 1994, p. 214). Ultimately, this corpus of writing suggests that there is indeed a symbolic geography in the southern Balkans, supplementing the material one, in which threads of significant meaning stretch between Constantinople

and the consciousness of all Orthodox peoples—a symbolic geography that has remained indelible.

6.5 Byzantine administration

The theocratic nature of the Byzantine and subsequently the Ottoman regime were central to the emergence of this symbolic geography. Christian Orthodox worship and ritual and the Byzantine state become coeval even before the schism of the Church into a Catholic Western one and an Orthodox, Apostolic one in the East. The Byzantine state and the Church did not partake in political–military contests of the sort that settled the issue of political primacy in Western Europe between popes and Holy Roman emperors. In spite of its own share of religious strife, overall the Patriarchate and imperial authority established a condominium in the East: the Emperor was secular sovereign by the grace of God, invested thus by the Patriarch; and the Patriarch was selected and invested by the Emperor. The Church enjoyed great privileges and administrative autonomy and controlled extensive estates throughout the Empire. Monasteries were established by imperial *chrysoboulai* (edicts) and endowed lavishly at the time of foundation both by the Crown and the nobility. The monasteries became further enriched through bequests and programmes of land acquisition, so-called *metochia*, which often included dozens of villages. In brief, the wealth and territorial sway of the Church was rivalled only by those of the Crown.

The ultimate ecclesiastical authority rested with the Patriarch of Constantinople. While he was, in theory, *primus inter pares* among the Orthodox patriarchs of Alexander, Antioch and Jerusalem, and the churches of Asia Minor, Dalmatia, Missia, Wallachia, Moldavia, Bulgaria, Serbia, Russia Muskovy and Crimea, the Patriarch of Constantinople was effectively supreme due to his connection to the process of imperial investiture. This suggests a political–hieratic geography of

Orthodoxy, with the Patriarchate of Constantinople at the pivot of power, dispensing ecclesiastical privileges and creating standards of conduct for subordinate players of the Church. The Ottoman conquest, however, brought the condominium between Church and Crown to an end. The Ottoman Sultan was, in the Arabic tradition, the defender of Islam, and his religious and secular authority could not be and was not shared. For purposes of political expediency, however, a new regime of accommodation with the Church was created, according to which the Patriarch of Constantinople retained his primacy among the Church's leadership and received signifiant additional religious, administrative and judicial *veratia* (privileges) which trickled down to the subject Christian populations (Koukkou, 1971, pp. 46–57). Muhammed II, therefore, transformed his hand-picked Patriarch Gennadius Scholarius from plainly head of the Orthodox Church to *ethnarch*, or leader of the Christian Orthodox people (Gennadiou, 1931, p. 241). The fusion of religious authority with secular administrative responsibility in the office of the Patriarch was to establish in the minds of Orthodox Balkan peoples the sense of religion as a legitimate basis for political territoriality. The Patriarch of Constantinople thus found himself at the head of a newly empowered polity, the spatial character of which coincided with the spatial distribution of Orthodox peoples and not with a territorial unit as was the case with political empowerment in Western Europe.

Following the sultanic *veratia*, the sway of the Orthodox Patriarchate of Constantinople in the running of the affairs of all Christian Orthodox Ottoman subjects, regardless of their linguistic affiliation, was unquestionable and extraordinary. The management of the Orthodox polity was accomplished with the assistance of a patriarchal 'court' which attracted distinguished Greeks of Constantinople—the Phanariotes. Moreover, the 'court's' influence extended to the management of the Empire in general through the close relationship between the Phanariote civil service and the Sublime Porte. Koukkou (1971, pp. 112–64) reports on the critical performance of Phanariotes

as *terjumani*, ultimately Ottoman foreign ministers, governors of Wallachia and Moldavia, and high-level administrators. The political influence of the Greek bankers of Constantinople was such that to a great extent they controlled the finances of the Empire and were expected to offer assistance in times of crisis. In spite of their deep attachment to the Orthodox faith, their political allegiances rested squarely with the Divan (Privy Council), thus prescribing a kind of national identity that was inconsistent with Western European notions of how national allegiances are constructed. Religious practice belonged to the private and spiritual realms and was managed by the Patriarch in accordance with the millet system, whereas the public realm was managed by the Sultanate. The different realms functioned independently. Autochthony, or in this case the self-image of being an inalienable part of a territory, was, therefore, much more solidly anchored through religious dogma and practice than through the elaboration of Western-style nationalism, citizens' rights and ethno-linguism.

6.5.1 Legal systems

An investigation of 838 imperial *firmans* (edicts), *veratia* (grants of privilege), court decisions, *bouyioundi* (commands) and administrative decisions dating from 1466 to 1912, suggests tremendous continuity in the hegemony of the Orthodox patriarchal administration and an entrenchment of church land tenure traditions, which confirm the fusion of management of ecclesiastical and secular affairs. While there are great similarities in the subject-matter, language and protocol between Byzantine imperial *chrysoboulai* and sultanic *firmans* directed towards Roumeliot millet subjects (which by definition included both Greeks and Slavs), the critical difference is the licence given to the Church to regulate Orthodox society. For example, in two *firmans* dated 21 April and 28 July 1732, the Sultan orders the *kadi* (judge) of Thessaloníki to respect the powers of the Patriarchate and allow it to run the affairs of the 'Tsaouss' monastery (probably the Vlatadon monastery) (HAM, 1952, *firmans* nos 153–4). In a *firman* from *c.* 1807, the *kaemakames* (governor) of Roumeli recommended to Selim Bey, governor of Thessaloníki, that it should not be necessary to retain hostages from the 20 monasteries of Mount Athos as a precautionary measure following the Serbian insurrection, because Mount Athos is under the strict control of the Patriarchate (HAM, 1952, *firman* no. 278). It is important to understand, however, that the *veratia* to the various millets of the Empire had to be reconfirmed following every royal succession, and their ultimate interpretation was at the discretion of the Sultan. In a *firman* dated 2 January 1709, the governor of Roumeli berated the Christians and Jews of Thessaloníki to the local *kadi* for renovating churches and synagogues in the city without first procuring imperial permits, although the management of church estates falls within the jurisdiction of millet *veratia* (HAM, 1952, *firman* no. 73).

6.5.2 Multiple land tenures

The archipelago of churches and monasteries and their dependencies during both the Byzantine and the Ottoman periods was thus one of the pillars of territorial signification. Their persuasiveness, right to control material wealth, ability to impose feudal standards of land tenure, especially after the thirteenth century, persistence in the landscape and ability to stamp that landscape with formulaic architecture and planning, all spoke of a standard process of control and signification. This process, on the one hand, exemplified the despotic nature of the Church–Divan arrangement, and on the other spoke to all Orthodox subjects in the same visual and social language, which gradually nurtured ideas of a 'Greater' Greece, Serbia, Bulgaria and, currently, Macedonia.

The continuous influence of organised Orthodoxy and Islam on the material and social landscape of the Empire relates obliquely to land tenure. Byzantine feudal-style land tenure gave way, under the Ottomans, to a new complex system according to which all conquered lands reverted to the Divan. The Sultan made land concessions based mainly on rights of usufruct.

The new system afforded the Divan maximum ability to reward or to penalise its people. A system of life-*timars* (military fiefs), which eventually turned into hereditary land grants in conquered territories, was established to benefit the *sipahis*, or cavalry class. Islamic religious and philanthropic institutions, the so-called *wakf* or *vakoufia*, are closely reminiscent of Byzantine era ecclesiastical institutions, and especially monasteries, in being tax-exempted and independently able to amass lands and wealth through bequests and acquisitions. Their proliferation and prosperity further entrenched in the southern Balkans religion-based processes of social and landscape control, although, following the nationalist revolution of 1821 and the creation of the Kingdom of Greece in 1830, Ottoman land tenure and monastic prerogatives quickly succumbed to Bavarian efficiency. Under the direction of Bavarian King Othon of Greece, the state sought to rationalise the vast wealth and lands of the Church by challenging all aspects of Ottoman-era ecclesiastical autonomy.

Whereas Constantinople proper, as the seat of the Patriarch and one of the geographic and symbolic anchors of the Orthodox faith, was physically removed from Macedonia, Mount Athos was within it. The Athonite monastic community founded in the middle of the eighth century became ultimately—by the tenth—a forward Orthodox and imperial bastion into the strategic region of Macedonia, extending its influence throughout the Macedonian mainland through an extensive network of *metochia*, or Athonite-affiliated monastic dependencies. Moreover, Athos was qualitatively different from Constantinople, since it functioned as a meditation chamber for all of Orthodoxy. No heterodox or schismatics are, or ever were, admitted to its monastic ranks. Most importantly, however, the Athonite community included a Bulgarian, a Serbian and a Russian monastery, as well as a Romanian retreat, among the 20 monasteries and the dozens of hermitages which still function there. The presence of these 'heterochthonous' (by Greek standards) monastic communities in Athos suggests that the peninsula was and continues to be a symbolic *axis mundi* that belongs to all Orthodox Christians and not only to the Greek Orthodox who have run the Ecumenical Patriarchate during and since Byzantium. Through their establishment on Mount Athos, they mediate the Bulgarian, Serbian and even Russian signification of the Macedonian territory. It is of some considerable importance that in 1993 the Russian Orthodox Church applied, and received permission, to found a new monastery on the site of the deserted hermitage of St Elias on Athos.

During the 1821 Greek uprising against the Ottomans, the Athonite monasteries (Greek, Serbian, Russian) spoke in one voice. The archives of the Megiste Lavra monastery yield a rich correspondence among the 20 large monasteries concerning their stance in the face of the uprising. Even in the most incriminating of communications about the digging of defensive trenches, the hiding of revolutionaries, the expedition of monks as combatants to the mainland, and the fabrication of gunpowder, there is no discussion of, or distinction by, nationality (Archives of Megiste Lavra (AML), for example, letters of 18 and 22 June and 9 and 10 July 1821; Lavriotes, 1966). When the Ottoman authorities eventually punished them, they also did not make any distinctions among them: they executed all the monks of the Greek monastery of Karakallou, as readily as they executed the membership of the Russian one of Panteleimon (AML, calendar of brother Pahomios, entry of Tuesday, 19 June 1823; Lavriotes, 1966). After 1870, therefore, the Bulgarian Exarchate—although representing an *administrative* schism from Constantinople—could continue to lay a claim to Macedonia—even Greek-inhabited southern Macedonia—partly because it shared sites such as the Orthodox *axis mundi* of Athos.

6.6 Conclusion

In Macedonia, *religion* and *not* linguistic affiliation reinforces what appear in Western European nationalist terms a set of absurd, and

overlapping, territorial claims. Western analyses of these claims have consistently focused on the evocation by Greeks, Bulgarians, Serbs, Albanians—and now Macedonians—of some long-past ephemeral instances of political/military hegemony. They neglect, however, to explore clearly not the presence, but the ability of pre-Christian traditions and Orthodoxy to produce permutations of a single religion-based autochthony for the different peoples of Macedonia.

The Byzantines found it expedient to decentralise the tools of territorial signification through the promotion of standard, script-supported vernaculars. Their objective was to diffuse Orthodox Christianity and their political influence among the Slavs, the Albanians and the Vlachs. The end result was that each of the peoples were allowed to elaborate a permutation of the fundamental notion of autochthony that defined Macedonia as universally Orthodox Christian and politically unitary.

The willingness of the Sultanate to sustain the tradition of linguistic and parochial pluralism through the millet system further affirmed this general notion of Macedonian autochthony. The formalising of standard vernacular languages, and the emergence of a press, theatre and literature in these vernaculars during the nineteenth century were critical for consolidating the national identity of each following independence, but these processes should be seen as separate and imported from the West. It is then a single idea of autochthony, or symbolic appropriation of territory, achieved through the manipulation of pre-Christian and Christian Orthodox symbols, sites and folk traditions that has produced as many subjective histories of Macedonia as there are antagonists.

Anthropologist Robert Cantwell (1993) defines 'the unconscious learning and mimicry that arise among people in the realm of social relations, which includes most of what we call "culture"', as 'ethnomimesis'. Although Cantwell employs the concept to describe the ways through which peoples of different cultures come to cross-fertilise their folk traditions through observation, it is also fitting in the case of Macedonia. We can use it as a further literary means to describe the proliferation of subjective Macedonian histories and conflicting land–society relationships: the temporal and spatial spread of a single fundamental notion of autochthony and process of territorial signification taught, imitated and consequently diffused through the region-wide practice of Christian Orthodox traditions and reinforced by dynastic linkages and Balkan geopolitics.

6.7 References

Afigenov, D., 1994, To gegonos tis alosis mesa sta Rosika chronika, in Chryssos, E., ed., *E alosi tis polis*, Akritas, Athens, pp. 221–46,

Angelopolous, A., 1980, *Voreios Makedonia. O ellinismos tis Stromnitsis*, Idryma Meleton Hersonesou tou Aimou (Institute for the Study of the Haemos Peninsula), Thessaloníki.

Brandmüller, W., 1994, E antidrasi tis Romis stin ptosi tis Konstantinoupoleos, in Chryssos, E., ed., *E alosi tis polis*, Akritas, Athens, pp. 167–90.

Cantwell, R., 1993, *Ethnomimesis, folklore and the representation of culture*, University of North Carolina Press, Chapel Hill, NC.

Connor, W. R., 1985, The razing of the house in Greek society, *Transactions of the American Philological Association*, **115**, 79–102.

Gennadiou, I., 1931, *Ta idiaitera dikaiomata tou oekoumenikou petriarchiou kai e thesis autou enanti ton allon orthodoxon Ekklesion*, Constantinople.

HAM (Historical Archives of Macedonia), 1952, Thessaloníki archive 1695–1912, vol. A, Ioannes Vasdravellis for Makedonike Vivliotheki, Thessaloníki.

Kalic, J., 1994, E Servia kai e ptosi tis Konstantinopolis, in Chryssos, E., ed., *E alosi tis polis*, Akritas, Athens, pp. 193–206.

Koukkou, E., 1971, *Diamorphosis tis Ellinikis koinonias kata tin tourkokrateia, tomos A, Ta pronomia tou patriarchiou kai e phanariotiki koinonia*, Etnikon Kentron Koinonikon Erevnon (National Centre of Social Research), Athens.

Lavriotes, A., 1966, *Eggrapha Agiou Orous tis megalis Ellinikis Epanastaseos, tomos A: 1821–1832* [AML], Ekdoseis Mavridi, Athens.

Moulinier, L., 1952, *Le pur et l'impur*, Paris.

Ostrogorsky, G., 1969, *History of the Byzantine State*, Rutgers University Press, New Brunswick, NJ.

Parker, R., 1983, *Miasma*, Oxford University Press, Oxford.

Tapkova-Zaimova, V., Miltenova, A., 1994, E alosi tis Polis kai e istorikoapokalyptiki logotechnia tis Voulgarias, in Chryssos, E., ed., *E alosi tis polis*, Akritas, Athens, pp. 209–18.

Vakalopoulos, K., 1988, *Modern history of Macedonia 1830–1912*, Barbounakis, Athens.

Wilkinson, H. R., 1951, *Maps and politics: a review of the ethnographic cartography of Macedonia*, Liverpool University Press, Liverpool.

7

Macedonian cultural and national identity

Theano S. Terkenli

7.1 Introduction

The causes of the 'Macedonia' problem are to be found in the recent (in historical terms) misguided definition of various Macedonias in nationalistic terms, in lieu of viewing them as one geographical entity, best understood in terms of a collective home for its people. The fact that this geographical entity has been fiercely guarded by fiery patriotism and nascent nationalism has further inflamed the current state of political instability in the Balkans.

This chapter attempts to probe into the roots of the Macedonian 'problem', because this has ceased to be a theoretical question removed from everyday reality, and has become a very pressing issue on which peace in the Balkans rests to a great degree. At the core of the problem lie negotiations for political legitimacy on the basis of nationalist affiliation. The primary objective of this chapter is to show that cultural identity is the wrong basis on which to negotiate political legitimacy on

nationalistic grounds. Instead, Macedonia, the home, must be seen as a geographical region, functioning as such in terms of its economic cohesion and internal subcultural and micro-social interactions.[1]

This chapter, then, is a critical evaluation of past political actions in the recent history of Macedonia, a history tightly interwoven with European nationalist movements. The central goal of this chapter is to attempt an understanding of Macedonian identity in terms of its meaning for the locals who consider it their collective home, with a heavier, albeit not exclusive, reliance on evidence from Greek

---

1. At the outset, I would like to make clear that I do not advocate a future creation of a single autonomous Macedonian nation-state. Far from that, I believe that such an attempt not only would be catastrophic to Balkan peace and European political stability, but that it also rests very far from the aspirations, interests and goals of the region's people.

Reconstructing the Balkans: A Geography of the New Southeast Europe. Edited by Derek Hall and Darrick Danta.
©1996 John Wiley & Sons Ltd

history, politics and cultural life.[1] Secondarily, the chapter will briefly sketch processes, contingencies and misperceptions surrounding Macedonian identity. The discussion is focused on the concept of home, because of the multiple valuable insights that the concept affords the study of cultural identity.

In the process of imagining new social worlds or legitimating existing ones, humans produce hegemonic ideas, as well as dominating classes and cultural boundaries. One such ideological construct is the creation of national identities, which start out as nationalist ideologies, that is, as perceptions of what the nation is or should be (Connor, 1992, p. 49; Fox, 1990, p. 4). Nationalist ideologies may, then, gain public meaning and be put into action. For purposes of this discussion, nationalism is defined as a set of ideological precepts focused on ordering, evaluating and homogenising internal heterogeneity, and partially on situating a politically defined territory (the state), its people (the nation), and its culture in an international arena (Williams, 1990, p. 128). The ongoing construction of a cultural identity with which to substantiate national identity has been central to this process:

some aspect of a common culture has always been central to the delineation of national identity. This chapter will address the question of how culture is expressed in the formation of national identity, and much less how cultural identity comes to be in the first place (i.e. 'what is Macedonian cultural identity?'). Culture is seen here as a set of understandings and a consciousness under active construction, by which individuals interpret the world around them (Fox, 1990, p. 4). As such, it represents a 'tool kit' or set of scenarios used by individuals or groups of individuals to stage their everyday lives, and by political factors to legitimate their positions. National cultures, thus, are not inevitable outputs of once and for all socialisation processes, but continual processes and outcomes, expressed through everyday lives, and rooted in historical factors and power structures at various levels. Because national cultures originate in everyday lives at the personal and at the collective level, it is useful to begin our analysis of Macedonian cultural identity with the aid of the idea of personal and collective homes.

7.2 Geographies of home: the creation of subcultural identities

Personal and collective geographies and regions of 'home', like any other type of geographical region, are culturally construed and contingent on place, time and society. As such, geographies of 'home' necessarily express and promote the way of life contingent on local sociocultural conditions. 'Home' has been defined first and foremost as a spatial context and the basis of one of the most fundamental geographical dichotomies: 'home' versus 'non-home'. Based on the fundamental dichotomy created by personal geographies between 'us' and 'them', we construct home at different scales. Personal homes may be closely linked to and articulated by familial and communal associations. Collective homes are delineated by ethnic, nationalistic, civic or ideological parameters. Most human knowledge is created through comparison or

---

1. I use the term Macedonia, in singular or plural, outside of quotations (which would indicate my siding with a particular political position on the national identity of Macedonia), simply out of respect for feelings of belonging or attachment of local populations to various 'Macedonias'. My personal belief, however, is that former southern Yugoslavian Macedonian cultural, and consequently national, identity (including the usurping of the name Macedonia and of its ancient symbols) has been deliberately fabricated on misguided principles by political factors for political purposes (US Department of State, 1947; Stalin, 1945). An elaboration of this position, which has already been well documented (Sfetas and Kentrotis, 1994, pp. 47–67), lies beyond the scope of this chapter. I will simply clarify my disclaimer by establishing for purposes of further discussion that I consider contemporary inhabitants of northern Greece first as Greeks, and contemporary inhabitants of the Republic of Skopje first as former Yugoslavians, and second as whatever the people of these two countries might elect to call themselves, with due respect to the historically established cultural identities of others.

juxtaposition. Personal, national or subgroup identities cannot exist in a contextual vacuum. We define ourselves always *vis-à-vis* another. We assign the unfamiliar, the foreign, to 'them', the 'other'. Elsewhere (Koop, 1993), I have suggested that the essence of 'home' lies in the repetitive, regular investment of meaning in a context that, through some measure of control, we personalise or identify with. In this way, it is the sense of personalisation of our immediate environment, expressed as some measure of power, control over, or simply identification with, that transforms place into home. This element of control, power or some other form of identification with or personalisation of a context is the first essential element in the transformation of space or place into home. I will proceed to use this element in order to gain some insight into 'Macedonia' as a collective geographical home.

Macedonia's 'ethnic mosaic', the harmonious symbiosis (Angelopoulos, 1992, p. 195) of distinct communities of Greeks, Turks, Slavs, Jews, Kutsovlachs, Gypsies and others, became problematic with the decline of the Ottoman Empire and the rise of Balkan nationalisms in the late nineteenth century. Macedonia became contested territory and ceased being a common home to these nationalities with the rediscovery of:

1. Its strategic position between the Balkans and the Aegean, and between Central Europe and Asia;
2. The dynamic port city of Thessaloníki;
3. Its fertile lands amidst a mountainous landmass.

Both in its recent history and in contemporary times, northern Greece (Μακεδονία[1]) has repeatedly proclaimed its Greekness and its unequivocal identification with the state of Greece, both from a grass-roots level and from higher political levels (Koliopoulos and Hasiotis,

1992, pp. 366–9; Kondis *et al.*, 1993). The claim to Macedonia by northern Greeks as 'theirs', that is, as their home in close conjunction with their Greek identity, has been declared in no uncertain terms, both at the regional core, Thessaloníki, and at the regional periphery, in its border prefectures, towns and villages. Macedonia thus has been declared on the basis both of a collective, grass-roots affiliation and of an economic relationship, as a geographical home context (Kofos, 1992, p. 170) that has been under direct Greek economic control for several decades, even centuries.

The spectacular demonstration, organised by Thessaloníki's civic and religious authorities in the spring of 1994 to support the Greek identity of the Macedonian department of Greece, brought together almost a sixth of the population of the country. The demonstration that took place, the speeches that accompanied it, and the street parties that followed vehemently proclaimed the Greekness of Μακεδονία with patriotic songs, Greek flags, ancient symbols, and folk-dances in a highly charged atmosphere. The slogans that the people chanted and the banners that they held echoed their larger claims: 'Our name is Macedonia, our rights are not negotiable', 'Because we are Macedonian Greeks', 'Macedonia is Greece itself', 'We are Greeks, worthy of our country and of our ancestors', and so on. The indigenous populations of the (more contested) northern Greek territories have also protested their identity in the face of the polyglot and often synchretic character of local traditions.

Economic factors have been instrumental in claiming Μακεδονία as a collective home. Before nationalism destroyed the possibility of horizontal linkages based on class solidarity and economic interests, the Greek inhabitants of Macedonia 'initially had very little concern about displacing non-Greek merchants, even those with Bulgarian leanings. They were rather conservative and indeed reluctant to lose their clients' (Gounaris, 1993a, p. 515). The growing political unrest and quest for an ethnic identity in the recent history of the various ethnic commu-

1. I employ the local Greek term 'Μακεδονία' to signify the northernmost department of modern-day Greece, in distinction to the larger, original historico-geographical territory of Macedonia, or the various other 'Macedonias' in question.

nities of Μακεδονία may be attributed to their increased commercial role and consequent economic security. All along, in the recent history of various Macedonias, we have similar evidence as to the predominant economic basis of claims to the region and to a Macedonian identity, as would be expected in the case of a collective homeland providing sustenance for its people.

Repetition or cyclicality is the second essential element in the transformation of place or space into home; it refers to the everyday or periodic return to places and faces that we call home, as well as to habitual routines and personal or collective rites of home. The historical factor is central to the construction of an idea of home, because habits that unfold in specific contexts and are repeated differentiate these locales or sets of circumstances from the rest of the known world. This element of personal or collective history, fundamental to the delineation of home, and expressed through regular repetitive patterns, is superimposed on the spatial and on the social in the creation and re-creation of home contexts. Besides personal or political control over Μακεδονία, the home, historical claims have been made both at a macro-historical and at a subcultural (family-lineage) level on Μακεδονία as a group home.

Some of the slogans chanted at a spring 1994 demonstration in Thessaloníki declared: 'Μακεδόνες [the inhabitants of Μακεδονία] are armed with their history', 'Alexander, rise: you are being robbed of your Μακεδονία', 'Down with the thieves of history', and so on. These latter slogans refer to the well-known debate between Greece and the Former Yugoslav Republic of Macedonia (FYROM) about the legitimacy of the name 'Macedonia' for the southernmost republic of the former country. At the family and at the village level, interviews with local people of the village Hrisa in northern Greece revealed that group identity, which informs individual identity in the larger community of 1522 people, is defined in terms (a) of ancestral territory or 'home', and (b) of belonging to a particular lineage (Drettas, 1977, p. 64). Specifically, the author mentions that respondents

speak of those in the same lineage as 'ours', a term that indicates affiliation with a common home. As supported by other scholars (Gounaris, 1993b, p. 196), it is thus not the common culture in terms of the local dialect, but rather the common genealogical parentage that ensures a collective identity in terms of a common home. As we shall examine below, with national identity construction the myth of common ethnic ancestry, of genealogy, has replaced as a linking mechanism the continuity of residence in the forefathers' land (Gounaris, 1993b, p. 191).

7.3 National identity construction: in the name of a cultural identity

At this point, it would be helpful to provide a brief outline of the construction of various Macedonian nationalisms, as they have been manifested at different geographical scales in the course of recent history (Koliopoulos and Hasiotis, 1992). The three major players in the scramble for Macedonia at the state level have been, at least in the course of this century, Bulgaria, Greece and Yugoslavia.

Macedonia became a particularly heterogeneous region during the Byzantine Empire: before the turn of the twentieth century the situation regarding any type of collective identification was hazy. National consciousness was understandably underdeveloped among rural populations up to the importation of the concept of nationalism into the Balkans from Western Europe around the end of the nineteenth and the beginning of the twentieth century. In 1912–13, during the First Balkan War, the three salient players in the scramble for Macedonia, Bulgarians, Greeks and Serbs, united against the common oppressor, the Turks, and 'liberated' Macedonia. In 1913, during the Second Balkan War, Greece allied with Serbia against Bulgaria over the Macedonian question. In 1918, at the Treaty of Bucharest, after the victory of the Allied forces in the First World War, Macedonia was finally divided: 50% went to Greece, 40% to Serbia and 10% to Bulgaria. On 30 April 1945, the Federal State of Macedonia was founded by President Tito of Yugoslavia as the southernmost member of the new Yugoslavian federation (Center for Macedonians Abroad, 1991, pp. 19–46). Meanwhile, there have been several attempts in the course of the Macedonian existence by locals and/or various Eastern European political factors, including the former Soviet Union, to unite all Macedonians into an independent state. Such attempts have always been opposed by Greek governments, as have any other external nationalistic claims or the inclusion of any derivative of the word 'Macedonia' in the name of any territorial entity within Yugoslavia. This has led to the current impasse in naming the newly emergent southern republic of former Yugoslavia.

The grounds for nationalistic, that is, territorial, claims put forward by the different actors in the Macedonian scramble have invariably developed from distinctive 'Macedonian national cultures', defined according to each actor's political motives (Public Record Office, 1941). In each case, nationalistic political ideologies preceded the construction of national identities, which ensued either voluntarily or coercively (Sfetas and Kentrotis, 1994, p. 47–67; The Citizens' Movement, 1993). In the creation, for example, of a separate Yugoslavian Macedonian republic, culture was seen by Tito as the space to let out the nationalistic steam in terms of 'differences', in order to secure a homogenised and centralised economic, political and national organisation of power. This notion of difference of 'us' from 'them' has always been central to the creation of nations, as in the creation of homes. I will now briefly turn to the ways that cultural identity has been deployed in the construction of national identity, through the exertion of political power from the top down.

Before the end of the First World War, in order to base their claims on Macedonia, the Bulgarian state engaged in linguistic propaganda to reinforce and highlight the Bulgarian linguistic elements in the mixture established as 'the Macedonian language'. The Greeks, on the other hand, were stressing that during Ottoman rule over Macedonia, the 'high culture' of the area was predominantly in the hands of Greeks in larger urban centres (Angelopoulos, 1992, p. 195), while the Greek language was the commercial *lingua franca*, and the language of the common Orthodox Church. Most of the rural subjects of the Turkish Empire, on the other hand, seem to have been Slavic speakers. Here, again, political intervention came to straighten out historical uncertainty and cultural 'shortcomings': Greek dictatorship from 1936 to 1941 engaged in a widespread campaign to change family names into Greek ones, as part of the 'neutralisation' process of the nation-state. Similar statist tactics were used towards the Turkish and Muslim names of the citizens in Bulgaria. At the international level, the former Soviet Union has also played a central role in the instigation of the idea of Macedonian national identity by actively supporting an independent Macedonian nation-state, allegedly for strategic purposes, i.e. access to the Aegean. Such tactics reflect the artificiality of the 'Macedonian national identity'. At a local level, members of the small slavophone minority that survives in northern Greece, referred to as 'Slavo-Macedonians' by other Greeks, call themselves 'Macedonian' in order to be distinguished from Greeks of other regions of the country, but overwhelmingly consider themselves Greek (Angelopoulos, 1992, p. 199; Pyrzas, 1994) and the original Macedonians of the region. They, too, strategically choose the performance of their national identity, depending on political pressures.

The acknowledgement that ethnic heritage, accompanied by local linguistic particularities, is not instrumental or even helpful in the historical delineation of identity in the case of Macedonia (Mavrogordatos, 1983, p. 247) is exemplified by the

existence of a multitude of historical evidence that certifies that members of the same family, related to various degrees, may belong to different ethnic groups, and, under armed pressure, the fluidity of ethnic affiliation [has been] the rule rather than the exception for a large part of the [Greek] slavophone population (Gounaris, 1993b, p. 200).

Often, depending on who the interviewer is, the answer may be 'I am Greek' in Bulgarian. Similarly, folkloric research attests to common customs among the various ethnic subgroups that have shared Macedonia, the geographical home, and, in particular, to local dances that greatly resemble those of neighbouring states (Pyrzas, 1994). Since 1912, each ethnic group has developed its own ethnologically pure forms of dance. More evidence about harmonious coexistence and intercultural sharing (Kondis *et al.*, 1993, p. 18) may also be found in the history of the 'Macedonian struggle' for the liberation of northern Greece from the Turks. For instance, history quotes some fighters for the annexation of northern Greece with the rest of the country as non-Greek speakers (Pyrzas, 1994). These fighters considered themselves Greek, none the less, and died in the name of Greece (Angelopoulos, 1992, p. 198).

Second, besides political affiliation and ethnic control of a common territory, historical claims have been predominantly deployed in the construction of a Macedonian national identity out of 'a Macedonian national culture'. Nationalism seeks to secure the forefathers' home by any means possible. As would be expected, all players in the scramble for Macedonia have resorted to that rationale, and each one of them has constructed a historical continuum theory: Greeks basing their claims on the ancient Greek kingdom of Philip II and Alexander the Great; Serbians on the medieval kingdom of Stephan Dušan (reigning over the territories for almost a century); and Bulgarians on the medieval kingdom of Tsar Samuel. The reality of who comprised just the Greek-speaking groups of Macedonia at the turn of the century is startling and flies in the face of any attempt to construct neat and simplistic models of ethnic affiliation (Mavrogordatos and Chamoudopoulos, 1931; Vlachos, 1945).

Up to the twentieth century, indigenous cultural identity did not have much to do with difference from an 'Other'. Rather, the position would be best described as transculturation, syncretism or identification with a multitude of cultural or subcultural institutions and social networks. Thessaloníki itself acquired its clear-cut ethnic cultural identity only after 1912; before that date the city was culturally indistinguishable from its surrounding villages. Within the city of Thessaloníki, as well as in other northern Greek settlements, Greek subjects may often primarily align themselves with parental ethnic affiliations deriving from their ancestral identity, rather than with Greek ethnicity. Pondii, the descendants of immigrants from parts of the former Soviet Union bordering the Black Sea, are such a case.

This odd amalgam has constituted Macedonia, the crossroads of cultures, where culture was usurped in order to legitimate political identity. Macedonia thus became the scrabble board where the impossibly arbitrary task of nation-building has been most blatantly revealed, where a collective home was dismantled and where ferocious nationalism, a principle of chaos and disorder, took its place.

7.4 The new cultural identity of global homogenisation: the resolution of the Macedonian problem?

The preceding analysis exposed the tentative and subjective nature of cultural identity construction for nationalistic purposes. Cultural productions of public identity are too often simplified and straight-jacketed in order to fit preconceived sociocultural ideas or ulterior political motives. The national and the cultural are reduced to the agent seeking to legitimise identity, in the same way that home, in our days, is apparently being reduced to the self, or a way of life and a state of being. The latter indication is one of the outcomes of a cross-cultural comparison between ideas of home (Koop, 1993), which suggests that, in contemporary Western society, the weakening of exclusive identification with place and social group reduces home to a mere accumulation of conscious and unconscious habitual routines.

The 'us' retreats into the self, the individual, or shrinks in scale and becomes more compelling, as in the current surge of nationalisms around the world. When other institutions of cultural or collective identity, such as community, family and religious affiliation become less relevant in social life, nationalism, the artificial principle, takes the place of identity construction at the collective level (Kedourie, 1993, p. 96).

Research on the concept of home (Koop, 1993) points to the fact that in more modernised and 'developed' societies, prevailing notions of home centre on the self and on the accumulation of personal habitual routines (whether these are thoughts, activities or patterns of feelings). In more 'traditional' settings, the meaning of home is based on physical surroundings. The city of Thessaloníki, compared to small-town settings in Greece and in the USA, and to a city of comparable size in the USA, clearly seems to belong, on the basis of respondents' answers about their ideas of home, to the more modernised, 'developed' categories. In other words, interviews with locals of Thessaloníki expose a loss of their physical community as home, whereas individual residential and lifestyle circumstances seem to take precedence over group home and identity. Where in the past individuals and homes were defined on the basis of shared group characteristics, under the present economic order, Thessaloníki, the core of Μακεδονία, is no longer much different in its tendency towards individualism and the glorification of lifestyle than the rest of the modern and post-modern world. Furthermore, within the city, ethnic and cultural difference on the basis of genealogical affiliation is no longer relevant (Pyrzas, 1994), as εντοπιότητα (being an indigenous resident of the region) has attenuated with the spread of modernity and Western culture in the Balkans. Finally, the contemporary trend towards a global homogenising culture has obviously begun to touch the lives of small-town Μακεδόνες as well.

Unquestionably, cultural identity is the wrong basis on which to negotiate political legitimacy. On the other hand, in the contested border territories, the idea of home, primarily in the form of parental lineage, provides much insight into locals' connection to their life environment and circumstances. Parental lineage seems to assume the meaning of belonging that residence and economic interrelations in a common geographical area used to carry.

In terms of nationalistic repercussions, perhaps the most significant question that we are left with is: does the loss of place-bound homes in current times, and the fact that εντοπιότητα is no longer relevant to the delineation of a common home in the case of Thessaloníki, point to a future where Macedonia may cease to be a problem? I would like to speculate on why it would certainly be premature to offer an answer to such a wishful question, despite the fact that Woodrow Wilson's ideas of the nation-state seem to be increasingly challenged in our days of cultural homogenisation. The more our homes expand with the current disintegration of spatial boundaries and the globalisation of relations, the more we turn to our nation, community or private space to secure our distinctiveness. We turn to whatever points of reference are closest to us and most unquestionable, such as our private space or our daily routines, in order to protect our identity. Home shrinks to the most secure level of intimacy. At the same time, however, attachment to home becomes stronger, especially to those parts of home that seem most endangered by time–space compression, pointing to a dialectical relationship between breadth of home contexts and human attachment to them (Koop, 1993). In this way, it seems that Macedonian national identity is stronger and more prominent where the 'we' is more clearly delineated and claimed (at the core/centre) rather than at the border, where the 'we' is more uneasy, disjointed and unresolved. Macedonia, the border, has been claimed by each centre, Athens, Belgrade or Skopje, and Sofia, for fear of losing or questioning their core: Greek identity, Serbian identity and Bulgarian identity. As exemplified by demonstrations, casual conversation and overall preoccupation with the issue, the division between 'us' and 'them' is starker in terms of nationalistic claims at the centre than at the periphery, where the notion of home, in terms of a clear-cut and distinctive cultural identity, is inclusive rather than exclusive. In this way, the question of identity at the border does not seem to be a cause of anxiety, as it is at the core.[1]

7.5 Conclusion

Nation-states have been defined, on the basis of real or imagined common culture, as formal regions in control of a territory. Their existence depends on the stability of their borders. Borders have historically defined regions, and cores have felt threatened when borders were ambiguously delineated or contested. Rather, depending on their degree of westernisation, nations should be viewed as home systems, or as nodal configurations, similarly to collective home contexts characterised by varying degrees of attachment throughout their extent. The political context of human belonging and attachment should thus be seen as a collage of overlapping and ever-transforming subcultural or personal affiliations and relations, which acquire differential intensity in space, time and society. As such, political definition of Macedonian identity is bound for a reassessment with the ongoing spread of one overarching, homogenising Western way of life that seems to be engulfing the rest of the world and rendering national identity and collective homes, as we have known them thus far, irrelevant in the post-modern world. The resolution of the Macedonian problem ultimately lies not in how we conceive Macedonian identity, but in how we reach common ground on conceptions of home in a fast-changing world.

---

1. The perceived possibility of border turmoil or redefinition, which might endanger established home contexts, explains the fears and anxieties instilled among Greek subjects in the larger urban centres of Μακεδονία.

7.6 References

Angelopoulos, A., 1992, Population distribution of Greece today according to language, national consciousness and religion, in *Macedonia: past and present*, Institute for Balkan Studies, Thessaloníki, pp. 195–204.

Center for Macedonians Abroad and Society for Macedonian Studies, 1991, *Macedonia: history and politics*, Ekdotiki Athinon, Athens.

Citizens' Movement, The, 1993, *Borders, symbols, stability: issues relating to the recognition of the former Yugoslav Republic of Macedonia*, Photosyn, Athens.

Connor, W., 1992, The nation and its myth, in Smith, A., ed., *Ethnicity and nationalism*, E. J. Brill, Leiden, pp. 48–57.

Drettas, J.-G., 1977, Un example de contacts interethniques en Macedoine, village de Hrisa (Gréce), *Études Balkaniques*, **3**.

Fox, R. G., 1990, Introduction, in Fox, R. G., ed., *Nationalist ideologies and the production of national cultures*, American Ethnological Society Monograph Series, vol. 2, American Anthropological Association, Washington, DC, pp. 1–14.

Gounaris, B., 1993a, Salonica, *Fernand Braudel Center Review*, **16**, 499–518.

Gounaris, B., 1993b, Ethnic groups and political parties in Macedonia during the Balkan Wars, in *Greece in the Balkan Wars 1910–1914*, Society for the Greek Literary and Historical Archive, Athens, pp. 189–202.

Kedourie, E., 1993, *Nationalism*, Basil Blackwell, Oxford, 4th edn.

Kofos, E., 1992, The Macedonian question: the politics of mutation, in *Macedonia: past and present*, Institute for Balkan Studies, Thessaloníki, pp. 169–84.

Koliopoulos, I., Hasiotis, I., 1992, *Modern and contemporary Macedonia: history–economy–society–civilization*, Paratiritis, Thessaloníki.

Kondis, B., Kentrotis, K., Sfetas, S., Stefanidis, Y. D., eds, 1993, *Resurgent irredentism, documents on Skopje 'Macedonian' nationalist aspirations (1934–1992)*, Institute for Balkan Studies, Thessaloníki.

Koop, T. T., 1993, The idea of home: a cross-cultural comparison, unpublished doctoral dissertation, Department of Geography, University of Minnesota, Minneapolis.

Mavrogordatos, G.Th., 1983, *Stillborn republic: social coalitions and party strategies in Greece, 1922–1936*, University of California Press, Berkeley.

Mavrogordatos, M. I., Chamoudopoulos, A. Ch., 1931, *Macedonia: demographic and economic study*, Papadopoulos-Marinellis, Thessaloníki.

Public Record Office, 1941, FO 371/33128, R1650/1650/7, Bulgarian irredentism, study by Foreign Research and Press Service, Balliol College, Oxford, 4 December 1941.

Pyrzas, K., 1994, *Personal interview*, Center for Macedonians Abroad, 8 January.

Sfetas, S., Kentrotis, K., 1994, *Skopia: in search for an identity and international acclaim*, Institute for Balkan Studies, Thessaloníki.

Stalin, 1945, Personal letter to Dimitrov, Moscow, 9 January, in Kondis, B. *et al.*, 1993, *Resurgent irredentism: documents on Skopje 'Macedonian' nationalist aspirations (1934–1992)*, Institute for Balkan Studies, Thessaloníki, p. 44.

US Department of State, 1947, Letter to the British Embassy, in Kondis, B. *et al.*, 1993, *Resurgent irredentism: documents on Skopje 'Macedonian' nationalist aspirations (1934–1992)*, Institute for Balkan Studies, Thessaloníki, pp. 43–4.

Vlachos, N., 1945, *Ethnic composition of the parts of Macedonia and western Thrace belonging to Greece*, Aetos, Athens.

Williams, B. F., 1990, Nationalism, traditionalism, and the problem of cultural inauthenticity, in Fox, R. G., ed., *Nationalist ideologies and the production of national cultures*, American Ethnological Society Monograph Series, vol. 2, American Anthropological Association, Washington, DC, pp. 112–29.

8

Slovenian responses to new regional development opportunities

Anton Gosar

8.1 Introduction

Since international recognition in 1992, Central Europe's youngest nation-state has been looking towards European integration (Klemenčič, 1992; Vrišer, 1994). Slovenia's geopolitical location within Europe is of great significance: it borders EU member Italy, the recent EU member Austria, the aspiring EU member Hungary, and the state of Croatia, another independent entity from the former Yugoslav federation. Due to war in the Balkans, the major route from the Mediterranean towards the Danubian basin (Italy–Hungary) has been promoted in place of the previous economic growth axis along the EU traffic corridor of Germany–Greece. In this chapter, major characteristics of recent changes in Slovenia's links with Europe are discussed: EU development scenarios; Slovenian road and rail projects; foreign investments in the Slovenian economy; and the contemporary regional development problems of Slovenia, particularly along its borders.

8.2 Slovenia and modern Europe

The country's international borders are of particular geographical significance. That with:

1. Croatia is the border among former administrative entities of the Yugoslav federation and at the same time a border between European countries at peace and European countries at war;
2. Italy separates Slovenia from the benefits and duties of Western alliances (EU/NATO/WEU);
3. Austria divides similar natural conditions (the Alps) and diverse socio-economic systems (Austria being a former EFTA member);
4. Hungary constituted part of the Iron Curtain of the socialist bloc (after 1948), as a consequence of which cross-border links are, in comparison to other neighbouring states, less developed despite mutual economic interest.

Culturally, Slovenia is the most westerly part of the Slavic island of south-central Europe, bordering Romance, German, Ugric and South Slavic nations. Since the country's natural composition is of equal diversity, as it encompasses the ecosystems of the Alps, the Mediterranean, the Danubian (also Pannonian) plains, and the central karst areas of Europe, Slovenia is justifiably characterised as a major transitional area of the continent (Figure 8.1).

Reconstructing the Balkans: A Geography of the New Southeast Europe. Edited by Derek Hall and Darrick Danta.
©1996 John Wiley & Sons Ltd

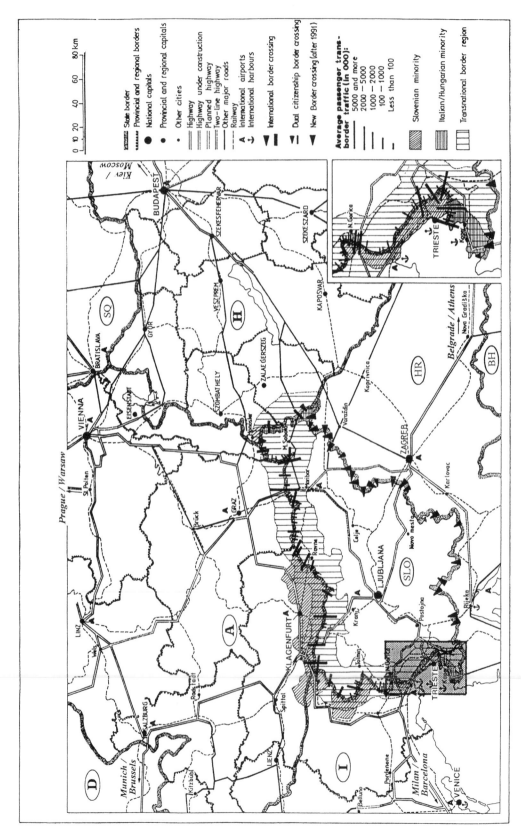

Figure 8.1 *Slovenia and its neighbours: transport, border crossing points and minorities*

Legend:

State border

Provincial and regional borders

● National capitals

• Provincial and regional capitals

· Other cities

Highway

Highway under construction

Planned highway

Two-line highway

Other major roads

Railway

International airports

International harbours

International border crossing

Dual citizenship border crossing

New Border crossing (after 1991)

Average passenger trans-border traffic (in 000):

5000 and more

2000 – 5000

1000 – 2000

100 – 1000

Less than 100

Slovenian minority

Italian/Hungarian minority

Transnational border region

Slovenia's geopolitical position within Europe is therefore of particular importance.

A major force of European restructuring in the 1980s was the European Community (EC) and in the 1990s continues as the European Union (EU). The 15 countries of Western Europe and Greece are not only economically prosperous but have developed goals of integration which seem suitable for most other member states. Petitions are placed by different countries to incorporate their nation-state and economy into the confederation. The applications of most of Slovenia's neighbouring countries have either been accepted or are being seriously considered. Italy is an EU founding member. Austria, a former EFTA member, was accepted as a full EU member state in January 1995. In Hungary, where restructuring towards a market economy and democracy has been rapid, basic policies are supportive of Western alliances. The fact that the country belongs to the Višegrad group of states (with the Czech Republic, Slovakia and Poland) will facilitate Hungary's smooth transition into the EU.

Part of Croatia's territory is occupied and claimed by the Serb quasi-state of Krajina. Because of the uncertainty of this dispute and the war in neighbouring Bosnia–Hercegovina, Croatia would currently appear to have only a slight chance of being treated equally with other petitioners for EU membership. The EU has granted Slovenia observer status and is supportive of the country's transformation processes, particularly in the fields of science and defence. Slovenia is part of the EU's EUREKA, TEMPUS and PHARE, and of NATO's Partnership for Peace development and cooperation programmes.

Constraining factors with regard to EU membership are related to Slovenia's past:

1. The five successor states of the former Yugoslav federation, Slovenia, Croatia, Bosnia–Hercegovina, Macedonia and 'rump' Yugoslavia (Serbia and Montenegro), have not agreed on the inheritance of the former entity.

2. The Communist regime of the previous multi-ethnic federation imposed laws of expropriation, for which former land and property owners living in neighbouring countries, especially Italy, are now seeking compensation and a quick settlement of previous injustices.

3. Slovenia's economy is the only growing economy of the former entity. Other parts of former Yugoslavia are involved in military disputes (Croatia, Bosnia–Hercegovina) or face sanctions imposed on them by the international community or neighbouring states ('rump' Yugoslavia and Macedonia). National and transnational financial institutions are keen to settle the US$16 billion loan given to former Yugoslavia by asking the only booming economy in the region to come forward with at least a third of the amount. Slovenia is willing to repay one-tenth of the former Yugoslavia's debts.

Slovenia is aware and supportive of all three major regional development frameworks being discussed in Brussels. These can be summarised as follows:

1. The European central axis model (London–Brussels–Frankfurt–Milan).
2. The isolated metropolitan regions model (e.g. the Milan metropolis, the Munich metropolitan area, the Vienna metropolitan area, the Budapest metropolitan area, etc.).
3. The interregional and intermetropolitan co-operation model (or core–axis model), which is in part a combination of both the above.

Recent Slovenian regional development plans and actions suggest that the government is in favour of the third scenario. Understandably, priority is given to the model calling for interregional cooperation (Piry, 1992; Klemenčič and Ravbar, 1993). Within this model, Slovenia could realise its own objectives and develop economic and political sovereignty most easily. Otherwise, the youngest nation-state in south–central Europe would be forced to adapt other development policies particularly those of neighbouring states and regions. In

101

this case Slovenia's territory of 20 256 km^2 and 2.1 million inhabitants would be asked to adapt its economy to the interests of Milan, Lombardy and Italy or to be part of the outer ring of the Budapest, Vienna or Munich metropolis.

8.3 Slovenia's development scenarios

Slovenia's transport routes are central to the interests of Brussels, and two proposed major European traffic corridors and development arteries would further impact on the economy, society and appearance of the country if planning proceeds according to EU scenarios (Černe, 1992). The war in the Balkan peninsula has interrupted the air, rail and North Sea–eastern Mediterranean (Hamburg–Athens) highway corridor, which links the EU member state Greece with the core area of the Union. As the Yugoslav conflict continued, interest in developing this route diminished not only in Brussels but in Slovenia as well, very much to the chagrin of the Croatian government.

On the other hand, the opening of borders towards Central/Eastern Europe has introduced new markets and preferential zones of development. In this respect, priority has been given to plans for the improvement of traffic conditions and construction of highways along the South to Central European Barcelona–Kiev corridor. The reinforcement of this route could bring economic benefits to Eastern and Central Europe and, in particular, to Slovenia and Hungary. For the first time in history a direct, modern traffic artery would link the Danubian and the Mediterranean basins. Koper, Trieste, Venice, as well as Rijeka, as Mediterranean ports, would support the central part of this development artery stretching from Spain and France through Italy, Slovenia and Hungary to the Ukrainian and Russian lowlands. Along the way, the Slovenian population centre and production axis of Ljubljana–Maribor could be further developed. The Slovenian port of Koper, with 4.9 million tonnes

transshipment annually, is particularly well placed to benefit from such a development. Hungarian, Slovakian and Austrian firms have already established major partnerships with Koper. Since some German firms, such as BMW, have also recently become Koper's business partners, jealous neighbours now refer to this sole Slovenian Mediterranean port as the 'Bavarian Hong Kong' (Gerenčer, 1993).

In 1993 an agreement was reached to construct a 19 km stretch of railway (Murska Sobota–Hodoš–Zalaloevoe) which would establish for the first time since the Second World War a direct linkage between the Slovenian and the Hungarian rail systems. Ironically, the new traffic line is to be built partly on the path of the old railway, which was closed and later removed due to the Iron Curtain. The World Bank is supportive of this construction and other improvements to the Slovenian rail system. In 1993 the train timetable for the first time in history introduced a direct Budapest–Trieste–Venice (at present crossing Croatian territory) passenger train. Between Ljubljana and Budapest a roll-on roll-off service for trucks was introduced. Border formalities are undertaken at the train's bordering points, thereby eliminating up to five hours' waiting at border crossings.

In Slovenia, plans are under way to construct 318 km of four-lane highway between 1995 and 1999 (Kmetič, 1993). All link Italy with Hungary and southeastern Austria. The investment, US$1.496 million, will be financed largely by Slovenian funds. A special road fuel tax was introduced for this purpose. The Italian government and firms, as well as the world's major financial institutions, have also promised to help. Plans to improve the highways from Austria towards Belgrade (the Tauern/Phyrn route) have been shelved, often to the disappointment of Slovenes as well. The well-constructed and recently (1992) opened 7864 m Karawanken Tunnel (Ljubljana–Salzburg–Munich) will have no straight four-lane highway continuation (Figure 8.2).

To develop functions that would be supportive of the EU, Slovenia must first develop a basic

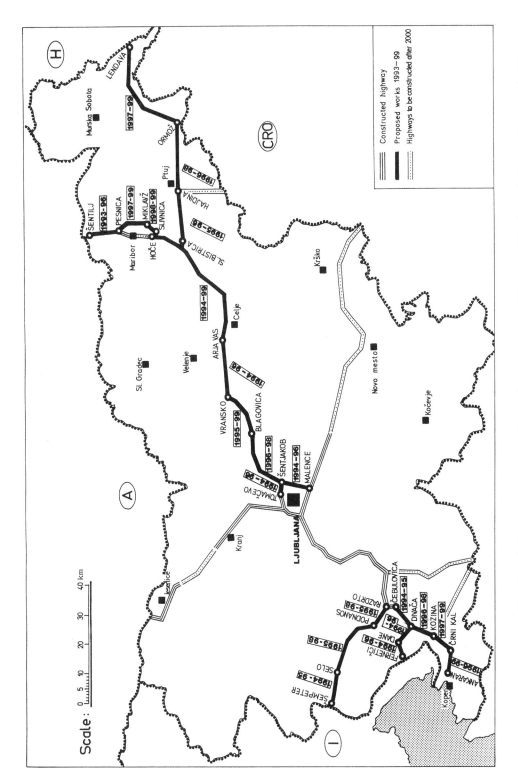

Figure 8.2 *Slovenia: proposed four-lane highway construction, 1993–99. Source: Slovenian Ministry of Traffic and Communications (1993)*

infrastructure. Rail, roads, telecommunications and energy lines (gas, electricity) are Slovenia's first priority. If there is little improvement Slovenia might end up an obstacle to European integration and a burden to its neighbours.

One way to improve the country's economy would be to encourage the development of transnational functional regions, disregarding administrative borders and physical barriers (Maier, 1986). The rudiments of cross-border cooperation were put in place in the northern Adriatic region as early as the 1970s. In the province of Friuli-Venezia Guilia and in Slovenia special funds were provided to enable linked economic growth. Information on the complementarity of production was jointly offered to the border provinces of Italy, Austria and Slovenia. Joint ventures of Slovenes in Italy and Austria and of Italians and Austrians in Slovenia now have almost a quarter-century-long tradition. For example, Slovenian Elan skis are produced in Austria's border region of Carinthia, while Italian Benetton textiles and Austrian Milka confectionery are made in Slovenia's border areas.

In 1993, 692 firms in Slovenia received foreign capital: 170 larger foreign investors (more than DM200 000) have invested DM936.3 million in the Slovenian economy (Mrozek, 1992; Jakomin, 1993). Most investments are related to services (banks), followed by electronic component producers and, in regard to the transitional character of the area, to trade, traffic and warehouse firms. One hundred and ninety enterprises in Slovenia are owned completely by foreigners, while 109 have joint venture status. Decisions to invest have been influenced by:

- an existing presence in the Slovenian (and former Yugoslavian) market
- increased perceived profits
- a skilled labour force
- lower costs of production

Most foreign investments are geographically located in cities along the V-shaped Jesenice–Ljubljana–Maribor central manufacturing axis (Figure 8.3). German and Austrian firms such as Siemens, Henkel and Semperit most often have signed cooperation agreements with producers located in this traditional urban/industrial core of Slovenia. Austrian banks and supermarkets and Italian financial and commercial institutions have opened branch offices in major cities. Foreign businesses seldom choose locations in peripheral, rural areas and particularly not along borders; some are located there, but to the disappointment of many they are owned not by investors from the neighbouring town or region across the border, but very often by a transnational corporation. One such example is the Adidas shoe production at Turnišče, just a few kilometres from the Hungarian border. The general policy of past governments of Slovenia to be supportive of polycentric and peripheral (industrial) development appears to have been dropped.

8.4 Socio-geographical problems of the Slovenian border regions

Slovenia is a typical small European transitional country, and as such can be regarded entirely as a border region. It provides a smooth transition from the highly developed areas of Lombardy in Italy (northern Adriatic) to areas in an earlier development stage. Traffic on the country's transit routes in times of peace is heavy: 90.5 million travellers were registered in 1988 at 119 Slovenian border crossings. The new, as yet not exactly defined border with Croatia (546 km) has introduced 26 new border crossings. Two new border crossings with Hungary were added to the two existing ones following Slovenia's independence. Sadly, Slovenian regional planning has in part neglected border crossings and border regions as spatial elements of development. Border crossings can function as innovation cores and a border region can gain by being developed according to the needs of the neighbouring region in another state. The neglect of border regions is particularly obvious in the eastern portion of the country, along the Hungarian and Croatian border. This is in part

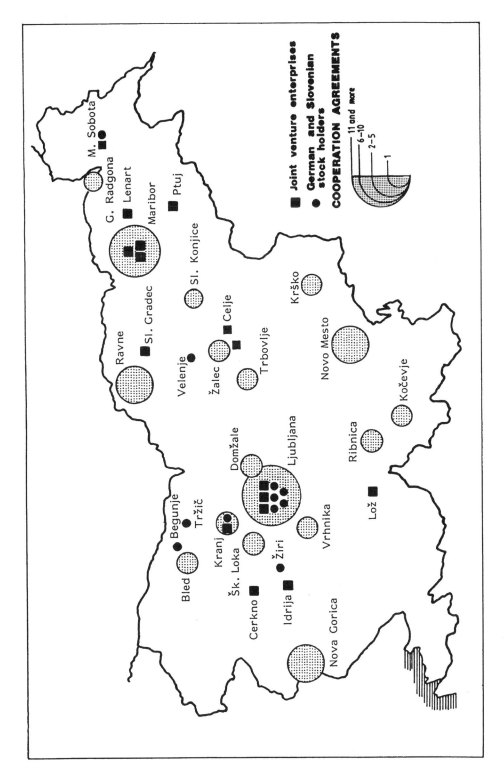

Figure 8.3 *Slovenian–German cooperation agreements and joint ventures, 1991*

105

understandable: the Slovene–Hungarian border was for decades a closed one, while the Slovene–Croatian border, separating former republics of the Yugoslav federation, was until recently not functioning as an international boundary since people could freely move and search for opportunities in core areas of the two autonomous entities of the multi-ethnic state. Almost 60% of all communes in Slovenia along the Slovene–Croatian border are demographically threatened and 87% of communes along the Hungarian border experience the same fate. Since some of them will be within the zone of the major EU corridor towards Eastern Europe, this could hinder overall development.

Border areas are sensitive to development. The ethnic composition of border areas is most often mixed and therefore interests of two or more cultures have to be recognised within development planning (Gosar, 1993). Often the economic interest of one or both bordering states is not identical with the interest of the region and the nationalities within it. Slovenia's border regions along the proposed corridor are ethnically mixed.

In the western portion, the Italian population has diminished in size from 21 336 (41% of the total population of the region) in 1948 to 2581 (5.1%) in 1961 and to 2751 (0.16%) in 1991. The new state border with Croatia has interrupted the established and functioning links between members and institutions of the Italian population of Istria. Non-Slovenes and Italians in the border region of Koper amount to almost 28% of the total population here. Increased immigration from other parts of former Yugoslavia made this area along the border with Italy ethnically mixed and sensitive to single culture development (Table 8.1).

The eastern portion of the proposed traffic corridor along the Hungarian border is settled by Slovenes, Hungarians, Roma (Gypsies) and Croats. The ethnically mixed area of Prekmurje was until 1919 within the Hungarian part of the Dual Monarchy. Immigrating Slovenes and their higher birth-rates constantly lowered the share (though not necessarily the absolute numbers) of the autochthonous Hungarian population in the border region. In 1910 Prekmurje had 14 637 Hungarians (81% of the total population of the region), in 1931 7407 (39%) settlers were of Hungarian origin, and in 1991 the Slovenian census authorities registered 7637 (8.5%) persons of Hungarian ethnicity (Table 8.2).

Slovenian border industrial development carried out in the 1970s in peripheral communes attracted labour from near and far. Croats from communes along the border were hired by several factories. In times of restructuring, enterprises in peripheral areas and along the more or less closed border with Croatia suffer most. In the communes of Lendava and Murska Sobota, on the Slovene–Hungarian and Slovene–Croatian borders, 5259 persons are registered as unemployed, placing both administrative entities on the top 10 list of unemployment. The 14.4% Slovenian unemployment average is well

Table 8.1 *Slovenia: the ethnic structure of border regions, 1961 and 1991*

Communes/Občine along:	All (000s)		All (%)		Croats (%)		Serbs (%)		Muslims (%)		Other (%)	
	1961	1991	1961	1991	1961	1991	1961	1991	1961	1991	1961	1991
Slovene–Italian border	10.0	31.0	7.2	17.2	50.4	28.9	18.1	17.0	0.2	7.3	36.2	51.8
Slovene–Austrian border	14.5	49.0	8.8	10.3	49.8	21.3	22.5	19.5	0.3	12.2	27.4	47.0
Slovene–Hungarian border	10.2	12.4	15.2	18.8	7.5	12.1	8.1	2.3	0.1	0.6	89.4	85.0
Slovene–Croatian border	30.1	55.6	9.4	14.7	37.8	30.5	10.7	11.3	0.2	5.2	51.4	58.0
Slovenia	69.3	239.0	4.4	12.2	45.4	22.7	19.6	20.0	0.7	11.2	34.3	46.0

Source: Yugoslav Census Reports, 1961, 1991.

Table 8.2 *Italian and Hungarian populations in Slovenia*

Communes/*Občine*	Italian			Hungarian		
	1948	1961	1991	1931	1961	1991
Piran	10 091	1 217	1 169	—	30	25
Izola	4 402	531	567	—	9	14
Koper	6 843	833	1 015	—	36	41
Murska Sobota	5	—	0	2 523	1 774	1 322
Lendava	20	3	0	11 542	8 115	6 315
Slovenia	21 714	3 072	3 064	14 429	10 498	8 503

— = No data.
Source: Yugoslav Census Reports, 1931, 1948, 1961, 1991.

surpassed here. In recent times of transition and devolution of Yugoslavia, minority populations are suffering most. Seasonal and part-time workers of non-Slovenian residence (and nationality) are most vulnerable in times of recession. The Croatian labour force in border communes has substantially diminished in size in recent years.

Care in the development of border regions is particularly required in regard to landownership and use (Belec, 1993). Experience from Austria and Italy, especially in the hinterland of Trieste and Villach, where Slovenes live as a minority, shows that development in the nation-state's or EU's interest (fast breeder reactor/highway construction/tourism) can damage the intentions of the local population and impact upon its culture. Both have occurred to the Slovenian ethnic group due to property confiscation.

8.5 Conclusion

Economic development executed in a single country's interest within a relatively small Europe can be hazardous to all, but particularly to the next-door neighbour. On the other hand, cooperation and consideration of mutual interests of cultures can produce benefits to the region, to the nation-state in question, and to neighbouring countries.

Slovenia is gradually resolving questions concerning its economic and political relationships with neighbouring states, notably:

1. The future of Slovenian firms as well as of past private investments in Croatia and in other parts of the former Yugoslavia, including some 20 000 second homes;
2. The ownership and use of joint projects, such as the Slovene–Croatian Westinghouse nuclear power plant near Krško, on Slovenian soil, and investments made by Slovenia's financial institutions and firms in power plants in Bosnia and in 200 commercial sites in Croatia, Serbia, Kosovo and Macedonia, and vice versa.

Growing nationalism is in part attributable to the past decade's huge labour immigration, recent refugee problems, and the loss of the once prosperous Yugoslavian market and Slovenian-owned property there. Furthermore, 238 968 foreigners—to a large extent former citizens of the Yugoslav federation—received Slovenian citizenship in 1991 and 1992; there are an additional 40 987 'guest workers', and 74 432 Slavic Muslim refugees from Bosnia are being hosted by the Slovenian government as the war rages just a few hundred kilometres away in their home country.

Slovenia is finding difficulty in promoting its economy as it attempts to replace the loss of the Yugoslav market of 20 million consumers (Gosar, 1991). The exchange of goods between former Yugoslav republics was greatly reduced after independence. The young nation-state's best partner of the former federation is Croatia, to where 9.5% of goods are exported and from where 7.4% are imported. Macedonia is the most important Balkan partner. More than 75% of trade takes place with Austria, Germany, Italy and France (in descending order of importance). The Austro-German impact is felt in almost every branch of the economy.

Recovering from a poor performance in 1992, Slovenia had a GNP per capita in 1993 of US$6494, far surpassing any other component of the former Yugoslavia. To financial partners Slovenia presents a number of unresolved problems, particularly with regard to the succession of Yugoslav debts. The thriving gambling industry along the Italian border may detract from the country's image, as do the nearby wars in Croatia and Bosnia; both factors lower investment attractiveness. Within Central Europe Slovenia ranks behind the Czech Republic, Hungary, Poland and Slovakia in terms of investment security. Unresolved problems may have a constraining effect on the future of European integration and the readiness of Slovenia to join the EU.

8.6 References

Belec, B., 1993, Grenzüberschreitende Grundbesitzvermischung und Beschäftigung-Beispiel der Gemeinden Nordostsloweniens an der Slowenisch–Kroatischen Grenze, *Dela*, **10**, 73–85.

Černe, A., 1992, European aspects of Slovenian transport system, *Slowenien auf dem Weg in die Marktwirtschaft, Arbeitsmaterialien zur Raumordnung und Raumplanung*, **108**, 24–9.

Gerenčer, I., 1993, Odprta pot proti morju, *Delo*, **35**, 8.

Gosar, A., 1991, Die neuen Markt- und Wirtschaftsstrategien in Slowenien, Jugoslawien, *Regionalforschung von Grenzüberschreitender Bedeutung: Kaernten–Slowenien/Kroatien*, *AMR INFO*, **22**, 25–38.

Gosar, A., 1993, Nationalities of Slovenia—changing ethnic structures in Central Europe, *GeoJournal*, **30**, 215–28.

Jakomin, A., 1993, Nemški partnerji so tudi največji tuji vlagatelji v slovensko gospodarstvo, *Republika*, **2**, 9–11.

Klemenčič, V., 1992, Gegenwärtige politische, soziale und wirtschaftsgeographische Probleme als Ausgangsbasis für die Integration Sloweniens in Europa, *Slowenien auf dem Weg in die Marktwirtschaft, Arbeitsmaterialien zur Raumordnung und Raumplanung*, **108**, 4–19.

Klemenčič, V., Ravbar, M., 1993, Actual problems of regional development in Slovenia, in *Development strategies in the Alpine–Adriatic region*, Centre for Regional Studies, Pécs, pp. 143–65.

Kmetič, F., 1993, Gradnja avtocest do preloma tisočletja, *Motorevija*, **37**, 10–11.

Maier, J., 1986, Ausländische Investitionen und ihre Auswirkungen aus der Sicht der Regionalwissenschaften, *Wirtschaftliche Zusammenarbeit zwischen Ländern verschiedener gesellschaftlicher Systeme, Arbeitsmaterialien zur Raumordnung und Raumplanung*, **47**, 1–7.

Mrozek, Th., 1992, Auswirkungen von kooperationen Bundesdeutscher/Bayrischer und Slowenischer Unternehmen im Rahmen von Joint-Venture, *Slowenien auf dem Weg in die Marktwirtschaft, Arbeitsmaterialien zur Raumordnung und Raumplanung*, **108**, 102–28.

Piry, I., 1992, Možnosti preoblikovanja politike regionalnega razvoja na primeru Slovenije, *Geographica Slovenica*, **23**, 223–47.

Vrišer, I., 1994, Einige wirtschaftsgeographische Überlegungen über die möglichen Beziehungen der Nachfolgestaaten Jugoslawiens zur europäischen Gemeinschaft, *Südosteuropa und die europäische Integration, Südosteuropa Aktuell*, **18**, 65–85.

9

Slovenian national identity exemplified

Michael Chapman

9.1 Introduction

This chapter explores some aspects of cultural identity in the newly independent and democratic Republic of Slovenia. Slovenia is situated at the crossroads of the Balkans, and has undergone a dramatic transformation in its political and economic circumstances, but the continuing war elsewhere in the former Yugoslavia has often obscured the reconstruction of this Balkan state (Glenny, 1992). Yet Slovenia's transition can be seen as a rare success story for this troubled region (Pogacnik, 1991).

Slovenia has not only adopted Western European ideas of democracy but it has also pursued the principles of the free market. This process has not been without conflict and difficulty, however, and the aim of this chapter is to explore the importance of cultural identity in Slovenia and to place it within this changing economic and social context.

9.2 The sunny side of the Alps

Slovenes are an independent people with an individual language and identity, but until the events of June 1991 Slovenia had never been an independent nation-state. Located on the border between the Balkans and the old Austro-Hungarian Empire, Slovenia has had a turbulent and often bloody history. The country has been repeatedly invaded and conquered by Bavarian, Frankish, Czech, Hapsburg, Turkish, Italian and German armies. Given these incursions it is perhaps surprising that the Slovenes have successfully managed to protect and maintain their own language and cultural identity. Most Slovenes are Roman Catholic and religion, like language, is an important part of their national identity.

Slovenia became part of Yugoslavia in 1918 as a consequence of the Treaty of Versailles and as a matter of bureaucratic and geographical convenience. The Kingdom of the Serbs, Croats and Slovenes was seen as a buffer against possible German influence and interventionism in this strategic part of the Mediterranean. The result for the Balkans at the Treaty of Versailles was the effective creation of a Greater Serbia, but the mix of Serbs, Slovenes, Croats, Macedonians and Montenegrins on which it was based had an explosive potential for ethnic conflict.

During the Second World War Slovenia was divided between German, Italian and Hungarian occupation. Following the war, Slovenia gained considerable autonomy and prosperity under the regime of the partisan hero Josip Broz (Tito). In

Reconstructing the Balkans: A Geography of the New Southeast Europe. Edited by Derek Hall and Darrick Danta.
©1996 John Wiley & Sons Ltd

order to keep the factions apart, Tito ruled with both a fist of iron and extreme diplomacy. Any opposition to his authority was ruthlessly suppressed. On his death in 1980 no apparent heir had the same political skill or determination to rule over the federation, and the subsequent rotating presidency between the republics was to prove impractical. The early 1980s witnessed increasing tensions between the republics, and as the fall of Communist systems elsewhere in Central and Eastern Europe began in 1989, it was only a matter of time before the first Yugoslavian republics would declare independence.

On 25 June 1991 the Slovene Assembly passed the Sovereignty Acts which proclaimed Slovenia as an independent country. On 26 June new signs and flags were hoisted at Slovenian border crossings. The Yugoslav federal army reacted and a 10-day war enveloped Slovenia. At the instigation of the EC a three-month moratorium was declared and the Slovene Assembly suspended the implementation of the Sovereignty Acts. On 8 October 1991 Slovenia finally cut all links with the former Yugoslavia and entered a new period of independence, with a new currency, control of border crossings and the passing of a new constitution on 23 December 1991. Germany was the first country to recognise the new independent state, and was soon followed by Sweden and Iceland on 19 December 1991 and by the rest of the EC members on 15 January 1992.

Slovenia is situated at the crossroads of Europe, between Austria to the north, Italy to the west and Croatia and Hungary to the east. The country is relatively small in size (20 251 km²) with a population of approximately 2 million inhabitants, representing only 8% of the total population of the former state of Yugoslavia. Slovenia has a modest coastline of 47 km, and much of the country is rural in nature, with 82% of the land classified as non-urbanised (Table 9.1).

9.3 Economic structure

In economic terms Slovenia accounted for 20% of Yugoslavian GDP and 30% of its exports before independence. This underlines the economic

importance of the region to the Yugoslavian economy and explains why Slovenia had a high standard of living compared with other republics.

The economy consisted of a number of key manufacturing industries including furniture, paper, footwear, electrical equipment and transport road vehicles (Table 9.2), and had a substantial export trade in such goods. Due to import duties and taxation, Slovenian products were less expensive than Western goods and therefore had a high demand in the Yugoslav domestic market. The fragmentation of the federation and the political tension between

Table 9.1 *Slovenia: outline land use*

Total area	20 251 km²
Coastline	47 km
Land use	*% of land area*
Forests	50
Grassland	17
Fields and gardens	12
Orchards and vineyards	3

Source: Statistical Office of the Republic of Slovenia, 1991.

Table 9.2 *Slovenia: workforce and GNP by economic sector, 1990*

	% workforce	% GNP
Industry and mining	59	53
Agriculture and fishing	2	4
Forestry	1	
Water management	0.3	
Construction	9	6
Transport and communications	8	6
Trade	12	20
Catering and tourism	4	3
Crafts and services	4	2
Housing—municipal services	2	
Finance and business	6	4
Education and culture	8	
Medical and social services	9	
Local communities	5	
Other		4
Total	100	100

Source: Slovenian Ministry of Science and Technology (1992).

Serbia and the other republics has meant that Slovenia has lost the majority of its 'internal' market.

The tourist industry has been affected by the transition to independence. Although seen as a means to promote economic growth the industry has suffered as 95% of the Adriatic coast belongs to the republics of Croatia and Montenegro. The coastline has been a major destination for foreign tourists and for Slovenians themselves, but the major infrastructure systems which ran through the former Yugoslavia are now disrupted due to the creation of new political boundaries and the continued war, as discussed in the preceding chapter. It will take some years before the tourist trade ever realises the same potential it had before the break-up of the former Yugoslavian federation.

The transition to independence has caused an element of political and economic uncertainty in the Republic of Slovenia. One consequence of the economic transition to a free market system has been the rapid increase in the level of unemployment in the country. Before independence unemployment was considered inconsequential as the state provided employment opportunities. The rapid dislocation of the old centrally planned economic system meant that unemployment reached 95 000 or 12% of the labour force, by March 1992. In 1994, unemployment stood at approximately 14% of the labour force and stems from the increasing number of bankruptcies of former state-controlled large companies. As the government intends to continue on its path of economic liberalisation, further privatisation programmes of former state industries are expected, but it has been constantly criticised by a Slovenian public suffering from this pain-now-growth-later economic and monetary policy. The Slovenian government has limited financial resources at its disposal, and it has been reasonably successful in servicing its external debt. Slovenia is a member of the International Monetary Fund and the World Bank. Both of these institutions have estimated Slovenia's federal debt to be smaller than first feared. Membership of these financial institutions

helped to give legitimacy to the financial sovereignty of the country as much as admission to the UN did for the country's political sovereignty.

A fundamental concern in the economic liberalisation of former Communist Central and East European countries has been the sheer pervasiveness of the old-style centrally planned command economy system. Although Slovenia has been better placed than many of its eastern neighbours, attempts to unravel these economies have become a complex and time-consuming economic and social objective. The adoption of free market principles and the introduction of a system which allocates resources via pricing signals has resulted in the necessity to establish new and unfamiliar institutional frameworks. Modern infrastructures have been required and new rules and laws have been introduced in order to activate a market-based system. There has been a need to define property rights and impose a system to enforce contracts.

Smaller in area than Belgium, Wales or the state of Maryland, Slovenia has undergone substantial urban expansion in the last decade, with the development of regional centres and the growth of smaller settlements of approximately 10 000 in population. Despite this expansion provincial towns remain relatively small, their size reflecting the essentially rural nature of Slovene society. Many Slovenes prefer to build their own homes and there is a preference for rural areas. However, with limited land resources at the country's disposal, there is a need to meet future housing demand by regenerating existing urban areas. The introduction of a market economy and the privatisation of the remaining public sector housing stock have led to a neglect by central government of housing provision and urban renewal strategies.

In 1991 the government introduced legislation to privatise the public sector housing stock. The tenure structure within Slovenia before independence was roughly half owner occupation, mainly in rural areas, and half public sector, concentrated in the cities, out of a total stock of some 678 590 dwellings. In 1991, the privatisation of public sector housing was undertaken by offering cash discounts and favourable lending criteria for those Slovenes wishing to purchase their own public rented accommodation. A prime objective was to induce as many Slovenes as possible to purchase their flats or homes with foreign currency payments, thereby enabling the Slovenian government to build up valuable currency reserves. In the first year after independence this was imperative in order that the domestic currency, the tolar, could be stabilised and the National Bank of Slovenia could be firmly established. Although expectations were high, only 40% of the public housing stock had been sold within the first year and only a fraction of the money gained from the privatisation programme was placed in the national development housing fund. No extra finance from central government was available for housing and urban renewal programmes, and housing expenditure had yet to be introduced into the national budget.

Slovenia now faces the problem of maintaining the existing public housing stock while also catering for specific housing needs of certain groups including the young, the elderly and the poor, and in providing an estimated 3000 new dwellings a year to match new housing demand. Since independence rehabilitation strategies have been geared towards the regeneration of city centres through improving housing supply. The demand for housing is, however, still greater than the existing supply, and as pressure develops for further urbanisation the identity of a polycentric settlement pattern and relatively evenly populated rural areas is now coming under threat.

9.4 Tourism and the Notranjski Kras region

The Notranjski Kras region is famous for its outstanding limestone geology and the word 'karst' which describes this type of land form is Slovene in origin. Attempts are being made to protect this environmentally rich region while also allowing for some development of specialised tourism and specially ecotourism activity. The key location in the Notranjski Kras is the town of Cerknica which lies to the southwest of the country and falls within a triangle between the centres of Ljubljana, Rijeka (Croatia) and Koper. The main physical feature of the karst area is the river basin of the Ljubljanica, which has a unique system of underground caves; the river itself appears above ground at seven different locations.

Key features of the Notranjski Kras which make it not only an important environmental area but also a prime attraction for tourism activity include:

1. Cerknisko Polje (Cerknisko Plain) and its intermittent lake, proposed as a natural heritage area under the RAMSAR international wetlands convention;
2. Cerknica lake, a breeding ground for about 90 species of birds.
3. The karst area, with a valuable and diversified underground habitat with well over 1000 underground caves.
4. Thirty endemic species of fauna recorded on the World Conservation Union (IUCN) 'Red' list of threatened animals.
5. The karst system of the River Ljubljanica with unique karst fields (*polje*), sink-holes and caves, (e.g. Krizna, Postonjska and Planinska Jama) on the northwest border of the Dinaric Mountains.
6. The largest uninterrupted, natural and intact woodland area on the border between the Dinaric and Alpine mountain chains, providing the most westerly remaining habitat of the European brown bear, the lynx and wolf.

It is not surprising, therefore, that attempts have been made to designate this area as a national park by the local authorities of Ilirska Bistrica, Postojna, Cerknica and Logatec, an area which covers 1672 km^2 with 60 000 inhabitants in over 272 settlements. These have agreed that the establishment of the park is the best policy for the long-term sustainable development of the region.

As Hall (1991) points out, tourism has gained increased importance as a mechanism to assist the process of economic transformation in many Central and East European countries. National borders have become more flexible and the influx of Western tourists is considered a valuable source of hard currency. The tourist industry can assist in the upgrading of local infrastructure and services which might otherwise not have been forthcoming from central government departments. Given the perceived economic opportunities, it is not surprising that the tourism sector is considered by many local inhabitants as a 'pot of gold' ready for the taking. The Notranjska Kras itself provides a series of tourism opportunities which can cater for several tourist market niches, and in particular 'ecotourism'. The region's outstanding natural environment provides an obvious attraction for domestic and international visitors alike. The karst topography alone will attract many researchers and specialists each year to the region. Other specialist tourism activities can be found all the year round and include winter downhill and cross-country skiing and skating, and in the summer months, walking and climbing in one of the last remaining extensive natural woodlands in the whole of Europe.

The Notranjski Kras has a delicate ecosystem, and the success of this system has been the balance between nature and human activity. The local inhabitants have contributed to this balance by respecting the environment and they practise traditional farming methods. Given the tourism potential, attempts are being made to plan and to preserve the spatial, social and cultural identity of the area. A local environmental group (AREA) has established a management team who are lobbying to implement such a plan for the Notranjska Kras (Bratko *et al.*, 1993). Key elements of this plan include:

1. The identification and protection of important cultural landscapes and the natural and cultural heritage of the region;
2. Offering a voice in the decision-making process for local inhabitants;
3. Accepting that the impact human activity has on the landscape is important;
4. Identifying and addressing ecological issues.

However, there are a number of pressures and conflicts that have to be resolved if the plans for the region are to be successful. The first issue concerns spatial designation and empowerment. From the mid-1980s attempts have been made to secure a future for the Notranjska Kras, but since independence the government has been reluctant to give a high priority to the designation of the park. The second issue regards finance and the need to acquire funds from the tourist industry. As tourism is considered to be a key economic activity for the region, then a top priority should be the establishment of a sustainable tourism strategy. Powers are required to halt any further development in the area which might impact on the environment, and financial support is necessary to implement a sustainable development plan. The local inhabitants, although sceptical of the proposals, do see economic benefits, through the generation of local employment and income, as the country opens up to the pressure for tourism. The question remains as to whether the Notranjski Kras can be protected and maintained as a unique natural and cultural environment while the negative effects of tourism which are likely to damage this balance can be controlled without the loss of revenue which is so necessary for the implementation of this plan.

9.5 Conclusion

This chapter has identified certain aspects of the economic, social and political processes of reconstruction in the Republic of Slovenia. Of considerable importance to the Slovenian people has been the notion of cultural identity as a core foundation in the process of transition. The notion of place, locality and the way in which human activity and the natural environment interact is traditionally important to many Slovenes and is part of their own cultural heritage. The issue that is becoming very apparent since independence is the real economic and social cost that political and economic freedom has brought. Part of this process has involved a dramatic and rapid adoption of free market economics. With its comparatively high standard of living and industrial strength, Slovenia is better placed than the other former Yugoslav republics to adapt to change. Even so, this newly independent state is still economically vulnerable. The drive towards independence and the subsequent reconstruction of the country itself is based on a clear notion of identity. The dramatic shift to a free market economy and the speed with which this has been achieved, the adoption of principles such as privatisation and open competition are indirectly challenging this notion of identity and cultural heritage. The critical question for a small country, situated on the boundary of an ever-enlarging Europe, is whether the tide of economic change, globalisa-

tion and economic and political integration will, sooner rather than later, consume the very essence of the cultural fabric of Slovenia and thus destroy its real strength as an independent nation-state in the reconstruction of the Balkans.

9.6 References

Bratko, B. B., Mahne, L., Gosak, S., Dvorscak, K., 1993, *The Notranjska Park in the Republic of Slovenia*, EC Project Report, Cerknica.

Glenny, M., 1992, *The fall of Yugoslavia: the Third Balkan War*, Penguin, London.

Hall, D., ed., 1991, *Tourism and economic development in Eastern Europe and the Soviet Union*, Belhaven, London.

Pogacnik, A., 1991, Planning Slovenia as an independent state, *Town Planning Review*, **62**(3), 3–4.

Slovenian Ministry of Science and Technology, 1992, *Facts on Slovenia*, Ljubljana.

Section C
Neighbours in transition

Introduction

Derek Hall

C.1 Transition

Many spatial, structural, historical and other links exist between the problems of former Yugoslavia and immediate neighbours. This section attempts to address some of the more important and obvious of these links within the context of the neighbouring countries' experiences of post-Communist transition and restructuring. Given the uneven rates and patterns of post-Communist restructuring, and the varying relationships with the Yugoslav vortex, the emphases upon and between these themes necessarily vary from chapter to chapter.

In Chapter 11 Dean Rugg sees the potential for new transport links between the Adriatic and Black seas as presenting a challenge for Albania to regenerate itself as a 'gateway' to Eastern Europe and the Middle East. This is seen as particularly pertinent at the present time given the need for international trade and transport to circumvent Serbia and Bosnia. The potential for new spatial relationships is further explored by Stella Kostopoulou's focus on the changing role of the port city of Thessaloníki in Chapter 12. A 'natural' outlet for Serbia and southern former Yugoslavia, the port city is currently experiencing very mixed fortunes, with, on the one hand, the promise of new overland links with the Adriatic, but on the other the major constraints imposed by the UN embargo on Serbia and by the Greek blockade on FYROM. Greece's role in the economic and cultural reconstruction of the Balkans is potentially important and should not

be underestimated. The country's own political stance—its hostility to FYROM, continuing mutual distrust of Turkey and lukewarm attitude towards Albania—however, despite its EU and NATO memberships (see Chapter 18), is placing unnecessary obstacles in the way of regional progress and harming Greek economic interests along the way.

David Turnock's well-detailed exposition of changing regional development processes in Romania (Chapter 13) brings into sharp focus the continuing high importance of the rural sector in the Balkans, the impact and interaction of different levels of territorial–administrative organisation, and the way in which political and bureaucratic procedures may or may not keep pace with continually evolving economic and social processes.

Not surprisingly, the rural sector is also the focus for the next two chapters which highlight similar problems facing newly privatised farming in Romania and Bulgaria. In Chapter 14, using original survey data from Romania, Mieke Meurs emphasises that with the restitution of agricultural land to rural families, the lack of capital available, poor access to inputs, distribution and markets, and a minimum experience of innovation among small farmers have induced many of them to form cooperative production associations. Significant regional differences have emerged, but in many cases the associations appeared little different from old collective farms, with instances of the persistence of former leaders. Focusing on rural Bulgaria, Sarah Monk

Reconstructing the Balkans: A Geography of the New Southeast Europe. Edited by Derek Hall and Darrick Danta.
©1996 John Wiley & Sons Ltd

(Chapter 15) emphasises the multidimensional practical problems of land restitution and agricultural privatisation. These range from disputes over farm and administrative boundaries to the inadequacies of the legislative framework.

In Chapter 16, Boian Koulov takes the opportunity to employ the Bulgarian tourist industry as a vehicle for exploring questions of environmental protection within processes of economic restructuring. Although our knowledge of the environmental situation in the Balkans has been enhanced in recent years (e.g. Jancar, 1985; IUCN–EEP, 1990; Karpowicz, 1991, 1993; Carter and Turnock, 1993; Nefedova, 1994), the ecological implications of the upheavals consequent upon political and economic restructuring are as yet poorly understood. Koulov points to social disruption, economic naïvety, administrative confusion and contradiction, and corruption, which have brought about considerable damage to environmental protection, rehabilitation and enforcement mechanisms. He concludes, pessimistically, that the very resources upon which tourism, as the country's most important economic activity, was based, have experienced the greatest adverse environmental impacts.

One of the major and more obvious spatial linkages between the Yugoslav vortex and neighbouring countries has been the often complex pattern of refugee movements. As an immediate neighbour of the former Yugoslavia and of Romania, with ethnic ties in both, Hungary is examined as a place of refuge by Alan Dingsdale in Chapter 17. He provides an important analysis of refugee flows, settlement policies and the impacts of such processes on the host country, and some of the spatial, social and economic dimensions of repatriation. The issues raised in this chapter are ones which are unlikely to go away easily. Indeed, with continuing political and social instability in the Balkans and further east, and with increasing national, continental and global economic disparities, refugee problems and policies to cope with them are destined to rise towards the top of the agenda of the 'developed' nations as we move into the twenty-first century.

The first chapter (10) which follows in Section C addresses the question of Albanian identity and the potentially important role of the Albanian nation of 6–7 million people located in the eponymous state and its immediate neighbours.

C.2 References

Carter, F. W., Turnock, D. eds, 1993, *Environmental problems in Eastern Europe*, Routledge, London.

IUCN–EEP, 1990, *Protected areas in Eastern and Central Europe and the USSR; an interim review*, World Conservation Union, Cambridge.

Jancar, B., 1985, Environmental protection: 'the tragedy of the republics', in Ramet, P. ed., *Yugoslavia in the 1980s*, Westview, Boulder, Colo.

Karpowicz, Z. ed., 1991, *Environmental status reports: 1990. Vol. 2: Albania, Bulgaria, Romania, Yugoslavia*, World Conservation Union, Cambridge.

Karpowicz, Z., 1993, The challenge of ecotourism— application and prospects for implementation in the countries of Central and Eastern Europe and Russia, *Revue de Tourisme*, 3, 28–40.

Nefedova, T., 1994, Industrial development and the environment in Central and Eastern Europe, *European Urban and Regional Studies*, 1(2), 168–71.

10

Albanian identity and Balkan roles

Derek Hall

10.1 Introduction

This chapter focuses on the major dimensions of Albanian identity and its wider significance for Southeast Europe. Although one of the more distinctly unique peoples of the region, ethnic Albanians inhabit several contiguous territories which are vulnerable to tension and potential conflict. Albania itself continues to exhibit a degree of uncertainty concerning the country's future.

No larger than the size of Wales, Belgium or the state of Maryland, with a population of 3.3 million Albania was Southeast Europe's smallest state until the fragmentation of Yugoslavia. Now Macedonia (FYROM) and Slovenia are smaller by both population and area. Divided from FYROM by the Macedonian highland eastwards, from Montenegro and Kosovo by the Dinaric Alps to the north and from Greece by the Pindus Mountains southwards, much of Albania is itself upland (Ackerman, 1938; Bërxholi and Qiriazi, 1986, 1990; Bërxholi *et al.*, 1988). The Adriatic and Ionian seas set the country's western boundaries, and by so doing wash the only fertile coastal plain on the eastern Adriatic.

Roughly 40% of Albanian land is cultivable, together with a further 15% under irrigation. Much of the remaining land is forested (DeS,

1991; Hall, 1994), although substantial areas of hillside erosion exist in the country's central flysch 'badlands'. Albania has bountiful water resources, with upland annual precipitation levels being some of the highest in Europe at around 1500 mm. Average annual water flow is estimated at 42 000 million m³ (Frashëri, 1988). These resources only began to be developed late in the interwar period. Subsequently, the northern rivers were harnessed to an increasing extent, with hydropower eventually accounting for some 80% of the country's electricity needs. Water management has not always made best use of this resource, however, and in the late 1980s and early 1990s the country's economic and political life was critically affected by water shortages following a series of relatively dry winters.

Albania is relatively well endowed with mineral resources, although their exploitation has been inhibited by undercapitalisation, poor management and, more recently, domestic instability. Hydrocarbons and fuels, particularly petroleum and bitumen, can be found in the southwest of the country, while the northeast is characterised by metallic deposits, notably chromite, copper and ferrous nickel. Pockets of poor-quality coal are found in a number of locations in the centre and south of the country. Western multinational corporations are currently exploring

Reconstructing the Balkans: A Geography of the New Southeast Europe. Edited by Derek Hall and Darrick Danta.
©1996 John Wiley & Sons Ltd

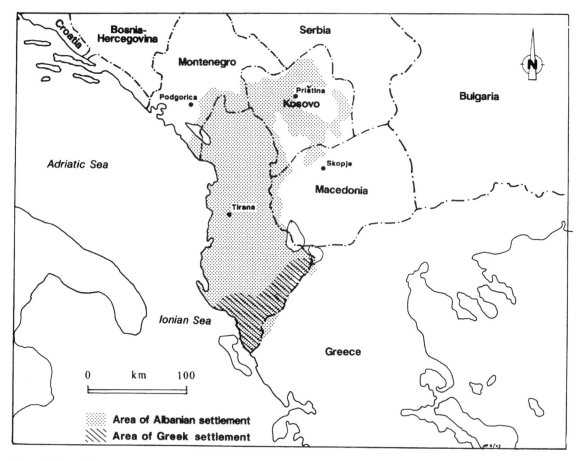

Figure 10.1 *Albanian-inhabited lands*

the country's southern continental shelf for further hydrocarbon resources. By the early 1990s annual output amounted to 2 million tonnes of coal and 1 million tonnes each of chromite, ferrous-nickel ore and copper ore (Bërxholi, 1990; *Mining Journal*, 1992). However, recent indications have suggested much lower levels of production.

10.2 State evolution

10.2.1 Albanian national awakening

Albanians claim direct descent from the Illyrian tribes who inhabited much of the southwest

Balkans. Their sense of identity and territoriality is based on a believed presence long predating Slav migrations to the area, and a long-term process of territorial compaction. Southern Illyria, roughly coinciding with present-day Albanian-inhabited lands (Figure 10.1), is said to have enjoyed a high level of economic, social and cultural development prior to Roman occupation (Buda, 1980). A gradual post-Roman unification of the more advanced Illyrian tribes and territories into a single state took place, although subsequent foreign invasions reduced the size of Albanian territory. The Arbër culture of the early Middle Ages further developed pre-Roman Illyrian elements (Anamali, 1969, 1972). Despite conquests by Bulgarians and Serbs in the

Plate 10.1 *The town of Ballsh in south–central Albania: industrialised under the Communists with an oil refinery and power station, it was poorly planned, badly polluted and is now part-derelict. Only the fringe buildings on the edge of town in the very foreground reveal any indigenous character (Derek Hall)*

ninth and tenth centuries which again diminished the extent of Albanian-inhabited lands, the term 'Albans' emerged in the eleventh century to incorporate an implicit territorial dimension. Although the schism of the Christian Church saw Roman Catholicism as the dominant faith of north Albanian lands and Orthodoxy as that of the south, subsequent Ottoman conquests were to introduce Islam to most Albanians (section 10.3.4).

As a consequence of the Serbian defeat at Kosovo Polje at the hands of the Turks in 1389, Albanians were able to penetrate western and northern Macedonia and to reach the southern Dalmatian coast at Ragusa (Dubrovnik). Some contend that significant numbers of Illyrian descendants had remained in these areas in the intervening years. Certainly from 1690 large numbers of Albanians (re)colonised the territories of Kosovo, Novi Pazar, Niš, Ipek (Peć), Djakovë and Gusinj.

Finally controlling all Albanian lands by the late fifteenth century, the Ottomans entrusted their administration to native pashas or beys (*begs*), who were played off one against another, as were highland chieftains (Skendi, 1967). Following the Greek revolution and growing opposition in northern Albania, however, the Turks introduced new administrative–territorial divisions of Albanian lands in an attempt to preclude a geographical basis for the development of an Albanian national identity. The north was placed within the Roumelian *eyalet* (province), with its centre at Monastir (Bitolj), and the south became part of the Janina *eyalet*.

As a nationalistic sentiment began to emerge in the mid-nineteenth century, Albanian lands were divided between *liva* (districts) based on the administrative centres of Shkodër, Prizren and Ipek, each with a governor under the auspices of an army general. A further territorial reorganisation in 1865 separated Albanians into three *vilayets* ('local governments'), based on Janina, Monastir and Shkodër. Each *vilayet* was sub-

Plate 10.2 *Some of the better appointed apartments built in Tirana during the 1970s with ground-floor shops. Large-scale clearance of typical Balkan single-storey dwellings and street widening schemes preceded their construction (Derek Hall)*

divided into a number of districts. Prior to the 1878 Berlin Congress, a fourth, Kosovo, *vilayet* was added to this framework to include the town of Novi Pazar and such Slav-inhabited areas as Niš, thereby counterbalancing and outweighing Albanian strength and influence.

By the 1870s, leading Albanians of all major faiths were voicing nationalist ideals over and above those of religious loyalty. An immediate objective was to prevent Montenegro, Serbia and Bulgaria annexing parts of Albania from a dismembered Ottoman Empire. Russian defeat of the Turks and the subsequent 1878 Treaty of San Stefano sought to incorporate Albanian lands into the newly independent Slav states of Bulgaria, Montenegro and Serbia, and to establish Russian dominance of the region. Both Austria–Hungary and Britain refused to accept such a situation, however, and the Congress of Berlin was called to reconsider the treaty.

10.2.2 The role of Kosovo

The importance of the Kosovo lands for Albanian cultural and political aspirations was emphasised when the first gathering to secure Albanian 'national' rights was held in Prizren in June 1878. This meeting gave birth to the Albanian League for the Defence of the Rights of the Albanian Nation. In referring to themselves as the Prizren League, Albanian nationalists employed the Turkish term *millet* (nation), indicating that they still perceived their place within the Ottoman imperial structure rather than seeking full independence.

Albanian and Serb counter-claims to Kosovo now entered the world stage, reinforced by ethnic, linguistic and religious differences. For Serbs, Kosovo represents the heartland of their nation and state. Serbian settlement was concentrated here from the seventh century.

Medieval Serbian kings were crowned in Prizren where Stefan Dušan (1331–55) established the seat of his empire. In 1346, when Dušan was crowned Emperor of the Serbs, Greeks, Bulgarians *and Albanians*, the Serbian bishopric of Peć (in Kosovo) was proclaimed a patriarchate, establishing the Serbian Church's independence of Constantinople (Durham, 1989). The Serbian Orthodox Church, an institution synonymous with the history and destiny of the Serbian nation, is thus rooted in Kosovo. The region's churches and monasteries continue to represent the Serbs' continuity with their medieval Slav state, emphasising Kosovo's central role in Serb national identity and heritage. The crucial defeat at Kosovo Polje in 1389 spawned such Serbian romantic literature and legend that over the centuries the débâcle has been transformed into a moral victory, and, most recently, a source of Serb nationalist fervour (see Chapter 3). Albanians in Kosovo are viewed by Serbs as latecomers and as Turkish surrogates, not least in helping to drive Serbs from the area in the seventeenth and eighteenth centuries (Jelavich, 1983).

Albanians claim a strong affinity with Kosovo since their Illyrian ancestors had inhabited the area at least three centuries before Slavs began to displace them in the region. Much later, in the later decades of the nineteenth century, Kosovo emerged as the cradle of an Albanian rebirth, the seat of literary inspiration and political will to pursue national freedom, after five centuries of Turkish domination (Prifti, 1978, pp. 223–5). Prizren was certainly the most active town in expressing Albanian nationalist sentiment.

10.2.3 Territoriality

The 1878 Berlin Congress ceded parts of northern Albania, including Kosovo, to Montenegro. Albanians attempted to prevent this, arguing that under Montenegrin control, the port of Ulcinj (Dulcino) could provide Russian access to the western Balkans and the Mediterranean. Albanian nationalists sought to set up a single Albanian *vilayet* (suggested by Britain) within the Ottoman lands. They attempted to repel Montenegrins in the north,

Greeks in the south, and Bulgars to the southeast, and seized Prizren, Prishtinë (Priština), Usküb (Skopje) and Dibër. Turkey responded with a swift reoccupation of these towns and the destruction of the Albanian League.

This failure emphasised the internal contradictions of Albanian national identity. Upland northern groups were often embroiled in localised disputes, and only rarely were they able to conceive of autonomy in broad national terms. The people of southern Albania, more settled economically and more open to external influence, were less opposed to Turkish administrative control (Skendi, 1953, p. 231).

None the less, the concept of territoriality—attachment to and protection of a given area by a self-identified group—possessed two important elements for Albanian national identity. The establishment of a unified territory acted as a rallying point for the expression of Albanian national geographical identity. Second, their homeland represented a vital asset to protect in the face of external territorial claims attempting to fill the vacuum of a crumbling Ottoman Empire.

By 1910, when Albanians again marched on Usküb and extracted several concessions from the Turks, Albanian nationalism had become a pawn in great power diplomacy. On 28 November 1912, amid the upheaval of the First Balkan War, Albanian leaders met in Vlorë to proclaim Albanian independence and to constitute a government of mixed religious affiliations (Skendi, 1967, p. 472). Italian and Austrian support quickly followed (Shaw and Shaw, 1977, p. 297), even though the new country lacked recognised land boundaries and most other attributes for self-determination.

Shortly afterwards, the London Conference of Ambassadors (1912–13) acknowledged Albanians to be a distinct people, with national traditions and ideals and deserving of self-determination (Barnes, 1918). Despite this, the conference ceded Kosovo to the Slavs, and not to the Albanian state which came into being on 29 July 1913 (Peacock, 1914). National pride was slighted by this separation: the new country's boundaries resulted from a series of compromises between the claims of Greece and Serbia and

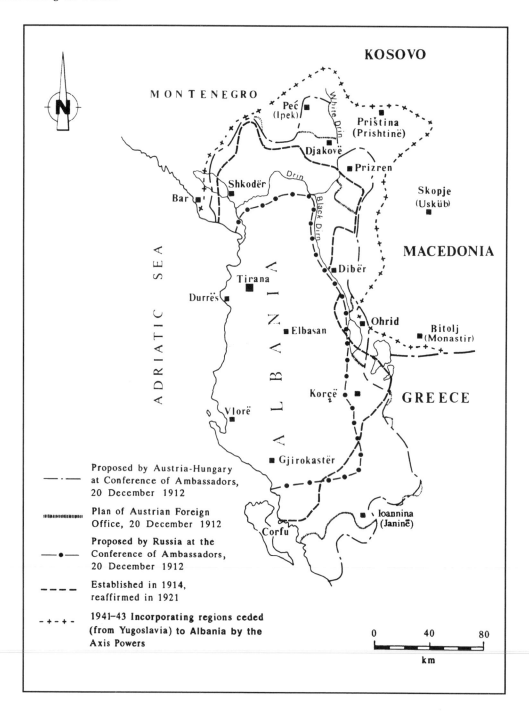

Figure 10.2 *Albania: alternative boundaries. Sources: Helmreich (1938, p. 256); Lendvai (1969, p. 174)*

those promoted by Austria and Italy, ostensibly on Albania's behalf (Figure 10.2). Little serious attempt was made to draw them in respect of either ethnic or economic considerations (Barnes, 1918, pp. 14–15; Giles, 1930).

During the First World War, the country was overrun by seven armies. In accordance with the 1915 'Secret Treaty' of London (whereby Britain, France and Russia convinced Italy to support them in the war), Italy sought a mandate over the port of Vlorë and central Albania. Although rebuffed at the Peace Conference, Italian ambitions were only thwarted by strong Albanian resistance and demonstrations in Italy itself. Woodrow Wilson's insistence on the principle of self-determination encouraged France to withdraw from northern and southeastern Albania. The country narrowly escaped partition (RIIA, 1939).

A national congress held at Lushnjë in January 1920 elected a parliament and government, and Albania joined the League of Nations later in the year. The country's borders were only finally confirmed in November 1921, after some minor concessions were made in favour of Yugoslavia. Athens' claim on all south Balkan lands inhabited by Orthodox Christians was cut short in 1922 when Greece was defeated by Turkey in Asia Minor (Stickney, 1926).

10.3 Ethnicity

10.3.1 Ethnic self-identity

While over 6 million ethnic Albanians inhabit several Balkan countries, Albania itself is relatively homogeneous. The April 1989 census (DeS, 1991, pp. 361, 370), declared 98% of the country's population to be ethnic Albanian. The remainder were made up of nearly 60 000 ethnic Greeks, some 5000 Slavs and over 1000 members of other ethnic groups, including Vlachs (Winnifrith, 1987) and Gypsies. The Greeks have lived in the Ionian districts of Himarë and Dhërmi, and from Gjirokastër southwards to the Greek border, across which many left the country during the early 1990s. The country's small Jewish community was airlifted to Israel in 1991. Aside from the possibility of any

statistical falsification, the combination of a very low level of emigration up to 1990, and a high ethnic Albanian growth rate has witnessed a gradual diminution of minority groups: from 8% of the total population in 1939 to 5% in 1961 and 2% in 1989. Such figures have always been contested: Greek sources have claimed up to 400 000 Orthodox Christians within the country as the Greek community.

Albanians believe themselves to be direct descendants of the pre-Hellenic, Hallstatt culture Illyrians. Illyrian tribes are thought to have inhabited the western Balkans since at least the second millennium BC. By the second century BC they had consolidated a state centred on present-day Shkodër. The term 'Albania' is believed to be derived from the Albanoi, an Illyrian tribe who inhabited present-day north-central Albania, and its application gradually spread to encompass other Illyrian groups, although the first known use is to be found in Latin dictionaries of the thirteenth century. In the Middle Ages the area was known as 'Arber' and its people as 'Arbëresh' (a name often used by ethnic Albanians in Italy and Greece). Following the Turkish occupation of the fifteenth century, Albanians began to refer to themselves as Shqiptarë and to their country as Shqipëri. The precise source is debated, however.

For at least several centuries, Albanians have experienced a cultural separation into two subgroups. To the north of the Shkumbin River and most characteristically in the remote northeast highlands, Gegs (Ghegs) have tended to live in small, dispersed settlements with social organisation based upon traditional clan loyalty.

Councils of elders, comprised of family headmen, have here maintained a semi-autonomous rule, regulating customary law, pasture, forest and water rights. They have also been responsible for overseeing the 'Law of Lek', which demands honour, hospitality and pursuit of retribution through the 'blood feud' (Durham, 1905, 1909; Mason *et al.*, 1945; Hasluck, 1954; Marmullaku, 1975, pp. 86–9; Lopasic, 1992). Even as late as the 1920s, 20% of male deaths in parts of the northeast could be attributed to blood feuds (Lendvai, 1969, p. 180). With valley bottoms acting as the boundaries between clan lands, communications in this part of the country have long been problematic, and the need for some men to hide from the threat of retribution has reduced the human resource potential of the region.

Inhabiting towns and villages in the plains and mountain basins to the south of the Shkumbin River, Tosks have been more susceptible to foreign influences: before 1990, most Albanian emigrants, particularly to Italy and the USA, were of Tosk origin. Although tribal organisation had largely disappeared in the south, until the eighteenth century some villages were made up of small clans headed by elected chieftains (Reméramd, 1928). Precluded from governmental positions by the Turks, Christian Tosks tended to join craft guilds, business and liberal professions, reflecting a more settled, economically oriented and outward-looking society than in the north. From the later nineteenth century, well-placed Tosk families sent their children to Western and Central Europe for their education.

The Muslim Geg, Ahmet Zogu, dominated Albanian political life in the interwar period, as prime minister, then as president, and, after having himself crowned in 1928, as King Zog I. The end of the Second World War, however, saw an emerging Communist leadership of predominantly southern origin, as exemplified by party secretary and commander-in-chief, Enver Hoxha, who was born in Gjirokastër (Dede *et al.*, 1986). The post-war regime's policy of attempting to mould a unitary Albanian nation saw the terms 'Geg' and 'Tosk' dropped from use.

10.3.2 The role of language

Nationality and religion did not coincide for the Albanians, such that language played a crucial role in projecting a national identity. It acted both as a common element and as a distinctive cultural and national trait separating Albanians from Turks, Greeks and Slavs, contributing to the 'national awakening' of the second half of the nineteenth century. This was particularly important as the Turks refused to accept Albanian as a medium of literature and instruction: in Albanian

lands, education was undertaken in Greek for Orthodox Christians and in Turkish or Arabic for Muslims.

Three dimensions were crucial in promoting language as the prime vehicle for Albanian national aspirations:

1. In structure and content Albanian holds an independent place within the Indo-European family, emphasising the ancient roots and separateness of the Albanian people;
2. Because of the Turkish proscriptions on the Albanian language and teaching, any written Albanian became a strong symbol of nationalist sentiment. Adoption of the Latin alphabet for the language's written form at the 1908 Albanian Congress at Monastir emphasised the Albanian national and cultural renewal and articulated a distinctiveness from Turks and Greeks;
3. The proscriptions on written Albanian saw the role of oral literature and traditions, myths and stories take on an important nationalist role. Vernacular folklore and tradition, songs, legends and epics were passed down orally from one generation to the next, sustaining a national identity and helping to maintain the Albanian language.

Difficult terrain, leading to isolation and poor communications, did encourage dialect differences across Albanian-speaking lands. Only in 1972 were uniform phonetic rules of spelling and a unified literary language formally adopted, incorporating the basic common elements of the Geg and Tosk dialects (EBNA, 1984, p. 74).

10.3.3 Other cultural symbols

Material culture has been important in complementing and moulding Albanian national identity (Hall, 1992). Archaeological evidence dates from Neolithic times, and a number of Bronze Age tumuli remain. Illyrian settlement began to be established in the fifth century BC, usually on strategic hilltops, and later fused with Greek influences. The Romans built roads, bridges and aqueducts, and from the fifth century defensive works and religious buildings were developed. Centres of artisan production grew in the Middle Ages, and following Turkish occupation, new architectural elements such as mosques and public baths were added. Individual urban settlements, such as Berat and Gjirokastër, and most rural regions had developed distinctive housing styles by the eighteenth century.

Although often revealing local and regional variation, domestic and military architecture, costume and textiles, wood, silver and ironworking, pottery, stone and visual art have all been promoted as elements of a 'national' culture.

'Shqipëri' is often thought to mean 'land of the eagles', a notion partly arising from the use of the double-headed eagle, the family emblem of the country's medieval national hero, Gjeorgj Kastrioti (Skënderbeg), a motif later adopted for the Albanian national flag. The son of an influential Catholic family from northern Albania, Skënderbeg was sent to the Sultan's court, became Islamicised, and fought with the Turks until defeated at Niš in 1443. Experiencing a profound transformation, Skënderbeg then returned to the family home at Krujë, denounced Islam and embarked upon a holy war against the Ottomans (Skendi, 1980). He helped mould a league of Albanian chieftains, who, after the 1444 Congress of Lezhë, became an effective military and political force (Wolff, 1956). Subsequently, he led his countrymen undefeated in battle against the Turks for almost a quarter of a century, receiving aid from the 'entire Catholic world whose cause he championed' (Noli, 1947, p. 2). His death in 1468 was followed by inevitable Ottoman victories.

Although the centuries of Ottoman domination which followed allowed the memory of the national hero to fade in the Balkans, Italo-Albanians, free from Islamic dominance, played an important role in perpetuating Skënderbeg's memory, to the extent that he became an inspiration for Italian unification. Skënderbeg's elevation to the role of Albanian national hero was attributable largely to the efforts of the writers of the later-nineteenth-century period of national revival (Skendi, 1968). He was promoted

as a major symbol of Albanian independence, uniting religious groups in a national ideal, even though this required Muslims to ignore the strongly anti-Islamic element of his struggles. Skënderbeg's inspiration was enlisted to reinforce stories, myths and legends promoting nationalist themes. For example, Naim Frashëri's *Skënderbeg* (1899), an epic poem depicting victories against the Turks, is seen as a watershed in the political significance of Albanian literature, whereby Skënderbeg's example performed a key role in generating the confidence necessary for achieving national independence and resisting foreign domination.

Although the interwar Zog regime appeared to draw on other sources of inspiration, the postwar Communists found it in their interests to harness the nationalist symbolism of Skënderbeg, whose presence, through statuary and 'heritage' site development was interwoven into the country's post-war development path, often implying a direct line of 'descent' between Skënderbeg and Hoxha as patriotic Albanian leaders.

10.3.4 Religion

Albanian national identity has coincided with race and language, rather than with religion. Geographically midway between Rome and Constantinople, Christian Albanian lands were divided between a Roman Catholic north and an Orthodox south following the eleventh-century schism. Religious differences, though marked, proved of little lasting importance in constraining Albanian national unity. Although Islamicisation followed the fifteenth-century Turkish conquests, the process was often slow, erratic and uneven (Skendi, 1956). Over the centuries, however, foreign, and particularly Western, perceptions of the Albanians tended to associate them with their Ottoman co-religionists, emphasising a negative role religion would hold for the nationalist cause.

None the less, by the end of the nineteenth century, the leading personalities of the Bektashi Islamic sect such as the Frashëri brothers emerged as effective Albanian nationalists with a sense of literary tradition. Bektashism was thought to have been introduced into Albania in the fifteenth century, and by the nineteenth century was embraced by perhaps a third of all Albanian Muslims. Despite its Shia sympathies, Bektashism presented a more tolerant form of Islam than the rigid prescriptions of the Turks, and became an appropriate, if paradoxical, vehicle for liberal intellectuals inspired by 'Western' notions of democracy and national self-determination.

Following national independence, the interwar period saw the Bektashi Order expelled from the now secular Turkey, to become an important influence in Albanian social and political life (Birge, 1937; Irwin, 1984; Norris, 1993).

However, the localised strength of Roman Catholicism in the north (Peacock, 1993) and of Orthodoxy in the south, together with the perceived 'external' associations of Albania's three major faiths, meant that religion was a prime target for a post-war Communist regime wishing to impose its own unifying emblems. Following a long period of attrition against organised religion, September 1967 saw Albania declaring itself an atheist state. This position was undermined, along with Communist power, at the end of 1990 (Starova, 1993), since when a national debate has ensued concerning the direction in which the country's development path should face—westward to Europe or eastward to the Islamic world. The extent to which foreign interests have been willing to finance the resurgence of particular faiths has merely acted to emphasise the divisive rather than unifying role of religion for Albanian self-identity.

10.3.5 The ethnic Greek minority

Ethnic Greeks who have lived in southern Albania claim antecedence of settlement dating back to prehistoric times. One Albanian line of argument, however, is that the Greeks were brought to the area as labourers under the Ottomans. Greeks refer to this region as 'Vorio

(northern) Epirus'. 'Epirus' in Greek means 'solid land', a territorial description which has political underpinnings in that it acts to differentiate the region from the Greek islands (Tachtsis, nd, p. 190). The region was detached when the major powers drew up Albania's borders in 1912. The 1914 Protocol of Corfu, however, ceded all of southern Albania to Greece. Although this was annulled by the 1921 Paris Ambassadors' Conference, the Greek government was reluctant to relinquish control of 14 villages in southwest Albania until international force was threatened in 1924. The subsequent Firenze Protocol of 1925 confirmed the present borders (C.H.G., 1946; Sigalos, 1963).

The League of Nations estimated the number of Greek speakers in Albania in the early 1920s to be between 35 000 and 40 000. In 1939, the Albanian authorities recognised a Greek minority of just 20 000, although the Greeks did have their own schools, representation on local councils and Members of Parliament. In contrast to the 1989 census figure of 58 758, a Greek community of 100 000–120 000, based on an extrapolation from the 1992 general election results in which the ethnic Greek party polled 54 000 votes, is a more likely figure.

The rehabilitation of religion since 1990 has seen religious argument in Albania increasingly interwoven with political and territorial considerations. Greek clerics allowed into the country to help rebuild Orthodox churches and other religious buildings were viewed by some Albanians as preaching division and secession (Paraskevopoulos, 1994). At one point, the Albanian president, Sali Berisha, accused the Greek government of fomenting unrest in the area.

Athens in turn criticised the Albanians for what it saw as mistreatment of the Greek minority which has possessed its own-language primary schools, but has also sought its own secondary schools and university education, economic 'decentralisation', and full representation in the police, judiciary, military and civil service (Hall, 1996a). Albanian Ministry of Education

Plate 10.3 *Few religious buildings survived the Communist period intact: this is one of two mosques in the southern town of Berat which were preserved as architectural monuments. Built in the 1550s, the Leaded Mosque has recently been subject to restoration work (Derek Hall)*

instructions in September 1993 allowed for Greek-language schools only in towns and villages designated as being located in minority-settled areas (Doyle, 1994). With the recent mobility of the southern population, not least the substantial emigration of ethnic Greeks, the definition of such areas has become a far from precise science.

Omonia, which was banned from standing as a political party in the country's 1992 general elections, and the Union for Human Rights, the two organisations representing Albania's ethnic Greeks, have been pressing for a degree of autonomy. They took their arguments to the OSCE commissioner for minorities, Max van der Stoel, when he visited Albania in July and August 1993 to investigate the situation of the Greek minority (Hall, 1996a).

Greece finds itself in a relatively strong position in this relationship as Albania requires Greek support to secure economic and political assistance from the EU. Much of the income derived from *émigré* worker remittances, upon which the Albanian domestic economy so heavily depends, comes from Albanians working in Greece. At the same time, however, with approximately US$50 million invested in around 100 joint ventures, Greek business interests require political and economic stability and ease of access across the border in order to be able to take advantage of increasing trading and investment opportunities available in Albania.

Following a visit by the Greek foreign minister, Karolos Papoulias, to Tirana in March 1995, therefore, relations improved. Albania committed itself to improving and respecting Greek minority rights within the country, and promised to introduce new educational legislation which would include the provision for private schools to be set up to teach the Greek language. In its turn, the Athens government appeared prepared to take action against Greek nationalist organisations advocating autonomy for the Greek community in Albania. Issues surrounding the situation of illegal Albanian immigrants in Greece and further rights for the Greek minority in Albania would be addressed by bilateral committees (EIU, 1995).

10.4 The role of the diaspora

10.4.1 *The diaspora*

In southern Albanian lands, large-scale emigration, especially to the Mezzogiorno and Sicily, followed the Turkish conquests of the fifteenth century and continued until the mid-eighteenth century. By 1907 there were recorded 208 410 Italo-Albanians, while a further 60 000 Albanians lived in the United States, notably around Boston and New York. Significant Albanian colonies had also been established in Bulgaria, Romania, Turkey and Egypt, with Albanian societies appearing in such far-flung centres as Buenos Aires and Odessa.

Italo-Albanians (who refer to themselves as Arbëresh), have played an important role in stimulating Albanian national identity: they

have helped develop a nationalist literature from the middle of the nineteenth century. Most adhere to the Uniate Church, preserving the Orthodox liturgy yet recognising the Pope, so as to appeal to both Catholic and Orthodox adherents. Towards the end of the nineteenth century the Arbëresh took on an implicitly political stance. Congresses were held in 1895 and 1897 in Calabria which called for a unified Albanian alphabet, the compilation of an Albanian dictionary, the foundation of an Albanian national society and the establishment of wide-ranging relations with Albania. Albanians themselves were suspicious of Italian political objectives. Within Italy, armed revolution was seen by some as the only way to gain Albanian independence. Thus although Italo-Albanians raised awareness of the Albanian question in Western Europe, a number of factors ultimately limited the movement's contribution to the achievement of Albanian self-determination.

Outside of Europe, nationalist impetus came from the Albanian colony in the United States, largely dominated by migrants from the Korçë region. An Albanian society was established in Buffalo, New York State, in 1905, and an Albanian weekly published in Boston supported the demands of the Albanian national leaders and called for the use of the Albanian language and the opening of Albanian schools in the homeland.

One irony of the Albanian struggle was that the very first Albanian Orthodox church was founded not in Albania, but in Boston, Massachusetts, in March 1908. Since 1880, the establishment of such an autocephalous church had been a prime aim of Albanian nationalists. In an event redolent with nationalist significance, American-educated Fan Noli, later to become Albanian prime minister, was ordained, as the first litany in Albanian was celebrated.

More recently, following political change in the early 1990s, the impact on the mother country of the diaspora has been uneven. Albanian Americans have invested in publishing, catering and transport, with some degree of success. Some of the first contracts for funding inward investment in tourism, property and economic development in the early 1990s were undertaken by Iliria Holdings, a group registered in Switzerland but fronted by Kosovars. The contracts were cancelled subsequently, however, and the Albanian government began investigations into the circumstances of the company. Any role Kosovars might have had as the country's economic saviours was considerably compromised by these events. Certainly, any potential the diaspora may possess in assisting Albania's post-Communist economic, social and political development has yet to be realised.

10.4.2 The domestic impact of recent emigration

Between 1990 and 1993, some 300 000 people—almost 10% of Albania's total population—succeeded in leaving the country, a large number of whom travelled to Greece and Italy to seek work, although many were forced to return. Emigrants in work (both legally and otherwise) outside of the country are now said to contribute remittances to the value of between US$300 million and US$1 billion (ATA, 7 October 1992; EIU, 1993, p. 32; Misha and Vinton, 1995), equivalent to several times the value of Albania's exports and up to a third of GDP. One obvious symbol of this new source of income and its conversion to conspicuous consumption has been the rapid growth of satellite dishes festooning otherwise often poorly provisioned homes. A rapid growth in car ownership has been fuelled by the large-scale import of used cars, secured in not always straightforward circumstances.

Several Albanian border villages and southern towns have been depopulated and much land has been left uncultivated. Many ethnic Greeks have left permanently. Some coastal villages have lost up to 80% of their inhabitants. The population of Qeparo, for example, dropped from 650 in 1991 to 130 in 1994, and schemes have subsequently been put forward to use the village's empty homes as accommodation for ecotourists (Fisher *et al.*, 1994; Farrow, 1995).

Large numbers of Albanians have crossed the border into Greece to obtain long-denied consumer goods, often in exchange for critically short food resources such as sheep or cattle (Dizdari, 1992). For some considerable time Albanians (in Albania) had suffered Europe's lowest living standards and the most prescriptive laws on private property ownership anywhere. They had existed in a vacuum between the consumer societies of Italy and Greece whose 'riches' had been brought into their homes in the 1980s via the television screen. Consumer goods were minimal, and the break-up of collective agrarian structures provided some families with farm animals surplus to their requirements, which have been used for barter to redress past material deprivations. This short-sighted, if understandable, position saw Albanian agriculture limping along at a subsistence level in the early 1990s, while at the same time food aid continued to be required to feed at least the urban population. Agriculture and the food industry have shown subsequent improvements since the land redistribution process has begun to settle down (Hall, 1996b).

10.5 Uncertainty

Albania is surrounded by uncertainty, both geographically and metaphorically. Adjacent Balkan lands within which ethnic Albanians reside—Kosovo, Macedonia, Montenegro and Greece—are either unstable, potentially unstable or hostile to Albania. Berisha is quoted as suggesting that although the Albanians were a divided nation of 7 million, less than half of whom actually lived in Albania, and that he had no wish to change borders by force, 'Albanians must have their space where they live' (Harris, 1994).

Although birth-control measures are now widely available, Albania's natural growth rate is around 2% per annum (compared to a European average of 0.4%) (ATA, 8 January 1994). Albania thus still has Europe's fastest-growing population, and more than half of its citizens are under 30 years of age. There is increasing competition for farmland, especially since privatisation. Many migrants from the country's harsh northeastern districts of Kukës and Dibër have moved south in search of better land and/or access to major urban areas, preferring the middle coastal lowlands and access to Tirana and/or Durrës. They have caused particular problems by occupying land adjacent to main roads; over 3000 illegal homes have been erected on the outskirts of the capital alone (Marrett, 1994). Such spontaneous movement to relatively fertile areas is also hampering the redistribution of agrarian land to its former tillers. The population of Tirana increased by about 5% during 1993, rising from 286 000 to 300 000 (ATA, 21 February 1994), fuelled by hitherto suppressed migratory tendencies.

This situation has been exacerbated by ethnic Albanian emigration from Kosovo following pressure from the Serbian authorities. By mid-1994 some 300 000 Albanians were estimated to have already fled Kosovo (Smith, 1994). Berisha reportedly would like to encourage Albanians from the north of the country to settle in the districts from which ethnic Greeks have emigrated, thus both satisfying land hunger and potentially diluting what is left of the minority population. With conflict on the doorstep, and the potential for a flood of refugees from Kosovo (Anon, 1994), the Albanian leadership cannot afford to heighten tensions in the region. A Belgrade announcement that 20 000 Krajina Serbs were to be resettled in Kosovo (*Novosti*, 13 August 1995) did provoke strong condemnation from Tirana (Barber, 1995). Generally, however, the Albanian government is aware of the danger of being drawn into conflict over Kosovo, and argues that the plight of the ethnic Albanians there should be addressed internationally as part of an overall peace plan for the former Yugoslavia. The future roles of the Albanian minorities in FYROM and Montenegro are a matter of some speculation.

Domestically, some economic progress is being made, albeit from a low base. Although chrome ore production fell by a sixth and copper ore production by a quarter (*BEE*, 8 May 1995), Albania showed the best relative economic recovery in Eastern Europe for the second

successive year with a 7% increase in GDP in 1994 (EBRD, 1995). The sustaining of such development indicators does, however, require social and political stability and confidence, both within and outside of the country.

10.6 References

Ackerman, E. A., 1938, Albania—a Balkan Switzerland, *The Journal of Geography*, **37**(7), 253–62.
Anamali, S., 1969, On the ancient culture of the Albanians, in Anon, *The Illyrians and the genesis of the Albanians*, Mihail Duri, Tirana.
Anamali, S., 1972, From the Illyrians to the Arbers, in Anon, *Convention of Illyrian studies*, Mihail Duri, Tirana.
Anon, 1994, Keeping out, *The Economist*, 21 May, pp. 42, 47.
ATA (Albanian Telegraph Agency) Tirana.
Barber, T., 1995, Albania condemns Serb plan for refugee 'colony', *The Independent*, 16 August.
Barnes, J. S., 1918, The future of the Albanian state, *Geographical Journal*, **52**, 12–27.
BEE (Business Eastern Europe), Economist Intelligence Unit, London, fortnightly.
Bërxholi, A., 1990, On the surface—flowers and leaves, underground—silver and gold, *New Albania*, **5**, 6–7.
Bërxholi, A., Qiriazi, P., 1986, *Albania: a geographic outline*, 8 Nëntori, Tirana.
Bërxholi, A., Qiriazi, P., 1990. *Republika Popullore Socialiste e Shqiperise: harte fizike*, Shtëpia Botuese e Librit Shkollor, Tirana.
Bërxholi, A. *et al.*, 1988, *Gjeografia e Shqipërisë*, Shtëpia Botuese e Librit Shkollor, Tirana.
Birge, J. K., 1937, *The Bektashi Order of Dervishes*, Luzac, London.
Buda, A., 1980, About some questions of the history of the formation of the Albanian people and of their language and culture, *Historical Studies*, **1**, 165–80.
C.H.G., 1946, Greek claims in southern Albania, *The World Today*, **2**, 488–94.
Dede, S. *et al.*, 1986, *Enver Hoxha 1908–1985*, Institute of Marxist-Leninist Studies at the Central Committee of the Party of Labour of Albania, Tirana.
DeS (Drejtoria e Statistikës), 1991, *Vjetari statistikor i Shqipërisë*, DeS, Tirana.
Dizdari, P., 1992, Pendimi është gjeja me vlerë në botë, *Tribuna Ekonomike Shqiptare*, **1**(5), 34.
Doyle, L., 1994, Tirana cracks whip over ethnic Greeks, *The Independent*, 15 June.
Durham, M. E., 1905, *The burden of the Balkans*, Nelson, London.
Durham, M. E., 1909, *High Albania*, Edward Arnold, London.

Durham, T., 1989, *Serbia: the rise and fall of a medieval empire*, William Sessions, York.

EBNA (Editorial Board of *New Albania*), 1984, *Albania*, 8 Nëntori, Tirana.

EBRD (European Bank for Reconstruction and Development), 1995, *Transition report update*, EBRD, London.

EIU (Economist Intelligence Unit), 1993, *Romania, Bulgaria, Albania: country report 4th quarter*, EIU, London.

EIU (Economist Intelligence Unit), 1995, *Romania, Bulgaria, Albania: country report 2nd quarter*, EIU, London.

Farrow, C., 1995, Qeparo—bringing people together, *In Focus*, **16**, 9–10.

Fisher, D., Mati, I., Whyles, G, 1994, *Ecotourism development in Albania*, Ecotourism Ltd/Aulona Sub Tour/Worldwide Fund for Nature UK, St Albans.

Frashëri, M., 1988, Hydric resources in the context of Albania's environmental protection problems, in Balkan Scientific Conference, *Environmental protection in the Balkans, abstracts*, Varna.

Giles, F. L., 1930, Boundary work in the Balkans, *Geographical Journal*, **75**, 300–12.

Hall, D. R., 1992, Albania's changing tourism environment, *Journal of Cultural Geography*, **12**(2), 33–41.

Hall, D. R., 1994, *Albania and the Albanians*, Frances Pinter, London.

Hall, D. R., 1996a, Recent developments in Greek–Albanian relations, *Mediterranean Politics*, **2**, 82–104.

Hall, D. R., 1996b, Rural change and migration in Albania, *GeoJournal*, **38**(2), 185–9.

Harris, P., 1994, Albania tries to hold its head up amid a sea of troubles, *Scotland on Sunday*, 14 August.

Hasluck, M., 1954, *The unwritten law in Albania*, Cambridge University Press, Cambridge.

Helmreich, E. C., 1938, *The diplomacy of the Balkan Wars 1912–1913*, MIT Press, Cambridge, Mass.

Irwin, Z. T., 1984, The fate of Islam in the Balkans, in Ramet, P., ed., *Religion and nationalism in Soviet and East European politics*, Duke University Press, Durham.

Jelavich, B., 1983, *History of the Balkans:* vol. I: *Eighteenth and nineteenth centuries*, Cambridge University Press, Cambridge.

Lendvai, P., 1969, *Eagles in cobwebs: nationalism and communism in the Balkans*, Macdonald, London.

Lopasic, A., 1992, Cultural values of the Albanians in the diaspora, in Winnifrith, T., ed., *Perspectives on Albania*, Macmillan, London, pp. 89–105.

Marmullaku, R., 1975, *Albania and the Albanians*, C. Hurst, London.

Marrett, M., 1994, Can Albania put its house in order? *The European*, 12 August.

Mason, K. *et al.*, 1945, *Albania*, Naval Intelligence Division, London.

Mining Journal, 1992, Albania, *Mining Journal*, supplement, 8 May.

Misha, G., Vinton, L., 1995, Big problems, small progress, *Business Eastern Europe*, **24**(18), 7.

Noli, F. S., 1947, *George Castrioti Scanderbeg*, International Universities Press, New York.

Norris, H. T., 1993, *Islam in the Balkans*, Hurst & Co., London.

Novosti, Belgrade, daily.

Paraskevopoulos, P., 1994, Keeping the lid on new Balkan row, *The Guardian*, 25 August.

Peacock, P., 1993, Roman Catholicism in North Albania, *Albanian Life*, **1**, 31–2.

Peacock, W., 1914, *Albania; the foundling state of Europe*, Chapman and Hall, London.

Prifti, P. R., 1978, *Socialist Albania since 1944*, MIT Press, Cambridge, Mass.

Reméramd, G., 1928, *Ali de Tebelen, Pacha de Janina 1744–1822*, Paul Geuthner, Paris.

RIIA (Royal Institute of International Affairs), 1939, *South East Europe: a political and economic survey*, RIIA, London.

Shaw, S. J., Shaw, E. K., 1977, *History of the Ottoman empire and modern Turkey*, Vol. II, Cambridge University Press, Cambridge and New York.

Sigalos, L., 1963, *The Greek claims on northern Epirus*, Argonaut, Chicago.

Skendi, S., 1953, Beginnings of Albanian nationalist and autonomous trends; the Albanian League, 1878–1881, *The American Slavic and East European Review*, **12**(2), 219–32.

Skendi, S., 1956, *Albania*, Stevens and Sons, London.

Skendi, S., 1967, *The Albanian national awakening*, Princeton University Press, Princeton.

Skendi, S., 1968, Skenderbeg and the Albanian national consciousness, *Südost-Forschungen*, **27**, 83–8.

Skendi, S., 1980, The complex environment of Skenderbeg's activity, in Skendi, S., ed., *Balkan cultural studies*, Columbia University Press, New York, pp. 167–86.

Smith, H., 1994, Serb grip tightens on 'holy' Kosovo, *The Guardian*, 26 July.

Starova, G., 1993, The religion of the Albanians in the Balkan and European context, *Balkan Forum*, **1**(4), 197–205.

Stickney, E. P., 1926, *Southern Albania or northern Epirus in European international affairs, 1912–23*, Stanford University Press, Stanford, Calif.

Tachtsis, K., nd, Epirus, in King, F., ed., *Introducing Greece*, Methuen, London, pp. 190–208.

Winnifrith, T., 1987, *The Vlachs*, Macmillan, London.

Wolff, R. L., 1956, *The Balkans in our time*, Harvard University Press, Harvard.

11

Albania as a gateway

Dean S. Rugg

11.1 Introduction

In 1937, Stadtmüller (1937–38. p. 366), a German geographer, stated that Albania's geopolitical role for 2000 years had been as a *Durchgangsland* (gateway) between the Adriatic Sea and the Balkan peninsula. In 1990, Cohen (1990, pp. 9–11), an American geographer, mentioned the relevance of the gateway concept in the changing geopolitical world. The purpose of this chapter is to analyse the connection between these two statements using Albania as a case study. Although common perceptions might discount the feasibility of the country being a gateway, Albania offers interesting opportunities for answering questions about the gateway concept. What are some of the characteristics of the concept? What sort of model can be developed to explain it? What is the contemporary role of such small states? Does the gateway concept as applied to Albania offer possibilities for understanding the restructuring of the Balkans—the focus of this book?

A strong theme in the history of Eastern Europe has been the dominance by external powers of these small states (Rugg, 1985). This theme was summarised by political geographer Harriet Wanklyn over half a century ago (1941, p. 27): can small states exist on their own without

being cat's-paws in world politics? Today, this question can be asked concerning the many new states that have emerged in the 'new world order', in contrast to the 1920s' 'New World' of Isaiah Bowman (1928). However, the question is most pertinent to the area in which Wanklyn first used it—Eastern Europe—where post-revolution developments illustrate that this shatter belt is still fulfilling its role as a laboratory for political geography.

Studies of gateway states are few, and Cohen does not delve into the background of the concept. One of the few uses of this concept for a state is by Burghardt (1962, pp. 279–84), who stated that Burgenland, a region on the eastern border of Austria that made the transition from a feudal to Western way of life, could serve as a bridge to Eastern Europe in the event of a Communist collapse. Gateway cities are mentioned more frequently than gateway states. In the late 1980s, Eaton (1989) applied the gateway city concept to the Midwest cities of the United States such as St Louis, where breaks in transport were crucial in developing concentrations of population. Kresl (1991) emphasises the role of connections in gateway cities. He differentiates between such cities serving as 'bridges' between two economies and those serving as 'points of access': Toronto and Hamburg are 'bridge cities',

Reconstructing the Balkans: A Geography of the New Southeast Europe. Edited by Derek Hall and Darrick Danta.
©1996 John Wiley & Sons Ltd

particularly now that the latter can take advantage of the collapse of the Iron Curtain to enlarge its hinterland; Copenhagen and Amsterdam are 'points of access' in which decision-making functions are paramount. Thus it appears that the role of gateway is enlarging from that of 'pass-through' to a place to 'come-together'.

A tentative model of the gateway concept for states focuses on the environment in which movement both within the political unit and to external areas is facilitated or hindered by physical and human geographical factors (Figure 11.1). Such movement thus can be restricted or free; normally the latter is rare. External movement includes relationships of the state with outside powers. Internal movement is related to the viability of the state, especially its degree of cohesion; the role of small states is a function of this territorial viability (Adhoc Committee on Political Geography, 1969, p. 64). Unfortunately, as we shall see, Albania's environment as a gateway has been dominated (a) by overdependence on outside powers who could shut off movement into and through the country, and (b) by a lack of cohesion that would prevent it from initiating movement. Thus, as Stadtmüller (1937–38, pp. 345–6) writes, the country has played largely a passive geopolitical role in the affairs of Balkan states.

11.2 Past aspects of Albania as a gateway state

Using the model shown in Figure 11.1, Albania's past role as a gateway state will be examined. Figure 11.2 illustrates some of the key internal aspects of the physical geography that have hindered all movement into and through the country. The dominant topographical features include the largest plain on the east coast of the Adriatic Sea backed by mountains exhibiting the highest relative relief in Europe, i.e. 70% of its area lies above the 300 m contour line. These mountains, a continuation of the Dinaric range of former Yugoslavia, represent a considerable barrier to communications, not only within the country in all directions but also to movement between the Adriatic coast and the interior of the Balkans. In the north, where the Albanian Alps remain the most inaccessible region of Europe, movement is especially restricted because of topography and poor roads. The terrain structure here resembles a huge dome with rivers radiating from a core and glaciated peaks rising to 2600 m. This is the land of the Gegs, who have followed a clan social structure. Further south in Albania, the major rivers break up the mountain structure into parallel blocks aligned in a northwest–southeast direction, improving accessibility and helping to explain why the Tosk groups of this area have tended to be more exposed to Westernising influences.

GATEWAY ENVIRONMENT

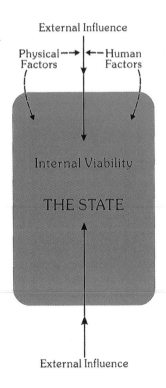

Figure 11.1 *The gateway environment*

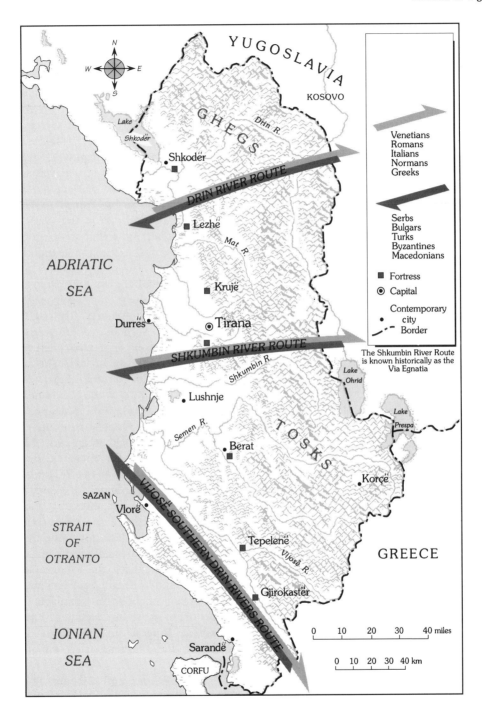

Figure 11.2 *Albania: historical gateway*

Owing to a process of deterioration from physical–human factors over a period of 2500 years, the Albanian Plain was also a barrier to movement until the Communist period. Braudel (1972, p. 67) explains that 'Mediterranean man has always had to fight against the swamps . . . this colonization is the distinguishing feature of its rural history'. In Albania, the deterioration was noted in 1920 when an Austrian geographer described the Myzeqe area, the largest portion of the plain, as 'a desolate wasteland covered with spreading water areas and impassable swamp forests . . . inundated in winter and dried up in summer' (Veith, 1920, p. 77). A cycle of land misuse included overcutting of mountain forests starting with Greeks and Romans, overgrazing on the increasingly barren slopes, followed by loss of soil in winter rains; the sediment in the streams caused flooding as gradients were reduced on reaching the plain. The result was floods, swamp and marsh conditions, and malaria.

Supplementing this process of deterioration in the plain from physical–human factors were the effects of land tenure during the latter part of Ottoman rule (Stavrianos, 1958, p. 138). In the eighteenth century, serfdom was introduced as fiefs were converted to private, heritable estates (*çiftliks*) raising export crops of corn, wheat and cotton. Rather than accept the new status of serfs, many peasants fled to the mountains and left areas of potentially productive land—those not marshy or flooded—abandoned and untilled. The result was a paradox of an underpopulated plain of swamp, fallow and pasture next to overpopulated mountains. Busch-Zantner (1938, p. 58) has provided considerable detail on this process. This pattern of land tenure changed little between the First and Second World Wars so that in early 1938 only 19% of the land in the plain was cultivated. It was left to the Communists to improve the plain through reclamation by drainage and irrigation—a major legacy of the Hoxha regime (Rugg, 1994, pp. 60–2). Cultivated land increased by 80%, and 60% of the arable land now is irrigated against only 10% in 1938. The malaria is gone.

Despite these barrier effects of mountains and plains in Albania through history, the country possesses three of the four major routes into the interior of the Balkans from the Adriatic Sea: via the Drin River to the Kosovo region of former Yugoslavia; the Shkumbin River to Macedonia and Thessaloníki (the major Greek port for the south Balkans); and the Vjosë–Drin (southern) rivers to Ióannina and Epirus (Figure 11.2). The fourth route is the Neretva River, which crosses Croatia into Bosnia leading to Sarajevo. In addition, the Serbs forced a Belgrade–Bar (Montenegro) railroad in the 1960–90 period to avoid Bosnian and Croatian territory.

The key to Albania's geopolitics was the Adriatic question—who would control access into and out of the Balkan peninsula from the direction of the sea? Once again, physical–human factors affected the role of gateway. Cvijić (1918), the famous Serbian geographer, emphasised three civilisations that controlled the historical geography of the peninsula. The first, Western civilisations like Greece and Venice, gained footholds for trade while Rome penetrated into the peninsula, building a system of roads along the four major routes mentioned previously. Thus, Albania served as an early gateway to the Balkans. Second, for most of 1500 years the oriental civilisations of the Balkans—Byzantium and Turkey—dominated the area and denied easy penetration for Adriatic powers via the Albanian routes. The third civilisation—the patriarchal—included not only the Slavs and Bulgars, but also the Illyrians, ancestors of the Albanians who used the topography to remain isolated and difficult to conquer and who maintained a separate language. Their tribal way of life, which included blood revenge, persisted longest in the north against both Adriatic and Balkan powers (Winnifrith, 1992, pp. 39, 47).

The Bulgarian and Serbian empires of the Middle Ages comprised much of the Balkan peninsula, even sealing off the interior from penetration by Adriatic powers. Stadtmüller (1937–38, p. 366) emphasises that Albania's location with routes inland made it a transit land or gateway for struggles between Adriatic and Balkan powers. Thus, the long geographical separation of coastal powers emerged (Greek, Roman, Norman, Venetian and Italian) from hinterland powers (Byzantine, Bulgarian, Serb, Turk and, only recently, Albanian) (Bowman, 1928, pp. 357–8). Relics of a line of fortresses built and rebuilt by representatives of both groups still exist along the margins of plain and mountains. These elements of physical and human geography are shown on Figure 11.2.

The most persistent relic of the geopolitical patterns of Albania as a gateway is the Via Egnatia, a Roman road following one of the major routes inland for over 3000 years along the Shkumbin River (O'Sullivan, 1972, p. 9). Yet, through all this period, the Albanian territory did not serve as a true gateway because movement was not free but predominantly one-way, either in or out. The goals of the Adriatic powers were not only control of this sea, but also access to Constantinople and to the resources of trade of the peninsula. The goals of the Balkan powers were to deny this access and to discourage footholds on the coast. This was true even in the 1930s, when Italy practically controlled Albania as a colony.

The 2000-year cycle of external dominance by either Adriatic or Balkan powers in Albania was broken with the rise of Communism after the Second World War. Then the geopolitics of its gateway role changed, but the question of Adriatic control remained crucial. Physical and human elements of geography continued to influence movement.

As a student in France during the interwar years, Enver Hoxha, the Communist leader who was to dominate Albania for over 35 years, became aware of the extent of the country's lag in economic development. He blamed the lag on the long period of Turkish and Italian exploitation and became obsessed with avoiding dependence on outside powers. This attitude helps to explain Albanian foreign policy up to 1990. Hoxha embraced a Stalinist programme of forced industrialisation that was designed to overcome the lack of development. However, his need for outside aid required help from other Communist powers. The brief attempt by Yugoslavia to make Albania a part of its federal structure reflected the old external pressure by a Balkan power, but failed because of Hoxha's use of the Soviet–Tito break to gain support from Moscow.

However, Albania's continued belief in the Stalinist model of Marxist development and unhappiness with its subordinate role in the Council for Mutual Economic Aid (CMEA or Comecon) caused it to turn to Chinese aid in 1961. Although economic aid was reduced, China remained the primary support for Albania until the 1970s, when China's new policy towards the West caused Albania to isolate itself and embark on a policy of self-reliance based on rather impressive resources of hydroelectric power, coal and oil, and metallic minerals of copper, chrome and iron-nickel. Throughout the entire period of Communism, Albania played no role as a true gateway, but reflected the continued importance of the Adriatic question by giving the Soviet Union and China footholds on the Mediterranean Sea; the Soviet Union even maintained a submarine base on Sazan Island near the port of Vlorë (Heiman, 1964).

The internal component of the gateway model (Figure 11.1) also illustrates the importance of physical and human factors in delaying Albania's establishment as a state with authority to control movement therein. The primary human factor was the lack of cohesion among the population of the country. The Albanians never had a medieval state or empire as a historical basis for nationalism as did the Bulgars, Serbs and even Macedonians. Instead, they utilised the rugged topography, especially in the north, to retain a fragmented clan society and looked to Skënderbeg, a hero who fought the Turks to a standstill in the fifteenth century, as the symbol of eventual independence. The poorly drained and malarial plain discouraged any seafaring role, and until 1990 they remained fairly passive—a part of other people's history (Winnifrith, 1992, p. 70).

During Ottoman times, nearly three-quarters of the Albanians converted to the Muslim religion in part because of the privileges connected with owning land. In the late nineteenth century, as ideas of nationalism appeared, Albanians depended on Turkey for protection against outside powers, who were waiting to seize portions of a newly independent but weak state. As Turkey, the 'sick man of Europe', collapsed, the Albanian Muslims feared being isolated by Christian states. Italy, Serbia and Greece all tried to gain parts of the area, but the Great Powers supported an independent Albania to deny these bordering powers access to this part of the Adriatic coast. America's Woodrow Wilson, moreover, was motivated to give Albanian opportunities for self-determination.

The cohesion of the new state continued to be hindered by the topography and by the fragmentation of tribes, religion and Geg–Tosk cleavage. Although excellent resources of metallic minerals and energy existed, the deterioration of the plain and the mountain barriers made development of a road system difficult. For example, Lane (1923, p. 52) emphasises how the population continued in the early 1920s to think as tribes while Tirana as a capital remained a vague concept. Zog, the primary interwar leader, had little success in solving the fragmentation. However, the Communists, especially after 1964 under Hoxha's ideological and cultural revolution, managed to reduce some of this fragmentation and facilitate interaction within the country by improving the roads and building the first railways; increasing literacy, especially for women; reducing the Geg–Tosk division by incorporating leaders of both groups in the party; and by abolishing all religious practices (Pano, 1992, pp. 38–9). Thus, the viability of the Albanian state improved despite the repressive atmosphere and barriers to movement into and out of the state. Albania did not serve as a gateway in either the interwar or Communist period.

In summary, Albania's role as a gateway state during more than 2000 years of history facilitated movement by external powers, either controlling or denying access between the Adriatic Sea and interior of the Balkan peninsula. Internally, the lack of cohesion as a nation delayed the growth of nationalism and led to Albania's passive role in gateway activity. With the 1990–91 'revolution', the possibilities of gateway activity began to improve.

11.3 Future aspects of Albania as a gateway state

Located along the borders of the world's geopolitical powers, some gateways are found in shatter-belt regions where zones of conflict have existed. The best-known shatter belt is Eastern Europe, where two world wars originated from the conflicting goals of imperialism and nationalism for great and small powers. Since the Second World War this zone had been quiet because of control by the Soviet Union. Now, however, since the revolutions of this area in the late 1980s and early 1990s, conflict has erupted again, especially from nationalistic goals. Samuel Huntington (1993, pp. 29–31) points out that the shatter belt of Eastern Europe, which he refers to as a 'fault line', still exhibits the contrast between 'progressive' Roman Catholic or Protestant West versus more backward Orthodox or Muslim East. Here, on the boundary between civilisations, flashpoints of conflict can occur. Cohen (1990) refers to three additional shatter belts—the Middle East, Southeast Asia and Sub-Saharan Africa—where conflict continues.

One of the keys to the role of Albania as a gateway is its status as a small state. Rothstein (1968, p. 29) states that

a small power is a state which recognizes that it cannot obtain security primarily by use of its own capabilities, and that it must rely fundamentally on the aid of other states, institutions, processes, or developments to do so.

Thus, small states occupy a subordinate position in the international system. We shall see that these characteristics of a small state will affect Albania's attempts to shift from an isolated situation based on self-reliance to a member of the international community.

Cohen (1990) sees opportunities for some small states or regions on the edges of geopolitical powers to serve as gateways. States like the Baltic nations, Hong Kong and Slovenia, or regions like Newfoundland, Alaska, British Columbia and Eastern Siberia, are optimally located for specialised manufacturing, trade, tourism and financial service functions, thus stimulating global economic, social and political interaction. Cohen also emphasises the role of such states in contributing to peace through increased flexibility of linkages within a large world system. Finally, he feels that such states or regions, by achieving independence, can accelerate the trend along these borders to change them from zones of conflict to zones of accommodation. One might add that the gateway state itself could become a true focus of two-way movement or interaction. We can apply this future gateway concept to Albania.

In applying the model of gateway states to the real world, Portugal is a possible parallel to Albania. MacDonald, in his 1993 (pp. 28, 74–5) study, feels that this state is an example of how a small entity has learned to deal with larger, more powerful states through the process of economic integration within a large organisation. DeMachete (1991, p. 9), a leading writer on Portuguese economics, called this state a gateway to Europe for US companies. Finally, Gumbel (1992) states that Portugal's recovery after revolution in the 1970s is a process Eastern European countries can emulate. He points out how the non-violent revolution allowed the country to shake off its authoritarian past and develop a stable democracy capable of modernisation within the EC.

Many of its pre-revolution characteristics resembled those of Albania, but EC membership enhanced Portugal's creditability among foreign investors, who were attracted by the country's tariff-free access to the rest of Europe, sunny beaches and wage levels about one-quarter those of Germany. Joint ventures are noticeable, such as the US$2.8 billion plant being built by Ford and Volkswagen with 30% subsidisation by Portugal from funds granted by the EC. The international sector has become crucial to Portugal with a stress on growth through exports

and improvement in the balance of payments. The EC connection has boosted morale because it has demonstrated the ability of the country to compete in the international system.

What about Albania's role as a future gateway state for the Balkans in terms of the external environment? Currently, such prospects are rather dim because of the geopolitical barriers to movement within the Balkan peninsula. The most serious problem is the antagonism towards Albania held by Balkan neighbours. Components of the former Yugoslavia have little basis for interaction with Albania. Montenegro has long coveted Shkodër as its natural geographic outlet, and at present the rail link to this city from Podgorica (formerly Titograd), completed in the 1980s, is closed. However, Albania has tried to drive a wedge between Montenegro and Serbia by engaging in talks regarding better relations. Second, Serbia's national policies threaten Kosovo, where some 2 million Albanians not only seem to be a threat to the Serbs but also occupy the historic land where national relics from the medieval period are located and where their most tragic defeat by the Turks took place in 1389. Thus far the Serbian government's attitude towards the Kosovars has been characterised by repression. Third, Macedonia is worried about the presence of Albanian minorities in the Tetovo area (also adjacent to Albania). Finally, Greek–Albanian antagonism is based on different perceptions regarding the Greek minority of some 60 000 (Figure 11.3). The Greeks feel there is discrimination, while the Albanians worry over Hellenisation of this southern region. As a result of this antagonism towards them, the Albanians have fears about security; for example, they were the first former Warsaw Pact power to request membership of NATO (Hall, 1996).

In the meantime, Hall (1994b) points out that, surprisingly, the need to circumvent the Balkan conflict may have improved Albania's opportunities to serves as a gateway to four Balkan states (Figure 11.4). Formerly, normal access into the Balkan peninsula came from the north via the rivers of the Danube and Morava, a route through Serbia which avoided the western barrier

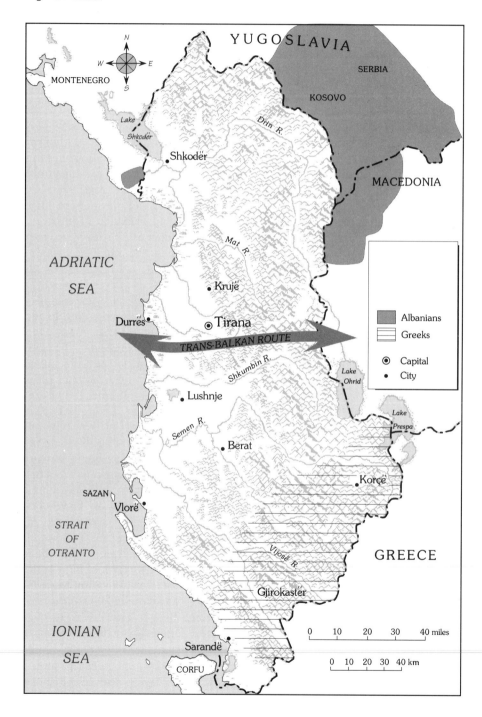

Figure 11.3 *Albania: present gateway*

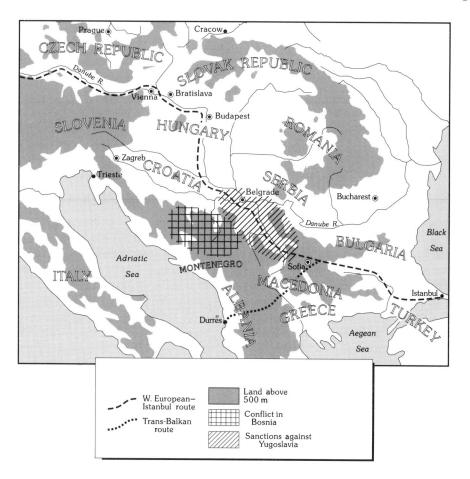

Figure 11.4 *Main Balkan routes*

of the Dinaric Alps. Now, however, conflict in Croatia and Bosnia together with sanctions against 'rump' Yugoslavia have closed this route. Thus, a need for new east–west links across the Balkans has stimulated considerable progress towards using the Albanian port of Durrës as a western focal point. Transport ministers of five countries—Albania, Macedonia, Bulgaria, Greece and Turkey—met on several occasions in 1993 and 1994 and discussed the need for improved long-distance interaction by road and rail from Durrës to Istanbul. Despite

the problem of the Albanian minority group in Macedonia, both countries see the advantage of using Durrës an an outlet to the west. At present, Macedonia is having to trade with the West via Bulgaria since Greece has closed its port of Thessaloníki over the 'Macedonia question'. Bulgaria and Turkey also desire greater interaction through the Balkans with the latter country feeling a tie to the large Muslim group in Albania. Greece, although having traditional feelings against both Macedonia and Bulgaria while giving support to Serbia, apparently did not want to be left out of the talks regarding improved transport links. One of these may be to Epirus.

At present, only a limited amount of aid has been acquired for initiating this trans-Balkan network. Some funds are available for improving the inadequate port facilities of Durrës and the narrow road to Macedonia, which will follow the old Via Egnatia along the Shkumbin River; the aim is to cut the transport time between Durrës and Istanbul from 30 hours to 10. Discussions have also been held regarding the completion of improved rail links along the same route. The Albanian rail system, about 800 km in total and constructed largely by inexperienced volunteer labour, now only averages speeds of 45 km per hour. The hydroelectric potential for electrifying the rails along the main east–west route to Pogradec has not been developed. An estimated US$200 million is necessary for rail renovation in Albania. The EC has granted funds for a telecommunications system, and a fibre-optic cable network along the Dinaric coast is being financed by eastern Adriatic countries plus Germany. With possible free port status, Durrës thus has the potential to be one of the busiest ports on the Adriatic Sea. But Hall (1994b, p.12) asks what happens if Serbia is re-admitted to the world community and the north–south routes into the Balkans again become dominant? Perhaps Albania's new role as a neutral east–west bridge, once begun and developed, would be hard to stop, considering the cultural links to Turkey and the Middle East symbolised by the importance of Islam in Albania's religious structure.

The aforementioned factors relate to the changing external environment in Albania and possibilities for a new gateway role in the Balkans. However, the internal environment of the country also has altered radically in the past three years and will influence gateway status (Biberaj, 1993; *Financial Times*, 1994; Hall, 1994a). Although cohesion within the country is still hindered by rugged terrain and a poor infrastructure of communications, progress is indicated by reforms aimed at establishing a genuine plural democracy and a free market economy. A law on constitutional provisions provides for separation of powers, guarantee of human rights and protection of private property. A legal framework for a market economy includes legislation concerning taxes, accounting, bankruptcy and a banking system. Overall, these changes illustrate a transformation from a closed artificial economy of inefficient plants and collective farms to an open economy of small farmers, traders and business people. Luthans and Lee (1994) call this transformation a paradigm shift—going back to zero and starting again in terms of economic reform. Such a shift, they say, was greater in Albania than in any of the former Communist states with the possible exception of Poland. What are some of the important aspects of this transformation that have affected the internal environment and gateway possibilities?

The first stage of the transformation involved emergency measures and shock therapy. Owing to the insecurity prevalent during the revolution, some 300 000 Albanians left the country of which only some that fled to Italy returned. The Italians initiated an emergency relief programme of 18 months designed to supply food, medical services and other necessities. Primary changes, however, took place after the victory of the Albanian Democratic Party in March 1992. Security and stability improved with the purging of Communist hardliners from the army and secret police. The biggest step, however, was the purge of the old economy by closing many large industrial complexes that were not only inefficient but also heavy polluters—the Elbasan iron and steel plant, the Tirana tractor factory and most of the metallic mineral mines. Salaries for the large number of unemployed people continued at 80%. The privatisation of collective and state farms caused turmoil in the countryside with looting and destruction of farm buildings, greenhouses and irrigation systems, and the cutting down of trees for fuel. Poverty was widespread in the country. However, the closing of industries, which led to a 60% decline in industrial production in the three years 1990–92, provided needed incentives for people to find work in agriculture and self-employment.

The new Albanian government, composed of relatively young people, is determined to integrate the country into the European mainstream, an attitude which not only resembles the early one in Portugal, but also has significant ramifications for gateway functions. The quick implementation of radical economic reforms in this poorest country of Europe involved reducing spending, making the currency (lek) fully convertible, and eliminating barriers to foreign trade. It also included attacking the most serious economic problem—the ending of subsidies and the liberalisation of prices with the exception of staple consumer goods, such as bread and milk. Sources of funds are remittances and foreign aid and investment. Remittances from Albanians overseas totalled US$150 million in 1992 and US$334 million in 1993. These funds not only covered the deficit that foreign aid had not supplied, but also raised income and the demand for goods, stimulated small-scale trade and investment, and allowed for the import of consumer goods and second-hand vehicles. The GDP increased an estimated 10% in 1993—the highest rate in Eastern Europe. Inflation dropped from 400 to 30%, and the government was able to reduce the 80% unemployment payments to 30%, which encouraged the jobless to find employment. Foreign aid amounted to over US$300 million in both 1992 and 1993. Finally, investments of US$200 million have been made, mostly from Italian and Greek entrepreneurs; these range from small kiosks to oil exploration along the Adriatic coast.

Early results from aid and private investment include joint ventures such as the Coca Cola plant (Albanian–Italian) and a hotel–business complex (Albanian–Slovene–Austrian), both in Tirana. The investments are guaranteed and profits can be repatriated freely. The average low wages of US$60–70 per month have led to shifts of Italian shoe and textile firms from East Asia, where wages are double and distances are much greater. Use of aid and investment funds for health, education and construction is also evident. Some 19 000 enterprises (mostly small shops and services) have been bought by operators from the Communist period and housing blocks are being turned over to their occupants at a minimal price. Gradually, aid and investment by 1994 led to capital accumulation for infrastructural and industrial projects, banking modernisation and institutional building. Recently, investment has looked at the need to develop the capital-technologically intensive mining industry and the establishment of tourism facilities. Finally, there are moves from joint government–private ventures to sole private investment schemes with fewer restrictions.

This economic reform has greatly affected agriculture. Privatisation of collective and state farms has been drastic, completely changing the rural landscape as some 500 000 peasants acquired small plots averaging 1.4 ha each. However, the incentives of ownership and eventual raising of bread prices led to a 1993 increase in food production of 15% and a projected rate of 8% for 1994. The rural population (65%) is making progress in feeding itself and producing surpluses for urban areas. Rural income has increased and food imports decreased except for sugar and cooking oil. A food-processing industry is emerging, and plans exist for the export of early fruits and vegetables. Meat and dairy products have increased from the day when the Communist restrictions on private plots reduced the number of livestock. Aid for agriculture in the amount of US$42 million has been provided by the World Bank, Japan and the Netherlands.

Much of this economic progress is now part of the landscape. Evident in the cities and towns are well-stocked markets and private food stalls, bustling streets with an avalanche of used cars, vans and trucks driven by 'inexperienced' operators, and new shops, kiosks and restaurants. In rural areas, the small plots are filled with peasants working by hand with scythes and creating mounds of drying wheat, roads are clogged with carts and cars, and some large fields from the past are still farmed using DDR Fortschritt tractors. Meat is sold along the roads. In both rural and urban areas, service stations are springing up.

However, barriers to progress still exist. Besides the threat of ethnic conflict over Albanians outside the borders, a democratic tradition is lacking, and there is little basis for a middle class or training in Western administration or legal codes. For example, Western companies have complained about the problems of decision-making connected with the attempts to rehabilitate the oil industry. Lack of capital has made attempts to privatise the old Communist industrial concerns very difficult. Barriers are also visible in the infrastructure, which is either lacking or crumbling; 70% of the country is largely inaccessible because of winding, narrow and pot-hole roads; only 1800 km are hard-topped (*Statistical Yearbook*, 1991, p. 269). Facilities at Durrës and other ports are antiquated, and only one small international airport exists at Rinas outside Tirana.

Although rural electrification programmes were carried through by the Communists, water and sewage facilities are minimal, especially in the large cities. Facilities like hotels, restaurants and service stations are far behind needs. Environmental effects of a half-century of Communism are seen in air and water pollution, several hundred thousand pillboxes constructed to repel an 'invasion', ageing factories, often vacant, and abandoned oil rigs with leaking storage tanks. Much of the housing built as blocks of flats during the Communist period needs to be replaced. Foreign investors have found that Albanians again prefer housing appropriate for extended families or village friends such as large villas or groups of villas.

Despite its backwardness, Albania has considerable potential in terms of resources and tourism. Its resources of metallic minerals (chrome, copper and nickel-iron) and energy (hydroelectric power, coal, oil and gas) are impressive for such a small country and, even though misused under Communism, are evaluated as worthy of rehabilitation and further development. Several foreign companies are exploring for oil along the Adriatic coast.

Perhaps most important is the potential for hydropower, which is responsible for 90% of Albania's electrical energy. The largest of the projects—three dams along the Drin River—has not only generated some 1.5 million kW of electricity but has also created reservoirs which permit crossing most of the country by boat in the shadow of the jagged peaks of the Albanian Alps. These views and other mountain scenery, plus the underdeveloped beaches and many historical monuments, make tourism a natural focus of future development. Creation of hotels along the coast is an early priority, but Western tourists would have to arrive by ship or plane; however, given peace in the former Yugoslavia, tourist movement by road from Western and Central Europe, much like the flood of tourists to the Yugoslav coast in the 1950s and 1960s, might occur. The potential in tourism for jobs and hard currency is excellent; in addition, foreign developers are exempt from a profits tax for the first five years. A prime area is the Albanian Riviera, where mountain scenery and historic places like Butrint (Roman) face the 3.2 km channel to the Greek island of Corfu; a daily ferry service now exists.

11.4 Conclusion

A model of the gateway process for a state as applied to Albania shows that this country historically has faced dominance by external powers, which led to either one-way movement into the Balkans or denial of this movement. Now, however, the pattern may be changing as Albania is benefiting from drastic implementation of economic reform measures after its revolution and need for east–west links across the Balkan peninsula around the Bosnian conflict in former Yugoslavia. Thus, external and internal aspects of gateway status are improving. Biberaj (1993, p. 382) believes that the keys are foreign investment, perseverance with reforms, and continued political stability. Membership in the EC is a distant goal. Even a Balkan or Adriatic federation or union seems implausible at this time, although the meetings of leaders of five Balkan countries could point in this direction. Gumbel (1992) points out that East European countries have a long way to go before reaching Portugal's stage; quite apart from EC membership, a modern administrative system and technocratic group are needed to work with similar units in other countries. In this way Albania could follow Kresl (1991) in becoming first a bridge (like Hamburg) and later a point of access for interaction (like Amsterdam), but well situated in terms of North Africa, the Middle East and the former Communist areas of Eastern Europe.

As a goal for small states, Portugal evidently has found the line between being dependent on a large international organisation like the EC and yet not losing its independence—a basic problem in Albania during its long struggle to throw off exploitation and overdependence on Turkey, Italy and the Communist powers. Perhaps Albania can also find this line and avoid Wanklyn's (1941) fear of a small state being a cat's-paw in world politics. The principles expressed by Edwards (1967, pp. 11–13), in connection with Luxembourg's role in Europe, are valid here:

Small states cannot exist in isolation . . . however strong the will to do so . . . and viability can be based on economic integration but there need be no loss of sovereignty.

For the first time in history, Albania might become a true gateway state.

11.5 Acknowledgements

The author acknowledges 1992 and 1993 grants from the International Research and Exchanges Board (IREX). He also appreciates cartographic work by Stephen Lavin and Les Howard of Map Press, Lincoln, Nebraska. The base map for Figures 11.2 and 11.3 is from Skendi (1956) and is used with the permission of the Greenwood Publishing Group, Westport, Conn.

11.6 References

Adhoc Committee on Political Geography, 1969, Studies in political geography, in Kasperson, R. E., Minghi, J. V., eds, *The structure of political geography*, Aldine, Chicago, pp. 57–65.

Biberaj, E., 1993, Albania's road to democracy, *Current History*, **92**, 381–5.

Bowman, I., 1928, *The new world: problems in political geography*, World Book Company, Yonkers, NY.

Braudel, F., 1972, *The Mediterranean and the Mediterranean world in the age of Philip II*, Harper and Row, New York.

Burghardt, A. F., 1962, *Borderland*, University of Wisconsin Press, Madison.

Busch-Zantner, R., 1938, *Agrarverfassung, Gesellschaft und Siedlung in Südosteuropa*, Beihefte zur Leipziger Vierteljahrsschrift für Südosteuropa, vol 3.

Cohen, S. B., 1990, The world geopolitical system in retrospect and prospect, *Journal of Geography*, **89**, 2–12.

Cvijić, J., 1918, The zones of civilization of the Balkan peninsula, *Geographical Review*, **5**, 470–82.

deMachete, R. C., 1991, Portugal: a gateway to Europe for U.S. companies, *Business America*, **112**, 9.

Eaton, L., 1989, *Gateway cities and other essays*, Iowa State Press, Ames.

Edwards, K. C., 1967, *Luxembourg: the survival of a small nation*, University of Nottingham, Nottingham.

Financial Times, 1994, Albania: special supplement, 21, July.

Gumbel, P., 1992, Portugal: a recovery that Eastern Europe can emulate, *Wall Street Journal*, 1 May.

Hall, D. R., 1994a, *Albania and the Albanians*, Pinter, London.

Hall, D. R., 1994b, Recent developments in Albania: transport links for whom? Paper presented at the annual meeting of the Association of American Geographers, San Franscisco, 30 March.

Hall, D. R., 1996, Recent developments in Greek–Albanian relations, *Mediterranean Politics*, **2**, 82–104.

Heiman, L., 1964, Peking's Adriatic stronghold, *East Europe*, **12**, 15–16.

Huntington, S., 1993, Civilizations in conflict, *Foreign Affairs*, **72**, 22–49.

Kresl, P. K., 1991, Gateway cities: a comparison of North America with the European community, *Ekistics*, **58**, 351–7.

Lane, R. W., 1923, *Peaks of Shala*, Harper, New York.

Luthans, F., Lee, S. M., 1994, There are lessons to be learned as Albania undergoes a paradigm shift, *International Journal of Organizational Analysis*, **2**, 5–17.

MacDonald, S. B., 1993, *European destiny, Atlantic transformations: Portuguese foreign policy under the Second Republic*, Transaction Publications, New Brunswick, NJ.

O'Sullivan, F., 1972, *The Egnation Way*, David and Charles, Newton Abbot.

Pano, N. C., 1992, Albania, in Held, J., ed., *The Columbia history of Eastern Europe in the twentieth century*, Columbia University Press, New York.

Rothstein, R. L., 1968, *Alliance and small powers*, Columbia University Press, New York.

Rugg, D. S., 1985, *Eastern Europe*, Longman, London.

Rugg, D. S., 1994, Communist legacies in the Albanian landscape, *Geographical Review*, **84**, 59–73.

Skendi, S., 1956, *Albania*, Stevens and Sons, London.

Stadtmüller, G., 1937–8, Landschaft und Geschichte in Albanisch-epirotischen Raum, *Revue Internationale des Études Balkaniques*, **3**, 345–70.

Statistical Yearbook of the Republic of Albania, 1991, Komisioni i Planet të Shtetit, Drejtoria e Statistikës, Tirana.

Stavrianos, L., 1958, *The Balkans since 1453*, Holt Rinehart, New York.

Veith, G., 1920, *Der Feldzug von Dyrrachium zwischen Caesar und Pompejus*, Vienna.

Wanklyn, H. G., 1941, *The eastern marchlands of Europe*, George Philip, London.

Winnifrith, T., 1992, *Perspectives on Albania*, Macmillan, London, St Martin's Press, New York.

12

Thessaloníki and Balkan realities

Stella Kostopoulou

12.1 Introduction

Since its founding, the city-port of Thessaloníki, the focal point of Macedonia (Greece), has been closely related to the economic and cultural life not only of its surrounding region, but also of the broader Balkan area. Recent global political and economic change has meant that EU economic policies have been reorientated towards closer cooperation with Central and East European countries and with the broader Mediterranean region, resulting in new forms of transnational, trans-border and transregional development policies.

Within this changing environment, Greece, the EU member country located at the crossroads of three continents, has also had to redefine its role and relationships with its Balkan, Black Sea and Mediterranean contexts. With the demise of cold war barriers, northern Greece can once again look northwards to its natural economic hinterland. Thessaloníki, the capital of northern Greece, strategically located in the most favourable geographical position where it can act as a bridge between the hinterland and the sea, is also in a position to recover its traditional role as a major economic centre in the Balkan region.

Thessaloníki has played a significant role in both Greek and world history for over 4000 years. As the largest port of the Balkan peninsula, Thessaloníki has always enjoyed strong natural advantages and has been an important centre of commerce, communications, administration and culture. The post-Communist destabilisation of the Balkans has made the opportunities for the exploitation of the city's special geopolitical position and its linkages with the rest of Europe and the Middle East even more apparent.

This chapter explores the evolution and changing role of Thessaloníki as a major economic centre for the Balkan region. It concludes by considering the place of both Thessaloníki and Greece in assisting a reconstruction of the Balkans.

12.2 Location and evolution of the city

Thessaloníki, situated at the inner recess of the Thermaikos Gulf, an inlet of the Aegean Sea, is strategically located at the southern end of the Axios–Morava corridor, where important trade routes have historically converged. The city lies on the slopes of the southwestern extension of the Balkan massif. To the south is a deep, spacious and protected harbour. The port is the terminal

Reconstructing the Balkans: A Geography of the New Southeast Europe. Edited by Derek Hall and Darrick Danta.
©1996 John Wiley & Sons Ltd

of a system of land communications. Indeed, the best natural route from the Aegean Sea to the central Balkans starts from the coast of the Thermaikos Gulf, and the best-known route linking the coastal plains of Albania and Macedonia (Greece), is that followed by the Via Egnatia, starting from the port city (Hammond, 1972). Thus, Thessaloníki can be seen as a 'gateway' from the sea to the Balkan peninsula, and situated on the shortest route between Central Europe and the Middle East.

The area of Thessaloníki is believed to have been inhabited since at least the beginning of the third millennium BC. The oldest known settlements of this region date from Neolithic times (Moutsopoulos, 1980). During the classical age the most important town near the shore was Therme, from which the bay derived its name, Thermaios, later Thermaikos (Papahadjis, 1957). Thessaloníki was founded on this site in 316 BC. In that epoch, with the conquests of Alexander the Great, Greek civilisation expanded to almost all the then known world. Macedonia, the land of Greek kings, needed a close contact with these far distant lands, and an extensive and wealthy hinterland required a natural outlet to the sea. Thessaloníki was that outlet, and subsequently a well-designed urban settlement was constructed (Vacalopoulos, 1963). The walled city comprised the area around and above its harbour which became the base for the mercantile marine and navy. Being not only a port but also a highway junction, Thessaloníki came to acquire particular significance as a commercial and cultural centre.

Following Roman occupation of Macedonia in the mid-second century BC, Thessaloníki was designated capital of the whole *Macedoniae Provinciae*. It was a 'free city' (*civitas libera*) and preserved the Greek language and its ethnic integrity, developing into the most populous city in Macedonia, as noted by Strabo. Thessaloníki's role as a major commercial city followed construction of the Via Egnatia (146–120 BC). As the shortest route from the Adriatic to Constantinople (Chapters 10 and 11), this road passed through the city. With the further extension of the Roman Empire to the east and

to the north, Thessaloníki became (a) a focal point of east–west and north–south communications, (b) the major trade centre for the Roman provinces in the Balkan peninsula, and (c) the most important port of the Roman Empire.

Throughout the Middle Ages, Thessaloníki was the second largest city of the Byzantine Empire and remained the most important commercial, administrative and cultural centre in the Balkans. As the busiest port in the peninsula, it was the city where Slav peoples came to exchange their products for goods originating from the Near and Far East. These commercial activities were further encouraged by the then navigability of the Axios River. The artistic, intellectual and religious influences exerted by Thessaloníki contributed decisively to the development of the Balkan peoples, who were converted to the Christian faith by the Thessalonian theologists Cyrill and Methodius (AD 836). In the thirteenth and fourteenth centuries, as the Byzantine Empire decayed, Thessaloníki's ties with the hinterland weakened, and trade diminished (Hoffman, 1968). Finally, Thessaloníki fell to the army of Murad II in 1430, after an earthquake had damaged the city walls. The city remained under Ottoman rule until 1912, when it was (re)incorporated into the Greek state.

During the Turkish occupation, Thessaloníki enjoyed the fruits of a politically united hinterland. Her trade, manipulated by shrewd and energetic merchants, was large and rivalled that of Constantinople, the capital of the Ottoman Empire. Balkan trade routes were of three types:

1. Maritime routes from Adriatic ports, which were of major importance during times of warfare in the interior;
2. Overland links from the ports of Ragusa (Dubrovnik), Dyrrachium (Durrës) and Thessaloníki to the important market towns of the interior;
3. Land routes from Germany (Hoffman, 1968).

By the end of the eighteenth century, the great powers which had commercially penetrated the Ottoman Empire, encouraged the development of a railway network to facilitate trade between Thessaloníki and Central Europe. The city was linked by rail with Skopje in 1871, and with Belgrade in 1880, thereby connecting it with the European railway network. Links to Monastir in 1893 and Istanbul in 1895 completed one Trans-Orient Express route. In 1916, the city was connected to the Greek railway network, which linked this city with Athens. As traffic increased, and new distribution channels were established, the last two decades of the nineteenth century saw Thessaloníki taking advantage of the fact that the port's hinterland extended over the whole of the Ottoman Empire in Europe.

Between 1878 and 1920 the political–geographical map of the Balkans was completely redrawn. The liberation of the city in 1912, the end of the Second Balkan War and the creation of new states in the Balkans changed the situation radically. The hinterland of Thessaloníki now became severely circumscribed by political boundaries. In response, the Greek government established a 'free zone' in 1923 and the 'Yugoslav free zone' six years later, both at the port of Thessaloníki, granting many privileges in order to stimulate trade and the development of manufacturing industry.

After the Second World War until 1989, Thessaloníki and its surrounding region was considered as Greece's natural northern defensive barrier in both economic and military terms against 'the threat from the north'. Economic development incentives for the region had little impact, and during the cold war period the city's role was diminished substantially.

12.3 Thessaloníki within a changing Balkan environment

The political and economic changes in the former socialist Balkan countries have created opportunities for the upgrading of Greece's regional role. The country would appear to hold significant potential advantages in assisting the economic development of the Balkans:

1. As a geographical bridge between the new states of the Balkans and Eastern Europe, the Middle East and the Mediterranean with Western Europe. Greece is the only EU member country in the region, and the only one that shares an extensive border with the Balkan countries (Frangaki-Tzaneti, 1991).
2. Historical, political, cultural and religious ties with Balkan and East European countries, not least through the Orthodox Church.
3. The structure of the Greek economy—small and medium-sized companies, trade, leading position in shipping and tourism, the growth of services—is favourable in order to offer support and assistance and technology transfer to the neighbouring countries.
4. A leading transport role, particularly in shipping. In this sector, Thessaloníki has an important position, being in close proximity to the restructuring Balkan markets. It has geographical advantages and modern mechanical equipment to handle increasing trade movement, and has the potential to develop into a major European port and a gateway between the EU and the countries of the Balkans and Central Europe.

Thus Greece can pursue the role of linking the Balkans and the developed Western economies, and in particular as an economic 'mediator' between the EU and the Balkans (Stamatoyannopoulos, 1992). Due to their geographical position, northern Greece and particularly Thessaloníki, are in the most favourable position to play a leading role in assisting closer cooperation. As Southeastern Europe and the Balkans hasten towards market economies, as the needs of commerce and industry become more varied, and as Greece's economic centre of gravity appears to be shifting slowly northwards, Macedonia (Greece), and particularly its capital city Thessaloníki, is once again becoming crucial to the whole region. Thessaloníki is the largest urban centre of the country in close proximity to the Balkan states and should again be able to consider the Balkans as its natural economic hinterland. It is the second largest urban area in

Greece, with a population of nearly 970 000 in 1991. Thessaloníki is the business, civic and cultural capital and transport node of northern Greece. It has the largest and oldest university in the country, and has been designated by the EU as 1997 European Cultural Capital.

Northern Greece accounts for 30% of the country's GNP, 54% of national exports, and contains nine of the country's ten industrial zones. Income growth in the region over the past decade has been more rapid than anywhere else in Greece. Today, the average per capita income for Macedonia is 90.5% of the national figure, while that for Thessaloníki is 95% (DCMT, 1992).

Thessaloníki constitutes the second largest concentration of industrial activity in the country: manufacturing employed 47% of the active population in the mid-1980s, when the figure for Greater Athens was 38% and for Greece as a whole 29%. Industrial activity is even more important than official figures indicate, since they exclude significant production activity that is carried out in small, usually unregistered, workshops and in homes (Chronaki *et al.*, 1993). Enterprises tend to be small or medium-sized, many of them located in industrial estates, including Sindos on the outskirts of Thessaloníki, one of the largest industrial zones in Greece (Springett, 1993).

As a major commercial centre, Thessaloníki is responsible for 73% of employment in wholesale trading in Macedonia and 15% of all Greece. The city is also the banking centre of northern Greece: of 478 branch offices in the region, 175 are located in Thessaloníki (DCMT, 1992). Being but one hour by car from the tourist area of Halkidiki, the city attracts foreign and domestic tourism. Thessaloníki and Halkidiki are particularly popular places and contain a majority of the 54 000 beds available in northern Greece (Kalaitzoglou, 1993).

Primarily, Thessaloníki is the focus of north–south and east–west overland, air and maritime transport and communications networks at both national and international level. The city's significance is closely linked with its port, one

of the most important in southern Europe, with a sphere of influence extending over a large part of Central and Eastern Europe and the eastern Mediterranean. The port serves as a major Balkan transit centre: it has, for example, infrastructural and labour advantages over such Balkan ports as Varna, Burgas, Constanţa, Rijeka, Koper and Durrës. Thessaloníki is the primary exporting and transit port of Greece, accounting for more than half of all Greek exports, and is second regarding total traffic. In addition, Thessaloníki is rapidly becoming one of the largest passenger ports in northern Greece, serving the Aegean islands. It is also situated on one of the country's main railway junctions, and the city's airport is the country's second most important. Thessaloníki's role as a major node within the trans-European networks will be re-emphasised when new transport infrastructure is established along the line of the ancient Via Egnatia and connecting road systems at the turn of the century.

12.4 The emerging role of Thessaloníki in the Balkans

The 1990s have seen substantial investments from Greek enterprises in the Balkan countries. Value of exports to the Balkans in 1994 reached almost US$1 billion, having risen from US$200 million at the beginning of the decade. More than 2000 Greek enterprises covering almost all sectors and services are active in the region (Table 12.1).

Greece is a major source of direct foreign investment in both Bulgaria and Albania. In the latter, Greece holds second position, after Italy, with 99 joint companies and investments worth up to US$120 million. In Bulgaria, Greece is the leading partner, with 700 joint companies and investments worth more than US$100 million. In Romania it holds twelfth position, with 858 joint companies and US$16 million invested in the country (NSS, 1993). Greek business people are also extending their activities in Moldova, Ukraine, the countries of the Caucasus and the Russian federation.

Table 12.1 *Trade between Greece and selected Balkan countries, 1990–93*

Year	Albania				Bulgaria				Romania			
	Exports		Imports		Exports		Imports		Exports		Imports	
	a	b	a	b	a	b	a	b	a	b	a	b
1990	2 825	—	1 947	—	8 896	—	17 300	—	9 396	—	11 412	—
1991	2 226	−21	2 165	+11	16 001	+80	20 396	+64	15 459	+65	16 797	+47
1992	7 869	+254	3 449	+59	31 880	+99	30 705	+8	20 479	+32	12 960	−23
1993	24 842	+216	2 902	−16	59 431	+86	36 814	+20	18 135	−11	13 166	+2
Total 1990–93	37 762		10 463		116 208		105 215		63 469		54 335	

a = value in million drachmas; b = annual percentage change.
Source: NSS of Greece (various).

As a meeting point of Greek and Balkan entrepreneurial activities, Thessaloníki's international trade fairs command increasing attention. In 1992, for example, the European Trade Forum attracted 1122 companies from 21 countries of the EU, Eastern Europe and the Balkans (Springett, 1993). Additional impetus to the emergence of Thessaloníki as a Balkan financial centre and exporter of financial services is being provided by several developments in the city:

1. Opening of the stock exchange centre in September 1995;
2. The choice of the city as headquarters of the Balkan and Black Sea Enterprise Centre, a joint public–private sector initiative that will provide support for Greek and Balkan small and medium-sized enterprises;
3. The location here of the Black Sea Trade and Development Bank;
4. The setting up of the European Centre for Development of Professional Training (CEDEFOP);
5. The creation of the Balkan Business Council and a Balkan Commercial Centre, to support and promote commercial cooperation in the region.

Through the provision of such commercial and organisational infrastructure, Thessaloníki is seeking to become the base of every EU organisation specialising in Balkan issues.

The structural changes in the economy of Balkan and East European countries are creating a situation which will allow commercial flows to seek their natural outlets, leading to an increase in the flow of trade through the port of Thessaloníki, especially for goods to the Middle East and Suez Canal. Thessaloníki seeks to become a strong development pole and major economic centre within a new dynamic 'regional market' (Katseli, 1994) incorporating the Balkans, the Black Sea and the eastern Mediterranean.

12.5 The future role of Thessaloníki in the Balkan region: challenges and obstacles

The second Thessaloníki conference on Greek–Balkan Business Cooperation, held in February 1995, concluded that northern Greece in general and Thessaloníki in particular should consolidate their claim as major actors in Balkan economics and business cooperation. Northern Greece can stimulate economic activity within the Balkans in a number of fields (Nikolinakos, 1992):

1. Trade exchanges, by providing consumer products and durable capital goods, as well as by absorbing goods produced by the Balkan countries, especially raw materials and minerals;

2. Industry, by creating joint companies and contributing to the modernisation of Balkan economies;
3. Organising the trade and distribution systems through the creation of autonomous or joint companies;
4. Transfer of technology and know-how, as well as in offering training and information services to senior executives and specialists;
5. Mediating between Balkan and EU companies, especially concerning issues of high technology.

The ability of northern Greek business to cooperate with enterprises from all parts of the world for activities in the wider area of the Balkans–Black Sea–Russia presents one of the most powerful incentives for the attraction of foreign investment to Greece and the creation of new forms of cooperation that would put to use the comparative advantages held by northern Greece. The activities of the private sector in the Balkans demonstrate particularly the need for economic and administrative decentralisation. Greek development has been Athens-centred for many decades. The vision of cooperation within the Balkans requires a region-based development model, with an emphasis on the role of northern Greece and its capital city, Thessaloníki.

Thessaloníki could act as a 'one-stop shop' to assist prospective investors in obtaining information, licences and authorisations, easing visa formalities, and in appreciating the priority attached by Balkan countries to preparing their economies for eventual EU membership. In this connection, Thessaloníki can be a 'nodal bridge' linking the EU and USA not only with the Balkan countries which seek EU membership but also with the Black Sea region and the Middle East, with much transit trade flowing through the port of Thessaloníki.

It is not enough, however, simply to express the will to be the bridge between the Balkans and the EU. A dynamic, long-term local and regional economic development policy is required within the framework of a national strategy, which in its turn must be a Balkan strategy, with European orientation the foundation stone of the common aims of Greece and the Balkans. Such a long-term Balkan economic strategy should be viewed as an important means for the growth, restructuring and modernisation of the Greek economy within the context of globalisation (Nikolinakos, 1992).

Initially, Greece seems to have handled the opportunities offered by the 'new' Balkan countries in a rather random and circumstantial manner. In spite of the encouraging activities of Greek business people and investors in the neighbouring Balkan countries, it seems that politically Greece has room to increase its influence in the region. The country has the potential to be an honest broker to the regional conflicts: although part of the region, it is not part of, nor party to, these conflicts.

12.6 Conclusions

Until recently, the role of Thessaloníki was determined to a large extent by its location within the national settlement hierarchy and to a lesser extent within the network of EU cities. Its geographical and historical importance as a major transport node were circumscribed by the cold war. Since 1989, however, a gradual but challenging change in the city's role has come about in response to new geopolitical and economic realities. Because of its geographical location and economic strength, Thessaloníki can expand its historical role as a central trading point, and become a transport and transit centre again.

Thessaloníki and the northern Greece region can now act as an EU bridge, a factor which would contribute to the stabilisation of the region and benefit the people of Europe and beyond.

12.7 References

Chronaki, Z., Hadjimichalis, C., Labrianidis, L., Vaiou, D., 1993, Diffused industrialization in Thessaloníki: from expansion to crisis, *International Journal of Urban and Regional Research*, **17**, 178–94.

DCMT (Development Centre for Macedonia and Thrace), 1992, *Macedonia and Thrace: a profile*, DCMT, Thessaloníki.

Frangaki-Tzaneti, E., 1991, The position of Greece in the Balkans today, *Trade with Greece*, **99**, 32–86.

Hammond, N. G. L., 1972, *A history of Macedonia*, Vol. 1: *Historical geography and prehistory*, Oxford University Press, Oxford.

Hoffman, G. W., 1968, Thessaloníki: the impact of a changing hinterland, *East European Quarterly*, **2**(1), 1–27.

Kalaitzoglou, A., 1993, Northern Greece, tip of the export spear, *Greek American Trade*, **30**(6), 30–5.

Katseli, L., 1994, Development strategy and entrepreneurial activities, *Epiloguie*, **103–4**, 360–4.

Moutsopoulos, N. K., 1980, *Thessaloníki 1900–1917*, Molho Publications, Thessaloníki.

Nikolinakos, M., 1992, The economic role of Greece in the Balkans and Eastern Europe, *Greek Economy*, **6**, 56–7.

NSS (National Statistical Service of Greece), annual, *Statistical yearbook of Greece*, NSS, Athens.

Papahadjis, N., 1957, *Monuments of Thessaloníki*, S. Molho, Thessaloníki.

Springett, C., 1993, Gateway to the Balkans, *Greek American Trade*, **30**(3), 18–24.

Stamatoyannopoulos, D., 1992, The role of Greece in the wider area, *Greek Economy*, **6**, 64–6.

Vacalopoulos, A., 1963, *A history of Thessaloníki*, Institute of Balkan Studies, Thessaloníki.

13

Romania: regional development in transition

David Turnock

13.1 Introduction

Following the experience of socialism when internal administrative areas were more or less passive receptacles for the allocation of capital under central planning, it seems entirely appropriate to examine the prospects for a new era of regional development driven much more significantly by local initiative. Central planning has been abandoned and with it many of the grandiose plans initiated by the former regime (Sampson, 1984), including major canal and water diversion projects. But given the traumatic effects of the transition, the regions of Romania can hardly survive and develop through the consolidation of their existing economic circumstances. While adjustment is complicated in all the former socialist countries, progress in market reform is all the more problematical in Romania through the disintegration of Yugoslavia and the breakdown in normal commercial relations with Serbia. But if the present economy and infrastructure are inadequate then central government has a continuing role in setting out the policy guidelines and creating enterprise organisations with specific regional responsibilities. No matter how minimal intervention may become, it is necessary to have an effective planning control system whereby development proposals can be evaluated by the local planning authorities. At the same time, however, the future role of the local authorities must be considered.

This chapter will concentrate on these basic issues, although it is recognised that there are other aspects of regional planning, such as the reorganisation of local government areas to reflect community awareness, the contributions of non-governmental research groups and transborder cooperation, which are being discussed elsewhere (Surd, 1991; Turnock, 1994).

The context can be set in terms of recovery from a system of excessive centralisation under socialism (Ben-Ner and Montias, 1991). A new civil society is being formed (Klingman, 1990), and electoral geographies reflect the pluralism of the new situation, despite the limited policy differences between many of the parties (Pop and Bodocan, 1991). Given the Romanian democratic tradition of 'making' elections, a chosen leader can expect wide support simply by virtue of holding the office. In voting for parliamentary representatives and local officials there is attraction towards effective administrators and debaters of intellectual capacity rather

Reconstructing the Balkans: A Geography of the New Southeast Europe. Edited by Derek Hall and Darrick Danta.
©1996 John Wiley & Sons Ltd

than to people of more modest calibre who are dismissed as 'opportunists'. The electorate is suspicious of radical programmes after the totalitarianism of the Communist system, and there is a mistrust of parties supporting rapid market reform.

Continued governmental intervention in the economy is expected especially by those in the state sector who feel insecure about their employment prospects. It is also expected by rural smallholders who are encouraged to support the present government for its restitution measures and who feel vulnerable in the face of opposition demands to remove subsidies, encourage investment and offer greater compensation to former farmers and landowners. The governing Social Democrats (formerly the Democratic National Salvation Front) can also gain support from nationalist groups, notably the Romania Mare Party, while the opposition forces (primarily the Democratic Convention (CD)) looking for more rapid reform, are constrained by the fragility of the present economic situation and the social problems which could follow from too rapid an overhaul of the state-owned enterprises (SOEs).

13.2 The economic situation

Changes in the economy are producing spatial variations which emerge most dramatically through limited social service provision (Hoffman, 1992) and patterns of unemployment. By August 1993 1.03 million people were unemployed, equivalent to 4.52% of the population or 13.92% of the number of people earning salaries. But rates are very variable when individual counties are considered (Figure 13.1). For unemployment in relation to population the lowest rates are in Gorj (1.79), Timiş (2.55), Bucharest (2.57) and Braşov (2.84); while the highest are in Bistriţa-Năsăud (13.07), Vaslui (9.41), Tulcea (8.27) and Neamţ (7.82). When unemployment is considered in relation to the number of salaries the lowest values are for Bucharest (5.89), Braşov (6.60), Timiş (7.04) and Prahova (9.53), while the highest figures apply to

Bistriţa-Năsăud (50.30), Vaslui (37.48), Botoşani (28.25) and Neamţ (27.01). The ratio between the highest and lowest values is 7.3 : 1 for the population and 8.5 : 1 for salaries.

Any thought that the economy could be left to develop spontaneously from the inherited base is being dashed by the scale of the recession which has seen overall production cut by half over three years. Major centres of heavy industry like Resita have seen steel production cut and pig iron production shut down altogether (Turnock, 1993c). The private sector has generated some 350 000 jobs, but the economy is burdened by the need for taxation to support the less viable state enterprises which survive as long as bankruptcy legislation is delayed. It is likely that deindustrialisation will prove an irreversible process, but there is potential in some sectors and foreign investment may be expected (Popescu, 1993b). However, it has been very limited so far (US$700 million), with Romania attracting only about 5% of all the foreign investment in former Communist countries (excluding former Yugoslavia). Of this investment, 40% falls to the top 20 companies (averaging some US$1.2 million each), with the other 26 000 companies with foreign capital averaging just US$16 000. It is also significant that 70% of the companies with foreign capital have been created by Romanian expatriates, especially those from Germany, Italy and the USA (Briggs, 1993). Western investment is unevenly distributed within the country, favouring the large cities and advanced regions like the Prahova valley. Bucharest remains one of the most industrialised capitals in Europe, with a relatively large proportion of its total capacity located in the city's central area (Popescu, 1991–92). There is also an investment targeting of natural resources: oil companies are prospecting and timber resources may justify further investment in the production of furniture. Further, some Romanian exiles are investing in rural industry in order to support their home villages (Talanga, 1995).

In the countryside the revolution led to the abandonment of Ceauşescu's rural programme, and all settlements are now free to develop

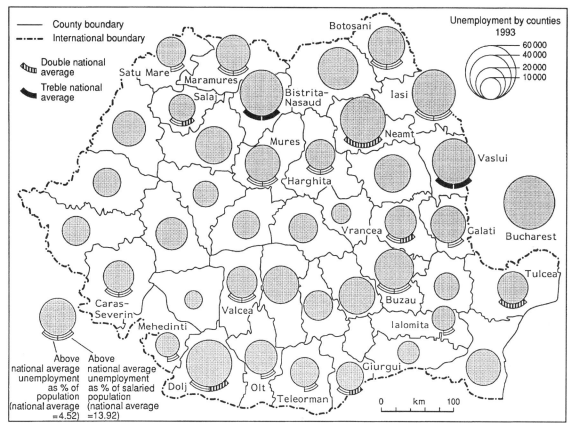

Figure 13.1 *Romania: unemployment, 1993. Source: National Commission for Statistics, Bucharest*

(Turnock, 1991a, 1993a). The value of the Romanian village has been emphasised in works published both within Romania (Dinorel-Stanculescu, 1993) and abroad (Iordache, 1990). House building has been prominent and all those involved in agriculture have benefited from privatisation of the former cooperative farms (Cooperative Agricole de Producţie (CAP)) under legislation passed in 1990 and 1991. Peasants whose families contributed land to the cooperatives have received holdings of up to 10.0 ha arable equivalent, while those farm workers without a claim have received 0.5 ha. Furthermore, people who lost their woodland through nationalisation can also seek restitution to the extent of 1.0 ha. But with some 5.06 million potential claimants and only 9.11 million ha available for distribution, it is obvious that the average holding will be below 2 ha (Turnock, 1993b). The complexity of the transition in agriculture is reflected in rural social tensions: there now seems to be a lack of the ease and contentment which characterised rural life in the past. There are social tensions between people who have received land (perhaps farmers occupying more than 10 ha; those with an urban background and lacking experience of agriculture) and others who worked for the CAP but who have no claim to a holding and who therefore receive no more than 0.5 ha, requiring them to work for others to make a living.

There is also a conflict between a subsistence approach to small farms (valued in terms of social security) and a market approach through efficient, low-cost food production (Fulea, 1993). Increased production of livestock is an important priority after the decline of recent years (Iacob, 1991). There is some evidence of a generation gap between the elderly farmers and the young people who have tended to drift away from the villages after leaving school. Some young people have returned to the countryside, motivated on the one hand by unemployment or uncertain prospects in the towns, and on the other by the opportunities in private farming and allied ancillary enterprises in the villages. However, unless such aspirants can immediately take over the running of a farm there may be little need for their labour. Young people finishing school in rural areas see agriculture as offering only limited opportunities compared to various forms of government service. Farm diversification is so important that some local families have provided for their children by extending their business into tourism. Small shops, hair salons, bars and restaurants are also possibilities where the capital and labour are available. This even extends to small industries such as sawmilling, baking (where a village is dependent for bread on a distant town) and other forms of food processing where local raw materials are available. There has been discussion in government of a settlement programme whereby young people would be placed on smallholdings of 3 ha, supported by a proportion of their former salary. The holdings would be gradually increased and financial support progressively withdrawn. But there is not enough land to justify this approach. The transition will be slow and difficult.

13.3 The role of the centre

Despite decentralisation, the centre remains very important because of the role of government and the work of the research institutes which hold so much of the professional expertise in the country. Government will have to consider initiatives which could have significance for particular regions while the institutes are assimilating Western development and planning concepts and suggesting ways in which they can be applied to Romanian conditions. While limited finance will inevitably limit the scope for regional programmes it is clear that there is a high level of intellectual ferment, so long constrained by the overriding importance of Communist Party pronouncements. But members of these institutes are making visits abroad more frequently and, moreover, the competition for research funding is stimulating researchers to publish thought-provoking papers in their journals in a bid to secure contracts from national and local government as well as from commercial enterprises. The wide-ranging nature of debate is all the more pronounced because of legislative delays which mean that most legal frameworks are still embryonic.

13.3.1 The case of the Commission for Mountainous Regions

This Comisia Zonei Montane (CZM) which is subordinate to the Ministry of Agriculture is emphasising the relevance of the principles of mountainology which have emerged from good practice in Alpine regions. The mountain areas of Romania are deemed to cover a total of 773 communes and towns in 27 counties, plus some portions of additional communes where individual villages satisfy the criteria for inclusion (Figure 13.2). Criteria for selection include high altitude (over 300–350 m) with slopes generally in excess of 15% and poor accessibility; in addition land must be used overwhelmingly for pastures, hayfields and forest (with at least 70% of the value of agricultural production consisting of animals—as opposed to crops—and with cattle and sheep predominant). The commission's review in the autumn of 1992 reported activity in agriculture, with efforts to improve the quality of pastures with the application of fertiliser and the correction of soil acidity, the planting of fruit trees and the promotion of the Pinzgau cattle breed. There is also a strong emphasis on the display of machinery suitable for small mountain farms at local agricultural shows: various

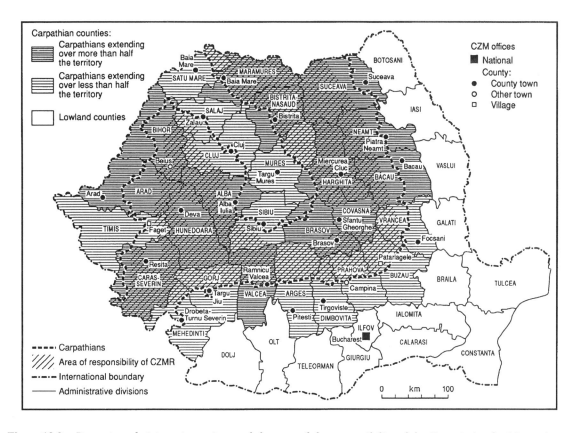

Figure 13.2 *Romania: administrative regions and the area of the responsibility of the Commission for Mountainous Regions. Source: Anuarul Statistic*

tractors and accessories are now supplied in the 18–45 hp range and very small machines for *motocultoare* (8–12 hp) are also available for very small hill farms.

The commission is also concerned with the improvement of rural services, including the extension of electricity supplies, and it also encourages research through the Institut de Montanologie at Cristian near Sibiu, with branches in three other distinct mountain regions—Gurahonţ (Arad), Panciu (Vrancea) and Saru Dornei (Suceava)—and model farms at Saru Dornei and Sibiu. Education in mountainology is provided in around 50 secondary, professional and technical schools; while there is also provision at five universities (Bucharest, Cluj, Craiova, Iaşi and Timişoara), plus the

special Facultatea de Montanologie at Vălenii de Munte. Model buildings are being publicised and the foreign contacts forged through Centrul International de Formare şi Inovare pentru Dezvoltarea Carpaţilor (CIFIDEC) are giving a number of farmers useful training and experience. For example, Valea Doftanei (Prahova) CZM has become involved in a pilot project for integrated local development; this deals with the growth of farm production (making more use of woodland fruits), additional processing for milk and meat, an improved fodder supply, more local industry and back-up from the local secondary school. It now seems that the concept will be applied more widely so that model localities will emerge in the counties of Alba, Băcau, Bistriţa-Năsăud, Suceava and Vâlcea.

But while this may offer a blueprint for the future, there is little capital for speedy implementation, and the commission has come in for a good deal of criticism because of its perceived ineffectiveness. Farmers are wary of programmes that originate in government, especially at a time when the political parties are divided over the question of association, which is strongly backed by the present Social Democrat government. Many mountain farmers are finding the market prices for their livestock are disappointing and the margins are insufficient to allow for land improvement and other investments, certainly at the high levels of interest currently in force. The situation is complicated by meat which is given away by the EC and by the heavy sales of livestock arising from the severe drought in the southwest of the country in 1993. Further difficulties arise in the livestock-rearing units which were set in the lowlands under Communism, associated with large agricultural trusts. Such units, now operating as independent businesses without their own fodder supply, are finding it difficult to survive, and the result is, once again, a flow of animals to the slaughter-houses and relatively low prices for farmers.

Tourism may be able to expand more rapidly in future (Talaba, 1991), and there could be a much stronger rural component than in the past (Stoica, 1990). The commission is strongly supportive and drawings for new three-storey houses (similar to those commonly found in the Carpathians of Poland and Slovakia) are being circulated. The need for high standards, enforced through a system of inspection, is appreciated. Other organisations are also getting involved. A private Federaţia Romana pentru Dezvoltare Montană (FRDM) has been formed to provide professional assistance to farmers in mountain regions who want to develop their business through projects involving new buildings, equipment (for food processing or crafts) and markets. The FRDM has specialists to evaluate projects in agrotourism, a sector in which some 550 households are now active. However, efforts need to be directed towards areas of outstanding potential and the commission's county programmes usual-ly include surveys of tourist potential. Thus in Prahova potential growth areas for agrotourism have been identified at Câmpina/Cheia, Slănic/Vălenii de Munte and Valea Doftanei, while in several counties there are local companies (such as Agromontana in Maramureş) to publicise the facilities available. Such organisations may operate at the commune level, as in the communes of Agapia, Bicazul Ardelean and Pipirig in Neamţ. Bran IMEX SRL is a particularly well-organised company which operates in the mountains close to Braşov where some 60 households are involved in providing accommodation; many of the houses are being improved and the company's services extend to transport from Bucharest and excursions in the locality.

13.3.2 A new planning control system

Considerable effort is being made to develop a new system of planning control which has been largely lacking in Romania so far. Under Communism, local authorities had very limited powers to control development provided for in the medium-term plans. But now it will be necessary for a developer to obtain a Certificat de Urbanism to declare that the project conforms to plans for the appropriate zone and is acceptable with regard to the area involved, to the design and to building materials as well as to the impact on traffic. In the case of large projects there will have to be a zonal study, an impact study and comment from the appropriate Comisia Locală pentru Urbanism and from specialists. The developer will then need Autorizaţia de Construire/Desfiinţare (for building or demolition) which will follow from consideration of the Certificat along with other documentation dealing with property titles and tax payments. Authorisation will relate to a specific period with further application needed if any extension is required.

The environmental input into planning control is likely to be much stronger in future. It is now widely accepted that there were inadequate safeguards in the past and much damage was caused (Hancu, 1990; Turnock, 1993b). This can be seen in manufacturing and the extractive industries (Iacob, 1992; Popescu, 1993a). Better protection will require special regimes as in the case of the Danube Delta with its Biosphere Reserve status (Gâştescu, 1993) which will greatly enhance its tourist potential in the long term (Niţu, 1990). But water management requires an effort in environmental conservation (Gâştescu, 1990) which can be provided by afforestation (Munteanu *et al.*, 1991) and small-scale hydropower projects (Haidu, 1991). Mountain pastures also require protection against heavy grazing and tourist pressure (Velcea *et al.*, 1993).

Planning control will operate in the context of a formidable array of plans. These will relate first to each local authority. The Plan de Amenajare a Teritoriului Municipal/Oraşenesc/Comunal (i.e. for municipalities, towns and rural communes) will deal with the present situation for population, infrastructure and zoning (highlighting the conflicts and malfunctions). It will consist of a written *memorial* and maps (a) for the whole area at 1 : 10 000–50 000; (b) for each zone at 1 : 5000–10 000 and (c) for each zone in detail at 1 : 100–1000. These plans will then be placed in context by plans for groups of local authorities (Plan de Amenjare a Teritoriului Interoraşenesc/Intercomunal) at a scale of 1 : 25 000–100 000. And in turn there will be three higher levels to the hierarchy with a Plan de Amenajare a Teritoriului Juḑeţean (or Municipiului Bucureşti), Zonal and Naţional. The recommended scales are 1 : 50 000–200 000, 1 : 50 000–500 000, and 1 : 500 000–1 000 000 respectively.

It will take a long time for all these documents to be produced. At the moment the necessary planning expertise is not available to local authorities even at the county level and the relevant Ministry of Public Works and Regional Development (Ministerul Lucrărilor Publice şi Amenajarea Teritoriului) is making full use of its planning institute in the capital: Urbanproiect Bucureşti. The staff have considerable experience of Western planning practice and the relevant concepts are being introduced. Thus the idea of

sustainable development has been discussed, linking the natural environment and its modifications with programmes for protection and minimisation of natural hazards with employment and income levels (Pascariu, 1993). Moreover, plans are being drawn up for priority areas such as the Jiu Valley mining area and Black Sea coast. It is perhaps unfortunate that the planning studies are so highly centralised, but there is consultation with the relevant authorities and with local experts (as well as other institutes in Bucharest) and it is the local authorities who will eventually make the decisions.

It is hardly possible to make an exhaustive study of the physical plans being drawn up, but the maps for each *judeţ* and for the country as a whole are already taking shape. The county maps deal with population distribution and settlement functions and the expected pattern for central places, working to a hierarchy of centres of county, zonal or inter-communal importance and identifying small towns with a weak economic base. Other problems are highlighted including water deficiency and environmental problems (erosion, flooding and pollution), overloaded communications and depopulation. Development plans emphasise the areas where environmental protection is needed (including national parks); this ties in with areas of high potential for tourism and other *zone agropedoclimatice* where irrigation work or some other kind of ameliorative action is needed. Proposals for further water storage and also for major road improvements are also shown, with particular emphasis on the corridor connecting Oradea with Cluj.

National maps have been drawn up for different aspects of the infrastructure and they show a great many projects for railways, roads and airports. The railway map highlights the principal routes which will need development to handle more international traffic operating at high speed (Cuncev, 1993; Floricel and Petrean, 1993). Other lines will also need increases in capacity through the duplication of tracks. This particular plan is remarkable in showing clear continuity with the programmes of the former Ceauşescu regime when rail transport was clearly

Plate 13.1 *The growth potential along the Danube valley remains considerable, with the scope for joint projects linking Romania with Bulgaria or Serbia. Here at the Iron Gates, the navigation and hydropower complex, built jointly by Romania and the former Yugoslavia, provides a frontier crossing (David Turnock)*

favoured over road improvements and higher levels of car ownership. Taken in conjunction with the county maps, it seems that all the great infrastructural programmes of the old regime (no doubt backed by civil servants still active in the bureaucracy) are being projected through the new generation of plans. This is not to say that they will be successful, but rather to suggest that while investment is limited through shortage of capital and the legislative backlog, there is scope for a mixing of old development priorities and new planning concepts, suggestive of exciting times ahead for the Romanian transition.

13.4 The role of local authorities

The local authorities have a key role in regional development and must look forward to more active involvement instead of passive adjustment

to central government requirements dominated by notions of equality that would try to bring shares of national industrial output in line with population (Cucu, 1980). However, their resources are limited, with most of their income (70.6% in 1991) coming from central government. Taxes are collected locally but most are remitted to the centre for reallocation. Therefore the debate about new forms of taxation (including VAT which was introduced in 1993, and more comprehensive taxes on agricultural resources) is flavoured by demands for greater local autonomy in fiscal matters. Income retained by local authorities comes from direct taxation, including taxes on property and privately owned land. But since the revolution these impositions have not increased in line with inflation and they have become increasingly nominal. There is also some revenue from business and commerce, encouraging some

Plate 13.2 *Environmental conservation will be given higher priority in future regional plans. This monastic complex on the edge of Iaşi was one of the historic buildings refurbished by the Communist regime (David Turnock)*

authorities to allow vacant space in public buildings (including primary schools) to be used for industrial purposes. With their limited budgets, the local authorities are struggling to pay all their employees and to maintain local cultural, medical, transport and other municipal services (including education from 1994). The deterioration in the roads over the last four years is an indication of the scale of the problem. In future greater financial autonomy, coupled with powers to set the rate at which certain taxes will be imposed (taxes on new building for example), will allow counties to compete for development projects like their Western counterparts. There will also be scope for competition through promotional activity and the development of good public relations, although this is not yet widely appreciated.

The country's statistical yearbooks now include financial information, and it emerges that local authorities were financed to the extent of 1200 lei per capita in 1989, 2160 in 1990 and 2580 in 1991. However, the rates varied considerably between counties with Bucharest being the area best endowed: 1980 lei per capita in 1989, 2800 in 1990 and 5350 in 1991 (respectively 1.65, 1.30 and 2.07 times the national average). Meanwhile the lowest rates of finance: 760 lei to Ialomiţa in 1989, 1450 lei for Teleorman in 1990 and 1390 lei for Teleorman again in 1991 are respectively 0.63, 0.67 and 0.53 times the national average. These variations reflect the differences in scale of the bureaucracies in counties where there are significant extra-*judeţ* functions in some cases. Thus in 1991 Bucharest's budget was 5359 lei per capita (for a total population of 2.35 million) compared with 2650 for the seven counties with cities of over 300 000 (total population 5.03 million), 2170 for the eight other counties which were also the cores of the pre-1968 regions (total population 5.32 million) and 2110 for the remaining 25 counties which have built up their bureaucracies since 1968 (total population 10.06 million) (Figure 13.3).

It is also interesting to see that the level of state subvention is high in Bucharest (78.7% of the

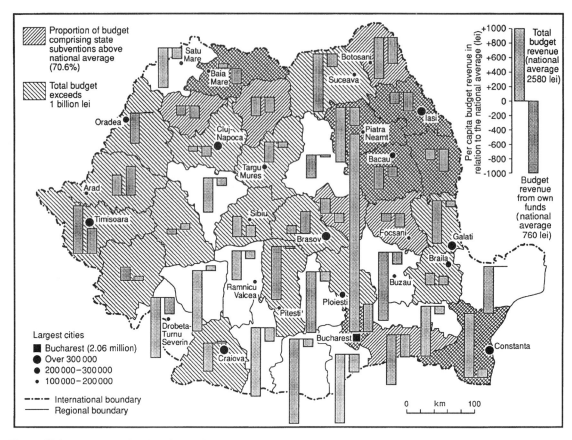

Figure 13.3 *Romania: local authority budgets, 1991. Source: Anuarul Statistic, 1992*

local authority's income) while the average for the other counties is 68.5, with a slightly higher rate in the 'new' counties—those created in 1968 through subdivision of the former regions—(69.1) than in the others (68.4 for those with large cities; and 67.2 for the rest). Twenty-four counties obtain less than the national average of 760 lei per capita of 'own funds', the lowest values being 400 lei for Botoşani, 450 for Călăraşi and Vaslui and 500 for Iaşi. Yet while 13 of the 24 receive an above-average proportion of their funds from state subventions, the remaining counties are further weakened by gaining a below-average proportion of their funds from the centre. In the cases where the proportion is more than five percentage points below the national average (Buzău, Dâmboviţa, Ialomiţa,

Olt and Teleorman), 10.47% of the country's population is supported by locally generated funds amounting to 8.26% of the national total while the total budget comprises only 6.65% of the national total. In the other cases where the state subventions are closer to the national rate, five comprise post-1968 administrative units (Alba, Giurgiu, Mehedinţi, Satu Mare and Vâlcea): 8.33% of the population is supported by 6.68% of locally generated funds and 6.33% of the national total for all local authority funding.

It is possible for local authorities to take initiatives in economic development but, so far, given limited funding and experience, the main energies are being devoted to securing the future for the large enterprises inherited from socialism which have already laid off a good many workers (Popescu, 1993b). The potentials of settlement systems will need to be assessed (Surd *et al.*, 1990). In the case of Vâlcea county, it is clear that there is an awareness of serious pollution problems from the chemical industry and the need to modernise plant rather than expand output. There is also an appreciation of the need for more light industry and especially food processing. Lying on the southern flanks of the southern Carpathians, Vâlcea is also an area of great potential for tourism, with a cluster of health resorts among which Călimăneşti-Caciu-lata and Govora have international reputations. But these centres, along with Baile Olănesti, need to attract foreign funding and modernise their facilities. The climatic resort of Voineasa in the Lotru Valley (arising out of the hydroelectric project) also has potential, with opportunities for winter sports around the Vidra reservoir where a new resort is being built. It is clear that the Ministry of Tourism and its research institute (Institutul de Cercetare pentru Turism) is determining priorities. However, the local authority's cooperation will be crucial in getting the infrastructure up to standard (and in particular in improving the roads from Voineasa to Vidra and in extending the main route westwards to Petroşani as well as northwards to Sebes and southwards to Novaci). Such projects need central government authorisation in the form of annual plans drawn up each autumn for the following calendar year. Local authorities are therefore developing their own strategies in collaboration with the centre, although they lack resources and expertise.

13.5 Conclusion

The end of state socialism has created a situation in which local decision-making is no longer constrained by the near-monopoly of the central government on planning and investment. Local developers, both individuals and local autho-rities, can now take initiatives. Foreign capitalists can make direct local contacts without the need to work through ministries and trading compa-nies in the centre. In theory this should open the way for the regions to promote themselves and so overcome the passivity to which they were reduced during the era of central planning. The regions will have to take a positive stance with economic programmes and promotional activity to sustain them. Otherwise potentials may not be appreciated and the distribution of (especially foreign) investment will continue to be highly uneven, with excessive emphasis placed on capital cities and the major regional centres. However, while the transition in Romania is relatively slow there is a remarkable ferment of ideas from which regional strategies can emerge. But regional identities have yet to be formed, and there is relatively little discussion about the future of local government areas and the potentials of different parts of the country. In the context of the 'super regions' of Europe, wider spatial perspectives to focus on the Balkan and Black Sea theatres need cultivation so that the southern part of the old Communist bloc in Eastern Europe can forge links across the former ideological divide and build a wider regional interest to balance those of the Alpine–Adriatic and Baltic groups.

13.6 References

Ben-Ner, A., Montias, J. M., 1991, The introduction of markets in a hypercentralised economy: the case of Romania, *Journal of Economic Perspectives*, **5**, 163–70.

Briggs, D., 1993, Romania: on the starting blocks or running out of steam? *Business Europa*, **1**(5), 7–17.

Cucu, V. S., 1980, Politica PCR de dezvoltare echilibrată a judeţelor RSR, *Terra*, **12**(4), 3–10.

Cuncev, C., 1993, Transporturile române si integrarea europeană, *Revista Căilor Ferate Române*, **38**(4), 28–30.

Dinorel-Stanculescu, T., 1983, Valorile culturale în arhitectura satului românesc, *Viitorul Social*, **12**, 311–21.

Floricel, G., Petrean, S., 1993, Pentru un program de viteze mari la CFR, *Revista Căilor Ferate Române*, **39**(4), 21–4.

Fulea, M., 1993, Specificul tranziţiei în economia de piaţa în agricultura României, *Sociologia Romaneasca*, **4**, 149–58.

Gâştescu, P., 1990, Water resources in the Romanian Carpathians and their management, *Revue Roumaine: Géographie*, **34**, 85–92.

Gâştescu, P., 1993, The Danube Delta: geographical characteristics and ecological recovery, *GeoJournal*, **29**, 57–67.

Haidu, I., 1991, *Potenţialul hidroenergetic al rîurilor mici din grupa nordică a Carpaţilor Orientali*, Universitatea A.I. Cuza Facultatea de Geologie–Geografie Rezumat Tezei de Doctorat, Iaşi.

Hancu, S., 1990, Calitatea mediului înconjurator în România: perspective de imbunătăţire, *Mediul Inconjurator*, **1**(1), 5–9.

Hoffman, O., 1992, Problemele protecţiei sociale în procesul tranziţiei în România, *Sociologia Romaneasca*, **3**, 263–72.

Iacob, G., 1991, Consideraţii geografice privind valorificarea fondului funciar şi cresterea animalelor în depresiunea Sibiului, *Terra*, **23**(1), 32–6.

Iacob, G., 1992, Dezvoltarea activităţilor minerometalurgice din regiunea Baia Mare-Baia Sprie şi gradul de poluare acestora, *Lucrările Seminarului Geografic 'Dimitrie Cantemir' Iaşi*, **10**, 245–62.

Iordache, G., 1990, Le rôle des communautés villageoises dans la vie spirituelle des Roumains, in Stahl, P. H., ed., *Études Roumaines et Aroumaines*, P. H. Stahl, Paris, pp. 69–73.

Klingman, G., 1990, Reclaiming the public: a reflection on creating civil society in Romania, *East European Politics and Society*, **4**, 393–438.

Munteanu, S. A. *et al.*, 1991, *Amenajarea bazinelor hidrografice torentiale prin lucrări silvice şi hidrotehnice*, Editura Academiei Române, Bucharest.

Niţu, M., 1990, Revitalizarea turismului în Delta Dunarii, *Tribuna Economică*, **1**(12), 12–14.

Pascariu, G., 1993, *A new framework concerning the sustainable development of human settlements*, Urbanproiect, Bucharest.

Pop, G. R., Bodocan, V., 1991, Opţiuni electorale pentru alegerea primarilor în Banat–Crisana–Maramureş and Transylvania, *Studia Universitatis Babeş-Bolyai: Geographia*, **36**(2), 66–75.

Popescu, C., 1991–92, Recent industrial changes in Bucharest, *Analele Universităţii Bucureşti: Geografie*, **40–41**, 85–9.

Popescu, C., 1993a, Mining versus environment in the newest coal basin of Romania, in Muica, C., Turnock, D., eds, *Geography and Conservation*, Geography Institute, Geographical International Seminars, Bucharest, pp. 103–8.

Popescu, C., 1993b, Romanian industry in transition, *GeoJournal*, **29**, 41–9.

Sampson, S., 1984, *National integration through socialist planning: an anthropological study of a Romanian new town*, East European Monographs, Boulder, Colo.

Stoica, G., 1990, Un viitor pentru satul traditional din România, *Revista Monumentelor Istorice*, **59**(2), 43–63.

Surd, V., 1991, Traditional forms of organising geographical space in Transylvania: 'The Lands', *Studia Universitatis Babeş-Bolyai: Geographia*, **36**(2), 75–80.

Surd, V. *et al.*, 1990, The typology of rural settlements in Tara Oasului, *Studia Universitatis Babeş-Bolyai: Geographia*, **35**(1), 69–75.

Talaba, I., 1991, *Turism in Carpaţii Orientali*, Editura pentru Turism, Bucharest.

Talanga, C., 1995, The restructuring of industrial activities in Romanian villages, in Turnock, D., ed., *Change in rural Romania*, Leicester University Geography Department Occasional Paper, Leicester.

Turnock, D., 1991a, The changing Romanian countryside: the Ceauşescu epoch and prospects for change following the revolution, *Environment and Planning: Government and Policy*, **9**, 319–40.

Turnock, D., 1991b, The planning of rural settlement in Romania, *Geographical Journal*, **157**, 251–64.

Turnock, D., 1993a, *Agricultural change in the Romanian Carpathians*, University of Leicester Faculty of Social Sciences, Discussion Papers in Geography no. 93/2.

Turnock, D., 1993b, Romania, in Carter, F. W., Turnock, D., eds, *Environmental problems in Eastern Europe*, Routledge, London, pp. 135–63.

Turnock, D., 1993c, The Resita industrial complex: perspectives in historical geography, *GeoJournal*, **29**, 83–102.

Turnock, D., 1994, *Regional development in the new Eastern Europe with special reference to Romania*, University of Leicester Faculty of Social Sciences, Discussion Papers in Geography no. 94/1, Leicester.

Velcea, V. *et al.*, 1993, Geographic elements regarding the environmental recovery in the Bucegi Mountains, in Muica, C., Turnock, D., eds, *Geography and conservation*, Geography Institute, International Geographical Seminars, Bucharest, pp. 119–21.

14

The persistence of collectivism: responses to land restitution in Romania

Mieke Meurs

14.1 Introduction

Throughout 1990 and 1991, debate raged in East and Central Europe over the most appropriate form of privatisation of the large public farms. Restitution was the form most commonly chosen. The Czech and Slovak republics, Hungary, Bulgaria and Romania all chose to privatise land through some version of the restitution of pre-war ownership. While politically popular, restitution has raised concern that it will create inefficient, small, labour-intensive farms, just at the moment that agriculture is opened up to global competition.

Rather than engaging in small-scale production, however, many households across East and Central Europe have responded by pooling their land into new forms of collective production. In Bulgaria, 46% of households surveyed in August 1992 expected to put their land in newly forming production cooperatives (Meurs and Spreeuw, 1994). In Romania, 62% of rural dwellers interviewed in 1991 expected to farm their land as part of a production association (*Survey Data*, 1991).

Examination of the Romanian survey data suggests that the decision to farm collectively can be explained, in part, as a response to the problem of creating viable private farms in the context of poorly developed and highly concentrated markets. Under the conditions prevailing in Romania during 1991–93, many individual producers were unable to secure access to the inputs, scale of production, and distribution networks necessary to form an efficient farming unit. The new collectives offered greater potential to do so. Both market development and farming requirements differ substantially by region, however, as a result of historical and geographical differences. This has produced significant regional differences in the emerging forms of agricultural production.

While offering benefits in terms of access to inputs and markets, the new associations appear somewhat slow to adjust to new market conditions. In many cases the associations are only minimally restructured versions of the old collective farms, with the old leadership still in place. Mechanisms to hold association leadership accountable to the membership and technical

Reconstructing the Balkans: A Geography of the New Southeast Europe. Edited by Derek Hall and Darrick Danta.
©1996 John Wiley & Sons Ltd

assistance to new management will be needed if the new associations are to remain competitive over the longer term.

14.2 Restitution and efficiency: household choice between cooperative and private farming

Fear that restitution would reduce efficiency was based on the assumptions that ownership and operation would coincide, and that smallholders with fragmented holdings would forego both economies of scale and the use of a capital stock designed for large-scale farming. In a world of perfect markets, an ownership structure based on smallholding would not threaten economies of scale or use of the capital stock. If smallholder production did not yield competitive returns, farm size could be adjusted through the lease or purchase of additional land and assets. Services of capital stock could be rented to those best able to employ machines.

During the transitional period, however, competitive markets have been slow to develop. Information and transaction costs are high, and monopoly power is prevalent. Under these conditions, individual producers find it hard to adjust asset use, production and technology to efficient levels. Credit markets, for example, may not permit access to technology and scale for all producers (Newbury, 1989; Stiglitz, 1993). Land markets may also be weakly developed, making it difficult for ownership to be separated from operation.

Monopolies in input supply and monopolistic distribution networks may also limit adjustment. Price distortions may affect the input mix that producers apply to their land, and price discrimination may favour one group of producers over another.

Under these conditions, many small individual producers may be unable to adjust their production efficiently through markets. Associations may serve as a means of transfering land from owners to potentially more efficient operators. Associations may also be better able to bargain with persisting monopolies. Where associations

have more collateral or less cultural resistance to borrowing, they may be in a better position to obtain loans (Paarlberg, 1992, p. 13).

While incentive problems have long been associated with collective forms of production, the benefits listed above may outweigh incentive costs, making associations a rational choice for households and a means of avoiding the inefficiency expected to accompany restitution. The role of associations will be particularly important in those regions where, for historical and geographical reasons, weak market development has a greater potential impact on efficiency. The speed with which individual agriculture emerges as an attractive alternative to associations will depend on how quickly markets develop, how resolutely governments insist on a level playing field for all forms of production, and how well the new associations adjust to market stimuli. But important regional differences in the pace of change are likely to persist.

14.3 Historical background

Prior to the Second World War, Romanian agriculture was characterised by a bimodal distribution of land, in which large (over 100 ha) and small (under 3 ha) peasant holdings coexisted. According to the census of 1941, holdings under 3 ha constituted 54% of all holdings of arable land, while holdings of 3–5 ha constituted another 20% of the total. Holdings over 100 ha accounted for well under 1% of holdings, but 14% of area. The average holding of 4.5 ha was further subdivided into an average of five parcels. Significant regional differences existed, however, with a viable middle peasantry concentrated among the ethnically Hungarian population in the old territories of Transylvania and Crisana (Roberts, 1951, pp. 58, 371).

Neither land nor labour markets appear to have been widely developed prior to 1945. According to the same census, 83% of holdings relied only on family labour. Over 71% of farms were owned completely by the cultivator, 28% were partially owned but included some additional land in métayage or lease, and less than 1% were wholly on lease (Roberts, 1951, p. 51).

During the pre-war period, Romanian small-holding was associated with backward production. In the late 1930s, Romania had the least mechanised agriculture in Eastern Europe. Bulgaria had twice as many machines per hectare as Romania, and Germany had 14 times as many (Madgearu, 1940, p. 58, cited in Roberts, 1951, p. 58). While the impact of a similar capital shortage in smallholder agriculture was reduced in Bulgaria through state-supported agricultural credit and service cooperatives, few such co-operatives were established in Romania.

A land reform implemented in March 1945, immediately after the creation of the Communist government, expropriated the land of German citizens and collaborators, absentee landholders and private land over 50 ha, as well as all machinery found on expropriated land. As of January, 1947, 1.4 million ha had been expropriated, and an average of 1.3 ha had been distributed to 800 000 peasant households holding less than 5 ha of land (Roberts, 1951, p. 294). At the time of collectivisation in 1948, however, the problem of fragmentation of Romanian landholding remained as severe as it had been in 1941. The large landholdings had been liquidated, but the amount distributed was inadequate to create viable peasantry.

Over the four decades of collective agriculture, a substantial amount of small, individual farming persisted, especially in mountainous areas. Some villages were never collectivised at all (Verdery, 1994): in 1980, individual farms controlled 4.8% of all arable land. In addition, household subsidiary plots of 0.10–0.25 ha approached 8% of arable land (Turnock, 1986, p. 184).

This household land was farmed partly in subsistence agriculture, but households were also encouraged to produce for sale to state purchasing agencies (Kideckel, 1993) and, to a certain degree, for peasant markets. Participation in peasant markets varied greatly by region, however, as will be seen below.

Alongside this residual small-scale production, collectivisation produced radical changes in the technology and scale of the majority of agricultural production. The stocks of both tractors and combines increased rapidly to an average of seven tractors and four combines per 100 ha under collective production. Production units grew to about 9000 ha in size (Romanian National Commission for Statistics, 1991). Most of the machinery was held in machine tractor stations (MTS), not on the collective farms.

14.4 The process of restitution

The Romanian Law on Land Resources was passed in February 1991. The law mandated redistribution of land held by the former collective farms, first to those who contributed land during collectivisation, and next (if available) to those who worked for the collective farm but did not contribute land. Land held by state farms would not be privatised. Households could claim a maximum of 10 ha, and heirs of original owners could claim on behalf of the owner. Since under Romanian law all offspring may inherit land, both men and women could receive land under the restitution. Romanians who received land through restitution can legally sell it, or buy up to a maximum holding of 100 ha per household. Family members and neighbours have rights of first refusal on agricultural land. Under this legal framework, many analysts feared a re-creation of the inefficient farming of the pre-war period.

An August 1991 survey by the World Bank and the government of Romania offers insight into the initial results of restitution. The survey included approximately 1200 rural households and 200 newly formed collective production associations in 19 of the 40 administrative units (*judeţs*). It included agricultural households, non-agricultural households and mixed households. The sample was designed to capture a representative cross-section of rural Romania, although it is not a strictly statistically representative sample. None of the *judeţs* along the Carpathian mountain range are included in the sample, although other mountainous areas, including *judeţs* along the Transylvanian Alps, are included.

Table 14.1 *Distribution of survey households by landholding size (N = 1243)*

Size (ha)	Current claimed ownership (%)	Currently farming in 1990 (%)	Claims		Expected land (%)	Intending to farm in 1992 (%)
			Prior owner (%)	Other claims (%)		
None	14	1	12	81	4	1
0–1	13	19	5	5	6	8
1–2	11	17	12	5	12	13
2–3	10	14	11	2	12	13
3–4	10	10	11	2	12	12
4–5	10	10	11	2	12	13
5–6	6	6	7	1	7	7
6–7	5	5	6	0	7	7
7–8	5	4	5	0	6	5
8–9	3	3	3	0	4	4
9–10	9	8	9	1	13	10
Over 10	4	4	6	1	5	7
Totals*	100	101	98	100	100	100

*Totals do not always add to 100% due to rounding.
Source: *Survey Data* (1991).

At the time of the survey, the old collective farms had recently been dissolved. Most land claims had been filed, households had taken possession of the land they expected to receive, but titles had not been distributed. The survey thus reflects changes under way, rather than a final outcome. As will be seen, however, the pace of change since 1991 has been slow. The major findings of the 1991 survey continue to offer significant insights into the process of rural transformation into the fourth year of the reform.

14.4.1 Landholding structure

Most households expected to receive smallholdings; 34% of households expected holdings of less than 3 ha, while 37% expected to claim 5–10 ha. The average expected size was 6 ha, and only 5% expected to claim over 10 ha (Table 14.1). The average size of the expected holdings differed greatly by *judeţ*, however, with the largest average holdings expected between the Carpathian Mountains and the western border with Hungary, where larger than average holdings predominated before the Second World War. Only 13% of households expected to

claim their land as a contiguous parcel; households expected an average of 4.3 parcels. Despite the small size of many holdings, little intention to lease or rent was reported in August 1991 (*Survey Data*, 1991).

14.4.2 New associations

Only 35% of households expected to farm their land individually. The majority of households (62%) expected to farm in an association of some type. Relatively few households (24%) expected to use a mixed strategy of placing some land in an association, while farming some individually, even though this mixed strategy corresponds most closely to the old arrangement of collective production alongside subsidiary household plots.

While the meaning of the term 'association' is still fluid, most associations resembled voluntary production cooperatives. In 74% of associations all workers were association members. Of the associations hiring non-member workers, 30% did so on a permanent basis, the other 70% hired either temporary or seasonal workers (*Survey Data*, 1991).

Not all members worked in the association, however. An average of 28% of members contributed only land to the association, 23% contributed only labour and 49% contributed both land and labour (*Survey Data*, 1991). Associations thus represent the main way in which owners transferred control of their land. In view of the small average plot size and high level of mechanisation in associations, the presence of non-working members is not surprising.

Non-working members received rent in cash or kind for the use of their land. In most cases, members' earnings for both land and labour contributions were linked to association performance. Only 11% of associations paid members only salary or wages, while 40% paid a share of earnings and 44% paid both salary and a share of net earnings. Hired workers' earnings were also frequently tied to association performance: only 34% received a salary or wages with no link to performance. Only 7% of associations paid a fixed rent for land, with the rest offering a share of output in kind, a share of net earnings, or both (*Survey Data*, 1991).

The new associations were large, but smaller than the old collective farms. Surveyed associations farmed an average of 1400 ha of land and had an average of approximately 300 members. The majority of members of the associations were members of the old collective farms, although a surprising number (31%) were not (*Survey Data*, 1991).

Most private farms, on the other hand, were small and poorly endowed. Private farming households expected to farm an average of 5.5 ha, with an average number of horses of 0.6 and of tractors of 0.2. Many resembled gardens more than farms (*Survey Data*, 1991).

14.4.3 Household choice between individual and associated farming

If the decision of a household to farm its land through an association is a response to problems in forming a viable private farm in the context of poor market development, the decision is expected to be influenced by the ability of the household to form an efficient farming unit under current conditions. This includes considerations of the farming capacity of the household, including household members' experience with private farming, age and education. The household's ability to form an efficient farming unit will also depend on the level of development of competitive markets for inputs and agricultural products, as well as the importance of economies of scale in local production.

Most households have some experience with private farming. In our sample, 5% of adults listed private farming as their main occupation in 1990 (prior to restitution), while 88% of the adults sampled listed private farming as their second occupation (*Survey Data*, 1991). On average, households had slightly more than two persons involved in private farming, but households planning to farm privately had significantly more members involved in farming (and more members) than did households expecting to farm in associations. Respondents in households planning to farm individually were slightly (but significantly) younger than those planning to farm in associations.

The extent to which private farming represented a commercial enterprise varied greatly by region, however. The *judeţs* of Alba, Cluj, Mureš and Salaj, all clustered to the northwest of the Carpathian and Transylvanian mountain ranges, reported the highest average agricultural incomes in 1990, while the *judeţs* of Brăila, Calaraši and Vaslui, clustered in the southeast, reported the lowest (*Survey Data*, 1991).

Because most households maintained some private agricultural production under collective agriculture, most households own basic agricultural tools and facilities. On the other hand, draft animals and mechanised agricultural equipment were still controlled by the MTS in 1991. About 25% of households owned a horse, 4% owned a buffalo and 19% owned beef cattle, which could perhaps be used as draft power, and only 12% of households owned a plough and 9% owned a tractor of some type. Associations had more capital: an average of 31 horses and 3.4 tractors per association (*Survey Data*, 1991).

Most households (93%), therefore, purchased some or all machine services from outside the household; 79% of households purchased all services from an association or MTS, while another 11% obtained some services from organisations, although dependence on machine services varied greatly by *judeţ*. The *judeţs* Alba, Cluj and Mureš, which reported the highest agricultural incomes in 1990, also reported the greatest ability to service their own land, with 27–34% of households providing some or all of their own services. *Judeţs* along the eastern coast, including Vaslui and Brăila, as well as Galaţi and Iaşi, reported the greatest dependence on others for machine services, with 0–3% of households providing at least some of their own services (*Survey Data*, 1991).

Households able to provide machine services for themselves are highly concentrated in a few *judeţs*. Only in Alba do more than 50% of the households provide some or all of their own services. Another five *judeţs* have more than 20% of households providing some or all of their own services. In Vaslui, all services were provided by organisations.

Households reported difficulties in securing other inputs as well. Spare parts for machinery, a perpetual problem under central planning, remained the biggest problem, with 52% of all households reporting that they were not able to purchase as many of these as needed. Fuel for machinery was the second most serious reported problem, but households also reported a need for greater amounts of fertiliser, young plants and animals, and feed (*Survey Data*, 1991).

Most (87%) of those reporting that they were unable to purchase adequate supplies of inputs blame high prices (*Survey Data*, 1991). This is true in all *judeţs*. Only 4% claimed that inadequate supply restricted their purchases. The most problematic items were those with high import content, and prices of these items have adjusted quickly towards world market levels. Households have not borrowed to obtain needed inputs, however. Almost no households reported borrowing for agricultural use.

Limited competition in marketing channels also poses problems for producer households. House-holds reported selling their products mainly to powerful state firms in 1991. Some alternative marketing channels were already emerging, however. Households reported selling 10–20% of most crops to private processing plants, and about half of marketed vegetables and meat directly to consumers (*Survey Data*, 1991).

Local crop specialisation can bring together a number of these factors. In regions where wheat and corn dominate, economies of scale are more significant than in vegetable or livestock regions. In these areas, small landholdings and limited access to machinery are likely to be important constraints on household production. In addition, grain crops are more likely to be stored and distributed through large state firms. Grain production is concentrated in the plains west and south of the Carpathian and Transylvanian Mountains, although more arable land than average is also under grain in Iaşi and Vaslui (Romanian National Commission for Statistics, 1991).

14.4.4 Household choice

Similarity in regional patterns of input problems, crop specialisation and landholding size reflect a range of ways in which limited evolution of competitive markets may continue to limit the viability of individual farming, and suggest that these factors are driving households' decision to cooperate. Statistical analyses of individual household choice yielded the following results.

A prevalence of grain farming in an area was found to correlate positively with associated farming. This may reflect the impact of economies of scale. This variable may also reflect the lack of competitive markets in machine services, however, as wheat and maize are among the most highly mechanised crops. Households themselves listed access to machinery as their first reason for choosing to farm as part of an association (*Survey Data*, 1991).

A household's greater supply of land and labour had the expected negative impact on the probability of choosing to farm in an association. Few households will receive enough land to organise large-scale grain production using the prevailing technology, but differences in expected land size none the less influence households' ability to organise viable production units independently.

Problems in securing sufficient inputs exerted positive impact on the probability of choosing to farm collectively. The impact of obtaining the inputs needed to farm on households' decisions reflects the lack of competition in input markets as well as their limited willingness or ability to rely on production credit. Households confirm that the associations are seen as a means of overcoming input problems: the abilities of associations to obtain fertiliser and seed are listed as the second and third most important reasons for joining. Associations appeared quite prepared to borrow to finance the inputs; 85% of associations expected to do so; outstanding debt does not appear to affect the ability or willingness to borrow (*Survey Data*, 1991).

Prior membership in a collective farm also had the expected positive impact on the decision to farm collectively in 1991. These results suggest that, although familiarity with collective production is a factor in households' decisions, the impact of weakly developed markets, including difficulties in adjusting farm size and input mix, as well as marketing problems are also significant.

14.4.5 Implications of choice for farm adjustment

Given the difficulties households face in forming viable farms, the associations play an important role in smoothing the transformation of collectivised agriculture. But the associations appear slow to adjust their behaviour to the demands of the emerging market economy.

Private households did not expect to reduce significantly the amount of land planted in 1992, but they did expect some significant changes in crop structure. Wheat and maize were expected to remain the two most important crops for households, with their share of planted area increasing slightly from 66% in 1991 to 71% in 1992. Soybeans, fodder crops, market vegetables and grapes were all expected to increase quickly, from an initial low level of production. Produc-

tion of other crops, including sugar-beet, barley and sunflowers, was expected to drop (*Survey Data*, 1991). In part, households appear to be responding to the new market stimuli, shifting from industrial (planners') crops, such as sunflowers and sugar-beet, to market vegetables.

In contrast, the majority (86%) of associations expected to expand overall agricultural production. More than half of the associations expected to expand production of wheat and maize. Sigificant numbers of associations also expected to increase both industrial crops (sugar-beet and sunflowers), and the more market-oriented vegetables and late potatoes. Associations did not expect to decrease production of any crops (*Survey Data*, 1991). Associations also expected to expand employment, despite reporting that they already had excess labour (*Survey Data*, 1991).

The overall expansion plans of associations suggest that they feel less contrained than do private farmers by existing market conditions. However, it is not clear that this optimism accurately reflects current market opportunities. Romanian GDP fell by over 15% per year in 1991 and 1992, then rose by 1% in 1993, and was expected to do so again in 1994. Official unemployment hovers around 10% (EIU, 1993, p. 8; 1994, p. 11). Export demand has also fallen, as Romania's major (post-socialist) trading partners undergo a similar economic collapse, and finding new agricultural export markets is difficult.

Under these conditions, associations' willingness to expand appears to continue the behaviour of output-maximising, centrally planned firms. While pay structures link rewards to farm performance, management does not yet appear motivated or able to adjust production decisions to current conditions. This will jeopardise the associations' viability as an alternative organisational form over the medium term, as state support is reduced and markets are opened to international competition.

14.5 Slow transition: 1992–93

Events since 1991 reveal a continuation of the patterns discussed above. A 1992 survey reveals even greater fragmentation of landownership than expected in the 1991 survey. While the percentage of landless households is slightly lower than expected (2.5% compared to 4%), the share of households with plots smaller than 3 ha is much larger than expected (63.6% compared to 30%), while the share of households holding 3–10 ha is much smaller than expected (32.4% compared to 61%). The share of households holding over 10 ha is also less than expected (Bulgaru *et al.*, 1992, p. 16).

The lack of emergence of a land market prevents consolidation of plots by individual owners. Many landholders are still waiting to receive titles (FBIS, 15 March 1993, p. 16), and this absence of legal title precludes sales. In addition, agricultural land has been exempted from taxation until 1996, so that households unable to use land efficiently may not be motivated to sell immediately.

Leasing has also not developed as an important means of reallocating land from owners to other operators, partly because of delays in establishing a legal basis for such leasing. The law on leasing of agricultural land had not passed until February 1993 (FBIS, 26 February 1993, p. 24). In the interim, some informal land leasing arrangements did arise, however. One estimate found that sharecropping arrangements had arisen on about 1% of arable land, and rental arrangements on about 4% (Bulgaru *et al.*, 1992).

The small private farmers also continue to face substantial barriers in securing adequate inputs. Many large state enterprises continue to operate as near-monopolies, as in the case of local MTSs or the Romanian cereal conglomerate Romcereal, which controls distribution of over 50% of domestic wheat production and imports, and maintains its own transport system.

The power of these firms is exacerbated by government and bank policy. The Agricultural Bank, preferring not to deal with individual farmers, instead extends agricultural credit to the large agricultural processing firms. The firms, in turn, serve as 'integrators', advancing credit in the form of inputs and cash on the basis of forward purchase contracts at fixed prices. Like the Agricultural Bank, the integrators prefer to deal with a small number of large partners—the associations.

Although the MTSs are now to be privatised, this may do little to increase competition in input markets, as the units are to be privatised as a whole, by selling shares to MTS workers and to associations. Where landholders can afford to buy into the MTS in substantial numbers, some improvement should occur in input delivery to this sector.

With so few changes in market conditions in Romania, many households continue to choose associations over private farming. Recent estimates suggest that 4050 associations have been registered, with an average of 193 members and 494 ha. In addition, an estimated 11 500 informal associations have also been organised, with an average of 63 members (Ianoş, 1992). An alternative estimate (Bulgaru *et al.*, 1992, p. 20) found that 23% of arable land was farmed in registered associations, and another 20% was farmed in informal associations, while households farmed about 49% (the other 8% was presumably still held by state farms). Private farmers tended to work smallholdings, averaging 2.5 ha in three parcels (Bulgaru *et al.*, 1992, p. 17).

14.6 Conclusion

Over the period 1990–93, ownership has been restored for a large portion of Romanian land. Many rural households face difficult conditions for private farming, however. Landholdings are small and fragmented, and land markets are not yet active. Access to inputs and equipment varies widely among *judeţs*, with many farmers dependent on large, powerful organisations for machine services and inputs. Production opportunities for small farmers are further limited by the dominant role of large state banks and firms in agricultural output markets.

Many households have chosen to recollectivise their land in new associations, and this decision is highly correlated, at both the regional and household level, with limitations on their ability to form a viable production unit. Associations compensate to some degree for poor development of markets by providing a means of consolidating land, as well as improving access to inputs, machinery and output distribution networks.

Adjustment by the associations to the new market conditions appears only partial, however. Associations report intentions to expand membership, production and borrowing, despite the depressed economic climate and the fact that many associations already report an excess of workers and inherited debt.

Further adjustments will be required if the new associations are to be a viable alternative to private farming over the longer term as markets develop. In particular, mechanisms to hold association management accountable to members for farm performance might encourage quicker adjustment. Technical assistance in the organisation of democratic governance structures, as well as new business plans, may also be necessary to smooth this adjustment and prevent further disruptions of the agricultural sector.

14.7 Acknowledgements

Much of the analysis in this chapter is drawn from research undertaken with Karen Brooks. Claudia Parliament participated in early analysis of the data. The Ministry of Agriculture and Food Industry of Romania facilitated survey design and data collection. Wim van Diepenbeck assisted in implementing the survey work. Darren Spreuuw and George Rwaga provided research assistance. Apparao Katikineni provided technical support for data analysis.

14.8 References

Bulgaru, M., *et al.*, 1992, *Probleme de baza ale agriculturii Romaniei*, Institute of Rural Economy and Sociology, Academy of Agricultural and Silvicultural Sciences, Bucharest.

EIU (Economist Intelligence Unit), 1993, *Country report: Romania, Bulgaria, Albania, 3rd quarter*, EIU, London.

EIU 1994, *Country report: Romania, Bulgaria, Albania, 3rd quarter*, EIU, London.

FBIS (Foreign Broadcast Information Service), *Daily Report*, Washington, DC.

Ianoş, I., 1992, Romanian agriculture in transition, typescript, Institute of Geography, Bucharest.

Kideckel, D., 1993, *The solitude of collectivism: region before the revolution*, Cornell University Press, Ithaca, NY.

Madgearu, V., 1940, *Evolutia economiei romanesti dupa razboiul mondial*, Bucharest.

Meurs, M., Spreeuw, D., 1994, *Rational peasants in Eastern Europe: household choice of organizational form in the agrarian transition*, American University Working Paper, Washington, DC.

Newbury, D., 1989, Agricultural institutions for insurance and stabilization, in Bardhan, P., ed., *The economic theory of agricultural institutions*, Clarendon Press, Oxford.

Paarlberg, P., 1992, *The evolving farm structure in Eastern Germany*, International Agricultural Trade Research Consortium Working Paper no. 92-9, Purdue University, Lafayette, Ind.

Roberts, H., 1951, *Rumania: political problems of an agrarian state*, Yale University Press, New Haven, Conn.

Romanian National Commission for Statistics, 1991, *Romanian statistical yearbook*, Bucharest.

Stiglitz, J., 1993, Incentives, organizational structures, and contractual choice in the reform of socialist agriculture, in Braverman, A., Avishay, A., Brooks, K., Csaki, C., *The agricultural transition in Central and Eastern Europe and the former USSR*, World Bank Symposium, Washington, DC.

Survey Data, 1991, World Bank and Romanian Government Survey, AGRAP Division, World Bank, Washington, DC.

Turnock, D., 1986, *The Romanian economy in the twentieth century*, Croom Helm, London.

Verdery, K., 1994, The elasticity of land: problems of property restitution in Transylvania, unpublished manuscript, Department of Anthropology, Johns Hopkins University, Baltimore, Md.

15

Problems of Bulgarian rural land reform

Sarah Monk

15.1 Introduction

This chapter considers the transformation of agriculture in Bulgaria from a state-run, monolithic, inefficient and outmoded system into a modern, fully decentralised and privatised sector that aims to be internationally competitive at least in the long term. Reforms introduced in 1990 and 1991 were designed to encourage the private ownership of land and the break-up of the collective farms. The reform of the agricultural sector involves a wide range of objectives, including not only farm output, but also input supply, agri-processing and marketing. This chapter, however, is concerned primarily with land reform. Land restitution is seen as a prior objective, and wider reform of the agricultural sector is not thought to be possible until this has been achieved.

Land reform in Bulgaria is taking place against a background of economic crisis. Annual inflation had been up to 300% (Milner, 1992) and is still of the order of 80%. Interest rates, although recently reduced, were 45% in September 1993. Output has fallen steeply in the early 1990s (Milner, 1993). In early 1994 unemployment was estimated at around 16%, but this national average figure hides pockets of extreme severity: around 40% of the unemployed are younger than 30 years old and about a third have never had a job.

The underlying problem is the way in which a centrally run economy can be transformed to a free market economy, and in particular how a free market in agriculture can be introduced. Agriculture is an important sector in any economy, but in Bulgaria it stirs deep-seated emotions concerning the nation's peasant roots and fears about food shortages. This is understandable, given recent shortages in Russia, Yugoslavia and Albania. Although such shortages have not yet affected Bulgaria, in the face of annual warnings, this does not make people's fears any less real.

There are additional reasons for concern. People are deeply worried about the fate of agriculture in the face of market competition, and the call for protection is strong. In the predemocratic economy, Bulgarian wheat supplied Russia and the former East Germany and, for example, the Bulgarian wine industry created highly successful export links with Western countries such as the UK.

The current situation is made more difficult when it is remembered that the original move to

Reconstructing the Balkans: A Geography of the New Southeast Europe. Edited by Derek Hall and Darrick Danta.
©1996 John Wiley & Sons Ltd

Communism came after a long war with severe suffering and deprivation. As in Britain, the first 30 years following the Second World War were a period of sustained growth. Living standards rose, and Bulgaria moved from a poor, largely peasant economy to a much wealthier and more modern state capitalist system—partly industrialised and with a modernised agriculture. It is usually easier to implement dramatic changes during a period of economic growth, a factor which may well have contributed to Communism's stability for so long.

With global recession and world trade at a post-war low, a dramatic change such as that from a state-run to a market economy is much more difficult to implement. It will undoubtedly make many people poorer, and the current levels of unemployment and inflation suggest that it is already doing so. The overall average unemployment figure of 16% in 1992 masked higher levels in the larger towns and cities. Female unemployment has been around 20% higher than male, and rising at a faster rate. Democracy is still fragile, and there is a real possibility that the impoverished people will vote the 'old guard' back into power at a future date if the new government cannot deliver.

The establishment of secure and tradable property rights in land is one of the most complex aspects of the transition to a market economy. A distinctive feature of Bulgaria's land reforms has been the decision to return the land to its 1946 owners. This is an explicitly political decision, as land restitution could have been undertaken in a number of alternative ways. This policy is difficult to implement, not least because long-term rural to urban migration has meant that some 40% of the 1946 owners, or their heirs, are no longer connected with the land in any way (Dinkov, 1992).

15.2 The problem

The former collective farms (TKZs) were vast and often encompassed as many as 20 villages and municipalities which themselves varied in

size from tiny hamlets to small country towns. In an attempt to modernise Bulgaria's agriculture, enormous agro-industrial complexes were formed at the end of the 1960s embracing agriculture-related industries such as canning factories, fodder units and food-processing plants (Entwistle, 1972). Although most of these complexes were disbanded during the 1980s when the industrial aspects became independent once more, there existed a huge technical, scientific and political bureaucracy to manage the vast collective farms that remained. The central headquarters of the state farm was generally located in the largest village, with local outposts in most of the others, although the precise arrangements varied with the size and extent of the farm. During the first decades after the Second World War, agriculture was 'modernised' and large sums of capital were spent on machinery, including heavy equipment such as tractors and combine harvesters. Enormous dairying complexes were built; and even in the mountain areas huge tobacco-drying plants were erected, some of which have never been used.

Under the previous system, the land and property rights of individual farmers and co-operatives had been expropriated by the state. The allocation and control of farm resources were centralised into a variety of state and collective agencies who were assumed to be more efficient, more knowledgeable and more able to serve the public interest than the individual farmers they replaced:

The result was a period of cavalier experimentation that severed the links of individual ownership and responsibility for land and farm assets (and even the jurisdictions of the various local authorities), enormously complicating current efforts to re-establish those rights (Hopcraft, 1992, p. 1).

The current reform programme recognises the problems that have been inherited from the previous system and attempts to match the complexity and the scale of the problems it seeks to address. These include not just the need to return expropriated land to private hands, but also the fact that the bureaucracy which ran the agricultural sector was itself removed from commercial incentives for cost-saving, efficiency or even investment—including the most basic investment of maintaining and improving the productivity of the land and related farm assets such as buildings, equipment and animals.

The result has been a systematic deterioration in the performance and productivity of Bulgarian agriculture relative to its potential, and the failure of the sector to respond innovatively to the opportunities for technical changes, and to the multiple market openings for its products (Hopcraft, 1992, p. 1).

The current reform programme thus has three main components:

1. To re-establish ownership rights over land and farm assets in a manner that is both speedy and perceived as being fair and legitimate.
2. To enable the establishment of free market institutions, including individual family farms, partnerships, cooperatives, joint stock companies and others in which owners may choose to manage their land and other assets.
3. To facilitate the full range of transactions between individuals and agencies, including outright sale, leasing, mortgaging, sharecropping and other arrangements that allow different agents to combine their land, finance, equipment, labour and other skills in order to farm the land. The central task is seen as establishing the legal, regulatory and information basis for making such transactions as secure and open as possible.

15.2.1 Land restitution

The first aspect of the reform programme is causing the greatest problems. There are two main issues: restitution of private property rights and the liquidation of the collective farms. Both of these have important political underpinnings and implications.

The government of 1990 introduced legislation designed to return all land within the aegis of the TKZs to the people who had owned the land in 1946 (or their heirs). New municipal land commissions were established in order to under-take this task. Land restitution was to take place on the basis of the 1946 boundaries wherever possible, and special arrangements were to be made where this was not feasible, usually because these boundaries had been obliterated (for example, by urban or highway development). An EC PHARE/World Bank report (PHARE/WBTF, 1992) argued that this aspect of land reform was a precondition for both the liquidation of the TKZs and the creation of a land market. In addition it noted that delay in land restitution was hampering agricultural production and investment, resulting in the neglect of orchards, irrigation systems and land protection.

In 1991 a new government (Union of Democratic Forces (UDF)) was elected which set about making further changes to the legislation in order to expedite the reform programme. The new Law on Ownership and Use of Farm Land (LOUFL) which had been promulgated in February 1991, was amended along with its implementing regulations in the spring of 1992. Most restrictions, such as those on the right to sell land, were removed from the earlier Act, and responsibility for implementation was transferred to the Ministry of Agriculture from the National Land Council, which was abolished. 'The task of organising a practical implementation mechanism is not yet finished and the prospects for a rapid transformation remain uncertain' (PHARE/WBTF, 1992, p. 3).

The main reasons for the delay have been complex:

1. In about a quarter of all cases, the boundaries between the former TKZs and between local authorities (communes) are in dispute because over the past 40 years administrative areas have been redefined three times. In addition the earliest TKZs have been amalgamated into larger concerns; agro-industrial complexes were created and then disbanded; and in most cases there is inadequate documentation or mapping of these changes. This conflict over boundaries between localities means that claimants to land often do not know in which

commune to file their claims, such that even the filing of land claims is incomplete.

2. Similarly, documentation concerning individual claims to land is missing or incomplete in many cases. This has led to multiple claims for the same land.

3. Some land is no longer available for restitution, because settlements have grown, railways and roads have been built, dams and irrigation systems have been introduced. Such developments have also interfered with the real former boundaries of 1946. So some claimants cannot be given their original land, and the allocation of alternative land of equal quality is likely to create problems and further disputes.

4. In disputes over decisions made by the municipal land commissions, claimants have no recourse except through the courts. This is expensive, and people do not always have faith that the outcome will be fair and just.

5. Administrators seem hidebound by the need for a full national cadastral survey as a prior condition for a land registration scheme, ignoring advice that existing methods and systems should be used unaltered in order to make progress with land restitution. A land registration scheme and a full national cadastre are two separate issues (although they can and should be combined at a later stage). Boundaries can be measured with a lower degree of accuracy than required for a full cadastre, using existing equipment. This would be sufficient to permit full and permanent title to land.

6. Computers to undertake land registration and processing claims are in short supply. Claims are being processed manually, which takes time. There is also a severe shortage of surveying equipment and trained staff to undertake the survey work deemed necessary to determine the 1946 boundaries.

7. There is no incentive for the municipal land commissions to speed up the process of land restitution. Rather, there is every incentive for them to delay the process for as long as possible. This is because such commissions are to be disbanded as soon as their task is

complete, and in the current economic climate their members are understandably unwilling to lose their jobs.

8. Some of the municipal land commissions are composed of members of the political opposition who are against such large-scale land reform and are deliberately presenting obstacles. In 1992 the Ministry of Agricultural Development conducted a performance review of the councils, and staff of about 140 of them have been replaced (Dinkov, 1992).

15.2.2 Liquidation of farm assets

The liquidation of the collective farms is carried out by liquidation committees. They are chaired by independent outsiders, but their composition includes some of the 'experts' from the old TKZ. Thus in Bansko, a collective in the southwest of Bulgaria, for example, the chair was (and still is) a forestry manager, and other members include the agronomist and the dairying expert from the old TKZ. Again there is the problem that when the task of liquidating the collective farm is completed, the members of the committee will be out of a job. In addition, while at Bansko all the committee members were reported to be in favour of the reforms, this is not the case in all parts of Bulgaria, and where there is local opposition the committee's task is made more difficult.

The functions of the committees are: (a) to continue to manage and run the collective farm and other former agricultural units during the interim period; (b) to determine the value of shares of all those who contributed to the original farm when it was first established; and (c) to liquidate the non-land assets of the farm according to what have been called 'unrealistically complex formulae' (PHARE/WBTF, 1992, p. 14).

A problem here is that accountancy as a profession is in its infancy in Bulgaria and therefore there is very little expertise in the valuation of assets. Furthermore, how can the assets be given a market value when there is no market for them? One solution has been to introduce open auctions, and to simplify the valuation of the non-land assets using values obtained from them. But even this is difficult because there has been no experience of auctions for so many years.

A second problem is that some collective farms in effect have no non-land assets. All they have are debts. In addition they are not only often in dispute with local authorities, but also with the separate state enterprises which were established under the Communist regime to 'own' all the machinery and transportation equipment of the TKZs. This equipment, including tractors and lorries, was originally 'transferred' from the farms into the control of the specialist agencies, but there are now disputes over which body actually owns the assets. The liquidation committees wish to retain such equipment within the local area.

A further problem is that in the cereal-growing areas the 1946 boundaries are considered totally inappropriate for modern cereal production. In 1946 Bulgaria was still basically a peasant economy, and individual landholdings were typically very small (0.16 ha on average) (Dinkov, 1992). To return to the 1946 boundaries is seen as retrogressive, and detrimental to the degree of modernisation in agriculture which has been achieved. Modernisation has been greater in cereal production than other sectors. Therefore many 1946 owners have attempted to form cooperatives, and to pool their land claims. But the UDF government has resisted this, as it has been suspicious of people's motives. There is much rumour that the 'old guard' still has a stronghold in many rural areas, and any moves to create cooperatives are viewed by the authorities as not to be trusted.

Foreign advisers have consistently recommended that the government accepts these pooled claims to land, if only on a temporary basis, until a proper land market can be established. When that happens, there will be a range of structures that can be adopted in order to purchase or lease land in various quantities, possibly including formal cooperatives. Meanwhile, another government was elected in October 1992, nominally 'non-party' but supported by the Bulgarian Socialist Party which includes many former Communists. Land reform is still 'political dynamite' (Milner, 1993, p. 35).

A further political reason for the delay in introducing a real market in land—foreign landownership is not permitted, and local people have no cash—lies in fears that too much would go to the Turks. There is also a rumour, so firmly believed that it has taken on the aspect of truth, that there is an overhang of 'red' money held abroad—stashed away in Swiss banks by corrupt party officials during the worst days of the old regime—and if markets were fully liberalised this money would flood into the country, further fuelling inflation and harming local people's interests.

15.3 Solutions

The main theme of this chapter is the problem of transforming agriculture from a state-run to a free market system. Even this is a misnomer, because all developed economies subsidise their agricultural sectors. But agricultural subsidies are expensive, have led to overproduction and have resulted in high prices to consumers. Notwithstanding the eventual nature of Bulgaria's agricultural sector, land reform is a priority. The legislation introduced to implement land reform is unduly complex, but the obstacles to land reform are also complex and should not be underestimated. They have been compounded by the frequent changes in government since 1990.

The agricultural strategy recommended by the PHARE/World Bank team (PHARE/WBTF, 1992) echoed recommendations made by other consultants. It is based on four main actions: (a) simplify and speed up the establishment of private property rights in agriculture and related industries; (b) complete the liberalisation of prices and trade; (c) promote a sustainable finance and credit system; and (d) stimulate institutional support for a commercially viable agriculture. This is based on the view that a competitive and healthy agricultural sector depends on people who are motivated to work hard to secure that end. The best motivation is seen to be provided by private property—that is, by ensuring that individuals have secure ownership or use rights in the land—and also by ensuring undistorted price signals so that farmers can make the right decisions over such activities as planting. Only in such circumstances, it is argued, will farmers be willing and able to borrow funds for working capital and investment—including seed and fertilisers. All this requires a legal and institutional framework which is currently lacking in Bulgaria.

15.3.1 Landownership rights

The restoration of landownership rights is seen as a priority, but should be kept separate from the process of finding suitable organisational forms for agriculture, such as limited companies, cooperatives or private farms. Instead, while the government should play the key role in restoring property rights, it should be up to individuals, groups and organisations to choose the form of agricultural organisation they prefer. This consideration is seen as important in moving the authorities, and indirectly the Bulgarian people, away from paternalistic, centralised decision-making and towards the ideology of a free market economy.

There are three main elements of restoring property rights: the restitution of land, the reallocation of non-land assets of collective farms through liquidation, and the privatisation of assets in related industries. All three are under way, but they should be refocused and accelerated. In July 1992, the government set itself the objective to settle land claims in detail sufficient to provide the basis for a legal title to 15–25% of applicants by December 1992 and to substantially complete the process by December 1993. This was seen as an ambitious target, and not surprisingly it has not been met, with only about half the applications having been settled within the allotted time. As the simplest claims will have been settled first, often it is more complex and difficult ones which have been left outstanding.

The municipal land commissions (MLCs) should be strengthened, replacing ineffective staff, and providing training and additional resources. Furthermore, the government should use publicity and public information to a much greater extent as a tool to help speed up the process. For example, a summary table and a map of Bulgaria showing progress in land surveys and reallocations of the 320 MLCs should be published on a regular basis (Dinkov, 1992).

Liquidation of collective farms should have been completed by the 1993 spring planting season without waiting for the full restoration of landownership rights but unsurprisingly it was not. New landowners should be encouraged to take over their land, and the assets of the collective farms should be auctioned off. Outstanding debts should be settled as a part of this process. However, there is considerable worry that totally free and open auctions might benefit outsiders and not the original contributors to the collective farm. Therefore it has been suggested (PHARE/WBTF, 1992, p. 16) that auctions could be based on coupons rather than money, with the additional proviso that the government may have to write off much of the debt. (Where this consists of unpaid taxes, the government is of course the main creditor.)

15.3.2 Privatisation of the food industry

The second priority, related to land reform, is the privatisation of the rest of the food industry—input supply, food processing and food distribution. This is essential to establish competitive markets in agriculture. Most agro-processing state-owned enterprises (SOEs) have been administratively reorganised into smaller units, but they tend to remain geographical monopolies because there is no competition from independent concerns, and are being registered as limited liability or joint stock companies. However, the government continues to intervene in price setting and in agricultural protection policy. There are good political reasons for this, not least galloping inflation, so that domestic prices for about 30 basic foodstuffs are being kept below world prices. One side-effect of this policy is that such administered prices tend to restrain competition and perpetuate the cost-plus pricing mentality of the past.

15.3.3 Price and trade liberalisation

Currently, controls on trade (mainly export quotas) are used to keep consumer prices of essential foods below world prices. But these restrictions isolate the domestic economy, much as during the Communist period. Despite the stated goal of guaranteeing prices for producers, the main effect is to repress producer prices and to obstruct the development of an open market-ing and trade system.

There is also a system of minimum export prices. This was designed to prevent inexper-ienced traders from buying at low domestic prices and undercutting prices for Bulgarian products on world markets. If trade constraints could really raise prices for Bulgarian exports, the most effective way would be through an export tax. But there is little scope for Bulgaria to influence international prices. An export tax would just reduce Bulgaria's share in world markets and repress prices for domestic producers.

15.3.4 Finance and credit

It is crucial for Bulgarian agriculture that finance and credit are available, both as working capital (seed and fertiliser) and for investment. At present investment in Bulgaria is repressed by uncertainty. The responsibility for investment decisions will remain unclear until the land reform process and liquidation of collectives is complete. Additional uncertainties will remain: high inflation and high nominal interest rates, reflecting macroeconomic instability, are deter-ring investment in agricultural production.

Clearly the current reform of the financial sector has disrupted the traditional flow of credit to agriculture. Commercial lending has declined dramatically because the unfinished land reform process leaves producers (farmers) without collateral. In the short term there is a need for special credit programmes to help overcome the shortage of working capital. But the government should not provide this as it would impose an unduly heavy budgetary burden and, rather like temporary price interventions, would serve to delay the continuing development of a proper system of credit. Instead, temporary land alloca-tions should be used as collateral for loans, and the use of future physical output should also be investigated (PHARE/WBTF, 1992, pp. 43–4). The current Civil Procedural Code should be revised so that private citizens can secure loans against the collateral of houses and agricultural land, and also so that creditors could, if necessary, sell the assets of defaulters.

15.3.5 Institutional support

There is a need for a fundamental change in institutional responsibilities. A wide range of functions previously undertaken by ministries, state agencies, SOEs and collective farms need to be taken over by private sector institutions, firms and farmers. The most efficient way to promote this is to restore and create private property rights. This involves building a legal framework which incorporates both contract law and bank-ruptcy law, and providing training and support services. It also requires information. There is a further problem of rural development in a broader sense, and the need to reduce regional disparities. However, it is clear that in the medium term at least, the best form of rural development is to develop and modernise the agricultural sector, and any regional aid should be administered and ideally financed by local government, although funding could be 'equal-ised' to some extent by diverting funds from wealthier to poorer authorities.

Reform of the agricultural sector, while a priority, is enmeshed within the wider reforms in other sectors of the economy. Institutional re-forms are thus vital for all of Bulgaria, not just agriculture. And within this process, land reform remains a clear priority.

15.4 Conclusions

The underlying problematic of this chapter is the question of how to move from a centrally run to a market economy without so disadvantaging certain groups as to jeopardise the new democracy, or worse still, arouse conflict.

In this context it is interesting to note that *The Economist* (Anon, 1992), predicted conflict in Bulgaria arising from ethnic antagonisms. The predictions were proved wrong; but the economic situation in Bulgaria is not so much improved as to remove the danger entirely. Clearly the transition period will continue to be stormy; and the agricultural sector and the related food industries are a crucial part of the transition.

The question is begged of what constitutes a market economy, especially in agriculture. Most teams of consultants selected by the EC PHARE programme seemed to agree that of all sectors agriculture should be free from subsidies and controls, because only then can the population benefit from lower world food prices. Yet all Western governments subsidise their agriculture.

A further question is the extent to which ownership is seen as crucial to the transition from a centrally run to a market economy. To the outside observer, a system of leasing or subcontracting the farming of land could also produce a market system. However, leasing and subcontracting still involve some form of property rights and for the system to work, these property rights must be fully supported in law. It is the lack of a wider supporting legal framework that is one of the major constraints on the development of a market system in agriculture in Bulgaria.

15.5 References

Anon, 1992, Macedonia: an old conflict, *The Economist*, 14 November.

Dinkov, A., 1992, *Personal interviews*, Bulgarian Minister for Agriculture, Sofia, 6 and 10 July.

Entwistle, E. W., 1972, Agro-industrial complexes in Bulgaria, *Geography*, **57**(3), 246–8.

Hopcraft, P., 1992, *Farm land and assets*, unpublished paper, The World Bank, Washington, DC.

Milner, M., 1992, An economy facing a lengthy sentence, *The Guardian*, 5 September.

Milner, M., 1993, Struggling economy threatens to keep Bulgaria out in the cold, *The Guardian*, 4 September.

PHARE/WBTF (World Bank Task Force), 1992, *An agricultural strategy for Bulgaria*, Agricultural Policy Analysis Unit, Bulgarian Ministry for Agricultural Development, Land Use and Land Restitution, Sofia.

16

Market reforms and environmental protection in the Bulgarian tourism industry

Boian Koulov

16.1 The Bulgarian tourism industry in transition: illusions and reality

International tourism in Bulgaria had enjoyed preferential treatment from the state since the late 1950s, when its large-scale development began. The ability of this 'hidden export' to generate hard currency was of primary importance to state decision-makers. The resulting tourist 'boom' put the population, especially along the Black Sea coast, in frequent contact with foreigners, including West Europeans. The greater exposure and increased acquaintance with market relations, as well as the favourable combination of natural resources and tourist infrastructure, created, after the 1989 political change, high expectations for rapid economic success among the local populace.

The results from both the 1990 and 1991 parliamentary elections (*The 1990 Elections in Bulgaria*; 'The October 1991 Elections') demonstrated that the population in counties with traditions in international tourism were, generally, more supportive of the rapid abolition of state ownership and regulation compared to

most other regions in the country. In the summer of 1992, at the time when, officially, over 50% of the labour force in the Black Sea resort town of Nesebar was unemployed, about 60% of the families opened trading stands, small shops, cafes, restaurants, bars and even picture and craft galleries in their houses and garages. The tourist season earnings generally had been enough to sustain the local population throughout the year. Thus, compared to industry for example, international tourism retained, even increased, its traditionally high economic status and created, especially in the smaller coastal counties, a 'comparative advantage' mentality, which assumed almost immediate affluence under the new market conditions. By 1993, over 3000 private companies were engaged in tourism in Bulgaria.

This favourable view of the tourism industry's economic adaptability was also shared and promoted by the national government ('Development of the tourist industry', 1990). Besides agriculture, international tourism was the first economic branch scheduled for privatisation; about 50% of all hotels, restaurants and other

Reconstructing the Balkans: A Geography of the New Southeast Europe. Edited by Derek Hall and Darrick Danta.
©1996 John Wiley & Sons Ltd

tourist facilities were expected to be privatised by 1995 (Dimitrov, 1993). Tourism's capacity to employ, directly and indirectly, significant labour resources, which numbered 120 000 in 1993 as opposed to 70 000 in 1989 (Dimitrov, 1993), its relatively short turnover cycle and its links to a wide spectrum of businesses, furthered expectations that it would be the development 'locomotive' at both the local and regional levels.

The analysis of the external conditions and internal developments within the tourism industry in the period 1990–94, however, showed reality to be more complex than state-level plans and local expectations. While the lion's share of Bulgaria's tourism market had traditionally been oriented towards Eastern European and Soviet tourists, the impact of the political and economic transformations there was not conducive to international tourism. In the 1990 and 1991 seasons, the sharp decrease in tourists from Eastern Europe was partially offset by an unusually high influx of Russians due to the lifting of their travel restrictions. However, although accurate data about the number of tourists cannot be provided because most of the visits are not registered to avoid taxation, the political and economic insecurity that later came with the fragmentation of the Soviet Union and the civil war in neighbouring Yugoslavia severely decreased the overall number of visitors. Another external factor contributing to the decline in the number of tourists to Bulgaria was the much broader choice of destinations (e.g. Spain, Cyprus, Greece, Italy) which East Europeans, freed from the numerous administrative and currency restrictions, enjoyed in the new political situation (Hall, 1991, 1992). In general, the 1989 upheaval in Eastern Europe and the dissolution of the Soviet Union had a negative influence on Bulgaria's international tourism: overnight stays by foreign tourists in 1990 were 12.8 million, but dropped to 4.7 million in 1991, 5.6 million in 1992, and 7.5 million in 1993 (*Statisticheski*, 1994).

The political instability and the continuously worsening economic conditions in Bulgaria also negatively affected the image of the Bulgarian tourism market. In addition, the administrators of Balkantourist, the former state monopoly in the international tourism business, allegedly attempted to dissuade potential Western buyers and to capitalise on discount prices at the pending privatisation of the tourism industry. For example, Balkantourist offices abroad refused to accept reservations and disseminated false information that hotels in Bulgaria were 'booked'. These activities corresponded to the similar strategy in industry, in which factory managers intentionally led factories into bankruptcy in order to buy them off at lower cost. This policy served also to justify the drastic personnel cuts needed as part of the pre-privatisation restructuring: in the period 1990–92, the number of offices abroad decreased from 27 to 10.

16.2 Market reforms at the local level: the tourism industry in Nesebar County

Over the last several decades, the tourism industry vividly demonstrated its development potential along the Bulgarian Black Sea coast. It had also played the primary role in sustaining the relative standard of living of Nesebar's population during the extremely difficult economic situation since 1990. Situated in the northern part of the Burgas district, this seaside county of approximately 15 000 people encompasses the largest Bulgarian resort with over 108 hotels: Slanchev bryag (*Statisticheski*, 1991). Such a large territorial concentration of tourist assets whetted substantial privatisation appetites, and provides a unique opportunity to study the introduction of market reforms and their environmental implications on the local level.

Besides Slanchev bryag, three additional case studies within the county are analysed in a comparative perspective: (1) the state hunting enterprise (SHE), (2) the town of Nesebar (the administrative centre of the county), and (3) the small seaside village of Vlas. In the cases of Vlas and Nesebar, the inquiry will focus on the changes in mostly private tourist businesses. In contrast, SHE and the Slanchev bryag resort provide examples of market reform effects on state firms of different size, profile and future status.

16.2.1 The Slanchev bryag (Sunny beach) resort

The former tourist complex, Slanchev bryag, is a case of a large state company under privatisation. Before 1989, the complex was a local branch of the Balkantourist state company. For over a decade, its administrative structure had been the focus of constant reorganisations, reflecting the national government's desire to increase economic performance. Under the Zhivkov regime, the changes were generally directed towards greater decentralisation to create a self-financing, self-managing firm. In that sense, the 13 November 1989 political change did not set a new goal. Greater emphasis, however, was placed on privatisation of the resort's fixed assets as a result of the changed political climate.

In 1990–91, privatisation was advertised as a 'panacea' for Slanchev bryag's economic and organisational problems, and few disputed its necessity. Conflicts arose, however, as to whether the centralised management structure of the resort should survive the resort's privatisation, and, in relation to that, which administrators and employees would retain their positions. Similar to other economic branches, the government established a so-called 'liquidation commission' to facilitate the transition to privatisation and placed at its head the former director-general of the Balkantourist–Slanchev bryag office. At the end of 1991, the commission divided the resort into 13 limited liability firms (LTDs), usually comprised of several neighbouring hotels and their adjoining restaurants. Some additional firms, such as 'Hotels, LTD' and 'Restaurants, LTD', were also set up, which consisted of the older and lesser attractive hotels and restaurants. Initially, these firms were scheduled to be privatised first.

The liquidation commission's actions, however, were shrouded with the familiar old veil of secrecy that had obscured organisational and personnel changes in the past. The resort was reorganised without any prior announcement, publicity, preset rules or regulations, auctions or trade union participation. The commission's excuse was the absence of privatisation legislation. As a consequence, the 'liquidators' were widely accused of having manipulated the process in order to avoid outside competition. Some alleged that part of the resort's property had been leased to banks (First Eastern International Bank) and money-laundering firms (Anzhel) under questionable financial terms (Kostova, 1994). Media reports and widespread rumours suggested that a newly established 'mafia' was ruining the resort and its image abroad in order to run it into the ground and then buy it at low cost from the state.

These 'crypto-privatisation' policies succeeded in preventing foreign investment. In 1991, the attempts of several Turkish businessmen to lease between three and five hotels were turned down because of the long-term character of the offer. The first and only foreign investor in Slanchev bryag was the British owner of the Red Lion public house, who secured a 50-year lease, which was later disputed by Nesebar County authorities.

In the beginning of July 1991 and 1992, the resort housed only about 7000 tourists though it had a total capacity of 27 000 beds. By the end of the month, the hotels were full, but the overall seasonal occupancy rate had drastically decreased in contrast to the pre-1989 period. Despite a twofold reduction of the service personnel in 1992, such cuts were not enough to produce a normal salary for the remaining employees. Cleaning personnel, for instance, were paid below the minimum salary, creating the appearance that the hotels were kept in operation only to prevent greater unemployment.

In spite of the pre-privatisation restructuring of Balkantourist, its top management level was retained in the form of a separate firm. In 1993, it controlled the resort's auxiliary services, which included the landscape and environmental protection department, education complex, laundry facilities, retail trade system, and the general maintenance and construction company. Although substantially transformed, this remaining Balkantourist firm was still best positioned to serve as the basis of a holding company—the widely preferred type of firm to manage the resort in the future.

16.2.2 The Nesebar state hunting enterprise

The Nesebar SHE is an example of a state enterprise that is not likely to be privatised in the immediate future. It was neither the largest nor the most successful enterprise of this kind in the Burgas district, and its attraction was due largely to its close proximity to both the town of Nesebar and the Slanchev bryag resort.

Bulgaria is recognised internationally for the qualities of its game hunting, which turned international hunting tourism into one of the most profitable branches of the tourist business in the country. Before 1989, as part of the centrally planned economic system, hunting tourism had a highly centralised and specialised structure; Balkantourist's Hunting and Angling Department enjoyed an uncontested monopoly in setting prices and marketing Bulgarian hunting and tourism abroad. All state hunting enterprises were managed by the firm Mourgash under the Ministry of Forestry, which also instituted the environmental regulations in the territory. Only about 25% of the area of the Nesebar SHE (a total of 8745 ha) was used for hunting, which demonstrates the priority given to wildlife preservation. The only other firm that offered hunting services to foreign tourists, Sokol, was affiliated with the Bulgarian Hunters and Anglers Union, which managed their own special hunting grounds.

Hunting enterprises enjoyed relatively high investment during Communist rule, since hunting was a particularly fashionable hobby among the *nomenklatura*. Although international hunting was a highly efficient tourist industry—in the 1980s, profitability in the Nesebar enterprise was

about 300%, not to mention the advantage of converting Bulgarian leva investments into hard currency earnings—the economic conditions in this sphere also considerably deteriorated following the overall downward trend in the Bulgarian economy after October 1989. The stigma of having been a *nomenklatura* sport fostered the perception that hunting was inessential, rather than an efficient branch of the tourism industry. As a result, investment in the industry practically ceased and its infrastructure gradually deteriorated. The organisational restructuring of Balkantourist further compounded such problems. With the state monopoly in international tourism broken, many new firms, Bulgarian as well as foreign, began to market hunting trips in Bulgaria abroad. However, among the Bulgarian firms, only Balkantourist possessed the necessary infrastructure and personnel to carry out this type of service.

In the early 1990s, the Nesebar SHE was able to sustain itself because several of its permanent clients, who had previously booked their trips through an intermediate organisation, now worked directly with the Nesebar SHE. The cooperation with Slanchev bryag was also of immense importance. The resort was diversifying its service mix by offering a number of ecologically sound activities, such as photo-hunting trips, visual hunting excursions and target practice with hunting rifles. Another result of the geographic proximity and the mutually beneficial collaboration between the resort and the hunting enterprise was the shared use of accommodation. This arrangement for the time being eliminated the need for the Nesebar SHE to invest in a new hunting lodge.

Nevertheless, the market reforms put much stronger pressure on the Nesebar SHE administration to demonstrate initiative and flexibility. The existing lodge was leased to a private firm for three years in exchange for its refurbishing. This special lease agreement allowed the firm to use the lodge only in the hunting off-season. Despite the sharply decreased number of tourists in 1992, the Nesebar SHE succeeded in earning the projected DM 150 000. Thus, it appeared as though the international hunting market would successfully regain its former economic position. There were legitimate concerns, however, that in the absence of future state subsidies, the enterprise would not be able to fulfil its major responsibilities towards the protection and rehabilitation of the forest and wildlife which, ironically, constituted its basic commercial resource. Accompanying the sharply increased prices of basic products and the continuing impoverishment of the majority of the population were dramatic escalations in incidents of poaching and illegal lumbering.

16.2.3 The town of Nesebar

Even before 1989, tourist business in the town of Nesebar was mostly private, which, with the advent of market relations, gave this extremely picturesque ancient port an edge over the large neighbouring resort. It was Slanchev bryag's proximity and regular public transportation links, however, that had transformed Nesebar into a popular tourist attraction—a supplement to the booming and, in peak season, over-crowded beach resort. The introduction of market reforms in the early 1990s did not substantially alter the mutually dependent relationship between the state resort, which attracted foreign tourists and linked the county to the national and world economy, and Nesebar, the county's administrative centre, which provided the natural and labour resources as well as the general infrastructure.

The post-1989 economic and political realities, however, produced distinctive adjustment strategies in the mostly private and unregulated tourist business in Nesebar compared to the nearby, large state-owned resort. Private entrepreneurship and tax evasion, which became the rule in this period of transition, enabled the town's residents to dramatically increase not only the quality, but the variety, of the tourist services offered. Thus, residents could successfully address the most persistent deficiency in the Bulgarian tourist industry—service quality.

However, the sudden almost total disappearance of the state during the transition stage brought about some unexpected and unwanted consequences. Prior to 1989, Slanchev bryag provided about 80% of the county's income. The symbiotic relationship between Nesebar and Slanchev bryag meant that the beach resort's difficulties could not but negatively affect the economy of the county as a whole. Despite Nesebar's relative success, county revenue decreased because the small stock of mostly private accommodation in this town of 8600 population (*Statisticheski*, 1991) could not compensate for the financial losses of the state-owned firm with over 27 000 hotel beds.

In the absence of a properly staffed tax collection system and an almost total lack of tax enforcement, authorities had difficulty effectively confronting mass tax evasion. Furthermore, new resource needs, associated with the market transition, coincided with the county's revenue crisis so the administration was forced to create new sources of funding. One typical example was the 2–3 million leva 'land for hospital' swap with the Trade bank 'Slanchev bryag', wherein the county provided the land and the building permit and the bank was to build and equip a hospital to serve both the tourist complex and the county. Furthermore, the sharp rise in criminal activity forced the restoration of the pre-1944 institution of county police. Four additional policemen were employed during the tourist season in an effort to bring the criminal activity (mostly burglary) under control.

County authorities sought to explain many of these difficulties as evidence of 'mental inertia', which stemmed from the old totalitarian ways of thinking. Accustomed to depending on and blaming the state for everything, residents displayed little initiative as far as the county problems were concerned. On the other hand, the oversimplified, vulgar perceptions of capitalism and the 'free' market also promoted widespread efforts to cheat the state in every way possible. For instance, to avoid control, most commercial transactions were conducted in cash, electricity was stolen from the national power grid, and street vendors simply refused to pay taxes as part of the pervasive drive to get rich 'overnight'.

In spite of the difficulties Nesebar encountered in the transition period, its private sector began to expand rapidly. This was most evident in the different business strategies adopted by Nesebar's private entrepreneurs versus those implemented by the administrators of the large state-owned tourist firms in Slanchev bryag. The state firm Balkantourist continued to run an accommodation bureau in Nesebar, though it could not compete with the town's private entrepreneurs and served an almost insignificant number of tourists. More significantly, even though the state-owned firm retained its international network through its offices abroad, it proved to be uncompetitive with the 'personalised' approach of Nesebar's private firms. In the summer of 1992, for example, Balkantourist had only attracted a small number of English tourists, far fewer than in previous years. At the same time, a number of private firms actively performed the function of tour operators, luring tourists to Nesebar's private lodgings. In 1991, this success was attributed largely to the Yugoslav market, but the war in that country quickly ended this promising relationship.

Two, presumably opposite, strategies could be identified in Nesebar's private tourist business in the period 1990–93. First, the 'personalised approach', which offered highly specialised service, mostly to Westerners, who traditionally visited the same houses every year or who were referred to relatives or acquaintances. This system showed very promising results: nearly one-third of the rooms in Nesebar were occupied through such host–client networks. The second business strategy employed by Nesebar's new private firms can be termed 'broad diversification' in that none specialised exclusively in tourism. The ensuing lack of specialisation, however, adversely influenced the quality of the tourist product. No organisation existed to establish and control standards and/or defend the interests of private lodging owners or tourists. In addition, the absence of experience in operating within a competitive environment

was evident in the rigid price inflexibility of Nesebar's private tourism. Despite the notably smaller number of tourists, prices showed little if any change. In the all-encompassing drive for quick profit, the prevailing attitude encouraged the 'robbing' of tourists rather than service and long-term planning.

Nevertheless, the tourist industry's confidence in its ability to act as a 'locomotive' of economic recovery along the coast made most Nesebar inhabitants feel quite optimistic about their future, despite the current crisis conditions. To a significant extent, their perceptions seemed rooted in the relative advantage of Nesebar's anthropogenic and natural resources and its tourist infrastructure. This quick to develop, strongly individualistic psychology pushed many to do 'anything it took' to succeed in the newly emergent and extremely competitive business environment.

16.2.4 The village of Vlas

This small village (about 1500 people) is representative of a multitude of villages and small towns along the Bulgarian Black Sea coast, whose 'sun, sea, sand'-type resources, together with the many new, unusually large houses are their most lucrative characteristics. Vlas's private tourist business was strongly dependent on special state–private contracts that had become obsolete with the introduction of the market reforms.

Before 1989, construction permits were extremely hard to obtain because of the strict building regulations in the coastal zone, imposed for environmental protection purposes. Thus, the location of such villages became an especially attractive asset for large industrial enterprises and other organisations. In search of sites for vacation houses and camping locations, many large trade union organisations often entered into 'land for housing' swaps with seaside villagers. The plants built very large (in some cases up to five-storey) houses, which the villagers owned, used and maintained. In exchange, villagers were contractually obliged to offer most of the rooms to the enterprise during part of the summer, for a period of 20–30 years, after which they were free to do with them as they wished. In addition, they could sell to the guests additional services, as well as fresh produce from their personal plots. These arrangements were welcomed by the villagers, since construction costs for these, in effect, small private hotels (which provided a substantial part of their annual income) would have otherwise been close to impossible. In the 1980s, construction costs for these houses ran as high as 100 000 leva, while the average annual salary varied between 2000 and 3000 leva.[1]

These private hotels, which today cost millions, had a guaranteed flow of tourists and a ready market for fresh produce without any transportation or packaging expenditures. In contrast to the nearby Slanchev bryag and, to a lesser extent, Nesebar, the tourists were predominantly Bulgarians, except in the cases when trade union cooperation existed with similar enterprises from the Soviet bloc states, producing tourist exchanges.

This unique form of cooperation between state and private interests abruptly changed after 1989, with the transition to a market economy. The precarious economic condition of the majority of the state industry, especially the largest enterprises, made the 'land for housing' swaps highly unlikely. In fact, the high inflation and legal uncertainty of the post-1989 period discouraged long-term financial commitments as a rule, while the pre-privatisation restructuring of state industry[2] led to major ownership problems related

to such agreements. The inability to sustain this kind of state–private cooperative arrangement suggests that new, market-based forms of utilisation of the tourist resources will have to be employed to sustain the tourist flows to the villages and small towns along the coast.

16.3 Roadblocks on the path to reform

Market reforms and the coinciding economic crisis transformed some old contradictions in the tourist industry and provoked the emergence of new ones. An all-encompassing survival and adjustment struggle took place on all levels of government over the control of market shares and state property ownership.

On the local level, the increasingly competitive commercial environment in the town of Nesebar led to contention between local and out-of-town street vendors. During the tourist season, Nesebar's population usually increased several times, leading many outside vendors to take advantage of the multitude of foreign and domestic tourists. In an effort to counter the increased competition, local vendors pressured town officials to withhold trade permits to outsiders. Authorities resisted, claiming that this act would deprive Nesebar of at least 90% of the artists, for example, who always had been an intrinsic element of the old town's charm.

Slanchev bryag, on the other hand, was troubled by numerous landownership conflicts arising from the land restitution reform. For instance, more than 50 years before, Nesebar county had granted a large part of what now is Slanchev bryag's territory as a marriage gift to the late Bulgarian Tsar, Boris III. Yet another part of Slanchev bryag, the 'Zora' villa zone, had been built on land that had been nationalised as late as 1968. The uncertainty about eventual ownership claims inhibited the pending privatisation of the resort.

Most revealing about the problems stemming from the introduction of market reforms in post-socialist Bulgaria, however, were the

---

1. Soft currency rates are set arbitrarily; according to the official rate at that time, 1 US$ was worth about 1 Bulgarian lev, or 3–4 leva on the black market.
2. The privatisation act provides two major privatisation techniques: (a) transformation of state-owned and municipal enterprises into joint-stock or limited liability companies and sale of interest and shares therein; and (b) the sale of entire enterprises or autonomous parts thereof. Preferential terms are provided for present or former employees of the enterprise under privatisation.

contradictions between the small county of Nesebar and the largest Bulgarian resort, Slanchev bryag. The resort had always been known as the 'goose that laid golden eggs'; however, the pending privatisation increased the economic attractiveness of its fixed assets more than ever. The Nesebar County administration, which had at least nominal jurisdiction over the resort, clearly intended to participate in its privatisation and future management. In 1992, the county authorities—the majority of whom had been elected on the anti-Communist Union of Democratic Forces (UDF) ballot—shared the view that the most efficient management structure for Slanchev bryag was a holding company. They argued that a 49% state ownership of the resort's fixed assets was needed to keep them from being 'snatched for nothing'. Thus, even the resort's pavements became contested ground between the county administration and the resort's firms. Nesebar authorities maintained that the right to issue vendor permits on county territory, which includes Slanchev bryag's streets, rested solely with them. In 1992 only, revenue from issued vendor permits in Slanchev bryag amounted to over 200 000 leva.[1] The county reached agreements with most of the local firms, but settled the remaining contests in court.

To counteract the perceived encroachments by outside parties, Slanchev bryag officials launched an effort to separate the resort, which has a permanent population of over 5000, from Nesebar County administratively and give it county status. Public discussions, demonstrations and other methods were employed to promote the separation proposal. In addition to some Members of Parliament, most of the resort's employees also supported the separation since it would have allowed them to buy, at low cost, the state-built apartments they currently rented, and thus settle permanently in the resort. Such measures were pursued by other resorts as well, prompting the Council of Ministers' November

1991 decree barring resorts from acquiring separate administrative status.

The district level of administration, represented by the city of Burgas, traditionally had also promoted its own interests in the multifaceted 'cold war' for control over Slanchev bryag. The majority of the resort's administrators lived in Burgas and preferred to bring in workers from outside the county, claiming this was the only way to have some leverage over what they called the 'Nesebar mafia'. Nesebar officials, however, argued that the county's population, which at the time comprised about 70% of the resort's personnel, could certainly meet all of Slanchev bryag's staffing needs.

Even in 1992, at the time when the anti-Communist UDF formed its own national government and appointed district administrations, the UDF-dominated Nesebar authorities complained bitterly about their incapacity to deal on equal footing with the Slanchev bryag resort. No longer based on party affiliation, their criticism and corruption charges were directed against the new political élite comprised of district officials, parliamentary members and cabinet ministers whose primary goal—according to county authorities—was to use their political influence for personal benefit. The disillusionment and scepticism, which clearly ran much deeper than the usual conflicts of interest between two levels of government, prompted serious negative implications for the success of the market transformation process in Bulgaria.

16.4 Environmental implications of the transition

The exceptionally high territorial and temporal concentration of tourists in the Bulgarian coastal zone had consistently raised ecological concerns, and was continually the subject of numerous national and regional programmes and plans (Development of the tourist industry, 1990; *Plan for integrated development*, 1990). The Green System and Environmental Protection Department in Slanchev bryag dates back to the early

---

1. In 1992, 1US$ was exchanged for about 22.5 Bulgarian leva.

1960s—the time when Bulgaria adopted its first environmental legislation. By the late 1980s, the department already employed over 150 workers and specialists operating on an annual budget of about 74 million leva. In addition to its primary activities, the department also managed a large dendrarium, which ensured the diversity of the resort's vegetation and served as an attraction for 'hobby' tourists.

In general, the post-1989 transition to a market economy adversely affected the environment of Nesebar County. In many cases, it brought to the surface capitalist ethics and policies, which often ran counter to environmental preservation. Private entrepreneurs, geared towards rapid profit maximisation at any cost, and many members of the political élite tended to regard environmental protection as naïve and preposterous. For example, in 1991 a restaurant was built on a sand dune in Slanchev bryag despite the explicit prohibition of any type of construction on the beach, and a flower garden of over 40 species was turned into an open-air bar overnight with devastating effect on vegetative diversity. Seeds and seedlings were wasted in total disregard of the natural environment—the resort's primary resource. Despite the drastic reduction in the number of tourists, all monitored ecological parameters in Slanchev bryag deteriorated in the 1989–93 period.

Market reforms brought about this effect largely through their impact on the protection and rehabilitation systems. Following the post-1989 changes in the state's priorities and the respective budget restructuring, the number of employees in the Nesebar SHE decreased considerably. These developments also reflected the constant reorganisations and personnel changes in the Committee of Forestry, which in 1992 combined forest preservation and lumber production in the same department. Such 'innovative' structural fusions of functions with opposing goals (also replicated at lower levels) were especially dangerous during the period of economic crisis, when short-term economic objectives tended to prevail. In addition, despite the stringent structural adjustment measures,

timber and meat (especially game) prices increased substantially, leading to escalations in illegal lumbering and poaching. Thus, the most valuable tourist resources in the Nesebar County experienced the greatest environmental shocks.

Most dangerous because of its demoralising effects, however, was the pervasive atmosphere of lawlessness and corruption in Bulgaria. The parallel existence of pre- and post-1989 laws and regulations, as well as inadequate enforcement resources, served as a serious stumbling block for environmental protection. Only the Burgas Regional Environmental Inspectorate, rather than its Slanchev bryag branch, could enforce regulations and act to ensure rehabilitation of the damaged habitat. Despite a 1992 adjustment, it was impossible for fees and sanctions to keep up with the pace of inflation, thus rendering them completely inadequate. Some newly adopted laws (Formation of state property, 1991) did not specify any financial obligations with respect to environmental protection. This allowed individuals to lease bars, cafes and restaurants at the expense of the state infrastructure and the resort's environment.

Ecological irresponsibility, however, was not typical only of aspiring *individual* capitalists. The managers of only 9 out of the 13 state firms created in 1991 to facilitate Slanchev bryag's privatisation agreed to financially support and maintain the resort's environmental protection system. The largest and most stable firms were the first to attempt to eliminate their ecological expenses. Their managers criticised the 'monopolism' of the Environmental Protection Department, and set up their own similar departments without any assessment as to the efficiency of managing the resort's environmental system on a piecemeal basis.

16.5 Conclusion

The post-1989 developments in Bulgaria's primary tourist markets, as well as the introduction of market reforms in an atmosphere of political instability and economic crisis, were the main factors behind the negative impacts of the transition at the local level. The abrupt, almost complete disappearance of the state during this period brought considerable damage to environmental protection, rehabilitation and enforcement mechanisms. Pervasive perceptions of lawlessness and corruption stimulated the sharp rise of criminal activity, negatively affecting the tourist industry and presenting a serious obstacle for environmental protection.

The rapidly increasing role of the private sector was accompanied by widespread oversimplified notions of capitalism and free market economics, which promoted extreme individualism and spurred a massive 'get rich quick' mentality. In this period of transition, ecological irresponsibility became the norm for many managers of state firms who waged their own 'war' of survival and adaptation. Particularly damaging for the environment were the 'crypto-privatisation' strategies and the positioning struggles for participation in privatisation.

Paradoxically, the very resources on which tourism—the leading economic activity in the country—was based experienced the greatest environmental shock. The long-term state strategies to preserve and rehabilitate natural resources were replaced by short-term private interests of capital accumulation. While the tourism industry's potential to regain its former status in the international market was preserved, the future sustainable development of this environmentally sensitive branch of the economy appeared unlikely without substantial state involvement in the protection and rehabilitation of the natural and anthropogenic resources of the coastal zone.

16.6 Acknowledgements

This study is part of a project on Environmental Implications of the Political and Economic Transition in Bulgaria, sponsored by the John D. and Catherine T. MacArthur Foundation. I wish to thank Mariana Asenova and Lori Lindburg for their assistance.

16.7 References

Development of the tourist industry as a priority in the national economy, 1990, Council of Ministers, decree 35, 10 April, *State Gazette*, Sofia.

Dimitrov, M., 1993, Good prospects for Bulgarian tourism, *Bulgaria*, Touristreklama, Sofia.

Formation of state property sole proprietor companies' act, 1991, Council of Ministers, decree 152, *State Gazette*, Sofia.

Hall, D., ed., 1991, *Tourism and economics in Eastern Europe and the Soviet Union*, Belhaven, London; Halsted, New York.

Hall, D., 1992, The challenge of international tourism in Eastern Europe, *Tourism Management*, **13**(1), 41–4.

Kostova, A., 1994, Razdavai i vladei e printsip, vlastvasht v 'Slanchev bryag', *Duma*, 27 January.

Plan for integrated development of the Bulgarian southern Black Sea coast, 1990, UN Department of Technical Cooperation and the Government of Bulgaria, Sofia.

Statisticheski Godishnik na NR Bulgaria, 1991, 1994, Central Statistical Agency, Sofia.

The 1990 Elections in Bulgaria, National Republican Institute for International Affairs, Washington, DC.

The October 1991 Elections, Report of the Bulgarian Association for Fair Elections and Civil Rights, unpublished manuscript.

17

Hungary as a place of refuge

Alan Dingsdale

17.1 Introduction

During the period of Communist governments in Central and Eastern Europe, the international movement of citizens was very strictly controlled. While sponsored group travel within the bloc was inexpensive and many people were able to afford collective visits to neighbouring countries, exit and entry visa and passport regulations ensured a strict monitoring of individual movement. Travel to Western Europe was highly constrained and further encumbered by the more practical restrictions imposed by shortage of Western currencies.

During the 1980s, Hungarian governments operated a more liberal regime than others in the region. Hungary was the first country to open its border to the West, to Austria. This action played an extremely important part in the exodus of East Germans via Hungary to Austria and thence to the Western, Federal Republic of Germany during the summer of 1990. This movement was itself a very significant element in the collapse of the Communist government of the DDR (German Democratic Republic) and the subsequent reunification of Germany.

With the collapse of Communist governments across Central and Eastern Europe, the opening of international borders and the relaxation or

abolition of restrictions on movement at least from the East raised the prospect of greater freedom of international movement within the region and between the region and Western Europe. Since 1989, Central and Eastern Europe has experienced an explosion of international movement, legal and illegal, for tourist, economic, political and refuge-seeking reasons. The location of Hungary at the crossroads of the whole of Europe has meant that much of the movement has involved both permanent stay and transit across its territory. Approximately 60 million crossings of the Hungarian border were made from mid-1989 to the end of 1990 (Berényi, 1992). These changes in Central and Eastern Europe, among other factors, have led to a changing attitude in Western Europe, where the various national governments and the EC collectively have changed their policy towards migrants and refugees.

Many aspects of the refugee situation are of interest. The purpose of this chapter is to sketch in the broad picture under three headings: (a) refugee waves coming to Hungary; (b) the development of the Hungarian government's policy for dealing with refugees; (c) the response of the international community. It is not proposed to examine in detail the conditions for refugees in Hungary, nor to present a detailed

Reconstructing the Balkans: A Geography of the New Southeast Europe. Edited by Derek Hall and Darrick Danta.
©1996 John Wiley & Sons Ltd

discussion of the territorial patterns and processes.

17.2 Refugee waves entering Hungary

According to the Office of Refugees and Migration Affairs, from the beginning of 1988 to the end of 1993 some 123 833 persons were registered in Hungary as asylum seekers. While this figure is reliable for those registered, it may greatly underestimate the actual number of refugees who entered the country. In particular, it probably underestimates those fleeing the conflict in former Yugoslavia, because no visa was required to enter Hungary from Yugoslavia. Many Croatians seeking temporary refuge probably never registered as refugees. The United Nations High Commission for Refugees (UNHCR) in Budapest (Cavalieri, 1993) suggest that perhaps twice as many people as registered actually fled temporarily from Yugoslavia to Hungary. In addition many refugees arriving in Hungary from Romania applied for Hungarian citizenship rather than refugee status (Dövényi, 1993). Citizenship was readily extended to anyone born of a Hungarian mother. According to Hungarian authors, legal and illegal immigration have grown in parallel and similar trends have been recognised in ethnic Hungarian and non-Hungarian patterns (Sik, 1990; Sik and Tóth, 1993). Interior Ministry figures suggest that some 50 000 people crossed the border illegally into Hungary between 1990 and 1992. Of these, 50% had been helped by people smugglers. Between January and November 1991 Hungary deported 28 000 border violators, and in the first half of 1992 the government was negotiating for agreements concerning illegal migrants with Austria, and had agreements with Czechoslovakia, Romania, Yugoslavia and the states of the former Soviet Union. A tripartite expulsion arrangement between Hungary, Austria and Romania had not been formally signed but was operating (Joly, 1992). However, according to the Ministry of Home Affairs, for the category of asylum seekers

legal immigration now greatly outweighs illegal immigration (Table 17.1). Additionally, approximately 10 000 Arab refugees from the Gulf War and 5000–6000 Chinese entered Hungary in 1990 (Berényi, 1992), but these groups do not seem to have been registered as asylum seekers.

Hungary acceded to the 1951 Geneva Convention on Refugees in October 1989. By November 1993 only 5629 of those entering the country and registering as asylum seekers had been recognised as refugees under the terms of the Geneva Convention and the associated 1967 New York Protocols. Table 17.2 shows the number and citizenship of those registering as refugees between 1988 and 1993. It clearly shows the two waves of refugees with which Hungary has had to cope. From 1988 to 1990 the first wave originated in Romania and in 1991 the great influx of the period came from the former Yugoslavia. Figure 17.1 shows the ethnic composition of refugees arriving in Hungary between 1988 and 1993: it is primarily ethnic Hungarian. The Romanians in the first wave and the Croats and Muslims in the second wave are only the surface features. The underlying movement is one of ethnic Hungarians living among minority communities outside Hungary 'returning' to live in Hungary.

These figures were also affected by the actions of the Hungarian government. At the beginning of October 1991, restrictions on entry to

Table 17.1 *Legal and illegal refugees entering Hungary, 1988–93*

Year	% Legal	% Illegal
1988	52.5	47.7
1989	20.6	79.4
1990	81.3	18.6
1991	88.4	11.6
1992	88.3	11.7
1993	98.3	1.7

Note: These figures refer to asylum seekers who registered with the Office of Refugees and record the manner in which they crossed the border into Hungary.
Source: Office of Refugee and Migration Affairs (1993).

Table 17.2 *Citizenship of refugees arriving in Hungary, 1988–93*

Year	Total	Romanian	Soviet	Yugoslav	Other
1988	13 173	13 173			
1989	17 448	17 365	50		33
1990	18 283	17 416	488		379
1991	53 359	3 728	738	48 485	408
1992	16 204	844	241	15 485	98
1993	5 366	548	168	4 593	57
Total	123 833	53 074	1685	68 099	975
%	100	42.86	1.36	54.99	0.79

Source: Office of Refugee and Migration Affairs (1993).

Hungary were introduced. Within one month 150 000 refugees had been refused entry and by April 1992 this figure had risen to 500 000, of whom 450 000 were Romanian citizens (Joly, 1992). In July 1992 Hungary closed its borders to those refugees from Bosnia who were being passed on by Croatia and Serbia.

Of the refugees entering Hungary between 1988 and mid-1990 only 8.2% wished to move on to a third country. Of these over 70% wanted to go to Germany. Perhaps not surprisingly 93% of the ethnic Germans coming to Hungary from Romania were in this category. The USA, Australia, Canada and Austria were the destination for others. By the beginning of 1991, some 6000 people had moved on to a third country.

The situation with refugees from Yugoslavia was different. Many from Croatia sought only

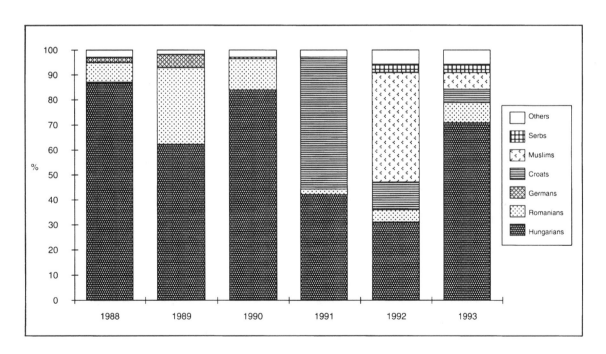

Figure 17.1 *The ethnic identity of refugees registered in Hungary, 1988–93*

temporary residence in Hungary, intending to return home once hostilities had ceased. However, those fleeing from Bosnia seem not to have wanted sanctuary in Hungary but rather to move to a third country. By June 1992 around 1000 Muslims had asked for temporary asylum in Hungary, but those wishing to pass through the country to Austria were reported as being substantial in number. However, the statistics from the border guards suggest that only about 2600 Bosnian Muslims had left for a third country, while reports from the municipalities suggest that 5000–6000 of the Croatian refugees left for third countries by the end of 1992 (Office of Refugee and Migration Affairs, 1993).

17.2.1 The Romanian wave

At the same time as East Germans were passing in large numbers through Hungary *en route* for West Germany, another stream of migrants was entering Hungary from the southeast. This group, however, did not intend to transit but in most cases to settle permanently in Hungary. These were refugees from the ethnic conflict in Romania. Ever since Transylvania was made part of Romania in 1919, the 2 million or so Hungarian minority living there has been subject to abuse, discrimination and cultural repression (Schopflin and Poulton, 1990). The 'systematisation' policy of the final years of the Ceauşescu regime, in which villages were bulldozed to the ground and their inhabitants moved to agro-industrial complexes, though condemned from outside as an example of flagrant ideological tyranny, was also characterised by a virulent strain of ethnic repression. The cultural life of Hungarians and other minorities living in ethnically mixed towns could easily be subverted by the Romanian majority. In the close-knit ethnically exclusive villages, however, the only way to overcome the rich minority culture was to destroy the built environment by which it was expressed and to move away the residents. This point of view was loudly expressed in Hungary and in the Western media (Dempsey, 1988), but it has been doubted by some British academic

authors (Lambert, 1989; Turnock, 1991). Unlike many Germans, Hungarians could not be bought out of Romania. Hungary did not have the financial resources or the constitutional imperative to repatriate the persecuted minority. In the late 1980s the simmering conflict between Hungarians and Romanians led to demonstrations in Budapest in support of the ethnic Hungarians in Romania and demands that the Hungarian government intercede with the Romanian government on their behalf. In 1989 demonstrations in Transylvania and the arrest of a leading Hungarian opponent of the Ceauşescu regime, Laszlo Tökes, began the sequence of events which eventually led to the fall and execution of Ceauşescu. In the 1989 cohort of arrivals in Hungary from Romania, 43% of men and 39% of women gave anti-Hungarian discrimination as the reason for leaving. A further 24% of men and 19% of women cited their material and political situation (Tóth, 1992). From the beginning of 1988 to mid-1990, of 31 310 refugees arriving in Hungary, 99.7% were Romanian citizens, although they belonged to several ethnic groups (Table 17.3).

Sik and Tóth (1993) analysed the first cohort to arrive in Hungary during 1988 and early 1989, and showed that the pattern of arrivals differed between the three main ethnic groups. This suggested a staggered process relating to ethnicity, with ethnic Hungarians coming first and in the greatest numbers, followed by ethnic Romanians and then ethnic Germans. However, the flow was not examined to show whether there was any clear territorial dimension at the district level.

17.2.2 The Yugoslav wave

Over recent years, strong economic links have been forged between Hungary and Yugoslavia, especially in the border regions. Hungary borders three former Yugoslav republics, Slovenia, Croatia and Serbia. Hungary has also been drawn into the political aspect of the Yugoslav conflict, supporting Slovenia and Croatia. Yugoslav Air Force jets strayed over Hungary in

Table 17.3 *Citizenship and nationality of refugees arriving in Hungary, 1988 to mid-1990*

Nationality	Total	Citizenship					
		Romanian	Bulgarian	Soviet	Yugoslav	Czech	Other
Bulgarian	16	15	1				
Czech	80	75				5	
Hungarian	23 147	23 103		6	1	27	10
Polish	4	2		2			
German	1 073	1 072		1			
Russian	5			5			
Slovak	8					8	
Gypsy	99	99					
Soviet	46	46					
Romanian	6 713	6 709					4
Serb	6	3			3		
Other	113	103					10
	31 310	31 227	1	14	4	40	24

Source: Central Statistical Office, Budapest.

1991 while attacking villages in Croatia. When the Prime Minister of Hungary, the late Jószef Antall, also pointed out that international treaties had been signed with Yugoslavia, not Serbia, it was interpreted by some as suggesting that Hungary might seek a revision of the international border with Serbia (Zametica, 1992). Other Hungarian ministers have also made statements concerning events in former Yugoslavia. But the closest ties arise from the ethnic links which are a central element in the conflict in Yugoslavia. There are 385 356 Hungarians living in Vojvodina, the northernmost autonomous region of Serbia, while 25 439 Hungarians live in Croatia, mainly in Slavonia. About 115 000 Croats and Serbs live in Hungary. Thus Hungary is inextricably bound with the warring groups of Yugoslavia, economically, politically and ethnically.

The fighting in Croatia in 1991 resulted in between 600 000 and 1 million persons becoming refugees. More than half of the displaced persons moved to other parts of Croatia and most of the remainder to other republics of the former Yugoslavia (Morokvasic, 1992). Of the 53 359 registered asylum seekers who entered Hungary in 1991, 48 485 were Yugoslav citizens. This was by far the biggest cohort of refugees entering the country between 1988 and 1992. The group was largely made up of Croats (58.9%) and Hungarians (39.0%). In 1992 the number of registered arrivals from Yugoslavia was only 15 030 and their ethnic composition had changed. Bosnian Muslims now accounted for the greatest proportion (47.5%), but Hungarians were still prominent (33.7%), while Croats (11.7%) were many fewer than in 1991. Some Serbs (2.9%) were also recorded. This shift in ethnic composition was, of course, directly related to the relocation of major hostilities from Croatia to Bosnia–Hercegovina. Table 17.4 shows the number and ethnic composition of refugees entering Hungary from Yugoslavia between 1991 and 1994.

Some British newspaper reports suggested that Hungary had taken in 40 000 refugees from Bosnia. Despite the non-registration of many, this figure is in marked contrast to the 15 030 who were actually registered by the Refugee Office. The substantial fall in registrations in 1992 reflects a change in Hungarian policy on admitting refugees. Throughout 1991 and the first half of 1992, Hungary operated an open-door policy. Even as many Western European countries closed their borders, Hungary maintained this. But in July 1992 Hungary changed its policy, closing the border to Bosnian refugees

Table 17.4 *Ethnic composition of refugees entering Hungary from Yugoslavia, 1991 to mid-1994*

Year	Total	Hungarian	Croat	Serb	Muslim	Other
1991	48 485	18 771	28 279	?	?	851
1992	15 030	5 065	1 758	436	7140	631
1993	4 427	3 688	102	152	369	116
1994*	1 333	1 081	26	42	108	76

*January–June.
Source: Office of Refugee and Migration Affairs (1993).

being passed on from Croatia and Serbia. Even so, Hungary still did not impose visa restrictions on individuals. This change of policy came because as Western countries refused to accept refugees from Bosnia, the Hungarian government was afraid that it could not cope with the influx. At the same time, the Hungarian government did not wish to participate in the organised deportation arranged by Serbs as part of the 'ethnic cleansing' of conquered districts of Bosnia.

When fighting flared up between Serbs (in the guise of the Yugoslav Army) and Croats in 1991, there were three theatres of engagement. One was in Dubrovnik, in the south. A second was along the Croatian–Bosnian border in Krajina, where a large Serbian minority was living. The other was along the border between Serbia and Croatia in eastern Slavonia. The latter theatre was known as the Baranya triangle and includes the towns of Osijek and Vukovar. This was the scene of some of the fiercest fighting. While Croats and Serbs predominate in this area, it is also populated by Hungarians and small minorities of Slovaks, Czechs, Ruthenians and Ukrainians.

Although a detailed analysis of the areas of origin of the 1991 asylum seekers in Hungary has not been undertaken, it is safe to assume that they came from this zone and adjoining districts of Vojvodina. Two streams have been recognised as originating from this area in 1991. The first came to Hungary in late July and August, the second in late September, when Vukovar had fallen to the Serbs and Osijek was under heavy attack. Once hostilities had eased in this theatre, some refugees returned home. Although the Baranya district as a whole was ethnically mixed, villages and often small towns were

ethnically exclusive. Even the biggest towns, Vukovar, and especially Osijek, while they contained several nationalities, had a predominance of Croats. The front line of December 1991, which became the cease-fire line of the Vance Plan and thus the boundary of the UN protected area meant that Hungarian-inhabited villages of the former Croatia were all located in the district occupied by Serb and Yugoslav Army units. By January 1992, 2500 Serbs had been moved into the area with 4000 more expected. The Deputy Prime Minister of the self-styled Serbian region of Slavonia, Baranya and western Srem said that 10 000–12 000 more Serbs could be accommodated (Joly, 1992). According to the Hungarian Refugee Office (Hrivnak, 1992), by early summer some 10 000–15 000 Croatian refugees had returned to Croatia from Hungary, but not to their original villages, because these had been occupied by Serbs.

17.3 The development of refugee policy

The refugee and migrant streams coming to Hungary raised new questions for immigration policy. Policy had to respond to the immediate situation, but also the preparation of a longer-term response was needed.

Reference has already been made to the Hungarian policy of imposing restrictions on mainly Romanian citizens in 1991, but of keeping the border open to refugees from the former Yugoslavia until July 1992; the border remains open to others from Eastern European countries, though not to refugees or migrants from outside

Europe. This has affected the numbers who actually entered the country.

When the first major waves of refugees began to arrive there was no legal or organisational framework to cope with them. In 1989 Hungary acceded to the Geneva Convention and enacted laws recognising refugee status. In the same year a Refugee Department was established in the Ministry of the Interior with headquarters in Budapest together with six regional offices. However, not until 1994 was a law promulgated to enact the framework for refugee policy (*Magyar Nemzet*, 1993).

Hungarian government policy for dealing with refugees, once accepted into the country, falls into two phases for each of the waves of refugees. The initial phase was to establish reception centres for refugees. In the case of the Romanian refugees, three centres were formed. Their location reflected the places of origin of the migrants and the magnet of Budapest, where many of the refugees wanted to settle. Because the number of migrants was relatively small and the flow fairly constant, three reception centres were sufficient to process them. In contrast, the much greater numbers and the suddenness of the flow from the former Yugoslavia made it necessary quickly to establish some 20 new reception camps. Even so, the vast majority of refugees from Croatia and Bosnia were not housed in such camps. Most refugees lived in local communities and received financial and other support from the authorities. During this period the settlement process was a spontaneous one as refugees found accommodation and jobs where they could. Dövényi (1993) identified two underlying principles of territorial distribution. First, the refugees have generally settled in districts near to the border across which they entered Hungary. Second, Budapest the capital and dominant urban centre, is very attractive to immigrants. These points are supported by a study of settled immigrants at the end of 1990 (Rédei, 1992), figures from which are presented as Figure 17.2. Almost half of the refugees were settled in Budapest with Pest County and the Romanian border counties of Csongrád, Békés

and Hajdu accounting for most of the remainder. This finding is supported by a survey of foreigners in Hungary conducted among 932 mayors in May–June 1992 (Kovács, 1993).

A second phase of policy with regard to the territorial aspect can be discerned. This also differed between the two streams, in relation to the different motivations of the asylum seekers. Because the Romanian refugees came to stay, it was necessary to elaborate a plan for their permanent absorption into Hungarian society. For the refugees from Croatia and Bosnia intending to stay only temporarily, schemes for voluntary repatriation were discussed.

In preparing a longer-term territorial policy for Romanian refugees, the Office of Refugee Affairs commissioned the Hungarian Geographical Research Institute to study the problem and to recommend suitable districts for the permanent settlement of refugees. The Geographical Institute team established three basic criteria (Dövényi, 1992): (a) the process should avoid tension between the settlers and the indigenous population; (b) close economic and social integration of the refugees into the local community must be achieved; and (c) the areas of settlement should offer advantages for both the host community and the newcomers.

The team identified districts which were suitable for refugee settlement, regarding these areas as neither the best nor the worst in the country. They had some social and economic problems, but the settlement of refugees could have some positive effects. These areas were investigated with regard to several important local conditions. Among these were population density, settlement types and level of development. More particularly, economic parameters such as land use and land use potential and the labour market were considered. Sociocultural factors such as housing availability and ethnic composition were also investigated. Past refugee policies were examined for the lessons they could teach.

The areas selected also complemented those in which refugee settlement had taken place spontaneously. This would have the effect of

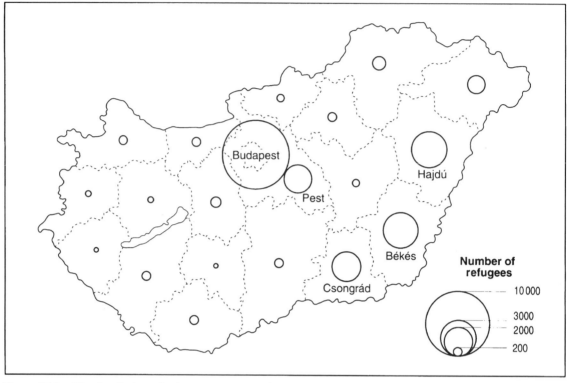

Figure 17.2 *The distribution of refugees in Hungary by county, December 1990. Source: Rédei (1992)*

spreading out the refugees more evenly over the country as a whole.

From this work the Geographical Research Institute researchers concluded that it was important to have an organised plan for settling refugees, and stressed the need to identify both suitable and unsuitable districts for settlement. They also emphasised the need for refugees to have a choice of places in which to settle. However, there should also be a system of financial incentives. Refugees choosing designated areas could receive financial help and those areas could also receive higher levels of general investment, which would help local residents. The study also recommended that a comprehensive system of information gathering about refugees should be established.

It is clear that the recommendations have implications for other aspects of internal policy. During the Communist period, spatial policy had

a low priority as governments thought in terms of economic sectors and social issues with areal differentiation and integration less utilised as concepts for policy. There is no particular evidence to suggest that the post-Communist government is prepared to place a high priority on territorial aspects of policy. Since refugee policy has many other elements demanding scarce resources, progress may be slow.

With regard to refugees from the former Yugoslavia, a different policy has been outlined. In February 1992 an attempt was made to negotiate a voluntary repatriation of some of this group. Representatives from Hungary, Croatia and UNHCR met to consider the possibility of displaced persons returning to Croatia. Figure 17.3 is redrawn from an unofficial categorisation of districts in Croatia made by the UNHCR liaison office in Zagreb for the possible repatriation of refugees. By the end

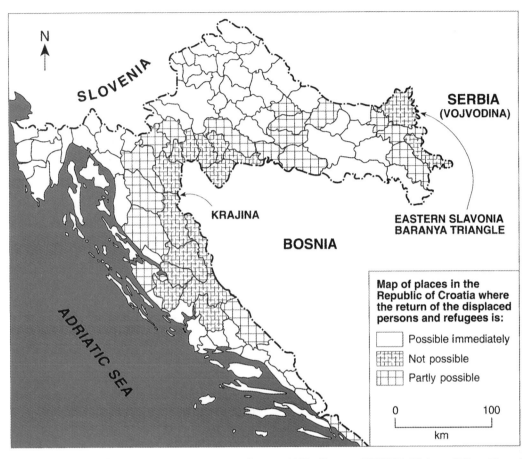

Figure 17.3 *Situation for returnees to Croatia, February 1992. Source: UNHCR Liaison Office, Zagreb and Budapest*

of April 1992 it seemed that circumstances had improved and concrete steps could be taken. However, even though the centre of hostilities had moved to Bosnia–Hercegovina, sporadic fighting continued in the Baranya triangle. Because of the economic embargo on Serbia and the war, the situation in Vojvodina had also deteriorated. These circumstances led to the abandonment of several voluntary attempts at repatriation (Office of Refugee and Migration Affairs, 1993). At the same time, the border between the Serb-controlled area and Hungary was closed. It is in this zone that most Croatian ethnic Hungarians lived. These are also the areas

which the UNHCR recognised as closed to voluntary repatriation.

These policies of settlement for one group and repatriation for the other made good sense in general from all points of view. The Romanian Hungarians wanted to be integrated into Hungarian society to build new homes, engage in gainful employment and identify with host communities. From the point of view of the Hungarian government, it was desirable to extend a welcome to ethnic Hungarians. At the same time, however, unemployment, housing shortages and the difficulties of ideological transformation have been manifold. Despite foreign assistance, refugees are a burden on the economy; if they are resettled, independent and gainfully employed, this burden is relieved. From the territorial point of view, however, it can be a problem if the government sees the immigrants as well suited to one kind of place while the immigrants want to be settled in another. Added to this is the attitude of local communities. So far, evidence suggests that Hungarian hosts have responded positively to the refugees (Kovács, 1993). There is some suggestion that solidarity with Romanian Hungarian refugees was weakening by 1991 (Csepeli and Zavecz, 1992). The attitude of local communities may ultimately be guided on the one hand by a wish to support Hungarian settlers from Romania as a matter of national identity, and on the other by a perceived threat to standards of living and access to scarce resources. Generally, village communities appear to have shown solidarity with new settlers. However, settlement of refugees in some areas should not be attempted as a solution to the depopulation that is occurring in them (Berényi, 1992).

A policy of voluntary repatriation of refugees from Croatia and Bosnia, when it can be achieved without threat to the returnees, is sensible from all points of view. The Hungarian government, with the assistance of the international community, can support refugees for only a short time and in rather poor conditions. But, will all Croat and ethnic Hungarians, let alone Bosnians, ever be able to return to their former homes? The interim cease-fire in eastern Croatia left substantial territory under Serb control. Its contiguity with Serbia meant that there would be pressure to incorporate it into a 'Greater Serbia'. Refugees would be dispossessed of land and housing and thus often employment and livelihood. These are not circumstances in which many would wish to return.

Further, a group of young men, unknown in number, are believed to have fled to Hungary to avoid military service. They are not, of course, registered as asylum seekers. It may be that they would not wish to return home even when hostilities have ceased.

For many immigrants, not only those from Romania and the former Yugoslav republics, Hungary may offer economic opportunities not so clearly available elsewhere in Central and Eastern Europe. As entry to Western Europe becomes increasingly difficult, this opens up the whole question of the further development of immigration policy.

17.4 The response of the international community

As many as 3.5 million people have been displaced by the Yugoslav conflict (Channel 4 Television, 1993). The Geneva Conference of July 1992 put the figure at about 2 million, of which approximately 1.8 million were from Bosnia. In comparison with some other European countries, and despite being in the front line, Hungary has received quite a modest total of refugees, especially from Bosnia. This picture is changed somewhat if the number of refugees per 1000 of native population is considered. One complaint of the Hungarian government has been that Western European countries, much wealthier than Hungary, have not borne their full share of the burden. The 'international community' has made Hungary's problem more difficult by hardening attitudes to receiving refugees from former Yugoslavia. Some Western countries have a very poor record, and, for example during the summer of 1993 Germany changed its constitution to restrict entry of asylum seekers. Many European countries closed their borders to refugees or severely tightened procedures. This made travel via Hungary to a third country very difficult. At the same time, however, we must recall that few refugees coming to Hungary actually wanted to travel to a third country or remain long in Hungary.

These general considerations aside, Hungary has received help in two ways. Official assistance from other governments has come via the UNHCR. In 1991 US$5 million was provided; in 1992 US$9 million; and in 1993 a further US$5 million. A sum of US$3.5 million was planned for 1994 (Cavaliéri, 1993). This help has been used for the administration of refugee centres, the provision of clothing and food, and for financial assistance to refugees. It was expected that the bulk of the 1994 funds would be used to maintain the weekly food-stamp grant of 1000 forint per refugee, and the remainder would subsidise domestic supplies, housing and medical expenses. At the same time, Hungary has received non-governmental help from many charities. This aid has arrived mainly in the form of clothing, shoes, blankets, medicines, food and household equipment, from internationally recognised sources such as the Red Cross, Lions and the Christian churches. But it has also come from private enterprises, small charities and individuals. An unpublished list provided by the Office for Refugees and Migration Affairs shows that in 1992 help given by this means to the Nagyatad refugee camp, the biggest in Hungary, came from 48 non-governmental organisations, with most EC countries and Austria, Switzerland, Norway, Czechoslovakia and Croatia represented.

By closing its borders to Romanian citizens in 1991 and Bosnian refugees in July 1992, Hungary in effect stopped the most critical problem that it had faced, that of numbers of refugees. Unless there is a flare-up of some other conflict in the region, Hungary is not likely to have to deal with such large numbers of refugees again. However, there is little doubt that a steady stream of asylum seekers or economic migrants will wish to enter Hungary in the future.

In acceding to the Geneva Convention, Hungary imposed a territorial restriction, refusing to recognise asylum seekers from outside of Europe. This territorial caveat was included because Hungary feared it might become an antechamber for non-Europeans trying to gain entry to the countries of the EU.

17.5 Conclusion

Foreigners living in Hungary include temporary residents such as 'guest workers', students and employees sent by their firms as well as refugees. The issue of foreigners living in Hungary is not a completely post-Communist phenomenon, but opening the borders has given it a new dimension. Without doubt the most difficult aspects of this dimension have arisen from the reconstruction of the Balkans. However, it must be borne in mind that the majority of entrants to Hungary are 'returning' Hungarians. This was true from the beginning in 1988 and became more pronounced with time: only in 1991 were ethnic Hungarians outnumbered by another nationality. It has also been re-emphasised by government policy, which, since 1991, has turned away many non-Hungarian would-be refugees.

Loescher (1992) has pointed out that refugees affect international relations in many ways, especially between the sending and receiving countries. In the case of Hungary, its transit location for many potential refugees and migrant flows will also be significant in its relations with other European states. The sharpest incidents so far have arisen from the reconstruction of the Balkans.

The Hungarian geographer György Enyedi (1992), in discussing East–Central Europe as a distinct European region, argued that Hungary was not part of the Balkans. However, Hungary has a common border with several Balkan states. Hungarian minorities are resident in numerous Balkan states. Hungary might also need to develop markets in the Balkans further for lack of markets elsewhere. The reconstruction of the Balkans must therefore impact upon Hungary in many ways. So far the biggest impact on Hungary from the violent change taking place there has been the arrival of refugees. Hungary has responded positively to this, and has hurriedly developed a policy which might have otherwise taken much longer to come into being. But the story has only just begun. As time goes on the refugee policy will become more closely related to 'normal' international relations and wider aspects of foreign policy considerations. So far, the policy has been shaped in the context of 'crisis management' and driven by humanitarian considerations. This will not be so in the future as the refugee or economic migrant factor is going to become a more prominent issue in the restructuring of the political geography of Europe.

17.6 References

Berényi, I., 1992, The socio-economic transformation and the consequences of the liberalisation of borders in Hungary, in Kertész, A., Kovács, Z., eds, *New perspectives in Hungarian geography*, Akadémia Kiadó, Budapest, pp. 45–58.

Cavalieri, J. P., 1993, Personal interview, Protection Officer, UNHCR, Budapest.

Channel 4 Television, 1993, *Bloody Bosnia*, broadcast, 3 August.

Csepeli, G., Zavecz, T., 1992, Conflicting bonds of nationality in Hungary: national identity, minority status, and ethnicity, *Innovation*, **5**(2), 77–94.

Dempsey, J., 1988, Hungary calls Rumanian farm plans 'idiotic', *Financial Times*, 22 August.

Dövényi, Z., 1992, A menekültkérdés néhány területi aspektusa Magyarországon, in Sik, E., ed., *Menekülők, vándorlók, szerencsét próbálók*, Hungarian Academy of Sciences, Political Science Research Institute, Budapest, pp. 83–95.

Dövényi, Z., 1993, *Some characteristics of international migration in Hungary*, unpublished manuscript, Budapest.

Enyedi, Gy, 1992, Turning points of urbanisation in East Central Europe, in Kertész, A., Kovács, Z., eds, *New perspectives in Hungarian geography*, Akadémiai Kiadó, Budapest, pp. 5–14.

Hrivnak, A., 1992, Personal interview, Counsellor, Hungarian Refugee Office, Budapest.

Joly, D., 1992, *Refugees—asylum in Europe?* Minority Rights Group, London.

Kocsis, K., 1993, *Az etnikai konfliktusok történetiföldrajzi háttere a volt Jugoslávia területén*, Teleki László Alapítvány, Budapest.

Kovács, R., 1993, Az 'idegenek' Magyarországontelepülések és menekültek, in Sik, E., ed., *Útkeresők*, Hungarian Academy of Sciences, Political Science Research Institute, Budapest, pp. 49–64.

Lambert, A., 1989, Return of the vampire, *Geographical Magazine*, **61**(2), 16–20.

Loescher, G., 1992, *Refugee movements and international security*, Adelphi Paper 268, International Institute for Strategic Studies, London.

Magyar Nemzet, 1993, Magyarország sokak számára Kánaán, interview with István Morvay, Head of the Office of Refugee and Migration Affairs, and former Minister for Refugee Affairs, 5 May.

Morokvasic, M., 1992, Yugoslav refugees, displaced persons and the civil war, *Refuge*, **11**(4), 3–6.

Office of Refugee and Migration Affairs, 1993, *Press release*, Ministry of Home Affairs, Budapest.

Rédei, L. Mária, 1992, Magyarországon tartózkodási engedélyt kérők összetételének alakulása az elmúlt évtizedekben és a folyamat demográfiai következményei, in Sik, E., ed., *Menekülők, vándorlók, szerencsét próbálók*, Hungarian Academy of Sciences, Political Science Research Institute, Budapest, pp. 75–82.

Schopflin, G., Poulton, H., 1990, *Romania's ethnic Hungarians*, Minority Rights Group, London.

Sik, E., 1990, *Menekültekről és menekülthullámokról (előtanulmány)*, Társadalomkutatási Informatikai Egyesültés, Budapest.

Sik, E., Tóth, J., 1993, Román származású menekültek Magyarországon, in Sik, E., ed., *Útkeresők*, Hungarian Academy of Sciences, Political Science Research Institute, pp. 23–38.

Tóth, O., 1992, Erdélyi menekült nők Magyarországon 1989-ben, in Sik, E., ed., *Menekülők, vándorlók szerencsét próbálók*, Hungarian Academy of Sciences, Political Science Research Institute, Budapest, pp. 65–74.

Turnock, D., 1991, The planning of rural settlement in Romania, *Geographical Journal*, **157**(3), 251–64.

Zametica, J., 1992, *The Yugoslav conflict*, Adelphi Paper 270, International Institute for Strategic Studies, London.

Section D
The broader context

18

The Balkans: a European challenge

Allan M. Williams

18.1 Introduction: from peace dividend to bitter harvest

Warren Christopher, the US Secretary of State, called the current crisis in the Balkans 'the problem from hell' (Fenske, 1993). This is most chillingly evident in the human tragedy in the former Yugoslavia, but the crisis also has wider implications for Europe as a whole. In 1989–91 a new era of opportunities seemed to be opening up for Europe; the ending of the cold war promised a peace dividend at the same time as the imminent completion of the Single Market and the Maastricht agreement seemed to be propelling the EU to Europe's centre stage, thereby providing hegemonic conditions for both political and economic development in the continent (Williams, 1994). Since then, the peace dividend has often seemed to have been transformed into a bitter harvest, with endemic economic and political transformation problems in Eastern and Central Europe, a loss of direction and purpose in the process of European integration, and deep divisions in the foreign and security policies of the EU.

The crisis in the former Yugoslavia has been closely intertwined with events on the larger European stage. It does, of course, epitomise the emergence of underlying ethnic and nationalistic tensions in post-cold war Europe. But it is also to some extent a cause of the loss of confidence in European institutions, as the challenges of the 'problem from hell' have overwhelmed both the institutional capacity of the EU, and the political will of individual Western European states. Moreover, the crisis in the former Yugoslavia has touched a seam of ancient religious conflicts, bound up with the history of external dominance of the Balkans by Turkey, which threatens to spill over national boundaries and engulf much of the larger surrounding region.

This chapter seeks to address some of these issues through consideration of three principal themes: the approach of the EU to the refugee crisis engendered by the conflicts in the former Yugoslavia, the weakness of the EU as a force in foreign affairs, relations with Turkey and the question of Islam, and the implications for the further enlargement of the EU.

18.2 Flight from 'the problem from hell': the European refugee space

The third pillar of the Maastricht Treaty is explicitly concerned with internal security matters in the EU specifically relating to the issue of freedom of movement across national

Reconstructing the Balkans: A Geography of the New Southeast Europe. Edited by Derek Hall and Darrick Danta.
©1996 John Wiley & Sons Ltd

boundaries. This was the climax of a succession of good intentions and measures to facilitate freedom of movement which date back to the Treaty of Rome itself. It is perhaps ironic that it was the massive outflow of refugees from the former Yugoslavia, which has a long history of labour migration links with the EU, which most clearly served to underline the intransigence of national sovereignty as against coordinated European-level action in this field.

Yugoslavia has long been linked to Western Europe by large-scale labour migration flows (King, 1994). The growth of emigration was particularly marked after the mid-1960s so that, briefly, in the late 1960s and early 1970s it was the single largest exporter of labour in Europe. Although overtaken thereafter by Turkey, Yugoslavia continued to be the second largest source of labour migrants from southern to northern Europe for the entire period down to the end of the cold war. In consequence, at the end of the 1980s there were large numbers of Yugoslavian workers and their families living throughout Western Europe: 611 000 in Germany, 117 000 in Switzerland, 70 000 in France and 40 000 in Sweden, according to the estimates of the OECD's SOPEMI reporting system. These were mostly labour migrants, seeking out higher wages than could be provided by their own national economic system, although the importance of political motivations should not be discounted.

From the mid-1970s, and again decisively in the early 1990s, economic conditions in northern Europe had led to reduced labour demand, even though emigration continued mainly via family reunification. In the 1980s, however, a substantial stream of asylum seekers was added to the earlier flows of labour migration. The numbers of asylum seekers from Yugoslavia rose from about 1000 per annum in the early 1980s to 24 000 by 1988, at which date they accounted for a quarter of all refugees from Central and Eastern Europe and the Soviet Union (Carter *et al.*, 1993). Not surprisingly, the geography of asylum seeking was broadly similar to that of labour migration. When conditions allowed, many refugees sought

to join existing large communities of expatriate Yugoslavians; as a result, about three-quarters applied for asylum in Germany. The crisis in the former Yugoslavia, and especially the conflicts in Croatia and Bosnia–Hercegovina have since changed the scale of the flow of emigration beyond recognition, but the geographical pattern remains essentially unaltered, leastways at the international level.

The greatest impact of the refugee crisis has, of course, been experienced in the former Yugoslavia, where there are an estimated 2 million people who have been displaced from their homes. For many the flight to safety involved moving to other locations within their own newly independent countries. However, large numbers have fled across borders into one of the other new republics of the former Yugoslavia. For example, in 1993 it was estimated that 573 000 refugees from Bosnia had fled to Croatia or Serbia, as part of a massive process of geographical resegregation along ethnic lines. Therefore, a region which has experienced a long history of population redistribution in response to conflict (Carter, 1977) has yet again witnessed the appalling scenes of refugees in flight, many of whom were unable to take with them more than a few belongings.

As exemplified in Chapter 17, despite the immense refugee tragedy which unfolded along the roads and lanes of the former Yugoslavia, it was the international dimension of asylum seeking which attracted wider attention. Towards the end of 1992, approximately 550 000 Yugoslavians had left the country as refugees; there were 220 000 in Germany, 70 000 in Switzerland, 60 000 in Sweden and 57 500 in Austria. This meant that social and political pressures on the receiving countries were, of course, highly polarised. The pressures continued to be highly concentrated in 1993 as is evident in the distribution of asylum seekers across Western Europe (see Figure 18.1(a)). These data are limited in that they refer only to arrivals in one year and to those going through the official registration channels, which therefore excludes most refugees from the former Yugoslavia.

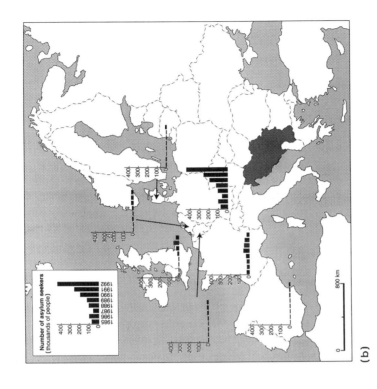

(b)

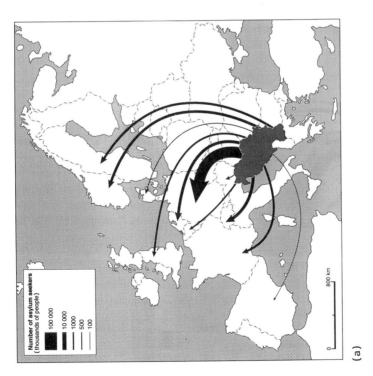

(a)

Figure 18.1 *Distribution of asylum seekers from the former Yugoslavia in Western Europe: (a) total flows; (b) yearly totals*

213

Table 18.1 *Asylum seekers from the former Yugoslavia, January–June 1994*

France	2 047 Former Yugoslavia
Germany	17 194 Serbia/Montenegro
	3 705 Bosnia–Hercegovina
Netherlands	4 277 Bosnia–Hercegovina
	2 363 Serbia/Montenegro
Norway	1 434 Former Yugoslavia
Sweden	4 681 Croatia
	1 540 Bosnia–Hercegovina
	1 388 Serbia/Montenegro
Switzerland	2 613 Serbia/Montenegro
	1 996 Bosnia–Hercegovina
UK	No data available

Source: ECRE (1994, pp. 8–10).

Nevertheless, the overwhelming focus on Germany, followed to a far lesser extent by the Scandinavian countries is clear, as is the relatively small number in the UK. Despite some reduction in the scale of these movements, refugees from the former Yugoslavia continued to arrive in large numbers during the first half of 1994 (Table 18.1).

Ethnic and linguistic ties, as well as proximity, have meant that Eastern as well as Western European countries have been the recipients of refugees from the former Yugoslavia, as forcefully depicted in Chapter 17.

Perhaps the most immediate international ramification was the testing of what can be termed the European refugee space, as defined by the willingness of individual European states to accept refugees fleeing the conflict in the former Yugoslavia. This was accentuated by the coincidence of the Yugoslavian crisis with a general increase in the numbers of asylum seekers, especially from Central and Eastern Europe. International comparisons are made difficult by the differences in definitions employed by individual states, and so the data presented in Figure 18.1(b) should be treated with caution. Nevertheless, they do confirm that there has been a marked increase in the number of asylum seekers officially registered in most European states. For example, in Germany the number increased from 73 800 in 1985 to 438 200 in 1992. Over the same period there were increases in the

UK from 6200 to 32 000 and in the Netherlands from 5600 to 20 300.

The overall response to such increases, almost without exception, has been a severe tightening of the conditions under which refugees can gain access to the European refugee space. In Europe as a whole, about two-thirds of all applicant asylum seekers were successful in 1980, but by 1990 this proportion had fallen to about one in ten (Baldwin-Edwards, 1991). The responses of individual countries have been varied. Perhaps most significant has been the German government's reframing of its relatively liberal refugee conventions (Article 16 of its Basic Law) in 1993. In Sweden, a tightening of controls on new asylum seekers was combined with an attempt to provide more generous treatment with large numbers of existing refugees from Bosnia. In June 1993 it was announced that a rapid and generous approach would be taken to some 40 000 Bosnian refugees. As a result, almost all these refugees received residence permits, with a further 30 000–40 000 relatives being entitled to join them under the terms for family reunification (ECRE, 1994).

In Britain, the UK government has taken an exceptionally tough line on asylum seeking, despite the desperate plight of the Bosnian refugees which has arisen directly from the largest violent political confrontation in post-war Europe. Crawley (1993, p. 23) writes that '. . . the British government has been a more than willing partner in the effort to close Europe's door to refugees'. The UK government sought to reduce the numbers of refugees at source, and the Immigration Act of 1987 imposed fines on airlines and shipping companies which carry people to Britain who do not have the required documentation.

The scale of the crisis in the former Yugoslavia is such that some governments have introduced emergency and exceptional laws and procedures, treating refugees from the former Yugoslavia as a special temporary category. There has been a general attempt to justify exclusion from the European refugee space by arguing that refugees should be kept as close to their original homes as possible, despite the clear evidence that neighbouring republics were already overwhelmed with their own refugee crises. This also perpetuates the myth—which is palpably untrue in many instances—that the refugees have home regions, let alone homes to which they will realistically be able to return in the near future. The net effect is that Western European governments have twice betrayed these refugees; by failing to intervene effectively in the process of ethnic cleansing and then failing to help the victims of this process.

The Yugoslavian refugee crisis has also challenged the ability of the EU to develop an autonomous role in the regulation of entry to the Union. The need for effective European-level policies with respect to refugees was inherent in the Single European Act which aimed to create freedom of movement across internal borders within the EU. This was given its most concrete form by the 1985 Schengen agreement which sought to remove border controls; this was signed initially by France, Germany, Belgium, Luxembourg and the Netherlands, and subsequently by Italy, Spain and Portugal. It was accepted that any such liberalisation would require a strengthening of border controls and a harmonisation of national rules on visas and, therefore, necessarily on procedures for granting asylum. This was recognised in the so-called third pillar of the Maastricht Treaty, which brought such policy within the competence of EU institutions, and also enabled intergovernmental cooperation on asylum, refugee and immigration issues. The scale of the refugee crisis in Yugoslavia, Somalia and elsewhere, together with dogged adherence to rights of national sovereignty in this realm, have meant that progress has been limited. The only way forward has been via the minimalist formula of recognising visas issued by other member states rather than—as hoped—by agreement on the harmonisation of rules across the EU.

The Yugoslavian crisis has served, therefore, to highlight the limitations to the EU's collective commitment to the third pillar of the Maastricht Treaty which deals with internal security. There

are good intentions in plenty, as is evident in the following extracts from an opinion of the Economic and Social Committee (European Communities, 1994, pp. 4–6):

People who face persecution by the state or are in physical danger because of their political convictions, nationality, ethnic group, race, or religious affiliation should be afforded protection in keeping with *the noblest European traditions* (emphasis added).

To avoid unfair burdens, consideration should be given to the evening out and if necessary redistribution of responsibilities within the EU. Whatever the redistribution method adopted, however, it should not lose sight of humanitarian considerations, and especially the basic principle of family unity.

Despite these fine sentiments, the EU has played little role in coordinating either aid to refugees or asylum policies. As a result, individual governments have acted primarily to minimise the numbers of asylum seekers granted residence, with Germany being left to receive a vastly disproportionate share of the population displaced by the crisis. In addition, the failure to harmonise rules means, however, that there continue to exist considerable national differences in the granting of visas to asylum seekers. The gateways to the European refugee space, therefore, are unevenly restricted. This is clearly incompatible in the longer term with the existence of freedom of movement within the Union, so that this represents an unfinished chapter of EU business.

Looking further ahead, it is clear that Europe has yet to see the full implications of the refugee crisis that has accompanied the crisis in the former Yugoslavia. In the most pessimistic scenario, the complete breakdown of the peace-building process and the renewal of conflict in Bosnia, spreading into neighbouring republics, may bring about a new and massive exodus of refugees who, almost inevitably, will look towards the refugee space of the EU for shelter. Even if this is avoided, and peace returns to the Balkans sooner rather than later, there is going to be a massive process of return migration. Return migration is not a new process in the Balkans, or indeed in southern Europe as a whole, but unlike the previous returns of labour migrants, this will be a return to a social and geographical situation wherein hundreds of thousands of homes are now either destroyed or relocated across new international boundaries. The EU and other international organisations will have to contribute to the process of reintegration in the region if they are to help to consolidate what will inevitably be a precarious peace.

18.3 European security and foreign policy: shattering an illusion

The end of the cold war required revision of what constitutes the threats to European security, and the most effective way to counter these. Initially, there was considerable euphoria that the cold war thaw would provide a peace dividend and reduce tension across Europe. However, the Balkan crisis has demonstrated the continued existence of threats to the security and defence of Europe, especially because of the re-emergence of long-suppressed inter-ethnic tensions pertaining to the mismatch between ethnic group aspirations and international territorial boundaries in Europe. As former British Foreign Secretary Douglas Hurd succinctly expressed it, 'the Cold War was unfriendly but stable' (Budd, 1993, p. 6). The ending of the cold war also called into question the relationship between the USA and its European allies, particularly as this coincided with renewed calls in the former for greater isolationism. With hindsight we can now see that the strategic demands of the cold war served to coalesce the potentially disparate interests of the Western allies, while submerging ethnic tensions in much of Central and Eastern Europe and the Soviet Union.

At about the same time as the cold war was coming to an end, the attempt to build common European defence and security mechanisms was gathering pace. This had its origins in the establishment of the EU's European political cooperation mechanism for co-ordinating foreign policy in the early 1970s. By the mid- to late 1980s the rapid shift to greater economic integration embodied in the Single European Market had led to a call for greater political union across a number of fronts including foreign and defence policies. This reached its apotheosis at Maastricht when it seemed that the 12 member states had taken a decisive step forward in December 1991 when they agreed a second pillar of the Treaty on European Union, committing themselves to 'a common foreign and security policy including the eventual framing of a common defence policy, which might in time lead to a common defence'. In the euphoria surrounding Maastricht it was easy to overlook the institutional weaknesses in what had been established. All that had been agreed were a set of general objectives such as promoting international cooperation and security. No individual country was likely to quarrel with this (Budd, 1993). The actual framing of a common policy, and the powers to decide what should and should not be matters of joint policy, and the detailed objectives of this, were left to the European Council, with its largely inglorious history of intergovernmentalism. There was also no substantial provision for defence other than the decision that the Western European Union (WEU) should be developed as the defence component of the EU; even this limited measure was constrained in that Ireland, Denmark and (until 1992) Greece were not signatories to the WEU.

The speed with which the parameters of international relations changed meant that these overwhelmed the cautious and modest attempt at institution building in the EU. Intergovernmentalism could provide no basis for tackling the multifarious foreign and defence issues which in their divergent appeal to sovereign national interests would cut across the attempt at collective policy-making and implementation. Almost simultaneously to the run-up to Maastricht, the first major challenge to the second pillar was brewing in the Balkans, and the crisis in the former Yugoslavia would soon stalk and confront the common foreign policy of the Treaty of European Union.

In the early stages of the crisis, such as during the attempts by the Croatian and Slovenian republics to secede from the Yugoslav republic in the course of 1991, the foreign policy responses were mostly directed along the familiar channels of national government diplomacy in Western Europe. However, the gravity of the crisis was such that a collective response was required of the EU. There were a number of pressing reasons for this: the proximity of the crisis to the external boundaries of the EU; the direct impact on a member state, Greece, which could become embroiled if the crisis spread to Macedonia and Albania; the disruption of trade as freight and passengers which once had flowed through Yugoslavia now had to be rerouted through Hungary; and the flow of refugees into the European refugee space (section 18.2).

At the same time, the EU was seen potentially to have a special role to play in the region. It was seen—indeed presented itself—as the centre of political and economic stability in Europe and as a bulwark of liberal democratic values. This was underlain by the historical role of EU and prospective EU member states (such as Austria) in the Balkans (Carter, 1977). The United States was also keen that the EU should adopt a greater political role in Europe, one that would be congruent with its enhanced status as an economic superpower. Not surprisingly, then, Slovenia and Croatia looked to the EU to play a key role in shaping both the new Europe and its broader security structures, that is, in creating the new territorial framework and political arrangements which would provide for the expression of their national aspirations.

The break-up of the former Yugoslavia was to prove the first, and hitherto the greatest, challenge to the second pillar of the Treaty of European Union. There is no denying the immense challenge of a conflict which has changed fundamentally in nature over time, leastways in the perceptions of external observers. Initially, this was seen as an internal conflict, and the EU set out to preserve the territorial integrity of federal Yugoslavia, not least because it feared that the redrawing of

boundaries could become contagious in a region where territoriality has been and is strongly contested. This approach, however, was to change during the course of late 1991 as Germany—for its own political reasons—began to pressurise the other member states to give early recognition to the new republics of Croatia and Slovenia. This threatened to shatter whatever semblance of unity the member states could hope to assemble. The EU responded by turning to political principles, and setting out the two principal criteria to be employed in granting recognition to the new states: they had to be democratic and respect human rights, and had also to recognise the rights of minorities. Again no member state could really object to such broad principles, especially as these had been used in the EU's largely negative response to Turkey's application for full membership (Eralp, 1993). Both the Commission and several of the member states hoped that it would provide a sufficiently broad umbrella to unite the foreign policies of the individual member states.

The attempt to create a collective approach was immediately put under pressure by continued German threats that it would pursue a national line on the recognition of Croatia and Slovenia if the EU as whole procrastinated in its common foreign policy. In an attempt to shore up the façade of unity, the EU in December 1991 decided to recognise Croatia and Slovenia as independent states. This was against the inclinations of the French and British governments and indeed of most of the member states, who feared that what they perceived to be precipitate action could inflame the position not only in former Yugoslavia but throughout the Balkans.

Irrespective of the lack of clear analysis of the implications of this territorial realignment, the EU's recognition of the new republics violated its own carefully crafted guiding political principles for recognition. Macedonia met both principles yet was not recognised, while Croatia did not meet either and was recognised. Expediency had triumphed over principle and perhaps even more importantly had cast the EU adrift without a clear course through the nationalist and ethnic tensions and aspirations which have since threatened to engulf parts of Central and Eastern Europe, and especially the former Soviet Union. For example, if we consider that, in a sense, Slovenia and Croatia represent case law for territorial sovereignty, then it could be possible to justify the partition of Bosnia, the integrity of former Yugoslavia or the independence of the Dalmation Serbs from Croatia. And if these principles were to be applied to former Yugoslavia, why not also to other minority groups occupying relatively well-defined territories within other Balkan or, indeed, any European states, including existing member states with long histories of nationalist claims and ethnic tensions?

There were no easy solutions available in 1991 and our criticisms benefit from the doubtful advantage of hindsight. It is possible to make out a counter-claim that the EU recognised Croatia and Slovenia at an early stage in the belief that firm leadership by the incipient regional super-power would end uncertainty, lead to acceptance of the new political geography of the region and reduce the possibility of violent conflict. However, even if this was true and was the primary motive for the early recognition, the EU does stand accused of treating the claims of two groups to sovereignty in isolation of all other claims and interests in former Yugoslavia let alone the remainder of the Balkans. Rarely can the history of a region have been so grossly neglected in what was posited as a political 'solution'.

There were immediate consequences of the EU's recognition of Slovenia and Croatia. Having become a major catalyst to territorial realignment, the Union was then propelled into the position of peace mediator in former Yugoslavia. Given its aspirations in respect of the second pillar of the Treaty of European Union, it is likely that this was not at first unwelcome. The inadequacy of its frail institutions for the enormity of the task was, however, soon exposed especially in respect of Bosnia. Having failed to broker a peace in Bosnia, there

was a rapid outbreak of conflict in that country in August 1992. There was consensus in the Western community that external intervention was required either to keep or to make a negotiated peace. This led to the idealistic suggestion that the EU should take responsibility for such an intervention force, especially if it was to be seen to share the responsibilities of 'global policing' with the USA. However, the WEU lacked the resources, the command structures and the operational experience to act on behalf of the EU. The limitations of EU pretensions were quickly and cruelly exposed, after it became clear that there was no alternative to UN involvement in both the peace negotiations and, through UNPROFOR, in peacekeeping and delivering humanitarian aid.

After EU pretensions had been stripped away, the traditional role of national governments was reaffirmed, especially that of the only two member states with the capacity for significant foreign military undertakings, the British and the French governments. These two countries, together with Germany, the USA and Russia have also formed the five-member contact group which has been most influential in seeking to broker a peace in Bosnia. However, they have had no more foreign policy success than the EU, so that Western European intervention in the crisis has appeared, at best, confused. The same applies to the leading role taken by the UN whose own mandate has resulted in a confused mixture of enforcement and peacekeeping activities (Higgins, 1993). This stopped—if only for a short time—the spread of armed conflict beyond Bosnia, but at a high price in terms of human suffering.

European Union intervention in the former Yugoslavia has also been hampered by Greece's, at times, uncompromising adherence to its national foreign policy interests at the expense of even a pretence of maintaining a common EU stance. The ending of the cold war could have heralded new trade and investment opportunities for Greece in the Balkans, but foreign policy in the early 1990s became entangled with traditional and previously submerged enmities over border security and ethnic minorities. Greece was at odds with Macedonia over its new name and its flag, leading to imposition of a Greek trade blockade in early 1994 and the Commission of the EU referring Greece to the European Court of Justice. In addition, Greece was at odds with the Albanian government over the treatment of ethnic Greeks, and with the EU over suspicions that it allowed violations of the UN trade sanctions on Serbia. All of this was grafted on to its long-standing disputes with Turkey over the partition of Cyprus, relations with the EU, and sovereignty in the Aegean Sea and airspace (Gürel, 1993). As a result of these disputes, Greece found itself increasingly isolated from its EU partners at a time when there was already growing disenchantment with Greece's failure to impose agreed economic policies in return for financial support. In effect, Greece was distancing itself from the very institution which provided the most substantial bulwark to its independence and influence.

By 1995 Greece had decided to step back from its isolationism and had launched a series of bridge-mending initiatives with its Balkan neighbours. Foreign Minister Carolos Papoulias visited Albania and Bulgaria and agreed to direct talks with Macedonia. As a result, at the time of writing Greece and Albania were set to sign a friendship agreement over the status of northern Epirus (a region in southern Albania with an ethnic Greek majority—see Chapter 10); the support of Bulgaria had been secured for construction of a Black Sea–Aegean oil pipeline from Russia; agreement had been secured for the Customs Union with Turkey in return for a timetable for Cyprus's membership of the EU; and negotiations were about to commence on recognition of Macedonia and ending of Greek trade sanctions. Even if solid progress is made in all of these areas, a number of potential disputes remain, including the issue of work permits for the Albanians working illegally in Greece, disputes with Bulgaria over shared use of the water of the Nestos River, and a whole raft of disputes with Turkey with whom relations remain distinctly frosty. Nevertheless, there

were some signs in 1995 that the foreign policy gap between Greece and the rest of the EU was narrowing, offering hope of a more collective approach to the security and diplomatic problems of the region.

Whatever the prospects for EU common policy in the future, the crisis in the former Yugoslavia has starkly highlighted the complex and overlapping set of international institutional affiliations in the region (Lawrence, 1994) (Figure 18.2). The 51-member Organisation for Security and Cooperation in Europe (OSCE) has the most comprehensive membership both in the region and in Europe as a whole, and its principal brief is to address issues related to pan-European security interests. Therefore, potentially, it could have been the most influential mediator in the crisis in the former Yugoslavia. However, in practice it has been riven with national interests (Russia, for example, has been reluctant to condemn its traditional ally Serbia) and has lacked the resources for any effective form of intervention. Instead, as long as the Russians, British and French continue to insist on their independent influences exerted via their seats on the UN Security Council, and as members of the five-nation contact group, the OSCE is unlikely to be able to exert any more than moral pressure.

NATO is the international body which has been most directly involved in the crisis, other than UNPROFOR. As an international organisation it lacks genuinely independent capacity, being subject to the will of its member states, and particularly of the USA. For most of its existence it has been dominated by the United States, which, in the post-cold war period, has sought to reduce its commitment to European security via a policy of greater burden-sharing with its European allies. The United States has not seen the crisis in the former Yugoslavia—unlike the Gulf War—as being central to its national interests. Instead, it insists that this is an arena where the Europeans should shoulder more of the burden of international 'policing'. There have been considerable disagreements between the United States and its European partners—especially France and the UK—over the role of

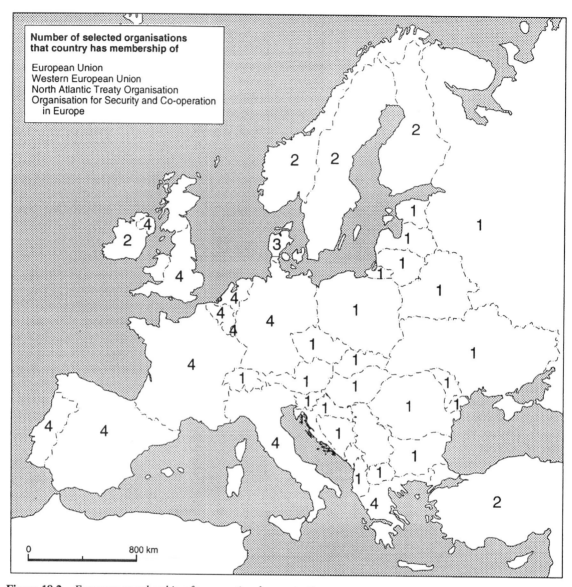

Figure 18.2 *European membership of supranational organisations*

NATO in the conflict. In the end NATO has been marginalised, being primarily restricted to trying to enforce the no-fly policy over Bosnia. The real impact of this on the course of the conflict has been limited. However, the Balkan crisis has been critical for NATO itself in that it has had to rethink its approach to operations outside of its area. When NATO planes in January 1994 intercepted and shot down Serbian aircraft, it was in fact the first ever 'out of area' combat mission by that organisation. Whether NATO could or would have played a greater role in the conflict if it had not been restricted by the overall command of UNPROFOR is debatable, for the scope of its actions would still have been constrained by Russian interests in the region, and by divisions among its leading member states.

The broader significance of the current crisis in the former Yugoslavia is that it could be an unfortunate model for further ethnic conflicts within and across international borders, which could undermine European security. In the most pessimistic scenario, there is the terrible prospect of a series of interlinked ethnic issues throughout and adjacent to the Balkans which could develop into outright conflicts. Furthermore, nationalism in Eastern Europe and the former USSR is different from that in Western Europe for there is no mediating framework of recent democratic traditions but instead a background of profound, deep and divisive economic and political transformation.

If this pessimistic scenario was to unfold, then the crisis in the former Yugoslavia has indicated very limited Western European political willpower, and indeed capacity, to intervene in any future attempts to realign territorial boundaries in Central and Eastern Europe. The British and French both have pretensions to be regional powers in the European arena, but in truth their military and political capacities are limited. A united Germany could have the economic, political and the military might for intervention, but its recent history is a major constraint on such a role. In the circumstances, only the EU, via the WEU, and NATO have the potential for significant intervention, but if and only if the lessons of the crisis in former Yugoslavia can be learnt and acted on.

NATO may well come to play a greater role in the region. In response to demands from the countries of Central and Eastern Europe for full membership of NATO since the end of the cold war, there have been closer links to the alliance. In 1991 they were offered the North Atlantic Cooperation Council, a form of diplomatic link; then in 1994 they were given a form of associate membership via the Partnership for Peace; and in December 1994 a study group was set up to consider the implications of full membership. From the perspective of the Central and Eastern European countries, NATO seems to offer great-

er security—perhaps against Russia, or even against each other. Whatever the real motives for their applications—and they may be as much political as security ones—there is the future potential for NATO to become embroiled in territorial and ethnic issues in Central and Eastern Europe. It is not a role for which it is well equipped, or comfortable with, as has been illustrated by the Kurdish issue within Turkey and the tensions between Turkey and Greece, both of whom are alliance members. The speed with which NATO membership becomes a reality is, however, still in question, not least because of Russian opposition to this eastern enlargement.

Turning to the EU, it is clear that the former Yugoslavia has provided a lesson in the realities of aspiring to superpower status. But perhaps we need not be unduly pessimistic about the future of the common security and foreign policies. The development of a collective approach must, of necessity, be a step-by-step process. Involvement in the war in Bosnia—however ineffectively—could prove to be a vital formative stage in the establishment of the second pillar. The eventual outcome is far from certain, not least because it is intrinsically linked with the question of the future course of political union. As Budd argues (1993, p. 35):

... in the intergovernmental compromises that are the hallmark of EC decision-making there are strict limits on its ability to transcend state interests and lowest common denominator policy-making, even where an institutional network has evolved to improve communication and the flow of foreign policy information and thereby minimise misunderstandings. States will be selective over those issues that they wish to see pursued via collective diplomacy.

Mortimer (1995, p. 20) takes an even bleaker view of the present strength of the second pillar, arguing that: 'The Maastricht structure might almost have been designed to make a common foreign policy impossible', because it sets out to deny any increase in powers for the Commission, the only single body capable of formulating and implementing a genuinely common set of policies. Instead, decision-making is left to the Council of Ministers, analysis is supposed to be provided by the Council's meagre secretariat resources, and implementation is 'left to the diplomatic service of whichever state, large or small is holding the presidency'. Arguably, then, a greater degree of federalism is a necessary precondition for an effective second pillar, and the 1996 Intergovernmental Conference will give some indication of whether this is a prospect for the medium or the longer term.

18.4 Turkey and the Balkans

In the former Yugoslavia alone there are an estimated 6 million Sunni Muslims, both of Turkish and non-Turkish origin. In numerical terms they were most significant (excepting the special case of Kosovo) in Bosnia–Hercegovina, where they represented an estimated 44% of the population. It was hardly surprising then that the Islamic countries, particularly Turkey, took a close interest in events in the Balkans. President Izetbegovic of Bosnia has expounded a belief in a moderate, secular Islam and also in the need for pan-Islamic solidarity among the world's Muslim communities. He has on several occasions made appeals to individual governments and to the Organisation of the Islamic Conference (OIC) for aid and intervention on behalf of his country. The responses of the leading Islamic countries have been mixed. Moderate Saudi Arabia has followed a cautious diplomatic course, seeking an international accord on Bosnia, supporting the successful efforts of the OIC to exclude the rump of the former Yugoslavia from the UN, and providing financial assistance for refugees in Albania and elsewhere. Iran, in contrast, outrightly condemns the West for the double standards it has shown in terms of its willingness to intervene on a massive scale in the Gulf crisis when its oil interests were threatened, and its reluctance to intervene as a peacemaking force in Bosnia. However, Turkey is the Islamic country most affected by the present crisis and this section of the chapter examines its relationship with the Balkans.

Before looking at Turkey's involvement with the Balkans in the 1990s, it is useful to make a brief historical diversion. Perhaps one of Turkey's principal legacies from the Atatürk period was the belief—widely adopted by its governing élites—in a European vocation and in non-interventionism. This has been avidly followed up to the 1990s, and both tenets were reinforced by the political climate of the cold war period which emphasised the inviolability of territorial sovereignty and the role of Turkey as an ally of the West, particularly of the USA. Turkey's relationships with the EU have waxed and waned over the years, but appeared to have been cemented by the 1963 Treaty of Association. In 1987 Turkey applied for full membership of the Community, but was rejected on the grounds of economic conditions, its size, human rights record and democratic credentials. There was also the underlying question of whether the EU was ready to accept as a member a country of 57 million Muslims. Turkey has also been dismayed that it has only been granted observer status in the EU, while Greece has been able to opt for full membership. In Turkish opinion this threatens to unbalance relationships and international security arrangements in the Aegean. It is against this background that Turkey has sought to reshape its international relations during the 1990s (Eralp, 1993).

Turkey's relationships with the Balkans have been sensitive in the extreme given the long Ottoman domination of the region. During the interwar years, Atatürk's government pursued careful, discrete and polite relations with its Balkan neighbours. After the Second World War, relationships became polarised: they were cool and minimal with Bulgaria and Romania, but warmed with Greece and Yugoslavia because of the perceived threat from the Soviet Union. Turkey actually signed a Treaty of Friendship and Cooperation with the latter two countries, but this fell into neglect, especially as relations with Greece deteriorated, nosediving after the 1974 partition of Cyprus. Turkey therefore continued largely to neglect the Balkans, instead concentrating on developing its political links with the EU and the USA. When the crisis in the former Yugoslavia first broke in the early 1990s, it received little attention in Turkey which was preoccupied with the conflict between Armenia and Azerbaijan, and with the potential for developing links with the Turkic republics.

Pressure at home, and the exposure of the 'ethnic cleansing' of Muslim communities in Bosnia were, however, to lead to a sharp shift in opinion. There were several reasons for this, including the legacy of scattered Turkish communities across the Balkans, the tie of religions especially as the West seemed unwilling or powerless to prevent Orthodox Christians from slaughtering Muslims, and pressure from the wider Muslim community especially the Turkic republics wherein Turkey was trying to establish itself as a role model for the newly established states. It also has considerable actual and potential trade interests in the region, especially with the gradual introduction of market reforms into the Balkans. Meanwhile, the government in Ankara has been under growing domestic pressure from fundamentalist elements and from right-wing parties such as the Welfare Party. Not surprisingly then, Turkish governments have been keen to be seen to take a keen interest in the events accompanying the disintegration of Yugoslavia.

As a member of NATO, of the OSCE and of the Council of Europe, Turkey has the capacity to exert some influence, in so far as these international institutions have any influence at all on events in the former Yugoslavia. Such a role is consistent with Turkey's aspirations to establish itself as a regional power, an aspiration which has strengthened since the EU was so discouraging in 1989 about its future accession. This regional role is broadly based and encompasses its relationships with the Middle Eastern countries, the Turkic-speaking republics and the Black Sea countries via the Black Sea Economic Cooperation project (Ataöv, 1993). Of all these roles, it is that in the Balkans which is of most immediate relevance to the future of Europe.

Although Turkey has taken a renewed interest in the Balkans in the 1990s, it has been relatively cautious in its approach, even with respect to the events accompanying the disintegration of Yugoslavia. It gave early diplomatic recognition to the newly independent Bosnian republic and signed economic and technical pacts with the Bosnian government in 1992. Turkey also offered troops to the UN for its mission in Bosnia, an offer which was accepted in 1993 after initial Greek resistance. Ankara has also been seeking a lifting of the arms embargo.

Turkey's involvement in the Balkans goes beyond the crisis in Bosnia. It has also consolidated its relationship with Albania, signing a military assistance treaty in 1992 and proposing the trans-Balkan railway project from Istanbul to the port of Durrës in Albania (see Chapter 11). Turkey has also been supportive of Macedonia's independence, not least because of the latter's conflict with Greece. It has also successfully rebuilt its relations with Bulgaria following the overthrow of the Zhivkov regime which had attempted a policy of forced assimilation of the Turkish minority in the 1980s.

In the face of these new international relations, Greece has become increasingly nervous of Turkey's role as a regional power and of the creation of what could be viewed as a pro-Turkey arc on its northern borders stretching from Albania to the Bosphorus. Greece is, of course, buttressed by its membership of NATO and of the EU (including the WEU), although as noted earlier, its recent diplomacy has not been well received by its European partners. Greece, however, does hold a trump card in this dangerous game of Balkan poker. Its membership of the EU puts it in a position to influence relations with the Balkan countries, especially in respect of Turkey. Its willingness to use this power has been amply illustrated by its long-standing veto (only overturned in 1995) of EU aid to Turkey, its delaying of the ratification of the Customs Union between Turkey and the EU and its threat to veto future membership for its traditional foe.

If the Bosnian crisis is a religious war, as most Islamic countries hold, then it is a conflagration which could spread with devastating effect to Albania, Kosovo and Macedonia, at the very least, and could draw in other larger regional powers such as Bulgaria. In the extreme case it might even involve Greece and Turkey in conflicts over Thrace with its approximately 200 000 Muslims. This is a matter of grave concern for the EU, whose overriding interest is in restoring stability to the Balkans, a region which lies across the EU's exposed southeastern and Mediterranean borders. Not only is regional stability a prerequisite for fruitful cooperation in the Balkans and the eastern Mediterranean, but a stable and harmonious Balkan region is a requirement for an enlarged and stable Europe.

18.5 The Balkans and the European Union

Some of the implications for Europe of 'the problem from hell' have already been discussed, particularly with respect to refugees, foreign and security policy, and the general political stability on the southeastern border of the EU. By way of conclusion, it is also important to realise how the Balkan crisis could have even wider ramifications, influencing the so-called 'architecture' of European union.

Since 1989 the EU has been faced with a new agenda, the search for a new institutional formula for its relationships with the states of Central and Eastern Europe in the post-cold war period. It has moved cautiously towards the idea of future full membership for many of these countries. Thus far it has signed a series of bilateral agreements with Poland, the Czech Republic, the Slovak Republic, Hungary, Poland, Romania and Bulgaria. These are essentially agreements to liberalise trade during the course of the 1990s with the aim, confirmed at the 1990 Copenhagen European Summit, of eventual membership of the EU. There can be little doubt that but for the violent disintegration of Yugoslavia, either the old republic or the newly independent states could have hoped for similar treatment. If, or perhaps when, such an enlargement occurs, it will lead to major changes in the north–south balance of the EU as well as, more obviously, in the east–west balance.

The process of enlargement, including the accession of the Balkan states, will bring about, of necessity, major changes in the EU. It is unlikely that enlargement can proceed without a substantial remodelling of the EU itself. Decision-making processes in an organisation of 20-plus members will have to change, and that almost inevitably will mean more majority voting and greater political union. This would suggest that widening cannot occur prior to a real deepening of EU structures. Yet there will also be pressures for the EU to move further towards an à la carte format so as to reconcile the divergent interests of both new and existing member states with its drive towards greater economic and political integration, which implies that some aspects of deepening will be selective. This was recognised in the initial framework document published by the Commission of the EU in preparation for the 1996 Intergovernmental Conference which is to review the Maastricht Treaty and the further stages of European integration. Among its priorities are the need to develop a truly common policy in line with its economic strength, the need to review the ineffective third pillar on justice and home affairs, and the extension of majority voting as a precondition for further enlargement.

This last point brings us to the timetable for future enlargement, about which the EU has been assiduously imprecise. At present, there is speculation, especially following the December 1994 meeting of the European Council, that the next enlargement of the EU will occur at the end of the century and that it will include the six East European countries with which the EU has signed bilateral accords, as well as Cyprus and Malta which have long-standing applications for membership. Accession of the Eastern European countries to the EU assumes that there will be substantial progress in their economic transformations, and there are far more uncertainties than certainties in this sphere. Perhaps the most realistic scenario is that the Višegrad Four (Poland, Hungary, Czech and Slovak republics) will become members some time before the Balkan applicants. The first new Balkan members—Bulgaria and Romania—are unlikely to become members until some time in the first two decades of the next century. Slovenia may become a member at the same time, if this has not already occurred in tandem with the Višegrad Four. Slovenia is an unusual applicant in that it is relatively small and prosperous (its GDP per capita is higher than that of Greece) and economically it could be absorbed relatively easily. However, its earlier accession could be hindered by property disputes with Italy or by reluctance to treat it differently from Croatia. Whatever the outcome, it is difficult to believe that Slovenia will not be in the first wave of accessions of the ex-Yugoslav republics. Thereafter, the predictions become even more speculative, as the EU has to face up to its interests and responsibilities in the Balkans at large. Turkey's membership is still to be decided on, Albania may decide to apply for membership, as—depending on the outcome of the present conflict—will some or all of the remaining republics of the former Yugoslavia. No timetable can be suggested for these latter countries until a permanent peaceful solution has been brokered in Bosnia, Croatia and Serbia.

In this scenario, the critical period for the Balkans will come in the first quarter of the twenty-first century. This will be when the EU really has to face up to the question of what kind of future Europe it envisages, and whether its relationships with the region will be as an external superpower or as a parent international organisation. At one level this involves a debate about the very nature of the EU as a federal as opposed to an intergovernmental organisation. At a much more basic level it raises questions that the EU has not openly confronted, such as the relationships between Greece and Macedonia, or Croatia and Serbia, becoming those between member states, or emigration from Montenegro and Turkey becoming internal to the single European market. Whatever the timetable, the task of redefining the relationship of the EU with the Balkans poses formidable questions, such as will make previous rounds of enlargement seem virtually controversy free.

18.6 References

Ataöv, T., 1993, Turkey, the CIS and Eastern Europe, in Balkir, C., Williams, A. M., eds, *Turkey and Europe*, Frances Pinter, London, pp. 191–200.

Baldwin-Edwards, M., 1991, Immigration after 1992, *Policy and Politics*, **19**(1), 617–36.

Budd, A., 1993, *The EC and foreign and security policy*, University of North London, European Dossier Series, No. 28, London.

Carter, F. W., 1977, *An historical geography of the Balkans*, Academic Press, London.

Carter, F. W., French, R. A., Salt, J., 1993, International migration between East and West in Europe, *Ethnic and Racial Studies*, **16**(3), 467–91.

Crawley, H., 1993, *The refugee crisis facing Western Europe*, University of Sussex, Research Paper No. 11 in Geography, Brighton.

ECRE (European Council on Refugees and Exiles), 1994, *Minutes and conference papers from the ECRE Biannual General Meeting, October 1st and 2nd*, ECRE, Geneva.

Eralp, A., 1993, Turkey and the EC in the changing post-war international system, in Balkir, C., Williams, A. M., eds, *Turkey and Europe*, Frances Pinter, London, pp. 24–44.

European Communities, 1994, *Opinion on the communication from the Commission to the Council and the European Parliament on immigration and asylum policies*, European Communities, Economic and Social Committee, Opinions and Reports, CES(94) 1008, Brussels.

Fenske, J., 1993, The West and 'the problem from hell', *Current History*, **92**(577), 353–6.

Gürel, S. S., 1993, Turkey and Greece: a difficult Aegean relationship, in Balkir, C., Williams, A. M., eds, *Turkey and Europe*, Frances Pinter, London, pp. 161–90.

Higgins, R., 1993, The new United Nations and former Yugoslavia, *International Affairs*, **69**, 465–83.

King, R., 1994, Migration and the single market for labour: an issue in regional development, in Blacksell, M., Williams, A. M., eds, *The European challenge: geography and development in the European Community*, Oxford University Press, Oxford, pp. 218–41.

Lawrence, P., 1994, European security: from euphoria to confusion, *European Security*, **3**, 217–35.

Mortimer, E., 1995, Euro-structures under one roof, *Financial Times*, 3 May.

Williams, A. M., 1994, *The European Community: the contradictions of integration*, Basil Blackwell, Oxford, 2nd edn.

19

Reconstructing the Balkans: the economic horizon

Derek Hall and Darrick Danta

19.1 Framework for reform

The early post-war emphasis placed upon industrialisation, and especially on the rapid adoption of heavy industry as the economic basis for the consolidation of a socialist state, was particularly significant in a corner of Europe notable for its low level of industrial and urban development (Hoffman, 1972; Gianaris, 1982; Lampe and Jackson, 1982). The claimed radical approach to economic planning introduced by the Communists initially appeared to promise a spatial and structural (re)distribution of economic activity which would both assist the modernisation of the region's economics and articulate socialist principles. In the latter case, instances of what Hamilton (1971a,b) referred to as adoptive—ideologically motivated—location decisions were particularly notable in Yugoslavia (Hamilton, 1968), where plants were located in upland, remote, backward and minority areas, apparently irrespective of raw material, transport, energy and market considerations.

The extent to which such location decisions typified the Balkans in particular and socialist Eastern Europe in general was a point of some debate (Turnock, 1978). None the less, post-war decades witnessed a changing emphasis in relation to the 'equity–efficiency trade-off', whereby relatively inefficient yet ideologically motivated location decisions gave way to those based on economic efficiency and regional and national competitive considerations. Yet both for demagogic reasons and because the Balkan societies were starting from a lower base than their East–Central European comrades, Romania and Albania in particular continued giving a high priority to heavy industrial development well into the 1980s. Although the statistical data are notoriously unreliable, regional inequalities would appear to have been reduced as investments were made in less well-endowed areas (Mihailović, 1972; Fuchs and Demko, 1979), but were by no means eliminated (Buckwalter, 1995).

The role of Soviet bloc coordination in the development of the Balkan space economy was variable. Although some manufacturing capacity in Bulgaria and Romania was located in relation to inputs delivered by the former Soviet Union, such considerations appeared to be less crucial than for the more economically advanced countries of East–Central Europe. In Yugoslavia, by contrast, a spatial diffusion of activity not only met ideological requirements but was seen

Reconstructing the Balkans: A Geography of the New Southeast Europe. Edited by Derek Hall and Darrick Danta.
©1996 John Wiley & Sons Ltd

as a strategic necessity in the face of potential hostility from the Soviet Union after 1948. The latter factor was significant in the dominance of the military–industrial establishment both here and in Albania.

Under state socialism, in return for the dogma of full employment, every able-bodied adult was expected to work, a Faustian contract whereby overmanning, inefficiency and a lack of tangible incentive were to symbolise a basic flaw in these countries' political economies (e.g. Koulov, 1992). With a low-wage formal economy—'they pretend to pay us and we pretend to work'—the second economy flourished (Haraszti, 1977; Kenedi, 1981), such that a social and economic duality came to dominate people's lives throughout much of Eastern Europe, although 'entrepreneurial' opportunities were more restricted in the less developed and more repressive states. In contrast to other governments of the region, Belgrade admitted to substantial unemployment, and undertook a number of agreements with West European countries in the mid-1960s to permit labour migration (notably to West Germany). Such propping up of the capitalist system by citizens of a supposed socialist country was condemned by Yugoslavia's neighbours.

All the while the region's infrastructure deteriorated and fell well behind Western standards. Now, the region has ambitious aspirations for infrastructure projects, both to upgrade regional and national systems to Western standards and to reorient their geographical emphasis westwards. Yet individual claims are both competing against each other and with those of East–Central Europe, where returns for investors are likely to be better in the shorter term. Further, while the resources of the multilateral lending agencies are painfully finite, commercial banks, conscious of the higher risks involved in Balkan infrastructure projects, are reluctant to extend finance for long-term investments without substantial guarantees. Governments are having to consider more creative financing options while consumers will find themselves paying higher prices for services provided (Calbreath, 1995, p. 39).

Confronting post-socialist transition from a less developed economic base, the loss of Soviet economic subsidies and markets for poor-quality goods and services was less dramatic in absolute terms for Southeast than for East–Central Europe. On the other hand, with narrower and less well-developed technological and skill bases, coupled to smaller and less sophisticated home markets, often contradictory legal frameworks and no small degree of corruption, the Balkan economies have not as readily found the flexibility and adaptability to meet changing circumstances. Further, the entrepreneurs of neighbouring 'Western' countries such as Greece, Turkey and Italy have been all too willing to fill commercial niches and short-term consumer requirements on an *ad hoc* basis which has not necessarily contributed to the natural progression and development of the Romanian, Bulgarian and Albanian national economies.

Economic reform can result in a fundamental redistribution of economic activities and their social consequences (e.g. Sziráczki and Windell, 1992). Regional variations in economic well-being are generally increasing in the Balkans as relative investment attractiveness influences domestic and foreign investors (Murphy, 1992). Necessary prerequisites for Balkan market economies include governmental monetary discipline, price liberalisation, asset privatisation and enterprise restructuring (Blanchard *et al.*, 1991; but see also Milanovich, 1991; Sjöberg and Wyzan, 1991; Gajo, 1992; Bogetic, 1993; Gacs *et al.*, 1993; Pashko, 1993; Rose, 1993). In the context of inflationary and unemployment pressures, with enterprises obliged to search for new markets, subsidies and price controls have mostly been abandoned. Legal and ethical codes, procedures for proper accountancy, bankruptcy and the enforcement of contracts, have been slow in evolving to establish a stable and legitimised context for formal commercial development comparable to Western practices. Currencies remain largely inconvertible, the second economy continues to flourish and cross-border petty trading, albeit complicated by sanctions against Serbia–Montenegro and the erstwhile Greek blockade of FYROM, helps to maintain the significance of the 'kiosk economy'.

None the less, signs have appeared that at least some of the Balkan states—both newly established and less recent in origin—are emerging from the post-socialist trauma (Table 19.1). Slovenia's economic recovery has been rapid, with recent high GDP growth and industrial output rates and an escape from the hyperinflation of 1990–92. The other apparently high growth economies of the region—Albania and rump Yugoslavia—are somewhat questionable: Albania's growth, apparently led by agriculture and services, is still none the less highly dependent upon foreign aid and diaspora remittances (Hall, 1995a), while the UN sanctions against Serbia–Montenegro and Belgrade's desperate requirement for foreign investment raise questions about the reliability of the statistical base here. Further, Slovenia's trade deficit is now more than compensated by a surplus on the services balance, particularly reflecting a stronger tourism revenue, a luxury not yet afforded to either Tirana or Belgrade.

Trade reorientation also appears to be an important factor in the economic transition of the Balkans: in 1994 some 60% of Slovenia's foreign trade was conducted with the EU compared to just 11% with the other states of the former Yugoslavia. For Romania, EU countries are also the most important trade partners, accounting for over half of both exports and imports compared to 1989 figures of 31% of exports and a mere 13% of imports (EIU, 1995j, p. 22). Albania's history of dependent (un)development appears to be reasserting itself as, for the first quarter of 1995, more than two-thirds of the country's exports—68%—went to Italy, and 40% of imports came from that source (with a further 23% originating from Greece) (EIU, 1995f, pp. 40–1).

By contrast, neighbouring Croatia's real GDP declined on average by 8% per annum between 1990 and 1994. Industrial production fell even faster, with the 1994 figure representing only just half that of 1989, as investment fell to just 16% of that year's level. However, Zagreb's fortunes

began to show signs of a turnaround in 1994, with a degree of stabilisation, a sharp fall in inflation and a rise in exports (ABECOR, 1995). Recovery continued into the first quarter of 1995, although subsequent conflict in the 'Krajina' and western Slavonia imposed a disruptive effect. Tourism earnings declined by 13% in the first half of 1995, with greater losses expected during the summer (EIU, 1995b, p. 17).

Paradoxically, popular opinion has tended to express support for reform but often not for the reformers, as the volatile political complexion of the region has revealed. It will take perhaps a generation or more for a cohort of political leaders to emerge who are not former Communists, demagogues or dubious entrepreneurs. Respectable citizens have watched their living standards decline as three (not necessarily unrelated) groups have tended to dominate new sources of wealth—the former *nomenklatura*, the 'mafia' and foreigners (e.g. Strauss, 1995). However, research on the role of the second economy in the transformation process is as yet poorly developed (e.g. Sik, 1994).

As central government has divested varying degrees of economic and political control, the roles of local authorities, regional and non-governmental bodies have become more crucial for regional development, particularly in the larger countries such as Romania. At the international level, increased regional access and circulation require:

1. The development of supranational regional cooperation—none of Alpe–Adria, Black Sea Economic Zone or Carpathian groups directly embrace all of the Balkan states;
2. Improvement of border access: frontier crossing delays of hours, even days, are still commonplace for road freight traffic;
3. General transport and communications upgrading.

The little more than US$20 billion invested by the West in Eastern Europe since 1989 (Table 19.2) is a minute portion of global foreign direct investment (FDI) flows. Initial advantage and relative stability have permitted East–Central

Table 19.1 *Balkan economic indicators, 1990–96*

	AL	BG	BH	CRO	MA	R	SLO	YU
a. 1990								
Real GDP growth (%)	nd	−9.1	1.6	−8.5	−9.9	−5.6	−4.7	−8.4
Average annual inflation (%)	0	23.8	nd	609	608	5.1	550	593
Unemployment (%)	9.8	1.7	21.2	11.1	22.0	nd	4.7	19.7
Industrial output (% change)	−7.5	−16.8	−8.0	−11.3	nd	−23.7	nd	−12.0
Agricultural output (% change)	0.1	nd	−5.1	nd	nd	−2.9	nd	−6.9
Imports ($bn)	0.2	3.3	1.9	5.2	1.5	9.1	4.7	6.8
Exports ($bn)	0.1	2.5	2.1	4.0	1.1	5.9	4.1	5.6
Trade balance ($bn)	−0.1	−0.8	0.2	−1.2	−0.4	−3.2	−0.6	−1.2
Total debt ($bn)	nd	10.9	nd	2.9	−0.1	1.2	1.4	nd
b. 1991								
Real GDP growth (%)	−10.0	−11.7	−37.0	−20.9	−10.7	−12.9	−8.1	−11.1
Average annual inflation (%)	36	339	117	123	121	175	118	121
Unemployment (%)	9.4	11.1	17.0	16.6	23.5	3.0	8.2	21.4
Industrial output (% change)	−37.0	−22.2	nd	−28.5	−17.2	−22.8	nd	−198.0
Agricultural output (% change)	−21.8	18.6	nd	−6.6	nd	1.0	nd	9.5
Imports ($bn)	0.3	3.8	nd	3.8	1.4	5.4	4.1	5.5
Exports ($bn)	0.2	3.7	nd	3.3	1.2	4.3	3.9	4.7
Trade balance ($bn)	−0.1	−0.1	nd	−0.5	−0.2	−1.1	−0.2	−0.8
Total debt ($bn)	nd	12.1	nd	2.7	−0.2	2.2	1.4	nd
c. 1992								
Real GDP growth (%)	−9.7	−5.4	nd	−9.7	−14.0	−13.6	−5.4	−27.0
Average annual inflation (%)	226	79	nd	665	1691	211	201	9237
Unemployment (%)	26.7	15.3	28.0	17.1	24.8	8.4	11.6	22.8
Industrial output (% change)	−44.0	−15.9	nd	−14.5	−15.8	−21.9	−2.8	−22.0
Agricultural output (% change)	−7.8	−13.9	nd	−56.0	nd	−13.8	nd	−17.7
Imports ($bn)	0.5	4.2	nd	4.5	1.2	5.8	6.1	3.9
Exports ($bn)	0.1	4.0	nd	4.6	1.2	4.4	6.7	2.5
Trade balance ($bn)	−0.4	−0.2	nd	0.1	0	−1.4	0.6	−1.4
Total debt ($bn)	0.6	12.2	nd	2.6	−0.2	3.5	1.2	5.6
d. 1993								
Real GDP growth (%)	11.0	−2.4	nd	−3.7	−14.1	1.3	1.3	−27.7
Average annual inflation (%)	85	73	nd	1517	335	256	32	116trn
Unemployment (%)	32.5	16.4	nd	18.4	29.0	10.2	14.5	50.0
Industrial output (% change)	−9.9	−6.9	nd	−6.0	−15.0	1.3	−2.8	−37.0
Agricultural output (% change)	14.4	−18.1	nd	34.8	−22.5	12.4	nd	−18.0
Imports ($bn)	0.6	4.6	nd	4.7	1.1	6.0	6.5	nd
Exports ($bn)	0.1	3.7	nd	3.9	1.0	4.9	6.1	nd
Trade balance ($bn)	−0.5	−0.9	nd	−0.8	−0.1	−1.1	−0.4	−1.0
Total debt ($bn)	0.8	12.3	nd	2.6	−0.8	4.5	1.2	5.6
e. 1994								
Real GDP growth (%)	7.4	1.4	nd	−0.8	−7.2	3.5	5.6	6.5
Average annual inflation (%)	20	97	nd	3	57	137	20	0
Unemployment (%)	35.0	13.4	nd	19.5	45.0	10.9	7.4	nd
Industrial output (% change)	−2.0	4.5	nd	−2.7	−20.0	3.3	6.4	1.2
Agricultural output (% change)	6.8	2.5	nd	nd	nd	0.2	nd	4.0
Imports ($bn)	0.7	4.0	nd	5.2	1.4	6.6	7.3	nd
Exports ($bn)	0.2	4.2	nd	4.3	1.1	6.2	6.8	nd
Trade balance ($bn)	−0.5	0.2	nd	−0.9	−0.3	−0.4	−0.5	nd
Total debt ($bn)	1.0	10.8	nd	3.9	0.9	5.5	1.3	5.6

(continued)

Table 19.1 *(continued)*

	AL	BG	BH	CRO	MA	R	SLO	YU
f. 1995 (estimates/forecasts)								
Real GDP growth (%)	6.2	2.4	nd	4.4	−1.0	3.4	5.5	5.0
Average annual inflation (%)	12	26	10	4	10	32	9	100
Unemployment (%)	20	11	nd	17	50	9	14	25
Industrial output (% change)	−8.0	8.0	nd	3.0	−3.0	10.0	12.4	3.5
Agricultural output (% change)	7.0	2.0	nd	nd	nd	5.5	nd	5.0
Imports ($bn)	0.8	4.5	nd	7.0	1.3	7.7	9.4	nd
Exports ($bn)	0.3	4.4	nd	5.0	1.1	7.1	8.5	nd
Trade balance ($bn)	−0.5	−0.1	nd	−2.0	−0.2	−1.5	−0.9	nd
Total debt ($bn)	0.5	11.7	nd	3.5	1.1	3.5	2.1	6.5
g. 1996 (forecasts)								
Real GDP growth (%)	5.8	3.0	nd	3.0	5.0	3.6	5.4	7.0
Average annual inflation (%)	10	25	nd	5	30	25	10	30
Unemployment (%)	18	11	nd	16	13	11	13	20
Industrial output (% change)	2.0	4.8	nd	4.0	10.0	5.0	4.9	5.0
Agricultural output (% change)	5.0	3.0	nd	nd	nd	3.0	nd	nd
Imports ($bn)	0.8	4.8	nd	8.4	nd	8.4	10.6	nd
Exports ($bn)	0.3	4.8	nd	5.6	nd	7.9	9.3	nd
Trade balance ($bn)	−0.5	0	nd	−2.8	nd	−0.5	−1.3	nd
Total debt ($bn)	1.0	12.5	nd	3.8	1.0	6.8	2.2	nd

Notes: $bn = billion US dollars; trn = trillion; AL = Albania; BG = Bulgaria; BH = Bosnia–Hercegovina; CRO = Croatia; MA = Former Yugoslav Republic of Macedonia (FYROM); R = Romania; SLO = Slovenia; YU = Federal Republic of Yugoslavia (Serbia and Montenegro).
Sources: EBRD (1995); EIU (1994, 1995a–j); Flint (1995); Kekic (1995); Lucas (1995a–c); Lucas and Lebl (1995); Misha and Lucas (1995); Misha and Vinton (1995); Vinton (1995). Authors' additional calculations.

Europe (Hungary, Poland, the Czech and Slovak republics) to attract the bulk of inward investment to former Communist Europe (Murphy, 1992; Gibb and Michalak, 1993; Michalak and Gibb, 1993; Michalak, 1995). By contrast, the countries of Southeast Europe, often ambivalent to systemic political and economic change, or embroiled in conflict, and with lower levels of economic and infrastructural development, have inspired limited confidence in potential Western and Asian investors in, and visitors to, the Balkans.

While entrepreneurial and environmental support for development has been assisted by the EU PHARE programme (and to a lesser extent by TEMPUS), and through unilateral arrangements such as the UK 'Know-how Fund', much foreign investment has been channelled via partnerships and joint ventures (Jermakowicz and Drazek, 1993): the automotive industry has become a prime example. Daewoo (South Korea) has invested an estimated US$500 million in the former Olcit factory in Craiova, Romania (Keay, 1995), and has sought investment diversification in the country through shipping, electronics and oil interests (Kapoor and Sweitzer, 1995). Land Rovers and pick-up trucks are to be assembled in former military plants in Bulgaria, with car production being inaugurated from September 1995. In Slovenia, Renault has invested US$180 million in a plant at Nove Mesto, to produce over 100 000 vehicles annually and capture one-third of the country's sales, as well as attacking the wider Central European market, following the company's failure to acquire the Czech Skoda enterprise (Rojec and Svetlicic, 1993).

Although foreign penetration of manufacturing and markets has been on a lesser scale than in East–Central Europe, Balkan production capability and markets are potentially very vulnerable and direct foreign investment may be regarded locally with some suspicion (Dobosiewicz,

Table 19.2 *Balkan and neighbouring countries: foreign direct investment, 1990–93*
A: $ million

	1990	1991	1992	1993	1990–93	% of total
Albania	—	—	19	20	39	0
Bulgaria	4	56	42	62	164	1
Czechoslovakia	188	592	1054	—	2600	21
Czech Republic	—	—	983	606	—	—
Slovak Republic	—	—	71	160	—	—
Hungary	311	1459	1471	2200	5441	44
Poland	88	117	284	350	839	7
Romania	−18	37	73	48	140	1
Russia	—	100	800	1100	2000	16

B: $ per capita

	1990–93	Most important source
Hungary	558	Belgium
Czech Republic	242	Germany
Estonia	139	Sweden
Slovenia	130	Germany
Slovakia	83	Austria
FYROM	45	—
Latvia	30	Russia
Poland	28	USA
Russia	20	USA
Croatia	19	—
Albania	18	Italy
Bulgaria	17	—
Lithuania	13	Russia
Moldova	10	Italy
Romania	9	France

Sources: Anon (1995, p. 96); Keay (1995, p. 31).

1992). The mutual loss of assured markets by the former component parts of Yugoslavia has added further vulnerability (Allcock and Milivojević, 1990; Cviic, 1991; Zarkovic, 1992; Bebler, 1993; Cvikl *et al.*, 1993; Uvalić, 1993; Cohen, 1995), although unlike much of the rest of the Balkans, an experienced class of entrepreneurs was already in place in the 1980s to assist subsequent small- and/or medium-size enterprise (SME) growth (Bartlett and Prašnikar, 1995).

An examination of patterns of private international investment in Bulgaria between 1989 and 1992 (Buckwalter, 1995) found that while the national capital Sofia enjoyed a leading role, there was no evidence of an increasing dominance. This suggested that growing international interest in the service sector of provincial cities could be compensating for investment decline in the manufacturing sector, as well as reflecting the slowness of reform processes and lingering Balkan bureaucratic obstacles to inward investment.

19.2 Rural challenges

Restoration of landownership to individual peasant families, at least in the short term, has brought substantial structural and spatial change in the Balkan countryside. Opening access to landownership for a maximum number of rural families, while accepting restitution claims from former landowners and their families, has highlighted a range of socio-economic issues rising from agrarian reform (see Chapters 13–15, and e.g. Turnock, 1993a,b; Buckwell *et al.*, 1994; Carter *et al.*, 1995):

1. The fragmentation and diminution of holding sizes following comprehensive redistribution has militated against capital investment, economies of scale and application of mechanisation and fertilisation, and has seen the need to fall back on an intensive use of often inexperienced family labour.
2. Some peasants have attempted to regain the same land that they or their forebears were forced to give up under the Communists. This has been particularly notable in upland Albania and Romania.

3. Rural–urban and rural–rural migration has been stimulated, particularly in those societies where rural populations had been restrained by policies preventing long-term migration.
4. Destruction of state farm, cooperative and other state-associated property and infrastructure was experienced in Albania in a rash of anti-state/party antagonism.
5. Delay in completing reform, particularly where disputes have arisen, has left some land uncultivated.
6. In some areas fragmentation has resulted in disruption to marketing and infrastructural maintenance.
7. Reductions in herd sizes have resulted from the abandonment of collective buildings with some stock units being separated from their fodder supply.
8. A substantial shift from cash crops to subsistence food production has taken place in response to a range of factors including fragmentation, lack of confidence in marketing arrangements, lack of access to capital and competition from cheap imported cash crops.
9. Former cooperative workers with no claim to land have found themselves unemployed.

Food self-sufficiency should be an attainable goal: before the Second World War the region was a significant agricultural exporter. New marketing systems are being developed to limit the retreat into subsistence farming, such that, for example, attention is being paid to the availability of fodder for private livestock herds. Informal cooperation has developed, and in some arable farming areas, notably in Romania, cooperative associations supported by the state have been created, particularly for the efficient deployment of machinery. As short-term expedients, not least in absorbing family-based labour, restitution and redistribution need to be followed by amalgamation and consolidation in order to improve efficiency and flexibility in the industry. This will entail not only further considerable spatial and structural change, but appropriate training and motivation for a new generation of farmers.

19.3 Industrial trends

Industrial output has fallen more steeply in the Balkans than in East–Central Europe and is generally taking longer to recover (e.g. Borensztein *et al.*, 1993): hesitant privatisation and political uncertainty, coupled with less developed infrastructures and neighbouring conflict, have limited investment confidence. A strong requirement for skills training and the development of market information systems remains (Hall, 1992b), although the transfer of 'entrepreneurs' from the state to the private sector, often armed with good contacts and overseas bank accounts, has been notable. Encouragement and promotion of inward investment, particularly in manufacturing, can emphasise:

1. Relatively cheap labour for producing goods for Western markets;
2. Trading links and experience with other East European countries and the Middle East;
3. Access to Balkan domestic markets where demand for improved quality is growing, despite often still very restricted disposable incomes.

Investment in both capital equipment and human resources continues to be a crucial requirement for the region's economic future. Encouragement of small industrial projects is being pursued through incubation schemes such as that of the aid-funded Lancashire Enterprises, stimulating the development of small businesses in Albania from an office in Tirana University, the Romanian Ministry of Research and Technology scheme for coordinating a programme for fledgling businesses, and the Bulgarian–German joint scheme setting up SME training centres in Pazardzhik, Stara Zagora and Pleven (BBC, 4 November 1993). Much of the limited capital available is being attracted to the tertiary sector, where financial return can be most readily accrued, notably in small-scale trade, retailing, catering, repairs and construction, and taxi services.

Share-ownership schemes have been, at best, flawed. Romania's attempt at voucher privatisation was compromised by the intervention of speculators. Less than 140 companies—one-sixth of all those mooted for privatisation in 1993— actually passed out of state hands in that year. An acceleration of the process, covering almost 3000 companies, was to take place in the following year, but significant numbers of these were not profitable (Carter *et al.*, 1995), and subsequent attempts to launch public participation in the privatisation process have been dogged by such inefficiencies as the government's inability to distribute subscription forms to the country's 700 share shops on time. In a 1995 poll commissioned by the opposition newspaper *Romania Libera*, almost 40% of those surveyed expressed little faith in the privatisation programme (Ballon, 1995, p. 20).

Environmental problems arising from the legacy of administrative disregard, dogmatic heavy industry and poor-quality fuels are likely to persist (Carter and Turnock, 1993). A survey of Bulgaria in 1993, for example, found that 17 regions, accounting for about 40% of the country's total population, experienced atmospheric conditions in which the presence of pollutants was above permissible levels (BBC, 21 October 1993). Concentrations of industrial dust, sulphur dioxide and other gases in the region have badly damaged the health of forests, crops, buildings and not least humans, as particularly expressed in bronchial and other ailments in children. Water pollution is also characteristic of a number of extensive catchments and coasts resulting from both onshore and offshore sources of degradation. Albania, for example, has yet to develop a sewage-treatment system, and in Bulgaria only one-third of the 187 municipal main drainage systems have effluent purification units. Such requirements should receive a high priority for Western investment, given the health, general environmental and economic benefits likely to accrue from them.

Although more stringent environmental legislation is in place, enforcement continues to be problematic. Increasing car ownership and consumer goods packaging have added new dimensions to environmental deterioration. Further, the environmental consequences of recent conflict in the region have been substantial (e.g. Richardson, 1995).

Reduction in capacity and of manpower in the large 'white elephant' plants which produced poor-quality goods and survived on heavy subsidies, has produced pockets of high unemployment, although where markets and appropriate finance have been available more sophisticated technology has been introduced: the steel industry, for example, has adopted Italian technology in relatively small-scale mills to make greater use of scrap. More so than in East–Central Europe, however, manufacturing in the Balkans has continued to be strongly influenced by government-supported monopolies (Schlack, 1993).

While dependence on low-quality lignite and later Soviet petroleum encouraged the East–Central European states to seek the nuclear energy option, in Southeast Europe there has been a more favourable local availability of hydroelectric power, oil and natural gas which have been harnessed together with a limited adoption of nuclear generation (Carter, 1970; Gurney, 1978; Turnock, 1989). Only Albania, with hydropower and hydrocarbon resources, is close to being self-sufficient. Somewhat ironically, a series of droughts in the late 1980s and early 1990s, severely restricting electricity generation, helped to bring that country to its economic knees, thereby contributing to subsequent political change. Western assistance for the oil and gas industry should improve energy source diversification. In Romania, the drive for self-sufficiency between 1982 and 1989 saw considerable deterioration of the energy infrastructure as spare parts could no longer be imported; import substitution was often undertaken with unreliable and inadequate equipment and materials (Patterson, 1994). As in Albania, industry received priority while domestic users often had their energy supplies cut or rationed, even in midwinter.

Two of the region's three countries active in the nuclear energy industry had links with the West prior to 1989. The Westinghouse 600 MW plant at Krsko in Slovenia was developed between Yugoslavia and a consortium of Western financial partners in a package which included assistance in uranium mining. Located close to the border with Croatia, it continues to function under an equal ownership cooperation agreement between Ljubljana and Zagreb. Romania's nuclear programme, inaugurated in the 1960s (employing British-sourced research equipment), was to embrace completion of the country's first reactor (a 700 MW CANDU model) at Cernavodă in 1995. By contrast, since the Chernobyl accident, the Western media have made much of the perceived technological shortcomings of Bulgaria's Soviet pressurised water reactor (PWR) technology nuclear plant at Kozlodui, upon which the country relies substantially for its electricity (Hall, 1989; Carter, 1990a). Improvements have been undertaken with European Bank for Reconstruction and Development (EBRD) funding, although a number of concerns remain.

A wide variety of technical assistance for the energy industry has followed political change, as exemplified in Romania (Table 19.3). A high priority for the region has been to link into the Union for Coordination of Production and Transmission of Electricity in Western Europe (UCPTE) grid system, which embraced the Czech, Hungarian, Polish and Slovak systems

in October 1995. Conflict in the former Yugoslavia severed UCPTE links to Greece, and the EU PHARE programme is examining the potential for creating a new connection through Hungary and Romania at an estimated cost of US$21 million as a higher priority than renewing the links across the former Yugoslavia (Calbreath, 1995).

19.4 Demographic and urban development

Thus far, relatively little research has been undertaken on post-socialist urban change in the Balkans. This is disappointing for two reasons.

First, a useful body of English language literature, often based on substantial and not always comfortable fieldwork, had been evolving on the nature and characteristics of towns and cities in Southeast Europe under the region's varying forms of state socialism. Our understanding of the structure of Bucharest owed much to the work of Turnock (1970, 1974, 1980, 1990a), while Carter (1973, 1979, 1986) in the cases of Sofia and Tirana, for example, was also able to synthesise a wide range of indigenous language research materials. Fisher's (1963) early work on Zagreb was also notable. The volume of contributions edited by French and Hamilton (1979: e.g. Hamilton and Burnett, 1979; Sampson, 1979) did much to set the agenda for

Table 19.3 *Selected international technical assistance programmes for the Romanian energy industry*

Source	Programme
Bechtel Corporation	Bucharest district heating system
L'École Polytechnique Fédérale, Lausanne	Digital simulation of district heating
Électricité de France	Load regulation
ENTUV, Essen	Training, supervision, refitting steam boilers
EU/EU PHARE	Energy efficiency and conservation
UCPTE/UNIPEDE	Linking Romania's grid with the rest of Europe
World Bank	Upgrading petroleum and gas sectors
World Bank	Refitting power stations

Source: Patterson (1994, pp. 159–66).

research into urban structure in the region in the 1980s. More general appraisals of urban characteristics focused on housing (Carter, 1990b; Hall, 1990b; Magnusson, 1990; Topham, 1990; Turnock, 1990b), urban demographic and social characteristics (Geco, 1970; Mirowski and Milnar, 1984); urban planning (Fuchs, 1980; Carter, 1987; Dawson, 1987; Hall, 1987; Turnock, 1987), new town development (Carter, 1975; Sampson, 1984; Hall, 1986; Turnock, 1986) as well as on wider processes of urbanisation (Pounds, 1971; Ronnas, 1982; Thomas, 1982).

Second, much research has been undertaken in recent years on post-socialist European urban and regional structure and change, but most of it has been concentrated in the more advanced societies of East–Central Europe, where trends may be more clear-cut, access is easier and databases are more readily available and reliable (e.g. Sýkora and Štěpánek, 1992; Ladányi, 1993; Leitmann, 1994; Pickvance, 1994).

A rapid swelling of the region's urban population (Table 19.4) is clearly taking place as the consequence both of the migratory impact of conflicts and political change and of a speeding up of rural to urban migratory processes, expressing a release of pent-up demand as former administrative constraints on rural populations have been removed, and reflecting economic restructuring. New urban forms are emerging, but in terms of spatial structure and built environment are less dramatic than some of the socialist period excesses (e.g. Danta, 1991, 1993).

Land value inflation has been much lower in the Balkans than in East–Central Europe, where values have risen to West European levels. Throughout much of the Balkans bureaucratic procedures and legal prohibitions have severely limited foreign participation in land and property ownership. Somewhat perversely, Albanian land prices have been inflated by Kosovar refugees using their savings to buy land for settlement, complicating an already disputatious process of land redistribution. Albania has been notable for the growth of spontaneous settlements, resulting from both domestic mobility and Kosovar

immigration, most readily observed in the Tirana–Durrës corridor. The particularly high concentration of defensive concrete bunkers in this region has provided ready-made accommodation for migrants. The larger bunkers, which could house 75 mm guns, have been repaired and refurbished, despite their lack of sanitation, with some being used to house small businesses (Reuter, 1993). Fuelled by such processes, the capital is expected to double its population size by the end of the decade, placing an impossible strain on an already beleaguered housing sector which, even by official estimates, has an immediate requirement for 150 000 new units in urban areas (Misha, 1995).

The region is generally regarded as having been under-urbanised under Communism, with the widespread incidence of longer-distance commuting being a tangible consequence (e.g. Fuchs and Demko, 1977, 1978). The urban tertiary sector remains underdeveloped, although the tangible consequences of the rise of the 'kiosk' economy can be found on the street corners and open spaces of many cities in the region. Housing privatisation, already gaining momentum under state socialism in the 1980s (Sillince, 1990; Turner *et al.*, 1992), has been implemented across the region, with Slovenia's programme having been notably swift and relatively successful (Sendi, 1995; see also Dekleva, 1994; Mandič, 1994; and Chapter 9 in this volume).

19.5 The position of women

The role of women in the region's transformation is crucial both economically and symbolically (Funk and Mueller, 1993, p. 2). Yet, apart from debates over abortion, little attention appears to be being paid to women's issues in Balkan reconstruction.

Under state socialism women carried a 'triple burden', being expected to function in three social roles: as mother and wife, as good worker or competent professional, and as social activitist (Petrova, 1993, p. 23). Certainly the planned provision of canteens at both workplace and

Table 19.4 *Balkan and neighbouring countries: demographic dimensions*
A: snapshot statistics

Country	Area ('000 km²)	Population						Life expectancy f/m*
		In millions	Density per km²	% change per year	Birth rate per '000	Death rate per '000	% Urban	
Albania	27	3.4	124	1.9	22	6	35	75/70
Bosnia–Hercegovina	51	4.4	86	0.5	14	6	38	73/68
Bulgaria	111	9.0	82	0.1	12	12	70	76/71
Croatia	57	4.9	86	0.4	12	11	54	74/67
Greece	129	10.3	80	0.5	12	10	63	79/74
Hungary	93	10.6	114	−0.1	12	13	60	75/68
Italy	294	58.1	198	0.2	11	11	69	80/73
Macedonia	25	2.2	88	1.1	17	7	54	72/68
Moldova	34	4.5	134	0.9	18	9	47	72/65
Romania	238	23.2	101	0.3	15	11	50	74/69
Serbia–Montenegro	102	10.5	103	0.5	15	9	48	73/68
Slovenia	20	2.0	99	0.5	13	10	60	75/67
Turkey	770	60.9	79	2.5	27	8	48	68/65

*Life expectancy at birth: females/males.
Source: Rayner *et al.* (1994, pp. 7–22).

B: Population change, 1990–94

	Mid-year population (millions)				
	1990	1991	1992	1993	1994*
Albania	3.25	3.29	3.36	3.36	3.37
Bosnia–Hercegovina	nd	nd	nd	nd	nd
Bulgaria	8.95	8.59	8.54	8.47	8.43
Croatia	4.76	4.78	4.79	nd	nd
Macedonia	nd	nd	2.06	2.07	2.09
Romania	23.21	23.19	22.79	22.75	22.72
Serbia–Montenegro	10.53	10.41	10.45	10.48	nd
Slovenia	2.00	2.00	2.00	1.99	1.99

*Estimates.
Sources: EIU (1995b, pp. 11, 19, 29, 36; 1995f, pp. 4, 30; 1995j, p. 3).

local residential area was meant, initially at least, to lighten women's load, as were launderettes and labour-saving devices. All of this presupposed that such chores were the woman's responsibility (e.g. see Nickel, 1989). Balkan patriarchal peasant tradition has provided a rich vein of conservatism conditioning gender relations today (Harsanyi, 1993; Todorova, 1993) and undermining socialist ideals earlier. Even in mid-1970s Stalinist Albania, a text sympathetic to the Tirana regime noted that while men were learning to take their full share of domestic responsibilities, they had not taken readily to such changes (Ash, 1974, pp. 236–7). Later, a 1986 Tirana University social survey of 450 city residents (Tarifa and Barjaba, 1986, 1990) found women overburdened with housework and child care, and thus marginalised in terms of cultural, professional and political activity. The additional hardships of Balkan life are often overlooked:

having to queue for bread at 4.30 a.m. before starting an eight-hour shift at 6 a.m. and of having to make small amounts of groceries last and please all of the family:

Every mother . . . can point to where communism failed, from the failures of the planned economy (and the consequent lack of food, milk), to the lack of apartments, child-care facilities, clothes, disposable diapers, or toilet paper. The banality of everyday life is where it has really failed, rather than on the level of ideology (Drakulić, 1992, p. 18).

The burden of persisting inadequate infra-structures, disruptions to supplies of water and energy and price inflation has largely been carried by women:

Jeta Kapllani stumbled out of bed at three o'clock yesterday morning, staggered half asleep from her fourth floor flat down the stairs to the ground floor carting pots, pans and buckets. She was fetching the day's water supply for her family of four, a chore that takes her 90 minutes before dawn every day. Power cuts and water shortages are endemic in Tirana. . . . The water—cold only—comes on every morning between three and five. . . . No self-respecting male would be seen dead doing 'woman's work' . . . (Traynor, 1993).

With political change came a re-evaluation of the question, posed across the erstwhile state socialist world, as to whether a woman's right to work, as guaranteed under Communist law and ideology, was indeed a form of emancipation or simply one more aspect of state exploitation. Women often felt forced to work outside of the home (in addition to the inevitable domestic chores), and were likely to be treated at the workplace within the confines of sexual stereo-types (Bren, 1992). Across Eastern Europe any development of women's roles took place within a vacuum, by dint of Communist Party diktat and largely without any commensurate compre-hensive change in social attitudes. Few women appeared to be able to attain significant political positions in their own right: wives of leaders often took key positions. Women's places on leading political, administrative and judicial organs were often based on a quota system rather than a recognition of merit, the proportion

usually being around one-third of the total places available (Childs, 1988, p. 251).

The reform process across the region has been eroding such advantages that women gained under the Communists while further damaging their current status (Einhorn, 1991; Weyr, 1992; Drakulić, 1993b; Milić, 1993; Petrova, 1993; see also Drakulić, 1990, 1993a). Indeed, in a region and era when newly established state systems are desperately seeking self-identity and justification, the return to the pre-Communist role of women can be seen as a symbol of the reappropriation of identity and culture (Funk and Mueller, 1993, p. 10; Harsanyi, 1993; Panova *et al.*, 1993; Todorova, 1993).

In particular, women have been unable to take advantage as readily as men of new economic opportunities. Women are reluctant to take on jobs with private firms that demand even more working hours and do not guarantee maternity leave or child-care benefits: the mechanics of the market economy do not value domestic work or child care. As unemployment has risen, women have been expected to be the first to be displaced (Rosenberg, 1991; Szalai, 1991; Bren, 1992; Williamson, 1992), and discrimination is often overt, in, for example, newspaper job advertise-ments for foreign joint ventures (Fong and Paul, 1992). Rising levels of crime against the person, not least rape, have accompanied an increase in crimes against property. Pornography is sold openly on the streets, and Balkan women's groups appear to have been slower to respond to new conditions than their sisters in East–Central Europe (e.g. Rieder, 1991; Bren, 1992).

While in the longer term (not inexpensive) freedoms of contraception, mobility and employ-ment and the inevitable onslaught of Western modernity on traditional values may assist an improvement in the position of Balkan women, in the short to medium term there are clearly other factors to diminish it: reactions against abortion, a prescriptive capitalist labour market and regressive social attitudes to accompany the return to tradition for national self-identity (Buckley, 1992; Corrin, 1992; Edmundson, 1992; Funk and Mueller, 1993). Most clearly, any reconstruction of the Balkans will be profoundly flawed if it embraces a subordination of women.

19.6 Opportunities for transport, travel and communications

As noted in Chapters 10–12, there has been much debate surrounding the development of Trans-Balkan road and rail communications linked with the growth of activity at Adriatic and Black Sea ports. This debate has a long pedigree (Beaver, 1941). During 1995, the weak link in the plans—Albania—saw considerable foreign support for the project. With the Tirana government itself committed to investing US$200 million in the country's infrastructure during the year, construction of the first leg of the US$128 million east–west highway from Durrës to the Greek and Macedonian borders, part financed by the EU, got under way (Misha, 1995). The EIB and EU PHARE programme are co-financing an expansion and upgrading of the ferry terminal facilities at Durrës. Post-socialist development there has seen ferry services offering ro-ro facilities increasing in frequency from one a week in 1992 to three a day in 1994. The EBRD is supporting a 55 ha industrial park for export-related businesses on the outskirts of Durrës, within 1 km of the new highway linking the port with Tirana. An Italian loan for rail infrastructure is to permit a doubling of train speeds between the two cities (EIU, 1995f, pp. 42–3). Routes to other Balkan ports have been projected for improvement through the Trans-European Motorway (TEM) and Trans-European Railway (TER) projects (Giannopoulos, 1984; Hall, 1992a; Hunya, 1995).

Since 1989 a sharp fall in railway freight tonnages has reflected a demise in industrial output and a reduced import of raw materials from the former Soviet Union. Shorter freight hauls, changing patterns and flow of commodities and commuting are demanding transport flexibility which rail may not be in a position to provide in the longer term.

In addition to a rapid growth in private motor vehicles, commercial road vehicles have also increased with private sector development and the generation of new haul patterns and working practices. Most notably, in 1994 the major German haulier Willi Betz bought 55% of the region's largest trucking enterprise, Somat of Bulgaria, introducing a seven-year US$48 million investment programme entailing the take-up of 1000 new Mercedes vehicles (Whitford, 1995). The virtual halving of Somat's workforce within three years has symbolised the human cost of restructuring in general and that of formerly state-run transport operations in particular, many of which have top-heavy management structures.

The transfer of goods from rail to road also represents a major element in structural change and a contribution to highway congestion. Rail infrastructures are both under-capitalised and often poorly managed, and have been adversely affected, both directly and indirectly, by the region's conflicts: for example, a third of Croatia's system has suffered war damage. International assistance is being employed to upgrade the technological infrastructure of the Albanian, Bulgarian and Romanian rail networks, but service rationalisation and organisational restructuring are required. Passenger services require considerable upgrading of speed, punctuality, interconnections and comfort. Just as the primary objective of international highway policy has been to establish linkage with the West rather than the originally targeted north–south connections of the 1977 TEM project, so within the TER framework Southeast Europe is looking to the longer-term possibility of high-speed train links extending from the West. In the mean time, however, most lines in the region fail to meet European standards and require considerable modernisation investment, for which, at best, only about a third of necessary funding is available locally (Hunya, 1995).

The consequent growth in cross-border road freight movement has contributed to congestion at frontier crossing points (Hickley *et al.*, 1995;

Hunya, 1995) at a time when international trends are pointing the way to removing barriers to trade and movement and when Western methods of logistics planning are being introduced into some Balkan operations. Motorways and dual carriageways are still few: recouping the cost of high-quality highway construction through the imposition of tolls (Hungary) or road use fees (Czech Republic) has been a recent characteristic of East–Central Europe (Hall, 1993c, d; Lavell, 1994), and Bulgaria was to have legislation in place by the end of 1995 to pave the way for tolls to be introduced along a 135 km stretch of the Sofia–Ploviv trunk route, part of the TEM from Western Europe to Istanbul. Supported by PHARE funding (with contracts going initially to UK and Spanish consultants), this first employment of road tolling in the Balkans is to take advantage of the fact that the road is used by some 85% of international motor traffic crossing Bulgaria. Tolling is later to be extended to the Sofia–Varna route (*EEM*, 12 May 1995, pp. 14–15). Thus far, however, the most advanced economies of the region, Slovenia and Croatia, have rejected the tolling option and are relying on loans from the European Investment Bank (EIB) and the European Bank for Reconstruction and Development (EBRD) respectively to support highway developments which are intended particularly to assist a reinvigoration of coastal tourism.

Highway infrastructure across the region tends still to be poor; roadside services have developed since 1989, but their quality is uneven. Potential danger and congestion are exacerbated by the presence of draught animals, under-powered motor vehicles and a burgeoning new generation of inexperienced drivers. Diversion of road freight traffic from the main Zagreb–Belgrade–Niš highway to alternative routes through Bulgaria, Romania and Hungary has acted to highlight shortcomings in the latter countries' infrastructures. The cost of just one new Danube road bridge between Bulgaria and Romania has been put at up to US$500 million (Calbreath, 1995).

Across Eastern Europe, air transport has experienced the twin processes of privatisation

and fleet modernisation as Western finance has been made available to encourage each state to divest itself of its flag carrier and each fleet to replace Soviet-built machines with Boeings and Airbuses (Symons, 1993). In the Balkans, however, only the Bulgarian airline Balkan falls squarely into this category. In the case of both Yugoslavia and Romania, Western aircraft were already employed to a large extent (McDonnell–Douglas and BAC-derived machines respectively) prior to 1989. Albania had no airline of its own under Communism, and the status of fleets carrying the Albanian flag in the 1990s has been questionable. A restructuring of the region's airlines' services, with the demise of long-haul flights to former socialist allies and an emphasis upon hub operation, has been complemented by an increase in Western airlines' flights to, and the spread of destinations within, the Balkans.

Air transport infrastructure upgrading, including the improvement of airports in both capital and provincial cities, has accompanied the privatisation of airport services in East–Central Europe (Hall, 1993c), but progress in this field has been slow in the Balkans. In Sofia and Bucharest, for example, state-operated freight-handling facilities are so stretched that cargo carriers recruit independent crews to take shipments to storage locations far from the airports (Calbreath, 1995). Modernisation of air traffic control systems and their integration into the European Air Traffic Services system via Eurocontrol has been a priority: in 1993, for example, Bulgaria received an ECU 30 million loan from the EIB for this purpose, while Siemens is heading a US$30 million refurbishment of Tirana's Rinas airport which will include an upgrading of ground-handling, radar and control equipment.

The new Balkan economies should be making heavy demands on the development of new telecommunications infrastructures, but while economic and political uncertainty continues to discourage those foreign businesses reliant on good telecommunications facilities from establishing themselves as a major presence in the region, so investment in those facilities will lag behind East–Central Europe, and the Balkan countries

Table 19.5 *Balkan and neighbouring countries: telecommunications availability, 1990/1993/2000*

	1990		1993	2000	
	Total phones (millions)	Per 100 population	Phone main lines per 100 population	Total phones (millions)	Per 100 population
Albania	0.02	0.5	2	0.02	0.4
Bulgaria	3.0	32	28	7.8	77
Hungary	1.8	17	15	2.4	22
Romania	nd	nd	11	nd	nd
Soviet Union	36.6	13		70.0	22
Moldova			12		
Russia	22.0*	15*	16		
Ukraine	8.0*	15*	15		
Yugoslavia	4.8	20		12.0	45
Croatia			21		
FYROM			16		
Serbia–Montenegro			19		
Slovenia			26		

*1991 figures.
Sources: Castle (1990, p. 20, from TRC, 1990); Chalmers *et al.* (1995, p. 39); Szaniawski (1995).

will find their position within the global market further disadvantaged. This was symbolised in January 1994 when the Trans-European Line (TEL), employing optical fibre cable, connected Budapest, Prague, Warsaw and Bratislava with Frankfurt (Hunya, 1995), to some extent replicating the high-speed rail and UCPTE electricity grid links which are beginning to enmesh East–Central Europe, but not the Balkans, with the West.

Ironically, however, local connections throughout the lands east of the Elbe remain poor. In the early stages of political change it was estimated (TRC, 1990) that the then Eastern Europe and Soviet Union would need to spend US$350 billion by the end of the decade on upgrading their telecommunications networks to a level shown in Table 19.5. Subsequent political fragmentation, economic recession and regional conflict leave such projections in doubt. Joint ventures have thus far been restricted to digital overlay networks (DONs), satellite links and mobile services, all aimed primarily at the business community (Szaniawski, 1995).

Outstanding coastal and mountain landscapes, climate, scenery and natural monuments provide Balkan tourism with a potential unrivalled in

Eastern Europe. Further, cultural and heritage sites are of immense value (Hall, 1990a, 1991b). Yet apart from the misleading figures for Albania (Hall, 1984, 1990c), international tourism development in the early 1990s in the former socialist countries of the Balkans was at best hesitant (Table 19.6). This could be attributable to the interaction of a wide range of factors: a lack of clarity of political change, continuing instability, a poor image of infrastructure and service provision, a generally lower degree of road transport accessibility from major West European markets, and a freeing of former Soviet bloc tourists from socialist vacation destinations (Hall, 1991b, 1992c,d, 1993a, 1995b). And of course patronage of established spas and coastal resorts in former Yugoslavia (e.g. Allcock, 1983, 1986, 1990, 1991) was disrupted, both by the break-up of the federation, turning Serbs away from the Croatian and Slovenian Adriatic, and by the subsequent conflict which had a wide-ranging indirect repulsion effect for intending tourists as well as the more obvious direct impact of inflicting heavy damage on Dubrovnik (Chapter 5), Sarajevo and other important centres.

Table 19.6 *Balkan and neighbouring countries: international tourism, 1980–93*
A: *visitor arrivals (millions)*

	1980	1985	1987	1989	1990	1991	1992	1993	% change 1985–89	1989–93
Albania	nd	nd	nd	0.01	0.03	0.01	0.02	0.05	—	69.1
Bulgaria	5.5	7.3	7.6	8.2	10.3	6.8	6.1	8.3	12.3	1.2
Greece	4.8	6.6	8.0	8.1	8.9	8.0	9.3	9.4	28.8	13.8
Hungary	14.0	15.1	19.0	24.9	37.6	33.3	33.5	40.6	64.9	38.7
Romania	6.7	4.8	5.1	4.9	6.5	5.4	6.3	5.8	2.1	15.5
Turkey	0.9	2.2	2.9	4.5	5.4	5.5	7.1	6.5	104.5	30.8
Yugoslavia	6.4	8.4	8.9	8.6	7.9	6.9			−4.1	
Bosnia–Hercegovina							nd	nd		
Croatia							2.0	2.4		
FYROM							0.1	0.1		−90.9
Serbia–Montenegro							0.2	0.1		
Slovenia							0.6	0.6		

B: *tourist receipts (US$ millions)*

	1980	1985	1987	1989	1990	1991	1992	1993	% change 1985–89	1989–93
Albania	nd	nd	nd	3	4	3	2	8	—	62.5
Bulgaria	260	343	494	495	320	44	215	307	44.3	−38.0
Greece	1734	1428	2268	1976	2587	2567	3255	3293	38.4	40.0
Hungary	504	512	784	542	824	1002	1231	1181	5.5	54.1
Romania	324	182	176	167	106	145	262	197	−8.2	15.2
Turkey	327	1482	1721	2557	3225	2654	3639	3959	72.5	35.4
Yugoslavia	1115	1061	1668	2230	2774	468			110.2	
Bosnia–Hercegovina							nd	nd		
Croatia							543	832		
FYROM							11	13		−28.2
Serbia–Montenegro							88	23		
Slovenia							671	734		

nd = no data.
Source: WTO (1993); WTO *Yearbooks*, 1991–95; authors' additional calculations.

Both in terms of tourist numbers and receipts, results were poor compared to those of Greece and Turkey and post-socialist East–Central Europe. As in other aspects of economic transition, an early revival could be detected in Slovenia, where diversification of the tourism product is being pursued, and in the mountain resorts of Romania (RMTT, 1990; Turnock, 1990c, 1991; Flint, 1993b); but, as noted earlier, persisting conflict has seriously constrained any tourism resurgence in Croatia. After an initial precipitous post-Communist decline in interna-

tional arrivals, Bulgaria (Flint, 1993a; Harrison, 1993) appears to have been benefiting from the deflection of coastal tourism away from Dalmatia, with a resurgence in both international tourist numbers and receipts for 1993.

The region's remaining important natural habitats, such as the Danube delta in Romania (Hall, 1991a, 1993b; Karpowicz, 1992; Hall and Kinnaird, 1993, 1994) and the Albanian coastal hinterlands (Hall, 1994) need reinforced protection measures and imaginative forms of 'ecotourism' development. However, attempts to involve local communities, particularly in 'sustainable' tourism development processes, have been constrained in some cases by the lack of experience of bottom-up development upon which citizens could draw (Hall, 1993b). The perceived economic panacea of international tourism is proving hard to resist for many Balkan decision-makers. Yet large-scale infrastructure developments, not necessarily benefiting the local population, will be required to fulfil current plans, and further heavy investment in training and management will be necessary to provide a much-needed improvement in quality of service.

Hotel privatisation is well advanced, and new construction is being undertaken in the capital cities. In Sofia, Hilton International is building a 300-bed hotel, while in Bucharest, a Romanian business family, referred to as 'influential' and 'controversial' figures, has secured the Bucharest Intercontinental hotel with a far lower bid than that of the Marriott US hotel chain. Marriott now plans two large developments in the city by the turn of the century, including a 35-storey hotel/conference/office centre. In Tirana, Austrian and Kuwaiti interests are opening two new complexes and the city's two pre-existing international grade hotels have been refurbished. It is significant, however, that much private investment in the Balkans' 'tourism' sector is being channelled into high-grade capital city hotels, as much a response to the shortage of quality accommodation for business persons and conferences than to any perceived upsurge in recreational demand.

Long-distance private travel by car is constrained by frontier delays, poor road surfaces, a lack of roadside services both for vehicles and passengers, the absence of good lower and middle-range accommodation in small towns, together with questions of insurance cover, particularly in parts of former Yugoslavia and Albania. Such accommodation, so widely available in Hungary, Poland and the Czech Republic, could be provided in tandem with the development of rural tourism, which is now a priority in Slovenia, for example. Further, newly established states may also need to do more to reinforce their

national identities and to generate a positive marketing image for tourism and more general investment purposes.

In catering and hospitality, the Black Sea countries have revealed some attractions for North American fast food and soft drinks interests. A Pepsico subsidiary, Pizza Hut, opened in 1994, the first of what was planned to be 15 restaurants in Bulgaria. Pepsico and Coca-Cola have been accompanied by a Swiss company to invest in a Bulgarian drinks container manufacturer. Coca-Cola has invested heavily in Romania, building bottling plants in several cities, including Bucharest and Braşov. McDonald's was due to open its first restaurant in the country by mid-1995.

With the elimination of hostile borders in a number of areas (and the destructive creation of others), opportunities for cross-border cooperation have been presented both in terms of tourism development (such as integrated day tours from Corfu to southern Albania), and for protecting environments hitherto located in inaccessible borderlands (Karpowicz, 1993; Hall and Kinnaird, 1994). Further, informal means of circumventing UN sanctions against rump Yugoslavia have stimulated not insignificant amounts of cross-border traffic. Together with substantial refugee flight, this has tended to distort further the region's international 'visitor' statistics. For example, more than 3000 Bulgarian motorists travelled into Serbia through the Vidin crossing-point to sell petrol during April 1994 (*BEE*, 6 June 1994). Indeed, despite sanctions, it was estimated that foreign investments worth around US$200 million made their way into Serbia–Montenegro during 1994 alone, with a large proportion coming from diaspora Serbs, such that the informal economy in rump Yugoslavia is reckoned to be equal to half the officially recorded GDP (Kekic, 1995).

19.7 Conclusion

Economic transition in the Balkans has proved more problematic and signs of collective economic well-being have been more elusive here than in the countries of East–Central Europe. The often cautious pace of reform is the result of a mix of political, economic and cultural factors. Urban unemployment and at least a short-term apparent decline in most people's living standards have resulted in such political expressions as the 'return' to power of socialists in Bulgaria, while farmers benefiting from restitution have been reinforced in their conservative position (Carter *et al.*, 1995).

Although the euphoria which followed the opening up of Eastern Europe was largely aimed at those countries of the region most adjacent to the West, a dissipation of the early optimism has seen international investors returning to less risky, more traditional markets such as Latin America and to the emerging areas of Southeast Asia (Keay, 1995). While the countries of the Balkans can still offer lower rents and wage levels than their East–Central European counterparts, such potential benefits are still being offset by shortcomings in infrastructure, legislative inconsistency and political uncertainty.

It is widely felt by investors that not until at least the turn of the millennium will there begin any widespread shift of investment to Eastern Europe in general and to Southeast Europe in particular (Anon, 1995). When that occurs, those regions most likely to feel the adverse effects will be the southern fringes of the EU, further exacerbating the problems of Greece, Spain and Portugal. Within 20 years, however, the wage disparities between the southern peripheries of Eastern and Western Europe may have largely disappeared, negating much of any original attraction of shifting investment towards the Balkans.

19.8 References

ABECOR, 1995, *Slovenia/Croatia*, ABECOR, Vienna.

Allcock, J. B., 1983, Tourism and social change in Dalmatia, *Journal of Development Studies*, **20**(1), 35–55.

Allcock, J. B., 1986, Yugoslavia's tourist trade: pot of gold or pig in a poke? *Annals of Tourism Research*, **13**(4), 565–88.

Allcock, J. B., 1990, Tourism and the private sector in Yugoslavia, in Allcock, J. B., Milivojević, M., eds, *Yugoslavia in transition*, Berg, Oxford.

Allcock, J. B., 1991, Yugoslavia, in Hall, D. R., ed., *Tourism and economic development in Eastern Europe and the Soviet Union*, Belhaven, London, Halsted, New York, pp. 236–58.

Allcock, J. B., Milivojević, M., eds, 1990, *Yugoslavia in transition*, Berg, Oxford.

Anon, 1995, Slow progress in the East, *EuroBusiness*, **2**(10), 96–8.

Ash, W., 1974, *Pickaxe and rifle*, Howard Baker, Wimbledon.

Ballon, M., 1995, Romanian privatisation: what a state, *Business Central Europe*, **3**(26), 19–20.

Bartlett, W., Prašnikar, J., 1995, Small firms and economic transformation in Slovenia, *Communist Economies and Economic Transformation*, **7**(1), 83–103.

BBC, *Summary of World Broadcasts: Eastern Europe economic reports*, BBC, London, weekly.

Beaver, S. H., 1941, Railways in the Balkan peninsula, *Geographical Journal*, **97**, 273–94.

Bebler, A., 1993, Yugoslavia's variety of communist federalism and her demise, *Communist and Post-communist Studies*, **26**(1), 72–86.

BEE (Business Eastern Europe), weekly, Economist Intelligence Unit, London.

Blanchard, O., Dornbusch, R., Krugman, P., Layard, R., Summers, L., 1991, *Reform in Eastern Europe*, MIT Press, Cambridge, Mass.

Bogetic, Z., 1993, The role of employee ownership in privatisation of state enterprises in Eastern and Central Europe, *Europe–Asia Studies*, **45**(3), 463–82.

Borensztein, E., Demekas, D., Ostry, J., 1993, An empirical analysis of the output declines in three Eastern European countries, *IMF Staff Papers*, **40**(1), 1–31.

Bren, P., 1992, The status of women in post-1989 Czechoslovakia, *RFE/RL Research Report*, **1**(41), 58–63.

Buckley, M., ed., 1992, *Perestroika and Soviet women*, Cambridge University Press, Cambridge.

Buckwalter, D. W., 1995, Spatial inequality in Bulgaria, *Professional Geographer*, **47**(3), 288–98.

Buckwell, A., *et al.*, eds, 1994, *The transformation of agriculture: a case study of Bulgaria*, Westview, Boulder, Colo.

Calbreath, D., 1995, Survey of infrastructure, *Business Central Europe*, **3**(26), 37–48.

Carter, F. W., 1970, Natural gas in Romania, *Geography*, **55**, 214–20.

Carter, F. W., 1973, *Post war functional and structural changes within the Sofia conurbation*, University College Department of Geography occasional paper 21, London.

Carter, F. W., 1975, Bulgaria's new towns, *Geography*, **60**, 133–6.

Carter, F. W., 1979, Prague and Sofia: an analysis of their changing internal city structure, in French, R. A., Hamilton, F. E. I., eds, *The socialist city: spatial structure and urban policy*, John Wiley, Chichester and New York, pp. 425–59.

Carter, F. W., 1986, Tirana, *Cities*, 3(4), 270–81.

Carter, F. W., 1987, Bulgaria, in Dawson, A. H., ed., *Planning in Eastern Europe*, Croom Helm, Beckenham, pp. 67–101.

Carter, F. W., 1990a, Bulgaria: geographical prognosis for a political eclipse, *Geography*, **75**(3), 263–5.

Carter, F. W., 1990b, Housing policy in Bulgaria, in Sillince, J. A. A., ed., *Housing policies in Eastern Europe and the Soviet Union*, Routledge, London and New York, pp. 170–227.

Carter, F. W., Hall, D. R., Turnock, D., Williams, A. M., Stevenson, I., Lowman, G., 1995, *Interpreting the Balkans*, Royal Geographical Society (with the Institute of British Geographers), Geographical Intelligence Paper No. 2, London.

Carter, F. W., Turnock, D., 1993, *Environmental problems in Eastern Europe*, Routledge, London.

Castle, T., 1990, East rings the changes for telecoms, *The European*, 27 July.

Chalmers, J., Cook, J., Cuthbert, H., Law, C. E., Lee, S., Simpson, P., 1995, Telecommunication survey, *Business Central Europe*, 3(24), 37–52.

Childs, D., 1988, *The GDR: Moscow's German ally*, Unwin Hyman, London, 2nd edn.

Cohen, L. J., 1995, *Broken bonds: the disintegration of Yugoslavia*, Westview, Boulder, Colo.

Corrin, C., ed., 1992, *Super women and the double burden*, Scarlet Press, London.

Cviic, C., 1991, *Remaking the Balkans*, Royal Institute of International Affairs/Frances Pinter, London.

Cvikl, M., Vodopivec, M., Kraft, E., 1993, Costs and benefits of independence: Slovenia, *Communist Economies and Economic Transformation*, **5**(3), 295–316.

Danta, D., 1991, Romania: view from the front, *Focus*, **41**(2), 17–20.

Danta, D., 1993, Ceauşescu's Bucharest, *Geographical Review*, **83**(2), 170–82.

Dawson, A. H., 1987, Yugoslavia, in Dawson, A. H., ed., *Planning in Eastern Europe*, Croom Helm, Beckenham, pp. 275–91.

Dekleva, B. V., 1994, Never-ending transition of housing policy in Slovenia, in Tanninen, T. *et al.*, eds, *Transitional housing systems*, Bauhaus, Dessau.

Dobosiewicz, Z., 1992, *Foreign investment in Eastern Europe*, Routledge, London.

Drakulić, S., 1990, The women who wait, *New Statesman and Society*, 31 August.

Drakulić, S., 1992, *How we survived communism and even laughed*, Hutchinson, London.

Drakulić, S., 1993a, *Balkan express: fragments from the other side of war*, Hutchinson, London.

Drakulić, S., 1993b, Women and the new democracy in the former Yugoslavia, in Funk, N., Mueller, M., eds, *Gender politics and post-communism*, Routledge, London, pp. 123–30.

EBRD (European Bank for Reconstruction and Development), 1995, *Transition report 1995*, EBRD, London.

Edmundson, L., ed., 1992, *Women and society in Russia and the Soviet Union*, Cambridge University Press, Cambridge.

EEM (East European Markets), fortnightly, Financial Times Newsletters, London.

Einhorn, B., 1991, Where have all the women gone? *Feminist Review*, **39**.

EIU (Economist Intelligence Unit), 1994, *Macedonia, Serbia–Montenegro: country profile 1993–94*, EIU, London.

EIU, 1995a, *Bosnia–Herzegovina, Croatia, Macedonia, Serbia–Montenegro, Slovenia: country report 1995, 2nd quarter*, EIU, London.

EIU, 1995b, *Bosnia–Herzegovina, Croatia, Macedonia, Serbia–Montenegro, Slovenia: country report 1995, 3rd quarter*, EIU, London.

EIU, 1995c,, *Bosnia–Herzegovina, Croatia, Slovenia: country profile 1994–95*, EIU, London.

EIU, 1995d, *Bulgaria, Albania: country profile 1994–95*, EIU, London.

EIU, 1995e, *Bulgaria, Albania: country report 1995, 2nd quarter*, EIU, London.

EIU, 1995f, *Bulgaria, Albania: country report 1995, 3rd quarter*, EIU, London.

EIU, 1995g, *Macedonia, Serbia–Montenegro: country profile 1994–95*, EIU, London.

EIU, 1995h, *Romania: country profile 1994–95*, EIU, London.

EIU, 1995i, *Romania: country report 1995, 2nd quarter*, EIU, London.

EIU, 1995j, *Romania: country report 1995, 3rd quarter*, EIU, London.

Fisher, J. C., 1963, Urban analysis: a case study of Zagreb, Yugoslavia, *Annals of the Association of American Geographers*, **53**, 266–84.

Flint, A., 1993a, Tourism: Bulgaria's first success story, *Business Eastern Europe*, **22**(34), 5.

Flint, A., 1993b, Romanian tourist market growing, *Business Eastern Europe*, **22**(38), 8.

Flint, A., 1995, Romania: growth strides, reform plods, *Business Eastern Europe*, **24**(26), 10.

Fong, M. S., Paul, G., 1992, *The changing role of women in employment in Eastern Europe*, International Bank for Reconstruction and Development, Washington, DC.

French, R. A., Hamilton, F. E. I., eds, 1979, *The socialist city: spatial structure and urban policy*, John Wiley, Chichester and New York.

Fuchs, R. J., 1980, Urban change in Eastern Europe: the limits to planning, *Urban Geography*, **1**, 81–94.

Fuchs, R. J., Demko, G. J., 1977, Spatial population policies in the socialist countries of Eastern Europe, *Social Science Quarterly*, **58**, 60–73.

Fuchs, R. J., Demko, G. J., 1978, The postwar mobility transition in Eastern Europe, *Geographical Review*, **68**, 171–82.

Fuchs, R. J., Demko, G. J., 1979, Geographic inequality under socialism, *Annals of the Association of American Geographers*, **69**(2), 304–18.

Funk, N., Mueller, M., eds, 1993, *Gender, politics and post-communism*, Routledge, London and New York.

Gacs, J., Karimov, I. A., Schneider, C. M., 1993, Small-scale privatisation in Eastern Europe and Russia: a historical and comparative perspective, *Communist Economies and Economic Transformation*, **5**(1), 61–86.

Gajo, A., 1992, Large-scale privatization: the key to the reform, *Albanian Economic Tribune*, **2**(6), 24–5.

Geco, P., 1970, L'accroissement de la population urbaine de la R. P. d'Albanie et sa répartition géographique, *Studia Albanica*, **2**, 161–82.

Gianaris, N. V., 1982, *The economies of the Balkan countries: Albania, Bulgaria, Greece, Romania, Turkey and Yugoslavia*, Praeger, New York.

Giannopoulos, G. A., 1984, Land transport in south-eastern Europe: situation and principles for improvement, *Transport Review*, **4**(1), 1–26.

Gibb, R., Michalak, W., 1993, The European Community and Central Europe: prospects for integration, *Geography*, **78**(1), 16–30.

Gurney, J., 1978, Energy needs in the Balkans: a source of conflict or cooperation? *The World Today*, **34**(2), 44–51.

Hall, D. R., 1984, Foreign tourism under socialism: the Albanian 'Stalinist' model, *Annals of Tourism Research*, **11**(4), 539–55.

Hall, D. R., 1986, New towns in Europe's rural corner, *Town and Country Planning*, **55**(9), 251–2.

Hall, D. R., 1987, Albania, in Dawson, A. H., ed., *Planning in Eastern Europe*, Croom Helm, Beckenham, pp. 35–65.

Hall, D. R., 1989, Planning Bulgaria's uncertain future, *Town and Country Planning*, **58**(12), 347–8.

Hall, D. R., 1990a, Eastern Europe opens its doors, *Geographical Magazine*, **62**(4), 10–15.

Hall, D. R., 1990b, Housing policy in Albania, in Sillince, J. A. A., ed., *Housing policies in Eastern Europe and the Soviet Union*, Routledge, London and New York, pp. 359–401.

Hall, D. R., 1990c, Stalinism and tourism: a study of Albania and North Korea, *Annals of Tourism Research*, **17**(1), 36–54.

Hall, D. R., 1991a, New hope for the Danube Delta, *Town and Country Planning*, **60**(12), 354–6.

Hall, D. R., ed., 1991b, *Tourism and economic development in Eastern Europe and the Soviet Union*, Belhaven, London and Halsted, New York.

Hall, D. R., 1992a, East European seaports in a restructured Europe, in Hoyle, B. S., Pinder, D. A., eds, *European port cities in transition*, Belhaven, London, pp. 98–115.

Hall, D. R., 1992b, Skills transfer for appropriate development, *Town and Country Planning*, **61**(3), 87–9.

Hall, D. R., 1992c, The challenge of international tourism in Eastern Europe, *Tourism Management*, **13**(2), 41–4.

Hall, D. R., 1992d, The changing face of international tourism in Central and Eastern Europe, *Progress in Tourism, Recreation and Hospitality Management*, **4**, 252–64.

Hall, D. R., 1993a, Eastern Europe, in Pompl, W., Lavery, P., eds, *Tourism in Europe: structures and developments*, CAB International, Wallingford, pp. 341–58.

Hall, D. R., 1993b, Ecotourism in the Danube Delta, *Revue de Tourisme*, **3**, 11–13.

Hall, D. R., ed., 1993c, Impacts of economic and political transition on the transport geography of Central and Eastern Europe, *Journal of Transport Geography*, **1**(1), 20–35.

Hall, D. R., ed., 1993d, *Transport and economic development in the new Central and Eastern Europe*, Belhaven, London.

Hall, D. R., 1994, *Albania and the Albanians*, Frances Pinter, London.

Hall, D. R., 1995a, Taking a lone stand, *Geographical*, **67**(4), 19–22.

Hall, D. R., 1995b, Tourism change in Central and Eastern Europe, in Montanari, A., Williams, A. M., eds, *European tourism: regions, spaces and restructuring*, John Wiley, London, pp. 221–44.

Hall, D. R., Kinnaird, V. H., 1993, Green tourism in Eastern Europe?, *Town and Country Planning*, **62**(6), 156–7.

Hall, D. R., Kinnaird, V. H., 1994, Eastern Europe, in Cater, E., Lowman, G., eds, *Ecotourism: a sustainable option?*, John Wiley, London, pp. 111–36.

Hamilton, F. E. I., 1968, *Yugoslavia: patterns of economic activity*, Bell, London.

Hamilton, F. E. I., 1971a, Decision making and industrial location in Eastern Europe, *Transactions of the Institute of British Geographers*, **52**, 77–94.

Hamilton, F. E. I., 1971b, The location of industry in East-central and South-east Europe, in Hoffman, G. W., ed., *Eastern Europe: essays in geographical problems*, Methuen, London, pp. 173–223.

Hamilton, F. E. I., Burnett, A. D., 1979, Social processes and residential structure, in French, R. A., Hamilton, F. E. I., eds, *The socialist city: spatial structure and urban policy*, John Wiley, Chichester and New York, pp. 263–304.

Haraszti, M., 1977, *A worker in a worker's state*, Penguin, Harmondsworth.

Harrison, D., 1993, Bulgarian tourism, state of uncertainty, *Annals of Tourism Research*, **20**(3), 519–34.

Harsanyi, D. P., 1993, Women in Romania, in Funk, N., Mueller, M., eds, *Gender, politics and post-communism*, Routledge, London and New York, pp. 39–52.

Hickley, C., Hill, J. D., McQuaid, D., Smrstik, C., Zarnecki, M., 1995, Bordering on the intolerable, *Business Eastern Europe*, **24**(13), 1–3.

Hoffman, G. W., 1972, *Regional development strategy in Southeast Europe: a comparative analysis of Albania, Bulgaria, Greece, Romania and Yugoslavia*, Praeger, New York.

Hunya, G., 1995, Transport and telecommunications infrastructure in transition, *Communist Economies and Economic Transformation*, **7**(3), 369–84.

Jermakowicz, W., Drazek, C., 1993, Joint venture laws in Eastern Europe: a comparative assessment, in Artisien, P., Rijec, M., Svetlicić, M., eds, *Foreign investment in Central and Eastern Europe*, St Martin's Press, New York, pp. 149–69.

Kapoor, M., Sweitzer, J., 1995, Daewoo's master plan, *Business Central Europe*, **3**(24), 29–30.

Karpowicz, Z., ed., 1992, *Environmental status reports. Vol. 4: Conservation status of the Danube Delta*, IUCN–EEP.

Karpowicz, Z., 1993, The challenge of ecotourism— application and prospects for implementation in the countries of Central and Eastern Europe and Russia, *Revue de Tourisme*, **3**, 28–40.

Keay, J., 1995, Unrewarded Eastern promise, *EuroBusiness*, **2**(10), 30–3.

Kekic, L., 1995, War profiteering, *Business Central Europe*, **3**(26), 15–18.

Kenedi, J., 1981, *Do it yourself*, Pluto Press, London.

Koulov, B., 1992, Tendencies in the administrative territorial development of Bulgaria (1878–1990), *Tijdschrift voor Economische en Sociale Geografie*, **83**(5), 390–401.

Ladányi, J., 1993, Patterns of residential segregation and the gypsy minority in Budapest, *International Journal of Urban and Regional Research*, **17**(1), 30–41.

Lampe, J. R., Jackson, M. R., 1982, *Balkan economic history, 1550–1950*, Indiana University Press, Bloomington.

Lavell, T., 1994, Toll motorway project ready to go, *Business Eastern Europe*, **23**(20), 5.

Leitmann, J., 1994, Katowice, *Cities*, **11**(3), 147–52.

Lucas, E., 1995a, Croatia: fruits of victory, *Business Eastern Europe*, **24**(47), 6.

Lucas, E., 1995b, FYR Macedonia: less bad than it looks, *Business Eastern Europe*, **24**(6), 4.

Lucas, E., 1995c, Romania: stable and starting expansion, *Business Eastern Europe*, **24**(5), 5.

Lucas, E., Lebl, A., 1995, Serbia–Montenegro: crippled, stable—and unreformed, *Business Eastern Europe*, **24**(11), 4.

Magnusson, L., 1990, Albania, in Mathéy, K., ed., *Housing policies in the socialist Third World*, Mansell, London and New York, pp. 315–21.

Mandič, S., 1994, Housing tenures in times of change: conversion debates in Slovenia, *Housing Studies*, **9**, 27–38.

Michalak, W., 1995, Foreign aid and Eastern Europe in the 'New World Order', *Tijdschrift voor Economische en Sociale Geografie*, **86**(3), 260–77.

Michalak, W., Gibb, R., 1993, Development of the transport system: prospects for East/West integration, in Hall, D. R., ed., *Transport and economic development in the new Central and Eastern Europe*, Belhaven, London, pp. 34–48.

Mihailović, K., 1972, *Regional development experiences and prospects in Eastern Europe*, Mouton, The Hague.

Milanovich, B., 1991, Privatisation in postcommunist societies, *Communist Economies and Economic Transformation*, **3**(1), 5–39.

Milić, A., 1993, Women and nationalism in the former Yugoslavia, in Funk, N., Mueller, M., eds, *Gender, politics and post-communism*, Routledge, London and New York, pp. 109–22.

Mirowski, W., Milnar, Z., 1984, *Urban social processes in Poland and Yugoslavia*, Polish Academy of Science, Warsaw.

Misha, G., 1995, Albania: spade work, *Business Eastern Europe*, **24**(37), 4.

Misha, G., Lucas, E., 1995, Albania: small, poor and promising, *Business Eastern Europe*, **24**(42), 6.

Misha, G., Vinton, L., 1995, Albania: big problems, small progress, *Business Eastern Europe*, **24**(18), 7.

Murphy, A. B., 1992, Western investment in East–Central Europe—emerging patterns and implications for state stability, *Professional Geographer*, **44**(3), 249–59.

Nickel, H. M., 1989, Sex-role socialization in relationships as a function of the division of labor: a sociological explanation for the reproduction of gender differences, in Rueschemeyer, M., Lemke, C., eds, *The quality of life in the German Democratic Republic*, M. E. Sharp, Armonk, NY.

Panova, R., Gavrilova, R., Merdzanska, C., 1993, Thinking gender: Bulgarian women's im/possibilities, in Funk, N., Mueller, M., eds, *Gender, politics and post-communism*, Routledge, London and New York, pp. 15–21.

Pashko, G., 1993, Inflation in Albania, *Communist Economies and Economic Transformation*, **5**(1), 115–26.

Patterson, W., 1994, *Rebuilding Romania: energy, efficiency and the economic transition*, The Royal Institute of International Affairs/Earthscan Publications, London.

Petrova, D., 1993, The winding road to emancipation in Bulgaria, in Funk, N., Mueller, M., eds, *Gender, politics and post-communism*, Routledge, London and New York, pp. 22–9.

Pickvance, C. G., 1994, Housing privatization and housing protest in the transition from state socialism: a comparative study of Budapest and Moscow, *International Journal of Urban and Regional Research*, **18**(3), 433–50.

Pounds, N. J. G., 1971, The urbanisation of East Central and Southeast Europe, in Hoffman, G. W., ed., *Eastern Europe: essays in geographical problems*, Methuen, London, pp. 54–82.

Rayner, C., *et al.*, eds, 1994, *Philip's geographical digest 1994–95*, Heinemann, Oxford.

Reuter, 1993, Home sweet bunker for Albanian migrants, *The Guardian*, 28 December.

Richardson, M., 1995, *Effects of war on the environment: Croatia*, E. & F. N. Spon, London.

Rieder, I., 1991, *Feminism and Eastern Europe*, Attic Press, Dublin.

RMTT (Romania Ministry of Trade and Tourism), 1990, *The programme of modernization and development of Romanian tourism in 1990–1992*, Ministry of Trade and Tourism, Bucharest.

Rojec, M., Svetlicic, M., 1993, Foreign investment in Slovenia: experience, prospects and policy options, *Communist Economies and Economic Transformation*, **5**(1), 103–14.

Ronnas, P., 1982, Centrally planned urbanization: the case of Romania, *Geografiska Annaler*, **64B**, 143–51.

Rose, R., 1993, Contradictions between micro- and macroeconomic goals in post-communist societies, *Europe–Asia Studies*, **45**(3), 419–44.

Rosenberg, D. J., 1991, Shock therapy: GDR women in transition from a socialist welfare state to a social market economy, *Signs: Journal of Women in Culture and Society*, **17**(1), 129–51.

Sampson, S. L., 1979, Urbanization—planned and unplanned: a case study of Braşov, Romania, in French, R. A., Hamilton, F. E. I., eds, *The socialist city: spatial structure and urban policy*, John Wiley, Chichester and New York, pp. 507–24.

Sampson, S., 1984, *National integration through socialist planning: an anthropological study of a Romanian new town*, Westview, Boulder, Colo.

Schlack, R. F., 1993, Going to market in Bulgaria: uphill on a knife edge, *Journal of Economic Issues*, **21**(2), 515–26.

Sendi, R., 1995, Housing reform and housing conflict: the privatization of public housing in the Republic of Slovenia in practice, *International Journal of Urban and Regional Research*, **19**(3), 435–51.

Sik, E., 1994, From the multicoloured to the black and white economy: the Hungarian second economy and the transformation, *International Journal of Urban and Regional Research*, **18**(1), 46–70.

Sillince, J. A. A., ed., 1990, *Housing policies in Eastern Europe and the Soviet Union*, Routledge, London and New York.

Sjöberg, Ö., Wyzan, M. L., 1991, *Economic change in the Balkan states: Albania, Bulgaria, Romania and Yugoslavia*, Frances Pinter, London.

Strauss, J., 1995, JR is alive and well and living in Romania, *The European*, 5 October.

Sýkora, L., Štěpánek, V., 1992, Prague, *Cities*, **9**(2), 91–100.

Symons, L. J., 1993, Restructuring the region's air industry, in Hall, D. R., ed., *Transport and economic development in the new Central and Eastern Europe*, Belhaven, London, pp. 67–81.

Szalai, J., 1991, Some aspects of the changing situation of women in Hungary, *Signs: Journal of Women in Culture and Society*, **17**(1), 152–70.

Szaniawski, K., 1995, Good in parts, *EuroBusiness*, **3**(5), 61–3.

Sziráczki, G., Windell, J., 1992, Impact of employment on disadvantaged groups in Hungary and Bulgaria, *International Labour Review*, **131**, 471–96.

Tarifa, F., Barjaba, K., 1986, Vështrim sociologjik mbi kohën e lirë të punonjësve, *Studime Politiko-Shoqërore*, **11**, 116–33.

Tarifa, F., Barjaba, K., 1990, Leisure in Tirana, *Albanian Life*, **48**, 11–15.

Thomas, C., 1982, Migration and urban growth in Yugoslavia, *East European Quarterly*, **16**(2), 199–216.

Todorova, M., 1993, The Bulgarian case: women's issues or feminist issues?, in Funk, N., Mueller, M., eds, *Gender, politics and post-communism*, Routledge, London and New York, pp. 30–8.

Topham, S., 1990, Housing policy in Yugoslavia, in Sillince, J. A. A., ed., *Housing policies in Eastern Europe and the Soviet Union*, Routledge, London and New York, pp. 402–39.

Traynor, I., 1993, Pouring cold water on Albania's lazy 'little pashas', *The Guardian*, 8 July.

TRC (Telecommunications Research Centre), 1990, *Eastern European telecommunications: regional assessment and analysis*, TRC, Chichester.

Turner, B. *et al.*, eds, 1992, *The reform of housing in Eastern Europe and the Soviet Union*, Routledge, London and New York.

Turnock, D., 1970, Bucharest: the selection and development of the Romanian capital, *Scottish Geographical Magazine*, **86**(1), 53–68.

Turnock, D., 1974, Urban development in a socialist city: Bucaresti, *Geography*, **59**, 344–8.

Turnock, D., 1978, *Studies in industrial geography: Eastern Europe*, Dawson, Folkestone.

Turnock, D., 1980, Bucharest: historical perspectives on the Romanian capital, *History Today*, **30**(8), 14–18.

Turnock, D., 1986, *The rural development programme in Romania with particular reference to the designation of new towns*, University of Leicester Department of Geography occasional paper 13, Leicester.

Turnock, D., 1987, Romania, in Dawson, A. H., ed., *Planning in Eastern Europe*, Croom Helm, Beckenham, pp. 229–73.

Turnock, D., 1989, *Eastern Europe: an economic and political geography*, Routledge, London and New York.

Turnock, D., 1990a, Bucharest, *Cities*, 7(2), 107–18.

Turnock, D., 1990b, Housing policy in Romania, in Sillince, J. A. A., ed., *Housing policies in Eastern Europe and the Soviet Union*, Routledge, London and New York, pp. 135–69.

Turnock, D., 1990c, Tourism in Romania: rural planning in the Carpathians, *Annals of Tourism Research*, **17**, 79–112.

Turnock, D., 1991, Romania, in Hall, D. R., ed., *Tourism and economic development in Eastern Europe and the Soviet Union*, Belhaven, London, and Halsted, New York, pp. 203–19.

Turnock, D., 1993a, *Agricultural change in the new Eastern Europe*, Stanley Thornes, Cheltenham.

Turnock, D., 1993b, *Agricultural change in the Romanian Carpathians*, University of Leicester Discussion Papers in Geography G93/2, Leicester.

Uvalić, M., 1993, The disintegration of Yugoslavia: its costs and benefits, *Communist Economies and Economic Transformation*, **5**(3), 273–94.

Vinton, L., 1995, Bulgaria: forward at a snail's pace, *Business Eastern Europe*, **24**(10), 3.

Weyr, T., 1992, Women's economic hardship in Albania, *Albanian Life*, **2**, 24.

Whitford, R., 1995, Road warriors, *Business Central Europe*, **3**(26), 27.

Williamson, A., 1992, Bringing down the other iron curtain, *The European*, 4 June.

WTO (World Tourism Organization), 1993, *Compendium of tourism statistics 1987–1991*, WTO, Madrid.

WTO, annual, *Yearbook of tourism statistics*, WTO, Madrid.

Zarkovic, M., 1992, Economic issues underlying secession: the case of Slovenia and Slovakia, *Communist Economies and Economic Transformation*, **4**(1), 111–34.

20

Forward into history

Darrick Danta and Derek Hall

20.1 Conceiving the Balkan future

As noted in the introductory chapters to this volume, any attempt to encompass a single conception of the Balkans is conspicuously flawed. As socio-economic disparities increase within and between societies of Southeast Europe, so, despite media attention being focused on 'Balkan' wars, it is becoming increasingly irrelevant to speak, pejoratively or otherwise, of 'Balkan nations' to imply that they share major common characteristics. Even the crude subjectivity of a table ranking East European states in terms of their 'transition prospects' (Table 20.1) (Lucas, 1995), reveals the disparate positions in terms of economic change held by the region's post-socialist states.

Slovenia, for example, is seen as 'a neglected success story', with the region's highest per capita GDP; indeed, if the take-up of credit card ownership is an indicator of economic development and 'Westernisation', then Slovenia (Vinton and Nathwani, 1995; see also Chapters 8 and 9), is out in front even compared to the rest of post-socialist Eastern Europe, with 35.3 cards per thousand population. Although this figure is only one-eighth that of France, it is still more than twice that for Hungary (15.9), the next closest post-socialist state.

Romania's size and relative stability (see Chapters 13 and 14) make it an increasingly attractive prospect for inward investment. Scepticism about Bulgaria's likely progress (Minassian, 1994; see also Chapters 15 and 16) is reflected in the country's relatively low level of foreign trade (Table 19.1).

Although revealing some of the highest recent growth figures, Albania's economy and political system, and indeed its population, are still among the most vulnerable in the region. Relations have improved with Greece, and the Council of Europe agreed to admit the country as a member. Yet misgivings have remained concerning the country's human rights performance and particularly the government's attitude towards press freedoms (EIU, 1995; Standish, 1995; see also Chapters 10 and 11). The parliamentary elections of March 1996 could encourage destabilising influences.

The restoration of relations between Greece and FYROM suggests potential for rapid economic recovery in the latter. A resumption of trade followed Athens' lifting of its 18-month-long unilateral blockade. Greece also promised to withdraw its veto on FYROM joining international institutions. In exchange, Skopje would drop the sunburst symbol from its flag, claimed by Greeks to have belonged to the

Reconstructing the Balkans: A Geography of the New Southeast Europe. Edited by Derek Hall and Darrick Danta.
©1996 John Wiley & Sons Ltd

Table 20.1 *Post-socialist transition progress*

Fast track quartet
** SLOVENIA
** Czech Republic
*** Poland
** Estonia
Second division
** Hungary
* Slovakia
*** CROATIA
** Latvia
** Lithuania
Large and hesitant
*** Russia
** Ukraine
** Kazakhstan
Lower Danube
*** ROMANIA
** BULGARIA
** SERBIA–MONTENEGRO
Small wonders
*** Moldova
*** FYROM
** ALBANIA
* Kyrgyzia
*** Armenia
*** Azerbaijan
*** Georgia
Tough prospects
** Uzbekistan
* Belarus
** Turkmenistan
War-ruined
*** BOSNIA–HERCEGOVINA
** Tajikistan

Key: *** = improvement; ** = no relative change; * = decline (in the third quarter of 1995 compared to the second quarter).
Note: Variables considered: macroeconomic performance, political stability, 'business climate' and 'reform-friendliness'.
Source: Lucas (1995, p. 1).

ancient house of Alexander the Great, and to rewrite some contentious clauses of its constitution which Athens claimed were implicitly irredentist (see Chapters 6 and 7; also Troebst, 1994).

While questions remain concerning the Tudjman regime's human rights record, Croatia's 'victory dividend' may yet be compromised by its financial and other commitments to Bosnian Croatian communities (Table 20.2).

A comprehensive reconstruction of Bosnia–Hercegovina could embrace six phases (Gow, 1995b):

1. Deployment of 60 000 members of the NATO implementation force for enforcing peace agreements;
2. Physical rebuilding of infrastructure: major international programmes would be required, and such reconstruction would generate local employment in the short term;
3. Economic regeneration, which could be led by the EU, emphasising a judicious use of local human and physical resources in both knitting the republic together and in developing trade with the outside world. But while a united Bosnia–Hercegovina has potential for significant economic strength through its minerals, manufacturing and forestry resources, economic sustainability would be very difficult under conditions of division (Metiljevic, 1995);
4. Political reconstruction, providing assistance for and after local general elections;

Table 20.2 *Recovery requirements of Bosnia–Hercegovina*

Sector	Cost ($m)		
Energy	613		
of which:		Electric power	330
		District heating	120
		Gas	95
		Coal	68
Health	392		
Transport	340		
Housing	310		
Water and sanitation	285		
Telecommunications	258		
Industry	220		
Agriculture	200		
Mine clearing	200		
Education	189		
Total	3007		

Note: These figures exclude costs associated with financial normalisation and arrears clearance and with emergency food aid.
Sources: Vinton (1995); World Bank (1995).

252

5. Social rehabilitation: including major programmes for education and training and the
reintegration of refugees;
6. Reconciliation: understanding and coming to
terms with the past.

The human cost of the wars of Yugoslav
succession can barely begin to be comprehended,
with just under three-quarters of all the 3.65
million displaced and war-affected citizens coming from Bosnia–Hercegovina (Table 20.3) (see
also Chapters 17 and 18). In terms of crude
economics, by the time of the Dayton peace
negotiations (see below) the Bosnian economy
had shrunk to just 25–30% of its 1990 size,
industrial output was down to 10–20% and per
capita GDP had been reduced from US$1900 to
a mere US$500 (Vinton, 1995; World Bank,
1995; see also Chapters 1 and 2). Considered to
have suffered a greater degree of destruction than
Germany at the end of the Second World War
(Gow, 1995a), Bosnia–Hercegovina, and its
reconstruction, will continue to act as a lightning
conductor for Balkan cultural, political and
economic tensions.

Four seminal events in the later stages of the
Bosnian conflict had proved decisive in both
finally undermining the UN role and hastening
some form of Balkan *modus vivendi*:

1. Seizure of UNPROFOR forces by Bosnian
Serbs for use as 'human shields';
2. The Croats' retaking by force of UN-patrolled
western Slavonia and the 'Krajina';
3. The Serbs' taking of the UN-guaranteed
Bosnian Muslim 'safe areas' of Srebrenica
and Zepa;
4. The August 1995 NATO bombing campaign
against Bosnian Serbs.

As the difference between peacekeeping and
peace enforcement had become dangerously
blurred UNPROFOR became the rather forlorn
symbol of inaction on behalf of the 'international
community' (Black, 1995).

The 10 articles, 11 annexes and 102 maps
comprising the arrangements for the future of
Bosnia–Hercegovina which emerged from the 21

Table 20.3 *Displaced and war-affected populations within the former Yugoslavia*

Source	Numbers ('000s)	% of total
Bosnia–Hercegovina	2702	73.9
of whom:	1300 displaced	
	1402 war-affected	
Croatia	463	12.7
of whom:	425 Croatia	
	38 E. Slavonia	
Rump Yugoslavia	449	12.3
of whom:	405 Serbia	
	44 Montenegro	
Slovenia	26	0.7
FYROM	15	0.4
Total	3655	

Sources: Valls (1995, p. 50), from UNHCR, Bosnian government and other sources.

days of negotiations in November 1995 at
Dayton, Ohio, and from subsequent gatherings
in London and Paris, were redolent of the
compromises reached following the century's
two world wars. All sides were war weary yet
far from happy with the outcome. While Bosnia–
Hercegovina was to remain a single state, thereby
conforming to the internationally held view that
borders should not be changed by force, it would
in fact comprise two entities: a so-called Muslim–
Croat federation with 51% of the former
republic's territory, including the capital Sarajevo and a 4 km wide corridor to the Muslim
enclave of Gorazde in eastern Bosnia (Figure
20.1(b)), and a Serb republic with 49% of the
land. The territorial configurations were significantly different from those drawn up by the
Contact Group in 1994 (Figure 20.1(a); see also
Chapter 2), and acknowledged the substantial
changes in military fortunes which had helped to
bring Serbs to the negotiating table.

A central government in Sarajevo, with a
parliament, court and central bank, would
incorporate features redolent of Yugoslavia's
past: a rotating presidency and the assignment
of posts nationally. Indeed, one of the tragedies
of the unravelling of Bosnia–Hercegovina was
that the republic had been the very embodiment

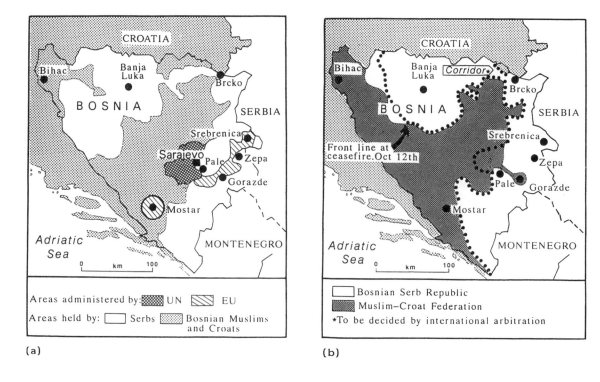

Figure 20.1 *Dividing Bosnia–Hercegovina for peaceful reconstruction? (a) The Contact Group proposal of July 1994; (b) The Dayton peace plan of November 1995*

of the Yugoslav multi-ethnic ideal, of different South Slav groups living side by side in harmony and with a common purpose.

Aside from the fragility of the peace plan's institutional framework, provision for three land corridors sounded dark echoes of past European peace settlements. A Gorazde corridor (Figure 20.1(b)) would link the eastern Bosnian Muslim enclave with Sarajevo, along which NATO forces would construct a highway through otherwise Serb territory; the maintenance of a Posavina corridor, a narrow strip of land linking Serb territories in eastern and western Bosnia, would pivot on Brcko, a Serb-held town subject to international arbitration to decide how wide the corridor should be. The Prevlak corridor would provide for Bosnian Serbs land access to the Adriatic Sea in the

extreme southeast corner of Bosnian territory, abutting Montenegro, a facility deeply resonant of Balkan history.

The provision that refugees would have the right to reclaim their homes or receive compensation appeared at best whimsical, both in respect of the refugees from Bosnia itself and those of the adjacent conflicts. For example, in August 1995 the Croatian president issued a decree imposing a three-month deadline on the reclamation of Serb homes (aimed at property in the 'Krajina' and western Slavonia), and legalising subsequent government confiscation of all abandoned property (Turnbull, 1995). Belgrade argued that, already crippled by UN economic sanctions, 200 000 refugees from the 'Krajina' would cost rump Yugoslavia more than US$420 million over the next six months.

In eastern Slavonia, still held by Serbs, and threatened for several months by Croat attack following Zagreb's military success in western Slavonia, an international force would demilitarise the area and permit it to be handed back to Croatia after two years. Tensions subsequently arose between the UN leadership and NATO concerning the location of responsibility for this activity.

That Sarajevo would come under wholly Muslim–Croat control met fierce opposition from the remaining 150 000 Serbs living in the capital. They feared that they would be subject to the same fate that befell Muslims at the hands of Bosnian Serbs in other previous 'safe areas'. It was particularly significant that the new road from Sarajevo to Goradze would need to start from the Serb-inhabited inner-city neighbourhood of Grbavica.

Just as the post-war division of Germany was meant to be an interim measure on the part of the four occupying powers, so Bosnia–Hercegovina was to be divided into three military sectors (US, UK, French: with no little historic irony a Russian force was to be stationed within the US sector), to allow NATO's 'implementation force' (IFOR) to enforce the Dayton plan and reinforce a 4 km wide demilitarised zone between the former warring parties. The criteria for withdrawal, however—successful separation of the warring parties, holding of national and local elections, successful completion of the arming and training of Bosnian government forces—required some degree of fine-tuning.

As Balkan and world leaders discussed the detail of territorial demarcation and trade-off in Dayton (Anon, 1995; Bogert, 1995; Borger and Freedland, 1995; Harris, 1995), and as David Owen published his account of three inconclusive years as a peace negotiator (Owen, 1995), one might have been forgiven for losing sight of the fact that the twentieth century was almost at an end. That the age of the information superhighway and world-wide web surfers could coexist with immense human suffering and barbarity resulting from historic, localised antagonisms, symbolises this most polarised and deconstructed age. Both history and geography may have been pronounced dead by postmodernist rhetoric, but they provide the very foundation upon which Balkan identity is perpetuated.

20.2 The end of the beginning

During the construction of this text, the editors were confronted by an ever-changing Balkan landscape and the challenges of how to cope with it in the production of a coherent volume: incorporate, ignore, select, abandon? At the same time both editors went through some degree of domestic upheaval; indeed, one of us survived being close to the epicentre of a major earthquake. Personal feelings are consciously subordinated in a work such as this for the sake of balance/objectivity/scientific integrity and other chimeras of academia. Yet neither could remain untouched by the events unravelling in the region: as we deliver the manuscript to the publisher and walk away to think through the next project, we are different persons from those who convened the conference sessions of 1994: our own identities have necessarily been re-evaluated in the process of generating these pages.

However Balkan history unfolds, the region will continue to be critical for European and indeed global relations and fortunes. At the turn of the millennium, when regions, countries and supranational groupings are characterised by ever-intense economic, technological and political linkages, a successful reconstruction of the Balkans—physically, psychologically, economically, socially and politically—is important for all of us.

20.3 References

Anon, 1995, Peace at last, at least for now, *The Economist*, 25 November.

Black, I., 1995, End of the UN's humiliating road in Balkans, *The Guardian*, 6 October.

Bogert, C., 1995, Last chance for a deal? *Newsweek*, 27 November.

Borger, J., Freedland, J., 1995, Tudjman hints at exchange of land, *The Guardian*, 18 November.

EIU (Economist Intelligence Unit), 1995, *Bulgaria, Albania: country report 3rd quarter*, EIU, London.

Gow, J., 1995a, Building on the peace, *War Report*, **38**, 26–7.

Gow, J., 1995b, How to raise the dead, *The Guardian*, 8 December.

Harris, P., 1995, Serbs may yet stand in the way, *Scotland on Sunday*, 26 November.

Lucas, E., 1995, Critical mass, *Business Eastern Europe*, **24**(39), 1.

Metiljevic, A., 1995, Who gets what, *War Report*, **38**, 30–1.

Minassian, G., 1994, The Bulgarian economy in transition: is there anything wrong with macro-economic policy? *Europe–Asia Studies*, **46**(2), 337–51.

Owen, D., 1995, *Balkan odyssey*, Victor Gollancz, London.

Standish, A., 1995, Albania's dark forces terrorise fledgling press, *The European*, 16 November.

Troebst, S., 1994, Macedonia in a hostile international and ethnopolitical environment (six scenarios), *Balkan Forum*, **7**(2), 25–44.

Turnbull, S., 1995, No peace for war's survivors, *The European*, 30 November.

Valls, P., 1995, The longer the wait, *War Report*, **38**, 50–1.

Vinton, L., 1995, Starting from scratch, *Business Eastern Europe*, **24**(43), 1.

Vinton, L., Nathwani, S., 1995, Card sharks, *Business Eastern Europe*, **24**(37), 1.

World Bank, 1995, *Rebuilding Bosnia and Herzegovina: a program for recovery and growth*, World Bank, Washington, DC.

Index

The BALKANS

AUSTRIA

Graz

Klagenfurt

Maribor

Nova Gorica Ljubljana

Trieste

SLOVENIA

Zagreb

Rijeka

Pula

CROATIA

Sava

KRAJINA

Una

Bihac

Banja Luka

BOSNIA &
HERZEGOVINA

Knin

Zenica

Split

Bosna

Neretva

Adriatic
Sea

Mostar

Dubrovnik

ITALY

L. Balaton

HUNGARY

Budapest

Danube

Tisza

Orade.

Drava

Pécs

Szeged

Arad

Subotica

Timişoara

VOJVODINA

Osijek

Novi Sad

Slavonski Brod

Vukovar

Belgrade

Tuzla

SERBIA

Srebrenica

Sarajevo
Pale Zepa

Goražde

Užice

Morava

Drina

YUGOSLAVIA

Niš

SANDJAK

Novi Pazar

MONTENEGRO

Podgorica

Priština

L. Shkodër

KOSOVO

Shkodër

Tetovo Skopje

ALBANIA

FYR MACE

Tirana

Prilep

Durrës

Elbasan

Ohrid

Bitola

L. Ohrid

L. Prespa

Flórina

Korçë

Sarandë

GREECE